What Makes Poor Countries Poor?

What Makes Poor Countries Poor?

Institutional Determinants of Development

Michael J. Trebilcock

University Professor and Chair in Law and Economics, University of Toronto, Canada

Mariana Mota Prado

Associate Professor, Faculty of Law, University of Toronto, Canada

Edward Elgar

Cheltenham, UK • Northampton, MA, USA

Published by
Edward Elgar Publishing Limited
The Lypiatts
15 Lansdown Road
Cheltenham
Glos GL50 2JA
UK

Edward Elgar Publishing, Inc.
William Pratt House
9 Dewey Court
Northampton
Massachusetts 01060
USA

A catalogue record for this book
is available from the British Library

Library of Congress Control Number: 2011932875

MIX
Paper from responsible sources
FSC® C018575

ISBN 978 0 85793 886 2 (cased)
978 0 85793 891 6 (paperback)

Typeset by Servis Filmsetting Ltd, Stockport, Cheshire
Printed and bound by MPG Books Group, UK

Contents

Preface

This book seeks to offer a concise overview of a field of studies that is often called 'law and development'. It focuses on the idea that institutions in general – and legal institutions in particular – matter for development, a topic that has generated a voluminous literature in the past ten years. This literature moves away from the assumption that development is primarily an economic problem, and one of its most relevant implications – as we argue in this book – is that lawyers have a very important role to play in this field of study. The central challenge faced by the field of law and development today is that we do not know how to reform dysfunctional institutions. While there is empirical evidence to support the argument that institutions matter for development,[1] a series of academic books that have assessed recent institutional reforms in developing countries come to the dismal conclusion that many – perhaps most – of these attempts have failed.[2] This book offers some insight into how lawyers and institution builders can best employ their skills to address some of the challenges of institutional reform.

The book starts with a brief overview of different concepts and theories of development, situating institutional theories within the larger academic debate on development. It then proceeds to discuss *why*, *whether* and *how* institutions matter in different fields of development. In the domestic sphere, we try to answer these questions by analysing institutional reforms in the public sector (rule of law, political regimes, bureaucracy) and the private sector (contracts, property rights and privatization). In the

[1] One example is the World Bank publication, *Governance Matters*, initially coordinated by Daniel Kauffman. More evidence has been provided in recent papers by other economists, such as Dani Rodrik from Harvard.

[2] Some examples include Thomas Carothers, *Promoting the Rule of Law Abroad: In Search of Knowledge* (Carnegie Endowment for International Peace, 2006); Kenneth Dam, *The Law-Growth Nexus: The Rule of Law and Economic Development* (Brookings Institution Press, 2006); Michael Trebilcock and Ron Daniels, *Rule of Law and Development: Charting the Fragile Path of Progress* (Cheltenham, UK: Edward Elgar Publishing, 2008). A more recent publication by Paul Dragos Aligica and Peter Boettke, *Challenging Institutional Analysis and Development: The Bloomington School* (Mercatus Books, 2009) focuses on the philosophical foundations of the institutional discourse.

international sphere, we discuss the importance of institutions for trade, foreign direct investment and foreign aid. In each chapter, we briefly review the theoretical claim that explains *why* certain institutions matter for a particular aspect of development, then we briefly review the empirical evidence available to assess *whether* those institutions indeed matter, and we conclude by discussing *how* the details of institutional design are likely to affect the efficacy of attempts to promote institutional reforms. Our general conclusion is that lawyers indeed have a role to play in these reforms, but this role lies in taking seriously the intricacies of institutional design, and producing solutions that are best suited to different contexts and realities.

The book is intended for readers seeking an accessible overview of the area. By highlighting the important role that lawyers can play in this field, it should be of particular interest to a legal audience, but should also be useful to anyone interested in a concise introduction to broader academic debates in the development field.

This project grew out of our course entitled Law, Institutions and Development taught at the University of Toronto, Faculty of Law. The course has been modified over the years and the current structure of the book is largely based on central themes of the course today. The process of building, shaping and polishing this course started long before we started co-teaching it in 2007. About a decade ago, Michael Trebilcock first taught this course with Kevin Davis, and continued later with another colleague, Ron Daniels. A great deal of the materials and analyses canvassed in this book were contributions by Kevin and Ron to the course in its pre-2007 version. Thus, both Kevin and Ron were involved (albeit indirectly) in the conception of this book and have significantly enriched it.

We could not have undertaken the intensive research and writing process of transforming a course into a book without the help of five very talented and extremely dedicated research assistants: Tess Bridgman, Natasha Kanerva, Jee Yeon Lim, Joanna Noronha and Michelle Segal. In addition to our research assistants, the JD, LLM and non-law graduate students from many countries around the world who have taken our course over the years have contributed invaluable insights into many issues addressed in this book. One doctoral student, Theresa Miedema, deserves a special thank you. She provided insightful comments on an earlier draft of Chapter 4 and was extremely generous in sharing with us parts of her doctoral dissertation on this subject and other unpublished work on ethnic conflict.

Last but not least, we are deeply grateful to Nadia Gulezko, our administrative assistant, for incorporating multiple rounds of revisions, keeping track of the latest drafts and for taking care of everything that was not related to the book project with her usual expedition and competence so as to minimize distractions we would otherwise have faced.

1. The ends and means of development

I. INTRODUCTION

The field of development theory and practice, at least in the post-World War II years, has been dominated primarily by economists. The central thesis of this book is that much of value can be added by incorporating a legal perspective in the development discourse. Lawyers with a particular interest in the interface between law and economics and related issues of political economy may have a significant contribution to make to the development field on issues of institutional design. Law as a discipline has always been preoccupied with processes and institutions by which laws and related policies are enacted, implemented and enforced. Hence, our perspective throughout this book is a focus on the relationship between law, institutions and development, but more particularly on the challenges that developing countries face in reforming their legal institutions, given the institutional legacies of history and the problems of path dependency that these legacies engender.

While, in many respects, our perspective is primarily concerned with the means of development – that is, how a society organizes itself institutionally to achieve its development objectives – one cannot entirely set to one side long-standing debates over the ends of development. In some respects, these contemporary debates are related to philosophical debates of what constitutes the good life and date back at least to the ancient Greeks. Although it is not the purpose of this chapter to provide an intellectual history of moral and political philosophy from the ancients onwards, or to espouse and defend any fully elaborated conception of the good life, one can at least identify some prominent strands in contemporary debates over the ends of development.[1] Without some definition on what these ends might be, it would be logically impossible to engage with the central theme of this book: the most appropriate means or mechanisms for vindicating those ends.

---

[1] See generally H.W. Arndt, *Economic Development: The History of an Idea* (Chicago: University of Chicago Press, 1989).

II. THE ENDS OF DEVELOPMENT

A number of classifications of countries – official and unofficial – exist, typically accompanied by various sub-classifications. One of the most conventional classifications identifies developing countries based on Gross Domestic Product (GDP) per capita. According to this classification, developing countries are all countries in the world except for the 40 or so members of the Organization for Economic Co-operation and Development (OECD) and other high income countries (such as some oil producing countries in the Middle East). This large universe of developing countries is typically sub-classified in various ways. For example, the World Bank distinguishes countries as low income; lower-middle income; upper-middle income; and high income countries. Low income countries are defined as having a per capita gross national income in 2010 of US$995 or less; lower-middle income countries have incomes between US$996 and US$3945; upper-middle income countries US US$3946 and US$12 195; and high income countries have incomes of US$12 196 or more.[2]

Implicit in such a classification of developing countries is the judgment that per capita income is what distinguishes developing countries from developed countries, and least developed from more developed countries. In such classification, the principal end of development might be inferred to be increasing per capita incomes. Indeed, in the early post-war decades, official multilateral development agencies such as the World Bank, many bilateral aid agencies, many governments in developing countries, and much scholarly discourse on development (especially in development economics) assumed that this was the primary end of development – that is, increasing per capita incomes and to that end maximizing rates of economic growth.[3]

In recent decades, dissatisfaction with such a narrow conception of development has been manifested in a number of quarters. For example, the United Nations Development Program (UNDP), in an annual series of Human Development Reports dating back to 1990,[4] has constructed a Human Development Index (HDI) based on three ends of development:

---

2 World Bank, 'Country Classification, Data and Statistics', available at http://data.worldbank.org/about/country-classifications (retrieved 13 April 2011).

3 Amartya Sen, 'Development, which way now?' (1983) 93:372 *The Economic Journal* at 745–62.

4 United Nations Development Programme, 'Origins of the human development approach' in *Human Development Reports*, available at http://hdr.undp.org/en/humandev/origins/ (retrieved 15 May 2009).

longevity, as measured by life expectancy at birth; knowledge, as measured by weighted average of adult literacy and mean years of schooling; and standard of living, as measured by per capita income.[5] While there is a strong positive correlation between per capita income and health and education status, this correlation is not perfect or tight. Rankings of developing countries often change significantly, either upwards or downwards, when health and education variables are incorporated along with a per capita income variable in this index.

In addition to the HDI, other indexes have been created. These indexes try to make visible various quantifiable indicators of development that are often overlooked in other indexes. They include social exclusion within OECD countries[6] and indicators of gender inequality,[7] for instance. More recently, the Oxford University's Oxford Poverty and Human Development Initiative (OPHI) joined the UNDP Human Development Report Office to create a new index to indicate the nature and quantify the extent of poverty. It is called the MPI, or Multidimensional Poverty Index.[8] The MPI examines a range of deprivations by using ten indicators at the household level (such as child mortality, years of schooling, and access to water, sanitation and electricity) to measure the same three critical dimensions of poverty as the HDI: education, health and living standard. This multidimensional approach to poverty reveals not only how many people are poor but also the nature and intensity of their poverty, which is relevant for policy design.[9] The percentage of people living in

---

5 United Nations Development Programme, 'The Human Development Index (HDI)' in *Human Development Reports*, available at http://hdr.undp.org/en/statistics/indices/hdi/ (retrieved May 15, 2009).

6 For example, the UNDP Human Poverty Index (HPI), introduced in the Human Development Report of 1997, is composed of the different features of deprivation in quality of life, such as a short life, lack of basic education and lack of access to resources. Within the HPI, the HPI-2 relates only to OECD countries, is derived separately from the Human Poverty Index for developing countries (HPI-1) and includes social exclusion as the fourth dimension of HPI-2 in order to better reflect socio-economic differences and the different measures of deprivation in the two groups. UNDP, ibid.

7 United Nations Development Programme, Human Development Reports, 'Gender-related Development Index (GDI) and Gender Empowerment Measure (GEM)' in *Human Development Reports*, available at http://hdr.undp.org/en/statistics/indices/.

8 This new index is featured in the 2010 UNDP Human Development Report, released in November 2010. Research findings are available online at http://www.ophi.org.uk.

9 Sabina Alkire and Maria Emma Santos, 'Acute Multidimensional Poverty: A New Index for Developing Countries' (2010) OPHI Working Paper No. 38 at 7.

poverty according to the MPI is higher than the percentage of people living on less than US$2 a day in 43 countries and lower than those living on less than US$1.25 a day in 25 countries. For example, in Ethiopia, 90 per cent of the population are MPI poor compared to 39 per cent classified as living in extreme poverty;[10] on the other hand, in Tanzania, 89 per cent of people live in extreme income poverty but only 65 per cent are MPI poor. This index captures access to key services such as sanitation and water in a more direct fashion, so the picture of deprivation seems to be a more accurate one: in some countries, services are available for free, while in others they are out of reach even for working people with an income.[11] Additionally, for the same reasons, the MPI can reveal the persistence of acute poverty in countries with strong economic growth, such as India.[12]

Another example of efforts to use more comprehensive measures to assess a country's level of development is exemplified by the eight Millenium Development Goals (MDGs) adopted in September 2000 by 189 members of the United Nations. In addition to defining these eight goals, the member countries of the UN also committed to a set of targets to be achieved by 2015 and defined indicators to monitor progress in achieving each of these goals:

1. Eradicate extreme poverty and hunger
   Target for 2015
   Halve the proportion of people living on less than $1 a day and those who suffer from hunger.
2. Achieve universal primary education
   Target for 2015
   Ensure that all boys and girls complete primary school.
3. Promote gender equality and empower women
   Target for 2005
   Eliminate gender disparities in primary and secondary education (preferred).
   Target for 2015
   Eliminate gender disparities at all levels.
4. Reduce child mortality
   Target for 2015

---

[10] The World Bank classifies extreme income poverty as living on less than US$1.25 a day. Available at http://web.worldbank.org/WBSITE/EXTERNAL/TOPICS/EXTPOVERTY/0,,contentMDK:20153855~menuPK:373757~pagePK:148956~piPK:216618~theSitePK:336992,00.html.

[11] Sabina Alkire and Maria Emma Santos, 'Multidimensional Poverty Index: 2010 Data. Research Brief' (July 2010) Oxford Poverty and Human Development Initiative. Available at http://www.ophi.org.uk/wp-content/uploads/OPHI-MPI-Brief.pdf, at 4.

[12] Ibid.

Reduce by two-thirds the mortality rate among children under five.

5. Improve maternal health
   Target for 2015
   Reduce by three-quarters the ratio of women dying in childbirth.
6. Combat HIV/AIDS, malaria and other diseases
   Target for 2015
   Halt and begin to reverse the spread of HIV/AIDS and the incidence of malaria and other major diseases.
7. Ensure environmental sustainability
   General target
   Integrate the principles of sustainable development into country policies and programs and reverse the loss of environmental resources.
   Target for 2015
   Reduce by half the proportion of people without access to safe drinking water.
   Target for 2020
   Achieve significant improvement in the lives of at least 100 million slum dwellers.
8. Develop a global partnership for development
   Targets
   - Develop further an open trading and financial system that includes a commitment to good governance, development and poverty reduction – nationally and internationally.
   - Address the special needs of the least developed countries and those of landlocked and small-island developing states.
   - Deal comprehensively with the debt problems of developing countries.
   - Develop decent and productive work for youth.
   - In cooperation with pharmaceutical companies, provide access to affordable essential drugs in developing countries.
   - In cooperation with the private sector, make available the benefits of new technologies – especially information and communication technologies.

Despite moving away from a strictly economic concept of development, both the HDI and the MDGs are mostly based on quantifiable variables, which can be measured periodically, and allow frequent comparison between different countries and their levels of development. In this respect, they are similar to income measures of GDP per capita.[13] The difference is that the multiplicity of variables in these two indexes makes it harder to draw clear-cut lines that distinguish developed from developing countries, such as the lines drawn by the World Bank between low, middle and high

---

[13] For a critique of these measures as the basis for an agenda for public policy-making, see Kerry Rittich, 'Governing by measuring: the Millennium Development Goals in global governance' in Helene Ruiz-Fabri, Rudiger Wolfrum and Jana Gogolin (eds), *Select Proceedings of the European Society of International Law*, Vol. 2, 463 (Hart Publishing, 2010).

income countries. For example, Vietnam, Chile and Cuba fare better on health and education (and in the overall HDI ranking) than other countries with the same level of income, whereas Bahrain, Angola and the United States do worse on health and education rankings than other countries with the same level of income.[14] Thus, by adding two variables that are not necessarily correlated with income (health and education), the HDI challenges our ability to draw a clear line separating who is developed and who is not.

Like measures of GDP per capita, the HDI and the MDGs are also embedded within a concept of development – one that might be multifaceted and less simplistic than GDP per capita, but still reveal a notion of what is development. At a conceptual level, the primacy of per capita income as an index of a country's state of development and maximization of rates of economic growth (and hence per capita income) as the primary end of development has been challenged by Amartya Sen, Nobel Laureate in Economics. In a widely celebrated book, *Development as Freedom*, Sen argues that the ends of development should be focused on promoting individual freedom, in the sense of enhancing the ability of individuals to choose to live lives that they have reason to value.[15] In Sen's view, to realize this objective various freedoms are important, including political freedoms, economic facilities, social opportunities, transparency guarantees and protective security. For Sen, freedom in these various dimensions constitutes both the means and ends of development in that they reflect a complementary and mutually reinforcing set of freedoms that promote more robust forms of individual agency and expand human capabilities, opportunities and functioning. The HDI partly reflects this concept of development. The MDGs, in turn, may not be easily associated with one particular author or concept of development, but it is clear that they have at least two novelties vis-à-vis other measures of development: a concern with gender equality, and a concern with environmental sustainability.

We accept that policies and institutions that increase per capita incomes

---

[14] UNDP, *supra* note 5. These discrepancies have persisted since 1990. See also UNDP, 'Defining and measuring human development', *Human Development Report* (1990) at 14–16. Available at http://hdr.undp.org/en/media/hdr_1990_en_front.pdf

[15] Amartya Sen, *Development as Freedom* (New York: Knopf, 1999). See also Martha C. Nussbaum, *Creating Capabilities: The Human Development Approach* (Cambridge, MA and London: Belknap-Harvard University Press, 2011); Martha Nussbaum, *Women and Human Development: The Capabilities Approach* (Cambridge University Press, 2000).

by increasing economic growth are instrumental in promoting development. But, following Sen, it cannot be the case that economic growth is the ultimate end of development or the exclusive means of promoting it. Economic growth is important for what it enables individuals, and the communities and societies of which they are members, to achieve in terms of their individual and collective conceptions of human well-being. In other words, focusing narrowly on economic growth as an end in and of itself – abstracting from what it enables members of a society, individually or collectively, to achieve (perhaps, as Sen would argue, in terms of enhanced human capabilities and functioning) – would be to accord economic growth a primacy in the conception of the ends of development that it cannot sustain. Nevertheless, it is important to recognize the opposing danger that the ends of development may become so diffuse that 'one sometimes wonders whether it now stands for anything more substantial than everyone's own utopia'.[16]

III. NON-INSTITUTIONAL THEORIES OF DEVELOPMENT

Debates about the means of achieving the ends of development have often reflected as much diversity of viewpoints as debates over the ends. In this section we provide a brief overview of a wide variety of theories regarding the means of development. The common feature among the theories described here is the fact that they ignore or reject the idea that institutions are important for development. Except for this common characteristic, these non-institutional theories of development differ radically from each other. At the risk of oversimplifying these differences, we have grouped a variety of non-institutional development theories under three major headings: (a) economic theories, (b) cultural theories, and (c) geographic theories. The following discussion will provide an overview of these theories and highlight their main policy implications.

Despite generally ignoring or rejecting the importance of institutions for development, most of these theories have an institutional connection. Some of them have institutional assumptions embedded in their models while others require functional institutions for their policy proposals to be effectuated. Thus, these so-called non-institutional theories have important institutional implications that are not always acknowledged or recognized.

---

[16] Arndt, *supra* note 1 at 165.

A. Economic Theories of Development

Over the post-war period, various schools of thought concerned with economic growth have come into and out of favour, including: capital fundamentalism; *dirigiste* central planning; neo-Marxist dependency theory; the Washington Consensus (the neoclassical model or market fundamentalism); endogenous growth theories; and eclectic combinations of all of the foregoing. Most of these theories simply assumed the relevant institutional capacity to implement the (highly divergent) policies that each theory espoused.

According to a class of theories known as the 'linear stages approach' or 'capital fundamentalism', countries need to mobilize domestic savings and foreign investment in order to generate sufficient investment to accelerate GDP growth.[17] Linear stages of growth theory was a branch of modernization theory, which was based on the view of developing countries as simply backward societies which must be brought into modern civilization through the evolutionary process of industrialization and economic development. The dominant theory of development in the 1950s and 1960s, it was initially developed by the economic historian, Walt W. Rostow, shortly after World War II, and was formulated as a capitalist response to Marxist development theory. Rostow's basic assumption was that there were pre-defined stages through which every country must proceed in order to achieve economic development, and developing nations could be located at a particular stage based on national growth and investment rates.[18] According to Rostow the most crucial need of developing countries was capital. However, some developing countries had very low rates of new capital formation, and were not able to save the resources required (15 to 20 per cent of GDP) to promote economic development. In this context, foreign aid (and to some extent foreign direct investment) were proposed as a solution to the savings gap.[19] A central policy implication of this theory was a state-centred approach to promoting savings and investments in early post-war development through state-created tax incentives for both private savings and investment in production by private companies, and high levels of investment in state-owned compa-

---

[17] Michael Todaro and Stephen Smith, *Economic Development* (Boston, San Francisco, New York: Addison Wesley, 2012, 11th edn) at 110–111.

[18] Rostow described the stages as follows: (a) traditional society; (b) preconditions for take-off into self-sustaining growth; (c) take-off; (d) the drive to modernity or maturity; (e) the age of high mass consumption.

[19] Todaro and Smith, *supra* note 17 at 114.

nies.[20] Thus, the 'capital fundamentalists' assumed a functioning state, bureaucracy, tax system, and other institutional features of an operational economy, but they did not address the problem of how to acquire these institutions.[21]

The linear stages approach to development was replaced in the 1970s with two other competing categories of theories: structural change theories and international dependence theories. In contrast to linear stages theory, these two sets of theories went beyond economic policies, addressing the need for political and social change in order to foster development. However, similar to 'capital fundamentalism', these theories also had institutional implications that were not addressed directly by their theoretical models.

Structural change theories argued that economic growth required that 'underdeveloped economies transform their domestic economic structures from a heavy emphasis on traditional subsistence agriculture to a more modern, more urbanized, and more industrially diverse manufacturing and service economy'.[22] This transformation required the state to implement policies to foster industrialization and mechanization of the agricultural sector, to provide a strong educational system to train the work force and enable rural workers to move to industrial sectors, and to undertake urban planning and make infrastructure investments to accommodate the growth of urban centres. These assumptions largely ignored the complex institutional framework that is required to enable the state to perform all these functions.

Dependency theories were primarily conceived in developing nations (especially in Latin America), and emerged largely in response to modernization theory and the capital fundamentalists' overly simplistic understanding of economic development. Dependency theories looked to external and historical influences as central to the state of domestic economic development but, similar to other economic theories, they also had important institutional connections that were not addressed in their models. The basic claim of these theories was that the international economic order is polarized and entails a relationship of dependence between the industrial centre and an agrarian periphery.[23] This claim assumed that

---

[20] Michael Trebilcock, 'What makes poor countries poor? The role of institutional capital in economic development' in Eduardo Buscaglia et al. (eds), *The Law and Economics of Development* (Connecticut: JAI Press, 1997) at 17.

[21] Pranab Bardhan, 'Symposium on the state and economic development' (1990) 4 *Journal of Economic Perspectives* at 3–7.

[22] Todaro and Smith, *supra* note 17 at 115.

[23] Ibid., at 122. See also Dennis Conway and Nikolas Heynen, 'Classical

exploitation of former colonies had remained, and in some cases had been intensified, after independence.

Some *dependencistas* were also influenced by Marxist ideas that the division between rich and poor is required to support the global capitalist system.[24] To eliminate dependency, these theorists advocated aggressive economic nationalism[25] grounded on import substitution industrialization (ISI), with high levels of tariff protection to restrict the flow of imports and to promote the development of local industries.[26] ISI policies assume a major role for the state, especially in making investments in infrastructure (transportation, energy and telecommunications) and in fostering industrialization in capital-intensive industries (the commanding heights of the economy). These theories, however, did not explore the fact that heavy state intervention in the economy assumes at least an efficient and competent bureaucracy and a functional executive branch. Moreover, the policies prescribed required effective laws and regulations, such as the tariffs and exchange controls on which the ISI model depended. Despite being central to dependency theories, these institutional connections were largely unexplored in the academic literature.

The neoclassical (or neoliberal) counter-revolution replaced the structural change and dependency theories, becoming the dominant paradigm in development theory in the 1980s and 1990s. The neoclassical model assumed that free markets could promote an efficient allocation of economic resources by creating efficient pricing signals, thus being labelled 'market fundamentalism'. This contrasted with the state-centred view of development assumed by most preceding theories. This model assumed that the state was often the source of the problem rather than the solution to challenges of development. In the late 1980s, the neoliberal theory was embodied in a set of policy prescriptions that became known as the 'Washington Consensus'.[27] The central tenets of the Consensus were:

---

dependency theories: from ECLA to André Gunder Frank', in V. Desai and R. Potter (eds), *The Companion to Development Studies* (London: Arnold, 2002) at 97.

[24] Todaro and Smith, *supra* note 17 at 123. See also Colin Clarke, 'The Latin American structuralists' in Desai and Potter, ibid., at 94.

[25] Brian Tamanaha, 'The lessons of law-and-development studies' (1995) 89:2 *American Journal of International Law* at 478.

[26] John Coatsworth, 'Structures, endownments and institutions in the economic history of Latin America' (2005) 40:3 *Latin America Research Review* at 126.

[27] For a brief history of the term, see John Williamson, 'The Washington Consensus as policy prescription for development' in Timothy Besley and Roberto Zagha (eds), *Development Challenges in the 1990s: Leading Policymakers Speak from Experience* (New York: World Bank/Oxford University Press, 2005) at 33–61.

macro-economic stability (fiscal discipline, tax reforms and reductions in public expenditures), liberalization (open trade and market deregulation), privatization, and policies to attract foreign direct investment (FDI) and stimulate private entrepreneurship (reduction of tax burdens, availability of credit for private investors, and fostering of competition within sectors). The Washington Consensus was closely followed by many Latin American countries, and more cautiously by developing countries in other regions.[28]

In common with its counterparts, however, neoliberal theories largely ignored the central role of the state – not in directly promoting development, but instead in providing the pre-conditions for markets to operate. Markets depend on a functioning legal system and effective regulation of capital markets, banking sectors, competition policies, the trade system, tax collection, and investment in infrastructure, healthcare and education, etc. The lack of attention to these institutional connections has been perceived to be one of the central reasons why many of these policies failed.[29]

Endogenous growth theory developed in response to the inability of the neoclassical model to explain rates of technological change and productivity growth, as well as the variable long-term growth rates experienced by different countries.[30] In contrast with neoclassical theories, endogenous theories of growth emphasize that 'economic growth is an endogenous outcome of an economic system, not the result of forces that impinge from outside'.[31] Endogeneity, in economics, refers to the fact that variables in a certain model are not independent – that is, changes in one variable will produce changes in another variable, and vice versa. Endogenous theories of growth thus claim that these variables, such as technological change, are

---

[28] V. Bulmer-Thomas, *The Economic History of Latin America since Independence (Vol.2)* (Cambridge: Cambridge University Press, 2003).

[29] Dani Rodrik, 'Goodbye Washington Consensus, hello Washington Confusion? A review of the World Bank's economic growth in the 1990s: learning from a decade of reform' (2006) 44:4 *Journal of Economic Literature*, 973–87. Other critiques include that the Consensus was too focused on GDP growth, while ignoring other important factors that influence living standards, especially those related to economic inequalities, and that the policies have had a negative impact on poverty levels and living standards of the poor. See Robin Broad and John Cavanagh, 'The death of the Washington Consensus' in Walden F. Bello, Nicola Bullard and Kamal Malhotra (eds), *Global Finance: New Thinking on Regulating Speculative Capital Markets* (London: Zed Books, 2000).

[30] Subrata Ghatak, *Introduction to Development Economics* (London, New York: Routledge, 2003, 4th edn) at 58.

[31] Paul M. Romer, 'The origins of endogenous growth' (1994) 8 *Journal of Economic Perspectives* at 3–22.

not independent: they impact on growth, which in turn impacts on them. As a result, 'economic growth involves a two way interaction between technology and economic life: technological progress transforms the very economic system that creates it'.[32] Endogenous growth theories seek to understand this interplay and how such interplay results in economic growth.[33]

For endogenous growth theories, technological change is an outcome of public and private investments in education (human capital), infrastructure, and research and development in knowledge-intensive industries.[34] This focus on technology is based largely on Joseph Schumpeter's work on the innovative process and technological change, which has been elaborated on by Arrow.[35] This introduced an endogenous theory of knowledge production whereby engaging in problem-solving generates both specific experience and general knowledge. This knowledge is a public good that can be re-used by other producers, leading to knowledge spillovers, which generate growth because productivity increases as knowledge is accumulated and disseminated. Competition for profits leads to improved products and production processes, which can also be understood as technological change/innovation, and technological change/innovation leads to more competition, thus generating economic growth endogenously by increasing productivity and human capital.[36] This theory explains why developed countries continue to experience high or increasing levels of growth, as 'the more you learn, the faster you learn things'.[37]

This theory leads to an important policy implication: there is room for state intervention to create incentives for accumulation of knowledge (human capital) and technological progress. In contrast to neoliberal theories, endogenous growth theory 'is somewhat more sympathetic to a more activist policy role for the state in realizing the dynamic economies associated with the introduction and exploitation of modern technology and its accompanying externalities and spillovers'.[38] In this analysis,

---

32 Philippe Aghion and Peter Howitt, *Endogenous Growth Theory* (Cambridge, MA: MIT Press, 1998) at 1.

33 Ibid.

34 Todaro and Smith, *supra* note 17 at 150.

35 Kenneth Arrow, 'The economic implications of learning by doing' (1962) 29 *Review of Economic Studies*.

36 Ghatak, *supra* note 30.

37 James M. Cypher and James L. Dietz, *The Process of Economic Development* (Taylor and Francis, 2008, 3rd edn) at 249.

38 Trebilcock, *supra* note 20 at 18.

private organizations are likely to under-invest in human capital generation, as some of the benefits from this expenditure are externalities that benefit society at large while the private organizations bear all the costs. Therefore government is advised to subsidize this gap between private investment and the socially optimal level of investment in human capital formation, research and training.[39] However, if human capital is a major engine of economic growth, then a 'brain drain' where highly skilled individuals emigrate from developing to developed countries may be a serious impediment to growth in developing countries. This will limit the effectiveness of increased educational attainment as a government policy to drive growth. Among economic theories of development, endogenous growth theory is perhaps the one that has most explicitly acknowledged the role of institutions in promoting economic development. However, they do not provide any insight into how to improve them.

As a result of the deficiencies of neoliberal policies, and contrary to mainstream arguments for less state intervention in the economy, a consensus has emerged: it is the *quality* of state intervention that matters, not necessarily its quantity. The quality of intervention, in turn, is now recognized as a function of the quality of a state's institutions.[40] Indeed, over the past decade or so, an institutional perspective on development has become increasingly prominent in development thinking, captured in the mantra, 'institutions matter' or 'governance matters'. The focus of this perspective is on how a state should organize itself through its political, bureaucratic, administrative and legal institutions to advance its development goals (however defined). We describe this perspective in more detail and the challenges it raises in Part IV of this chapter.

B. Cultural Theories of Development

The word culture does not have a singular or universal meaning, and can be used to describe a wide array of societal forces, such as formal and informal norms of behaviour, religious beliefs, informal codes of conduct, social habits and attitudes, or the existing value, moral or ethical system that prevails in a particular society. Despite these ambiguities, or perhaps because of them, the term has often been used in development theory. This section provides a general map of some of the many ways in which culture is associated with development in the academic literature.

---

39 Cypher and Dietz, *supra* note 37 at 249.
40 See, e.g., Trebilcock, *supra* note 20.

As discussed in Part II, there are different conceptions of development that reflect different interpretations of what is required to achieve human well-being. Despite their divergences, these conceptions of development have one thing in common: they assume that there is a universal core to either the conception of what the good life is (the ends of development), or what is needed to enable individuals to pursue a good life (the means of development). In contrast, some authors argue that societies have diverse, culturally defined conceptions of 'the good life' and how one goes about achieving it. This perspective asserts that different societies have different values and these differences should be respected, and as such there are no grounds for judging that the values of some societies are better than others.

The most radical versions of this argument claim that everything is culturally defined.[41] This can lead to questioning the validity of the entire development enterprise. For example, the radical relativist Escobar argues for the preservation of indigenous culture and against the use of Western (or any) standards as a benchmark, and claims that the imperialistic nature of the development discourse makes it comparable to discourses of colonization.[42] The idea that there is an incompatibility between Western and other cultures may assume a static and perhaps immutable view of culture, which presupposes that we cannot intentionally and purposively change culture. A stronger version of this argument claims that 'culture is destiny', that with or without intentional attempts to do so, culture will not change.[43]

At the other extreme of this debate, there are theorists who believe that culture is at the very core of conceptions of development and, as a consequence, only cultural reforms can promote development. According to these theorists, universal conceptions of development cannot be realized unless the culture of developing societies mimics the culture of developed nations, which are more congenial to development objectives. Thus, promoting Western conceptions of development and trying to implement

---

41 For a discussion of this, see Jack Donnelly, *Universal Human Rights in Theory and Practice* (Ithaca, NY: Cornell University Press: 2003) at 89–107.

42 A. Escobar, 'Introduction: development and the anthropology of modernity' in *Encountering Development: The Making and Unmaking of the Third World* (Princeton, NJ: Princeton University Press, 1995) at 3–20. The label 'radical relativist' is explained in more detail in R.A. Shweder, 'Moral maps, "First World" conceits, and the New Evangelists' in L. Harrison and S. Huntington, *Culture Matters* (New York, NY: Basic Books, 2000) at 158–76.

43 Kim Dae Jung, 'Is culture destiny? The myth of Asia's anti-democratic values' (1994) 73 *Foreign Affairs* 6.

liberal democracies in developing countries will not work unless there is a substantive cultural change in these societies. Harrison argues, for instance, that some societies have a progress-resistant cultural outlook that will prevent development unless they change these cultural traits.[44] However, Harrison can be accused of formulating a revamped version of modernization theory as his theory similarly assumes that development is achieved through evolutionary progress (distinguishing backward from modern societies) and uses this notion to claim that developing cultures should improve by becoming similar to developed cultures. Other scholars, such as Sen, may also be vulnerable to the criticism of proposing a modified version of modernization theory. Any discourse that suggests that there is something universal that all societies should aspire to (rationalism, human rights, democracy, etc) assumes that there are societies that are at more advanced stages of their evolution, and that they should serve as models to laggard societies.

In contrast to those who use a concept of culture to challenge conceptions of development, there are theorists who question the notion of culture as defined in the development literature. Scholars such as Tatsuo seek to deconstruct Western representations of the First and Third Worlds, questioning conceptions that try to establish clear lines to separate them. Tatsuo claims, for instance, that most of the debate about development and culture is built upon false dichotomies that separate Western cultures from other cultures. [45] If we abandon these dichotomies, Tatsuo argues

---

[44] Harrison argues that these cultures have the following outlook: they have religious beliefs that nurture irrationality, inhibit material progress, and are utopian; their views of destiny are informed by fatalism, resignation and sorcery; their members are focused on the present or on the past, not on the future, creating difficulty with planning and punctuality; wealth is conceived as a non-expandable resource and resource allocation is a zero sum game; knowledge is abstract, theoretical and cosmological, among other things. See Lawrence E. Harrison, *The Central Liberal Truth* (New York, NY: Oxford University Press, 2006); Harrison and Huntington, *supra* note 42.

[45] Tatsuo challenges the depiction of Asia as a Confucian (or Confucian-Islamic) society in contrast to a Christian (or Judeo-Christian) West by showing that religious and cultural diversity are important characteristics of the Asian region. He also challenges characterizations of Asia as communitarian, arguing that individualism is not alien to Asia in general and to Confucianism and Buddhism in particular. Tatsuo concludes that the idea of an 'Asian culture' ignores the complex reality of the region (and its religious, cultural, and socio-economic diversity), and also presents an oversimplified portrait of religious and cultural traditions (assuming that Confucianism is incompatible with individualism): Inuoe Tatsuo, 'Liberal democracy and Asian Orientalism' in J. Bauer and D. Bells (eds), *The East Asian Challenge for Human Rights* (Cambridge: Cambridge University Press, 1999).

that the tension and incompatibility between liberal democracy and 'Asian culture' largely disappears. A similar argument is developed by Amartya Sen in his book *Identity and Violence*.[46] According to him, identities have been often defined by singling out one aspect of a person's life, such as religion, when in fact a person may identify more strongly with other aspects of his or her character. Sen claims that the miniaturization of identities has created polarization between different ethnic and religious groups, and has been a source of ethnic and religious conflict around the world.

Culture can also be understood in light of the distinction drawn by Amartya Sen between the ends and the means of development. Cultural freedom can be conceived as a goal of the development process if one believes that the opportunity to engage in cultural activities is part of the basic freedoms that constitute a developed country (conceiving development as freedom).[47] In turn, culture can be conceived as a means to an end, viewed as a necessary component of the process that generates economic gains or increased freedom of choice.[48]

In addition, culture can interact with the ends and means of development in more indirect ways, which have important policy implications. As to ends, culture strongly influences value systems,[49] affecting what a given society will consider to be 'a good life', therefore impacting upon what a society considers to be the ultimate end of the development process. As to means, culture may be a relevant consideration when designing effective strategies to reach development goals. Culture can influence economic, political and social behaviour in substantial ways.[50] In economic terms, culture can influence levels of entrepreneurship, willingness to take risks and business ethics. In political terms, culture can impact on the frequency and quality of public discussion, civic interaction and engagement in deliberative processes. In social terms, culture can determine levels of solidarity and trust, as well as educational attainment, marital patterns, or expectations about others' behaviour. Thus, on this view, reforms that try to influence economic behaviour should take into account specific cultural characteristics that guide economic behaviour in particular societies. Similarly, attempts to promote political reforms, such as implementing a liberal democracy, must acknowledge that political behaviour is

---

[46] Amartya Sen, *Identity and Violence: The Illusion of Destiny* (New York: Norton, 2006).

[47] Amartya Sen, 'How does culture matter?', in Vijayendra Rao and Michael Walton (eds), *Culture and Public Action* (Stanford University Press: 2004) at 39.

[48] Ibid.

[49] Ibid., at 42–3.

[50] Ibid., at 39.

influenced by culture, and that the same political institutions might not function in the same way in different cultural contexts.

One of the conclusions that can be drawn from the influence of culture on human behaviour is that development policies need to be adjusted to divergent cultural contexts, and it is unlikely that one will be able to design a universal blueprint for all developing countries. This raises the question of whether it is possible to claim that there is a discipline or a field of study called law and development. The idea that development strategies and policies need to be tailored to particular contexts may suggest that the problem of development should be analysed on a case-by-case basis, with little or no room for generalizations.

However, culture is not the only factor that influences human behaviour.[51] Thus, there is room to develop some common strategies that transcend cultural divides. Despite cultural differences, many societies share important commonalities. Heterogeneous beliefs and practices will often exist within a given culture, and these dissenting voices can play an important role in questioning the maintenance and permanence of certain entrenched cultural traits.[52] Finally, culture is dynamic, making it difficult to draw conclusive distinctions between societies. Cultural change may occur endogenously, or may be linked to external forces arising from interaction with other cultures.[53] In other words, culture is not destiny. Policymakers should be mindful of cultural factors when designing development policies, but no society should be viewed as a prisoner of its existing cultural context.

In general, economists can be accused of not paying enough attention to culture as a relevant factor in human behaviour, and of not acknowledging its relevance for the development process.[54] There is, however, one important exception within this group: the new institutional economists,[55] who follow for the most part Douglass North's definition of institutions:

> Institutions are the rules of the game of a society, or, more formally, are the humanly devised constraints that structure human interactions. They are composed of formal rules (statute law, common law, regulation), informal constraints (conventions, norms of behaviour and self-imposed codes of conduct), and the enforcement characteristics of both.[56]

---

51 Ibid., at 43.

52 Ibid., at 43.

53 Ibid., at 43–44.

54 Ibid., at 37.

55 And, according to Sen, they are not the only ones. Adam Smith, John Stuart Mill and Alfred Marshall can also be cited as examples.

56 Douglass North, 'The new institutional economics and Third World

Most of what we refer to as culture is encompassed by what North calls 'informal institutions'. Thus, according to the new institutional economics, culture, together with formal institutions, influence human behaviour and structure social interactions.

However, institutional economists do not go much beyond acknowledging that culture influences human behaviour. It is not clear how, when and why it does so. The result is that culture is often treated as a black box in institutional analyses.[57] We do not know, for instance, to what extent the existence of formal institutions, such as the rule of law and democratic accountability depends on certain underlying cultural values, such as individualism and lack of hierarchical structures.[58] We also do not know if formal institutions can change culture and vice-versa.[59] And if these changes are possible, we do not know when and under which circumstances they are likely to take place.

This poses a major challenge for the advancement of our understanding of the problem of development. While institutional theories of development have become prominent in development discourse, without a thorough assessment of the role that culture plays in institutional stability and institutional change, reforms may have either limited success or unintended results. Culture is an important factor that is currently largely missing in the institutional reform puzzle.

C. Geographic Theories of Development

A third group of theories claims that development is largely dependent on the geographic location and condition of a country. These theories diverge, however, in their explanation of why geography matters, and whether it has a direct or indirect effect on development. This section will provide a brief overview of some of these geographic theories and discuss their policy implications.

---

development' in J. Harris et al. (eds), *Economics and Third World Development* (London: Routledge, 1995).

[57] D. Acemoğlu and S. Johnson, 'Unbundling institutions' (2005) 113 *Journal of Political Economy* 5.

[58] For an analysis suggesting that there is empirical evidence to support the idea that there is significant influence of culture on governance, see Amir Licht, Chana Goldschmidt and Shalom Schwartz, 'Culture rules: the foundations of the rule of law and other norms of governance' (2007) 35 *Journal of Comparative Economics* at 659–88.

[59] Harrison, for instance, argues that formal institutions do not change culture. It is necessary to modify culture before promoting institutional reforms. Harrison and Huntington, *supra* note 42.

Several basic claims are made to support the idea that geography can directly impact on a country's development, as well as a more recent approach – called economic geography – which attempts to show how geography interacts with a number of other factors, creating a dynamic in which economic activity is concentrated in certain areas despite the lack of relative geographic advantages. The first basic claim is based on climate: tropical countries are more likely to be underdeveloped. This might be so for a number of different reasons. Some scholars believe that tropical climates impact on productive economic activity, especially agriculture, because of the fragility and low fertility of tropical soils, high prevalence of crop pests and parasites, high evaporation and unstable supply of water, as well as ecological conditions favourable to infectious human diseases.[60] Others claim that tropical climates inhibit work because of hot weather and humidity,[61] or the abundance of easily obtainable, non-agriculturally produced food, which reduces the need to work hard and so creates a culture of idleness.[62]

The second claim is based on location: landlocked countries face significant barriers to engaging in trade, and therefore are significantly deprived of the economic benefits derived from international or inter-regional commercial activity.[63] According to Paul Collier, this can create a poverty trap whereby development prospects are limited because landlocked countries face impediments to integrating into the global economy, a problem which is particularly severe where the landlocked country's coastal neighbour has not invested sufficiently in the infrastructure necessary to allow its neighbour to transport goods to the coast where they can be traded intercontinentally. Collier describes these landlocked countries as 'hostages to their neighbours', especially where instability or violence restricts access to trade routes.[64] Further, impoverished neighbours are poor markets for

---

60 David E. Bloom and Jeffrey D. Sachs, 'Geography, demography, and economic growth in Africa' (1998) 29 *Brookings Papers on Economic Activity* at 207–96; Jeffrey D. Sachs, 'Tropical underdevelopment' (2000) Centre for International Development at Harvard University, Working Paper # 57.

61 D. Landes, *The Wealth and Poverty of Nations: Why Are Some So Rich and Others So Poor?* (New York: W.W. Norton, 1998).

62 William Easterly and Ross Levine, 'Tropics, germs, and crops: how endowments influence economic development' (2003) 50 *Journal of Monetary Economics* 1, at 7 (citing Machiavelli).

63 J. Sachs and A. Warner, 'Economic reform and the process of global integration', in William C. Brainard and George L. Perry (eds), *Brookings Papers on Economic Activity* (Brookings Institution Press, 1990).

64 Paul Collier, *The Bottom Billion* (Oxford: Oxford University Press, 2007) at 55.

a neighbouring country's goods, preventing landlocked countries from leveraging on the growth of their coastal neighbours.

The third claim is based on natural endowments. It is intuitive to assume that natural resource abundance would be more conducive to growth, and indeed natural wealth can positively impact on a country's development outlook. However, this is not necessarily the case:[65] the phenomenon of the 'resource curse' has shown that under certain circumstances abundance of natural resources will not lead to growth,[66] will foster rent seeking and corruption,[67] and may lead to an increased likelihood of civil conflict resulting from disputed resource ownership.[68] There is a general consensus that what determines whether or not a country will be able to utilize resource wealth to become rich is largely determined by the quality of its institutions.[69]

Engerman and Sokoloff make an alternative geographic claim which

---

65 Jeffrey Sachs and Andrew Warner, 'Natural resource abundance and economic growth' (1995) NBER Working Paper Series 5398 at 1–47; Richard Auty, *Sustaining Development in Mineral Economies: The Resource Curse Thesis* (London and New York: Routledge, 1993). See also Thorvaldur Gysfason, 'The International Economics of Natural Resources and Growth' (2007) CESifo Working Paper Series No. 1994.

66 Studies have shown that the negative economic impacts were caused by a phenomenon called 'Dutch Disease': W. Max Corden and J. Peter Neary, 'Booming sector and de-industrialisation in a small open economy' (1982) 92 *Economic Journal* 368, Royal Economic Society, at 825–48. See also Migara de Silva, 'The political economy of windfalls, the "Dutch Disease" – theory and evidence' (1994) John M. Olin School of Business Discussion Paper (Saint Louis: John M. Olin School of Business). For an overview of economic and political causes and possible solutions to the problem of the resource curse, see Macartan Humphreys, Jeffrey Sachs and Joseph Stiglitz (eds), *Escaping the Resource Curse* (New York: Columbia University Press, 2007).

67 Richard M. Auty (ed.), *Resource Abundance and Economic Development* (Oxford and New York: Oxford University Press, 2001); Terry Lyn Karl, 'Oil-led development: social, political and economic consequences' (2007) *CDDRL Working Papers*, at 36; Carlos Leite and Jens Weidman, 'Does Mother Nature corrupt – natural resources, corruption and economic growth' (1999) IMF Working Paper No. 99/85.

68 Michael T. Klare, *Resource Wars: The New Landscape of Global Conflict*, (New York: A Metropolitan/Owl Book, 2002). On the correlation between natural resource dependence and civil conflict, see Paul Collier and Anke Hoeffler, 'Resource rents, governance and conflict' (2005) 49:4 *Journal of Conflict Resolution* at 625–33.

69 See Halvor Mehlum, Karl Moene and Ragnar Torvik, 'Institutions and the resource curse' (2006) 116 *The Economic Journal* at 1–20. See also Daron Acemoğlu, 'An African success story: Botswana' in Dani Rodrik (ed.), *In Search of Prosperity* (Princeton, NJ: Princeton University Press: 2003); Collier, *supra* note 64.

supports the idea that geography has an indirect effect on development by influencing the emergence of strong or weak institutions. This theory points to certain resource endowments as creating high levels of inequality of wealth, human capital and political power, which work against the development of strong institutions. Instead of fostering developmentally beneficial institutions, high levels of inequality allow the growth of 'institutional structures that greatly advantage members of elite classes'.[70]

Another argument based on natural resources focuses on germs and crops. Diamond, in his book *Guns, Germs and Steel: The Fates of Human Societies*, shows that some nations, including European nations, developed resistance to germs acquired from farm animals, whereas others, such as colonized nations, did not have farm animals and therefore did not develop such resistance.[71] The spread of these germs at the time of colonization negatively impacted on the development prospects of colonized nations. Also, regions such as Africa had germs that restricted the use of farm animals, undermining their productivity. Further, some regions had plant species that could be easily domesticated into high-yielding food crops, such as grains. In contrast, other regions did not have species that would lend themselves so easily to cultivation.

Economic geography is still another theory of development, which focuses on economic models of the geography of development, looking at why economic development takes place in a certain area rather than another, despite the lack of relative geographic advantages. This differs from the approaches explained above, which use the inherent geographic location of a country to explain a history of underdevelopment. Economic geography seeks to explain such phenomena as the 'division of the world into industrial and nonindustrial countries, the emergence of regional inequality within developing countries, and the emergence of giant urban centers'.[72] The theory focuses on a combination of the forces of chance and necessity producing one of many possible equilibria, which benefits

---

[70] Stanley L. Engerman and Kenneth L. Sokoloff, 'Factor endowments, inequality, and paths of development among New World economies' (2000) 14: 3 *Journal of Economic Perspectives* at 217–32. See also Michael Ross, 'Does oil hinder democracy?' (2001) 53:3 *World Politics* at 325–61; Nathan Jensen and Leonard Wantchekon, 'Resource wealth and political regimes in Africa' (2004) 37:9 *Comparative Political Studies* at 816–41.

[71] Jared Diamond, *Guns, Germs, and Steel: The Fates of Human Societies* (New York: W.W. Norton and Co, 1997).

[72] Paul Krugman, 'The role of geography in development' (1999) 22:2 *International Regional Science Review* at 147.

a particular place over another. The World Development Report (2009) produced by the World Bank examines geographic disparities in wealth by utilizing three explanatory concepts from economic geography:

- density (a local measure of human concentration);
- distance (a national measure of distance to hubs of economic activity, i.e. transport costs); and
- division (an international measure of economic integration and the impermeability of economic borders).[73]

The report concludes that three spatial transformations, 'higher densities, shorter distances, and lower divisions', are necessary for development to occur.[74]

One of the most prominent proponents of geographic theories of development is Jeffrey Sachs. He claims that barriers to development include three features that are intrinsically connected to a country's geography:

- transportation costs (which can be especially high for landlocked countries);
- diseases (an acute problem in the tropics, where infectious diseases may deter investment); and
- poor soil fertility (which can be caused partly by torrential rains, such as those that occur in equatorial regions).[75]

Sachs acknowledges the importance of economic policy and institutions – such as trade openness, fiscal rectitude, and the rule of law – for development, but he believes that 'for much of the world, bad climates, poor soils and physical isolation are likely to hinder growth whatever happens to policy'.[76] The result is that tropical countries cannot eliminate poverty by

---

73 World Development Report 2009, 'Reshaping economic geography' (Washington: The World Bank, 2009). Available at http://econ.worldbank.org/WBSITE/EXTERNAL/EXTDEC/EXTRESEARCH/EXTWDRS/EXTWDR2009/0,,menuPK:4231145~pagePK:64167702~piPK:64167676~theSitePK:4231059,00.html.

74 Ibid., at 57.

75 Jeffrey Sachs, 'Institutions matter, but not for everything: the role of geography and resource endowments in development shouldn't be underestimated' (2003) *Finance and Development*. A similar argument is developed by Diamond, *supra* note 71.

76 J. Sachs, 'The limits of convergence: nature, nurture and growth' (14 June 1997) *The Economist*. See also John Luke Gallup, Jeffrey D. Sachs and Andrew

simply promoting good economic policies or institutional reforms.

This does not mean that geographic theories of development are deterministic. Sachs, among others, believes that geography is not the sole cause of underdevelopment. Instead, geographic factors create barriers to development, which in turn generate a low-level growth equilibrium or a poverty trap.[77] According to Sachs, the poverty trap can be overcome by investing in infrastructure to reduce transportation costs, agricultural technology to increase productivity, and improved health care services and treatment to reduce the burden of tropical diseases. In order to enable these investments to be made in resource poor countries, he argues that the developed world should increase foreign aid to poor countries, especially in Africa, to assist these countries in breaking out of the poverty traps in which they are currently stuck.[78] Once geographical barriers to development are addressed, institutions then become relevant.[79] However, reformers must first deal with geographical barriers, lest these more fundamental problems undermine any positive effects of institutional reforms.

The idea that well-governed poor nations can be caught in a poverty trap has been influential since the 1950s, and has long justified large foreign aid programs (as discussed earlier with reference to Rostow and modernization theory). This claim, however, is much disputed in the contemporary development literature. Some claim that there is no empirical evidence to support the existence of poverty traps.[80] Others provide a great deal of evidence that poor institutions, rather than geography, are the fundamental cause of underdevelopment, as discussed below. Some of these institutionalists include geographic factors as a secondary cause of a country's level of development.

Daron Acemoğlu, Simon Johnson and James A. Robinson (AJR) are among the many authors who support the idea that geographic factors play only an indirect role in development by affecting a country's

---

D. Mellinger, 'Geography and economic development' (December 1998) NBER Working Paper No. W6849. Available at SSRN: http://ssrn.com/abstract=145013.

77 Sachs, *supra* note 74; David E. Bloom, David Canning and Jaypee Sevilla, 'Geography and poverty traps' (2003) 8 *Journal of Economic Growth* at 355–78.

78 Jeffrey Sachs, *The End of Poverty* (New York: The Penguin Press, 2005) at 208.

79 Sachs, *supra* note 75.

80 William Easterly, 'Reliving the 1950s: the big push, poverty traps, and take-offs in economic development' (2006) 11 *Journal of Economic Growth* 289–318; Aart Kraay and Claudio Raddatz, 'Poverty traps, aid, and growth' (2007) 82 *Journal of Development Economics* at 315–47. But see Bloom et al., *supra* note 77 (showing that geography is not determinism, but it might influence poverty traps or low level equilibria).

institutions.[81] They argue that geographic factors affect the historical development of a country,[82] because the wealth that existed before colonizers arrived was influenced by geography, impacting on each country's overall development outcome. Geography influenced the types of institution that were implemented by colonizers: in regions with inhospitable climates, colonizers established extractive institutions to exploit natural resources (extractive societies); in regions with hospitable climates, colonizers created settler societies which developed strong institutions (neo-Europes). The institutional environment promoted at colonization had a dramatic impact on the development prospects of colonized countries. Well-functioning institutions encouraged investment in machinery, human capital and better technologies, fostering growth and development. AJR's argument differs from Sachs' argument, in that he concludes that geography has only an indirect effect on a country's level of development: development is determined by the institutional environment which is affected by geography.[83]

If institutions matter, countries should seek to create better institutions through institutional reforms in order to improve their development prospects. Sachs, however, criticizes this proposal as a convenient solution from a developed country perspective. Sachs points out that, according to institutional theories, 'the rich world has little, if any, financial responsibility for the poor because development failures are the result of institutional failures and not a lack of resources'.[84] Sachs claims that poor countries need money from developed countries in order to develop. However, this does not eliminate the institutional question. It is unlikely that a country can implement the ambitious policies Sachs calls for without

---

[81] Another important paper in this literature is Sokoloff and Engerman, *supra*. note 70. See also Easterly and Levine, *supra* note 62; and Dani Rodrik, Arvind Subramanian and Francesco Trebbi, 'Institutions rule: the primacy of institutions over geography and integration in economic development' (2004) 9 *Journal of Economic Growth* at 131–65.

[82] Daron Acemoğlu, S. Johnson and J. Robinson, 'The colonial origins of comparative development: an empirical investigation', 91 *American Economic Review* at 1369–401. For further evidence supporting AJR's hypothesis, see Easterly and Levine, 'Tropics, germs, and crops,' *supra* note 62 at 3–39.

[83] To prove this point, Acemoğlu uses colonization as a natural experiment to compare the relative effect of geography and institutions in the level of development of different countries. According to him, colonization is a good experiment because it provoked an exogenous variation on institutions, eliminating problems of reverse causality and mere correlation without causation: Daron Acemoğlu, 'Root causes' (June 2003) 40 *Finance and Development* 2.

[84] Sachs, *supra* note 75.

well-functioning institutions. Regardless of the specific policy arrangements, strong institutions are necessary for government policies to provide the necessary framework for effective development.

This Part has surveyed the major non-institutional development theories of the past 60 years, with a focus on their implications for institutional questions and institutional reform. There has been much controversy and criticism of development theory as it has evolved, which has spurred continuous debate in this field of study. However, there now seems to be a general consensus that institutions play an important role in promoting development (however conceived), as we discuss next.

IV. INSTITUTIONAL THEORIES OF DEVELOPMENT

As noted above, economic theories of development predominant in the past shared in common the characteristic of either disregarding the nature and quality of a developing country's domestic institutions or, alternatively, simply assuming that a country possessed the institutional capacity to implement the theories of development in question.[85] Pranab Bardhan has noted, 'in this [traditional development] literature the state was often left floating in some behavioral and organizational vacuum, making it easy to be used for a blanket endorsement of indiscrimate state intervention'. Cultural and geographic theories of development similarly tend to marginalize the importance of the character and quality of a country's institutions in advancing its development goals. Cultural theories tend to stress deeply embedded cultural beliefs and practices as a determinant of development (while being vague about whether or how these should be changed),[86] while geographic theories tend to emphasize natural endowments as a key determinant of development.[87] Both classes of theories have a deterministic quality that is much attenuated in institutional theories.

---

[85] Pranab Bardhan, 'Symposium on the State and Economic Development' (1990) 4 *Journal of Economic Perspectives* 3, 3–7. In the case of endogenous growth theory, while acknowledging the importance of institutions to development, little guidance is offered on how institutions can be improved.

[86] See e.g. Licht, Goldschmidt and Schwartz, *supra* note 58. But see Amy Cohen, 'Thinking with culture in law and development' (2009) 57 *Buffalo L. Rev.* 511.

[87] See e.g. Bloom and Sachs, *supra* note 60 at 207–96; Sachs, 'Tropical underdevelopment,' *supra* note 60. See also Landes, *supra* note 61; and Easterly and Levine, *supra* note 62 at 7.

The idea that institutions matter for development has both a theoretical and an empirical pedigree. The theoretical pedigree of institutionally focused development theory is based on a number of assumptions and arguments developed by a school of thought called New Institutional Economics (NIE), which attempts to explain the reasons for the development of institutions and their effect on economies.[88] The basic assumption of NIE is that people are rational actors who respond to incentives and these incentives are influenced, if not determined, by institutions that induce individuals and organizations to engage in productive activities – or the converse.[89] The empirical pedigree is based on cross-country studies that show strong correlations between institutional quality and growth and development around the world, while some studies claim to find empirical evidence that also supports causation from institutional quality to development.

The institutional perspective is compelling because it appears to identify important determinants of a given country's development prospects that are within that country's control, suggesting that governments should no longer consider themselves captive to factors such as history, culture, climate, geography, natural resource endowments or the international economic system. If this perspective is adopted, lawyers – who often conceive of themselves as institutional designers – should become important contributors to the development enterprise.

The institutional perspective on development raises a number of key questions, which are briefly addressed in this section. These questions are the following:

1. What exactly do we mean by 'institutions'?
2. Does empirical evidence support the claim that the nature and quality of a country's institutions are a major determinant of its development prospects?
3. Why do institutions matter for development?
4. Which institutions matter, and with respect to which conceptions of development?
5. Why do some countries have chronically bad institutions?
6. How can these countries acquire good institutions?

---

88 Geoffrey M. Hodgson, 'The approach of institutional economics' (1998) XXXVI *Journal of Economic Literature* at 168.

89 North, *supra* note 56.

A. The Definition of 'Institutions'

What is an institution? The term, as used in both the theoretical and the empirical literature, exhibits significant ambiguity.[90] For example, Douglass North defines 'institutions' as follows:

> Institutions are the rules of the game of a society, or, more formally, are the humanly devised constraints that structure human interactions. They are composed of formal rules (statute law, common law, regulation), informal constraints (conventions, norms of behaviour and self-imposed codes of conduct), and the enforcement characteristics of both. Organizations are the players: groups of individuals bound by a common purpose to achieve objectives. They include political bodies (political parties, the senate, a city council, a regulatory agency); economic bodies (firms, trade unions, family farms, cooperatives); social bodies (churches, clubs, athletic associations); and educational bodies (schools, colleges, vocational training centres).[91]

This definition has been highly influential academically, and is widely used by development scholars. However, from a lawyer's perspective, it is an odd definition of institutions.[92] Beyond a country's constitution, lawyers do not tend to think of institutions as the rules of the game. For example, the legally prescribed speed limit on a given highway is not considered to be an institution but rather a legal rule promulgated by one set of institutions, enforced by another and, in the event of disputes, adjudicated by yet another. Also, the distinction between institutions and organizations that North draws is idiosyncratic in that many of his forms of organization, like political bodies (political parties, the senate, a city council, a regulatory agency), are typically conceived of by lawyers as institutions charged either with making, administering or enforcing laws. Finally, by including informal constraints (cultural conventions, norms of behaviour and self-imposed codes of conduct) in his definition of institutions, North's conception of institutions becomes so all-encompassing that it includes almost any factor that may influence human behaviour and hence risks losing any operational content. For our purposes, if only by stipulation, we understand institutions to mean those organizations (formal and informal) that are charged or entrusted by a

---

[90] For an extensive survey of definitions of institutions, see Geoffrey M. Hodgson (2006) 'What are Institutions?' 40:1 *Journal of Economic Issues* at 1–25.

[91] North, *supra* note 56.

[92] Mariana M. Prado and Michael Trebilcock, 'Path dependence, development and the dynamics of institutional reform', (2009) 59 *University of Toronto Law Journal* 341.

society with making, administering, enforcing or adjudicating its laws or policies.

B. Do Institutions Matter?

At one level, this question invites an intuitive or axiomatic response. A central characteristic of 'failed states' is that few or none of the basic functions of the state are performed with even a minimal level of effectiveness, including such fundamental functions as maintaining some semblance of law and order, preventing mass starvation, and avoiding gross repression of or violence towards major segments of the population. 'Failed states' are characterized as such precisely because they lack functioning public institutions.[93]

At a somewhat less intuitive level, one can derive the importance of institutions to a country's development prospects by a process of elimination. This is the analytical strategy adopted by Mancur Olson in a widely cited paper.[94] In this paper, Olson evaluates access to the major factors of production by different countries and concludes that differential access to these factors cannot explain why some countries are rich and others poor. In terms of access to technology, Olson argues that most countries have roughly equivalent access to basic technological innovations and that their cost accounts for a tiny fraction of their GDP. With respect to access to land and natural resources, he argues that a high population-to-land ratio does not explain why some countries are rich and others poor – indeed, some of the richest countries in the world have some of the highest population densities and often lack major natural resources of their own. With respect to access to financial capital, capital in the contemporary world has become enormously mobile and will quickly gravitate to countries and activities where the marginal product of capital is highest. If one assumes that marginal returns to capital in capital-intensive developed countries are declining over time, capital would gravitate to countries with higher ratios of labour and lower ratios of capital where returns to capital would presumably be higher. Thus, according to Olson, none of these explanatory factors could adequately account for why some countries are rich and others are poor.

With respect to marketable human capital, it may be true that citizens

---

[93] Robert Rotberg, 'Failed states, collapsed, weak states: causes and indicators' in Robert Rotberg, *State Failure and State Weakness in a Time of Terror* (Washington, DC: Brookings Institution Press, 2003) at 6.

[94] Mancur Olson, 'Big bills left on the sidewalk: why some nations are rich and others poor' (1996) 10 *Journal of Economic Perspectives* 3.

of many developing countries possess less education and other forms of specialized human capital than citizens of developed countries, but Olson points out that most emigrants from these countries to developed countries typically increase their incomes substantially and immediately. If one assumes that employers in developed countries generally pay wages reflecting the marginal product of labour, this implies that these emigrants, even with their current stock of human capital, are much more productive in receiving countries than in their home countries. According to Olson, this is so presumably because of differences in the policy and institutional environments between these countries. In emphasizing the importance of differences in policies and institutions, Olson points to large differences in the growth record of countries during certain periods, despite the fact that these countries share common cultures and, for long periods of time, common histories: for example, North and South Korea, East and West Germany, China, Hong Kong and Taiwan.

More recently, led by the Governance Group at the World Bank, much more systematic cross-country econometric analyses of the impact of institutional quality on development outcomes have been undertaken.[95] The findings of this empirical perspective can be captured by examining one particularly influential study entitled 'Governance Matters', undertaken by Kaufmann, Kraay and Zoido-Lobaton, all of whom are affiliated with the World Bank. This regularly updated study is part of the World Bank's ongoing research on governance, which now covers about 200 countries.[96]

---

[95] For a helpful review of the empirical literature on this issue, see Ashok Chakravarti, *Aid, Institutions and Development: New Approaches to Growth, Governance and Poverty* (Cheltenham, UK: Edward Elgar Publishing, 2006).

[96] Daniel Kaufmann, Aart Kraay and Pablo Zoido-Lobaton, 'Governance Matters', World Bank Policy Research, Working Paper No. 2196 (Washington DC: World Bank, 1999) available at http://info.worldbank.org/governance/wgi/pdf/govmatters1.pdf; Daniel Kaufmann, 'Rethinking governance: empirical lessons challenge orthodoxy', Discussion Draft 11 March 2003 (Washington, DC: World Bank, 2002) available at http://siteresources.worldbank.org/INTWBIGOVANTCOR/Resources/rethink_gov_stanford.pdf; see also Daniel Kaufmann, Aart Kraay and Massimo Mastruzzi, 'Governance Matters IV: Governance Indicators for 1996–2004', World Bank Policy Research Group, Working Paper No. 3630, World Bank, 2005, available at http://www.worldbank.org/wbi/governance/pdf/GovMatters_IV_main.pdf; Daniel Kaufmann, Aart Kraay and Massimo Mastruzzi, 'Governance Matters VII: Aggregate and Individual Governance Indicators, 1996–2007' World Bank Policy Research, Working Paper No. 4654 (Washington, DC, World Bank, 2008), available at http://papers.ssrn.com/sol3/papers.cfm?abstract_id=718081; Daniel Kaufmann, 'Governance redux: the empirical challenge' in Xavier Sala-i-Martin (ed), *The Global Competitiveness Report 2003–2004*, (New York: Oxford University Press, 2004). See also World

The World Bank's Governance Project involves compiling a large number of subjective measures of institutional quality – meaning data obtained from either polls of country experts or surveys of residents – and grouping them into six clusters:

1. *Voice and accountability*: Measures the extent to which citizens of a country are able to participate in the selection of governments and combines indicators measuring 'various aspects of political process, civil liberties, political rights' and 'the independence of the media'.
2. *Political stability*: Measures 'perceptions of the likelihood that the government in power will be destabilized or overthrown by possibly unconstitutional and/or violent means'.
3. *Government effectiveness*: Measures the inputs required for the government to be able to produce and implement good policies. Combines 'perceptions of the quality of public service provision, the quality of bureaucracy, the competence of civil servants, the independence of civil service from political pressures, and the credibility of the government's commitment to policies'.
4. *Regulatory quality*: Includes measures of 'the incidence of market-unfriendly policies such as price controls or inadequate bank supervision as well as perceptions of the burden imposed by excessive regulation in areas such as foreign trade and business development'.
5. *Rule of law*: Includes measures of 'the extent to which agents have confidence in and abide by the rules of society. These include perceptions of the incidence of both violent and non-violent crime, effectiveness and predictability of the judiciary, and the enforceability of contracts.'
6. *Control of corruption*: Measures perceptions of corruption ranging from the frequency of 'additional payments to get things done' to the effects of corruption on the business environment. Corruption is defined as 'the exercise of public power for private gain'.

The authors of 'Governance Matters' created indexes that measure institutional quality along each of these six dimensions as well as a composite 'governance' index designed to measure the overall quality of governance in a society. They regressed three measures of development – per capita GDP, infant mortality and adult literacy – on these indices.[97] They found

---

Bank, *Where is the Wealth of Nations? Measuring Capital for the 21st Century* (Washington, DC: World Bank, 2007).

[97] For a critique of the variables employed in this and succeeding studies and

strong correlations (and asserted causal relationships) between each of their sub-indices of institutional quality, as well as a composite governance index, and their measures of development, hence their conclusion that 'governance matters'. In a more recent iteration of this work, Kaufmann reports:

> The effects of improved governance on income in the long run are found to be very large, with an estimated 400 percent improvement in per capita income associated with an improvement in governance by one standard deviation, and similar improvements in reducing child mortality and illiteracy. To illustrate, an improvement in the rule of law by one standard deviation from the current levels in Ukraine to those 'middling' levels prevailing in South Africa would lead to a fourfold increase in per capita income in the long run. A larger increase in the quality of the rule of law by two standard deviations in Ukraine (or in other countries in the former Soviet Union), to the much higher level in Slovenia or Spain, would further multiply this income per capita increase. Similar results emerge from other governance dimensions: a mere one standard deviation improvement in voice and accountability from the low level of Venezuela to that of South Korea, or in control of corruption from the low level of Indonesia to the middling level of Mexico, or from the level of Mexico to that of Costa Rica, would be associated with an estimated fourfold increase in per capita incomes, as well as similar improvements in reducing child mortality by 75 percent and major gains in literacy.[98]

Drawing on the Kaufmann et al. data, Rodrik, Subramanian and Trebbi estimate the respective contributions of institutions, geography and international trade (integration) in determining income levels around the world.[99] In their study the authors use a number of measures of institutional quality that capture the protection afforded to property rights as well as the strength of the rule of law. The authors find that the quality of institutions 'trumps' everything else. Conventional measures of geography are shown to have, at best, weak direct effects on income, although they have a strong indirect effect by influencing the quality of institutions. Similarly, in their analysis trade is almost always insignificant except for indirect effects on institutions. To convey a flavour of the striking nature of their findings, the authors conclude that 'an increase in institutional quality of one standard deviation, corresponding roughly to the difference between measured institutional quality in Bolivia and South Korea, produces a 2 log-points rise in per capita incomes, or a 6.4-fold difference

---

their definitions, see Kevin Davis, 'What can the rule of law variable tell us about rule of law reforms?' (2004) 26 *Michigan Journal of International Law* 141.

98 Kaufmann, 'Governance redux: the empirical challenge', *supra* note 96.

99 Rodrik, Subramanian and Trebbi, *supra* note 81 at 141.

– which, not coincidentally, is also roughly the income difference between the two countries'.[100]

A major challenge confronting these empirical studies is the problem of causation. Correlation does not imply causation: showing that all rich countries have good institutions does not prove that they are rich *because* they have good institutions. For instance, one can show that civil law countries fare better on average than common law countries in international soccer tournaments, but this does not mean that the soccer players' performance is determined by that country's legal regime.[101]

In addition to the possibility that strong institutions and wealth are unrelated but coexisting variables, it is also possible that wealth causes the development of strong institutions, rather than the reverse. For example, Glaeser, La Porta, Silane and Schleifer argue,[102] based on cross-country econometric evidence, that (a) human capital is a more basic source of growth than institutions, and (b) growth causes good institutions, because poor countries escape from poverty through good policies, often pursued by dictators, and these countries only subsequently improve their political and related institutions. In other words, they claim that the causal arrow flows from human capital and good policies to well-functioning institutions. However Kaufmann et al., in subsequent iterations of their work, test for and reject the possibility of reverse causation, concluding instead that the econometric evidence supports causation running from strong institutions to improvements in development indicators (including growth).[103]

It is also possible that the two factors, wealth and good institutions, influence each other – both being endogenous to a single system of development – and therefore the causal arrow flows in both directions: strong institutions ⇔ wealth. Therefore, both conclusions – that good institutions create wealth and wealth creates good institutions – may be correct.

There is, however, a more important limitation in these studies: the cross-country econometric measures provide very little operational guidance to policy reformers because of the level of abstractness employed in defining institutional variables. As Mary Shirley states,

---

[100] Ibid., at 136.

[101] Mark West, 'Legal determinants of World Cup success' (2009), Michigan Law and Economics Research Paper No. 02-009. Available at SSRN: http://papers.ssrn.com/sol3/papers.cfm?abstract_id=318940 or DOI: 10.2139/ssrn.318940

[102] Edward L. Glaeser, Rafael La Porta, Florencio Lopez-de-Silanes and Andrei Shleifer, 'Do institutions cause growth?' (2004) 9 *Journal of Economic Growth* 271.

[103] Daniel Kaufmann and Aart Kraay, 'Governance and growth, causality which way? Evidence for the world in brief', WBI. Washington, 2003, available at http://www.uoit.ca/sas/governeaceAndCorr/GovGrowth.pdf.

> [t]he measurement of institutions is still in its infancy. Although important regularities have been discovered, the current measures are not actionable. They are too crude to help aid agencies, policy-makers, and concerned citizens to design reforms and gauge their outcomes. The devil is truly in the detail, and the current set of measures may be seriously misleading about the micro-developments. Part of the fault for the weakness of the measures lies with researchers who have focused their attention and efforts on variables that can be used for cross-country growth regressions. Actionable variables are not likely to be useful for papers worthy of peer reviewed journals, but they are essential for a useful understanding of institutions.[104]

C. Why do Institutions Matter?

From an economic perspective focused on growth, the answer to this question turns on the nature of the economic incentives embodied in the institutional framework and whether they induce socially productive or unproductive activities. According to North, 'the institutional framework dictates the kinds of skills and knowledge perceived to have the maximum pay off . . . If the institutional matrix rewards piracy (or more generally redistributive activities) more than productive activity, then learning will take the form of learning to be better pirates'.[105] If one adopts more expansive conceptions of development (such as Sen's conception of development as freedom), certain institutions may matter not only because of consequentialist impacts on growth or other social indicators, but also for intrinsic or deontological reasons such as facilitating and ensuring various civil and political liberties – for example, freedom of expression, association and other democratic freedoms. Even if one adopts this perspective, however, empirical evaluation is still important in assessing whether institutions do in fact protect or advance the freedoms that are central to this perspective.

D. Which Institutions Matter?

Much of the recent scholarship espousing an institutional perspective on development is extraordinarily vague as to (a) which institutions matter to development, and (b) within classes of institutions, which institutional characteristics are conducive or antithetical to development. As we noted earlier, definitions of institutions are also often extraordinarily vague and ambiguous. Moreover, it is important to note that much of the recent institutional literature concludes that a host of context-specific factors

---

104 Mary Shirley, *Institutions and Development* (Cheltenham, UK: Edward Elgar, 2008) at 98.

105 North, *supra* note 56 at 17.

determine optimal institutional characteristics within classes of institutions. For example, although Francis Fukuyama has recently concluded that institutionalists have won the debate over the causes of underdevelopment 'hands down', and that institutions are the 'proximate causes of growth'.[106] He notes that public administration is not a science susceptible to formalization under a set of universal rules and principles[107] and that political institutions also are not susceptible to characterization in terms of optimal formal political arrangements.[108] According to Fukuyama, the full specification of a good set of institutions will be highly context-dependent, will change over time, and will interact with the informal norms, values and traditions of the society in which they are embedded.

Fukuyama is not alone in emphasizing the context-dependent nature of institutional design. Rodrik, Subramanian and Trebbi, in their paper 'Institutions rule', reach rather salutary, perhaps even sobering conclusions, despite the triumphalist title of the paper. For example, they find that while property rights may be an important determinant of development in all countries, the precise configuration of an optimal property rights regime is likely to be highly context-specific:

> Obviously, the presence of clear property rights for investors is a key, if not the key, element in the institutional environment that shapes economic performance. Our findings indicate that when investors believe their property rights are protected, the economy ends up richer. But nothing is implied about the actual form that property rights should take. We cannot even necessarily deduce that enacting a private property rights regime would produce superior results compared to alternative forms of property rights.
>
> . . . there is growing evidence that desirable institutional arrangements have a large element of context specificity, arising from differences in historical trajectories, geography, political economy, or other initial conditions.
>
> . . . there is much to be learned about what improving institutional quality means on the ground. This, we would like to suggest, is a wide open area of research. Cross-national studies are at present just a beginning that point us in the right direction.[109]

---

[106] Francis Fukuyama, 'Development and the limits of institutional design' in Global Development Network, St. Petersburg, Russia, 20 January 2006, unpublished conference paper, available at http://depot.gdnet.org:6666/gdnshare/pdf2/gdn_library/annual_conferences/seventh_annual_conference/Fukuyama_plenary1.pdf., at 1.

[107] Francis Fukuyama, *State-Building: Governance and World Order in the 21st Century*, (Ithaca, NY: Cornell University Press, 2004).

[108] Fukuyama, *supra* note 106.

[109] Rodrik, Subramanian and Trebbi, *supra* note 81. See more generally, Dani Rodrik, *One Economics, Many Recipes: Globalization, Institutions and Economic Growth* (Institutions for High-Quality Growth, 2007), Chapter 5.

In a similar vein, in a recent paper,[110] Rohini Pande and Christopher Udry state:

> Recent years have seen a remarkable and exciting revival of interest in the empirical analysis of how a broad set of institutions affects growth. The focus of the recent outpouring of research is on exploiting cross-country variation in 'institutional quality' to identify whether a causal effect runs from institutions to growth. These papers conclude that institutional quality is a significant determinant of a country's growth performance.
>
> These findings are of fundamental importance for development economists and policy practitioners in that they suggest that institutional quality may cause poor countries and people to stay poor. However, the economic interpretation and policy implications of these findings depends on understanding the specific channels through which institutions affect growth, and the reasons for institutional change or the lack thereof . . . We also conclude from our review that this literature has served its purpose and is essentially complete. The number of variables available as instrumental variables is limited, and their coarseness prevents close analysis of particular causal mechanisms from institutions to growth . . . This suggests that the research agenda identified by the institutions and growth literature is best furthered by the analysis of much more microdata than has typically been the norm in this literature.

Complementing her criticism that the current institutional measures are not useful to policymakers, Mary Shirley also makes a claim for more microdata in the form of case studies:

> Developing more useful measures of institutions will not be simple. Ultimately, consistent, comparative case studies will be crucial if we are to understand the complex nature of institutions and institutional change and develop more specific and accurate measures.[111]
>
> Comparative case studies are one way to discover the determinants of reform without sacrificing necessary institutional details . . . Unfortunately, case studies have a bad and not entirely undeserved reputation as *sui generis*, unscientific, devoid of theory and unworthy of publication in top academic journals . . . Even rigorous comparative cases will likely suffer from small sample problems, selection biases and the difficulty of constructing a counterfactual. Nevertheless, comparative case studies are worth the effort if we want to begin to unravel the determinants of institutional change. It seems unlikely that cross-country econometric studies can begin to develop more nuanced measures of institutions until they are informed by comparative case studies.[112]

---

110 Rohini Pande and Christopher Udry, 'Institutions and development: a view from below' (Yale University, 18 November 2005) in R. Blundell, W. Newey and T. Persson (eds), *Proceedings of the 9th World Congress of the Econometric Society* (Cambridge University Press).

111 Shirley, *supra* note 104 at 98.

112 Ibid., at 184.

In sum, while much empirical evidence supports the view that institutions matter for development, we know very little about which institutions matter, and what specific institutional characteristics within classes of institutions matter for development.

E. Why are Some Countries Afflicted with Persistently Bad Institutions?

According to most of the institutional literature reviewed above, countries that are afflicted with persistently bad institutions are (in Olson's words) leaving 'big bills on the sidewalk'. Why would societies engage in such myopic or self-destructive behaviour, particularly in an era where mass communications technologies make information highly accessible at low cost? Many members of these societies should be, and probably are, aware of the fact that alternative institutional arrangements in other countries appear to generate dramatically superior development outcomes. So why do bad institutions persist?

According to North, the reason is the phenomenon of 'path dependency', which describes how the reinforcement of a given set of arrangements over time raises the cost of changing them.[113] Most public institutions exhibit increasing returns to scale and network effects, making it very difficult for rival institutions that demonstrate superior qualities to emerge. Existing institutions also generate biased feedback loops that tend to confirm prior institutional expectations about existing institutional arrangements rather than providing exposure to and information about institutional alternatives. In addition, vested interests both within and outside existing institutional regimes often derive substantial benefits from these regimes, hence creating concentrated sources of resistance to institutional change. All of these factors, according to North, tend to create strong forms of institutional path dependency that often render radical institutional reform infeasible.[114] While occasionally revolutions occur or charismatic leaders emerge that may offer the prospects of a decisive break with the past, these contingencies are much more the exception rather than the rule. However, as Bardhan indicates, with the exception of North, the new institutional economists have not taken these issues very seriously.[115]

---

[113] For a helpful overview of path dependence theory and its applications, see Paul Pierson, 'Increasing returns, path dependence, and the study of politics' (2000) 94 *American Political Science Review* 251 at 252–7; our discussion below draws in part on Pierson's survey of the literature.

[114] Douglass North, *Institutions, Institutional Change and Economic Performance* (Cambridge University Press, 1990).

[115] Pranab Bardhan, *Scarcity, Conflicts, and Cooperation: Essays in the Political*

F. What can Countries with Bad Institutions do to Acquire Better Institutions?

To a large extent, responses to this question are constrained by responses to the previous question about the reasons for the persistence of bad institutions. Much advice that has been offered on this question borders on the banal. For example, Olson concludes: 'The best thing a society can do to increase its prosperity is to wise up.'[116] *The Economist*, in a survey article, suggests: 'Africa's people need to regain their self-confidence.'[117] These proposals do not offer much in the way of concrete, actionable reforms.

Serious thinking about this question needs to address the complexities of the path dependence dynamic described above. This is, however, a daunting endeavour and we still do not have a firm understanding of how to transform dysfunctional institutions. Indeed, Douglass North in a recent book states: 'To put it bluntly, we may know a lot about polities, but not how to fix them.'[118] This lack of knowledge on how to successfully promote institutional reforms is illustrated in a recent book on rule of law reform and development (co-authored by Michael Trebilcock), which describes the mixed to weak results of many rule of law reform initiatives in developing countries.[119] Recent faltering initiatives to install democratic regimes in many developing countries (such as Iraq and Afghanistan) provide further illustrations of these challenges.[120]

Thus, while economists have been influential recently in emphasizing the important role of institutions as a major determinant of development, they have made much more limited progress in illuminating strategies for overcoming these 'path dependency' obstacles. After a detailed recent review of the economic and political scholarly literature on path dependency,[121] we drew the following tentative implications that follow

---

and Institutional Economics of Development (Cambridge, MA: MIT Press, 2005), chapter 2.

116 Olson, *supra* note 94 at 21.

117 'Africa: the heart of the matter', *The Economist*, 13 May 2000 at 22–4.

118 Douglass North, *Understanding the Process of Economic Change* (Princeton, NJ: Princeton University Press: 2005) at 67.

119 Michael J. Trebilcock and Ronald J. Daniels, *Rule of Law and Development: Charting the Fragile Path of Progress* (Cheltenham, UK: Edward Elgar Publishing, 2008).

120 Georg Sorenson, *Democracy and Democratization: Processes and Prospects in a Changing World* (Westview Press, 2007, 3rd edn); Larry Diamond, *The Spirit of Democracy: The Struggle to Build Free Societies Throughout the World* (New York: Henry Holt and Co., 2008).

121 Prado and Trebilcock, *supra* note 92.

from attention to path dependence in formulating institutional reform strategies.

First, because of context-specific factors that explain the evolution of existing institutions (and networks of institutions), no one-size-fits-all blueprint for legal reform or broader institutional reform in developing countries is likely to be optimal. Other developing countries which share many of the same historical experiences and institutional characteristics as the country whose institutions are the focus of reform efforts are likely to be a more useful source of information, experience and ideas as to what is likely to work than other countries which share few of these common characteristics.[122] Future research on reform options, to be effective, will often have to be led by scholars within the countries in question complemented by scholars with relevant comparative expertise pursued through collaborative research initiatives.

Second, as a result of switching costs and institutional interdependencies, ambitious or highly innovative across-the-board political, bureaucratic or legal reforms carry significantly greater risk of failure than more modest or incremental reforms. Disillusionment with progress with democratic and rule of law reforms in many developing countries may, in this respect, reflect unrealistic expectations.

Third, if more ambitious or innovative institutional reforms are to be pursued successfully, they should focus on institutions that can be more easily detached from mutually reinforcing mechanisms, and become relatively free-standing, although even in such cases complementary reinforcing institutional reforms over time are likely to be necessary.

Fourth, detached, free-standing institutions, pilot programs or decentralized initiatives enlisting enthusiastic participants are likely to be more successful than across-the-board centralized reforms of existing institutions that conscript unwilling participants by imposing significant switching costs on them. Demonstration effects from pilot projects may subsequently persuade sceptics on either the demand or supply sides of the institutional reform equation that switching costs are not as large as previously assumed or that the benefits of incurring these costs are larger than expected. Such pilot projects also have the virtue of reversibility in the event that they generate unintended consequences, and thus entail lower risks.

Fifth, in reforms that are sensitive to switching costs from the institutional status quo, it is important to identify the different kinds of switching

---

[122] See Sharun Mukand and Dani Rodrik, 'In search of the Holy Grail: policy convergence, experimentation and economic performance' (2005) 95 *American Economic Review* 374.

costs that may be salient – whether they reflect political economy factors that have shaped and been reinforced by the initial choice of institutions; or reflect lack of financial or technical resources; or reflect learning effects; or reflect co-ordination or network effects; or reflect deeply entrenched cultural or religious beliefs or practices. While these factors can be conceived of as exogenous constraints on institutional reforms, one can equally view them as endogenous factors that have shaped the evolution of the institutional status quo. On either view, they will also significantly shape feasible margins of reforms, but in different ways.

Sixth, political and economic crises or catharses may provide opportunities for more radical institutional change, but also present risks of denial, deferral or repression, or precipitous adoption of ill-conceived policy or institutional choices in response to public consternation or disaffection. To mitigate these risks, the reform process must broaden the pool of policy ideas by enlisting previously marginalized constituencies and incorporating them into more enduring institutional reforms so as to create a new alignment of ideas, interests and institutions.

We are fully cognizant of the modesty of these conclusions. However, we take comfort from the fact that it reflects a similar modesty on the part of at least some of the more prominent New Institutionalists, such as Douglass North:

> Path dependence means that history matters. We cannot understand today's choices (and define them in the modelling of economic performance) without tracing the incremental evolution of institutions. But we are just beginning the serious task of exploring the implications of path dependence.[123]
>
> A major frontier of scholarly research is to do the empirical work necessary to identify the precise source of path dependence so that we can be more precise about its implications.[124]

V. CONCLUSION

Path dependence counsels attention to contextual and historical particularities in proposing institutional reforms. As with debates over the ends of development – which yield explicit or implicit divides between those who believe that there are certain core or universal elements in a normatively defensible conception of development and those who believe that such conceptions are highly culture- and context-specific – similarly with

---

123 North, *supra* note 56 at 100.
124 North, *supra* note 118 at 7.

respect to the means of development. Even if certain ends of development were thought to be universal, the different starting points or initial conditions of the large universe of developing countries may suggest that there will be very few universally effective blueprints with respect to substantive economic and social policies and the processes and institutions appropriate for implementing, administering and enforcing such policies. However, it may be argued that, at least amongst some groups of developing countries, some problems are sufficiently common that at least limited generalization is possible as to problem diagnoses and prescriptions. Espousing extreme forms of relativism as to the ends of development may lead to acceptance of or acquiescence in appalling abuses of power by tyrannical governments, including abuses of the most fundamental human rights by incumbent political regimes or rival factions vying for power, or traditional religious or cultural belief systems and practices that may be egregiously discriminatory towards major segments of the population, including women and ethnic and religious minorities.

As to the means of development, if one views differences as overwhelming any commonalities, then, as Arndt puts it, we are simply resigning ourselves to the proposition that each country should 'write its own history,'[125] and that nothing is to be learned through successes and failures of policies, processes and institutions in addressing similar problems in other developing countries, or at least other developing countries that share much in common in terms of economic, social, political, geographic and historical experience. Without some potential for at least cautious or qualified generalizations, the whole field of development as a scholarly or analytical enterprise is called into serious question.

---

125 Arndt, *supra* note 1 at 165.

2. The rule of law and development: in search of the Holy Grail

I. INTRODUCTION

Recent empirical research on the relationship between the nature and quality of a country's institutions and development outcomes purports to demonstrate, inter alia, that improvements in the rule of law are likely to have dramatic impacts on development outcomes. For example, as noted in Chapter 1, according to the World Bank, an improvement in the rule of law by one standard deviation from the current levels in the Ukraine to those middling levels prevailing in South Africa would lead to a fourfold increase in per capita income in the long run.[1]

Similarly, according to Rodrik et al., an 'increase in institutional quality' (measured largely in terms of the strength of private property rights and the rule of law) 'of one standard deviation, corresponding roughly to the difference between measured institutional quality in Bolivia and South Korea, produces a 2 log-points rise in per capita incomes, or a 6.4-fold difference'.[2]

Reflecting this view of the relationship between the rule of law and development, beginning in the 1990s there has been a massive surge in development assistance for law reform projects in developing and transition economies involving investments of many billions of dollars.[3] There has also been a major resurgence of scholarly interest in the relationship between law and development.

Proponents of an optimistic view of the relationship between the rule

---

[1] Daniel Kaufmann, 'Governance redux: the empirical challenge', in Xavier Sala-i-Martin (ed.), *The Global Competitiveness Report 2003–2004* (New York: Oxford University Press, 2004).

[2] Dani Rodrik, Arvind Subramanian and Francesco Trebbi, 'Institutions rule: the primacy of institutions over geography and integration in economic development' (2004) 9 *Journal of Economic Growth* 141.

[3] See David Trubek, 'The rule of law and development assistance: past, present and future', in David Trubek and Alvaro Santos (eds), *The New Law and Economic Development: A Critical Appraisal* (Cambridge: Cambridge University Press, 2006) at 74.

of law, or law more generally, and development have made extremely bold claims about the potentially beneficial impact of legal reforms. For example, in his influential book, *The Other Path*, Hernando de Soto makes claims such as: 'The legal system may be the main explanation in the difference in development that exists between industrialized countries and those that are not industrialized.'[4] He also argues that 'development is possible only if efficient legal institutions are available to all citizens'[5] and that 'the law is the most useful and deliberate instrument of change available to people'.[6]

In contrast, various law sceptics doubt the ability of legal reformers to identify appropriate legal reforms; consider that legal reforms often face potentially insurmountable economic, political and cultural obstacles; or argue that legal reform is often irrelevant because informal alternatives to law are of overriding importance as mechanisms of social control in many developing countries.[7] In this respect, sceptics point to the failure of the first law and development movement in the late 1950s to early 1970s – which we discuss in more detail in Part III of this chapter – and argue that we may be condemning ourselves to repeating earlier mistakes by ignoring the lessons of history.

In examining the relationship of law to development, several broad questions need to be addressed:

1. What is embraced or connoted by terms such as 'law', 'legal institutions' and 'the rule of law'?
2. Do law and legal institutions in fact significantly determine a country's development prospects (given particular conceptions of the ends of development)?
3. To the extent that they do, what explains why many countries have chronically poor law, legal institutions, or the rule of law (or in Mancur Olson's terms, why are they 'leaving big bills on the sidewalk')?[8]
4. If a country has chronically poor laws, legal institutions or rule of

---

4 Hernando de Soto, *The Other Path: The Invisible Revolution in the Third World* (New York: Basic Books, 1989) at 185.

5 Ibid., at 186.

6 Ibid., at 187.

7 See Kevin Davis and Michael J. Trebilcock, 'The relationship between law and development: optimists versus skeptics' (2008) 56 *American Journal of Comparative Law* 895.

8 Mancur Olson, 'Big bills left on the sidewalk' (1996) 10 *Journal of Economic Perspectives* 3.

law, what measures are both important and feasible in a law reform strategy?
5. What is the appropriate role for external actors in promoting rule of law reforms in developing countries?

II. THE DEFINITION OF LAW, LEGAL INSTITUTIONS AND THE RULE OF LAW

'Law' could connote an almost infinite number of areas of substantive law, from commercial and corporate law to tax law, family law, property law, contract law, administrative law, and so on. Nobody possesses the requisite expertise across all of these areas of substantive law to judge whether a country's substantive laws reveal deficiencies in one respect or another as evaluated against some conception of the ends of development. Instead, we will focus on the major classes of legal institutions which include courts, police, prosecutors, correctional institutions, specialized regulatory or law enforcement bodies, legal education institutions, professional regulatory bodies, and so on, and examine the characteristics of these institutions against various conceptions of the rule of law.

Problems of evaluation begin with widely divergent understandings of the content of the concept of the rule of law, which – despite the now fashionable pre-eminence accorded to it in many development circles – has in fact been the subject of long-standing normative debates and is highly contested terrain. According to Tamanaha, in a recent intellectual history of the rule of law, 'there are almost as many conceptions of the rule of law as there are people defending it'.[9] Michael Trebilcock and Ron Daniels have reviewed these debates in some detail in previous work.[10] For present purposes, it suffices to say that conceptions of the rule of law run the gamut from the deontological (protection of basic human rights) to the instrumental (protection of property rights and contracts to promote investment and growth), and from extremely 'thick' conceptions (that largely equate the rule of law with a just legal system, which in turn is largely elided with a just society), to very 'thin' or formalistic conceptions (that emphasize that laws should be publicly promulgated, be predictable in their application, apply to all citizens, including government officials, and be subject to some

---

[9] Brian Tamanaha, *On the Rule of Law: History, Politics, Theory* (Cambridge: Cambridge University Press, 2004) at 3.

[10] Michael J. Trebilcock and Ronald J. Daniels, *Rule of Law Reform and Development: Charting the Fragile Path of Progress* (Northampton, MA: Edward Elgar, 2008) Chapter 1.

form of neutral adjudication in the event of disputes as to their interpretation or application).

Objections to thick conceptions of the rule of law point out that such conceptions largely deprive the concept of the rule of law of any independent meaning by equating it with 'justice' in all its manifestations and hence particular conceptions of the ends of development rather than as a means of vindicating those ends.[11] Objections to thin conceptions of the rule of law point out that even grossly unjust or immoral societies, such as Nazi Germany or apartheid South Africa, might meet purely formalistic criteria, lacking, as these conceptions do, any elements of basic civil and political rights.[12] Intermediate conceptions of the rule of law are possible, which stress due process or natural justice values of the kind familiar to Western constitutional and administrative lawyers, as well as basic civil rights.[13]

It is important to identify the causal mechanisms that translate improvements in the quality of the rule of law into enhanced development outcomes. From an economic perspective, much of the literature emphasizes that protection of private property rights and enforcement of contracts translate into enhanced incentives to engage in productive investments and hence enhanced economic growth (as described in the next chapter). More generally, the stability and predictability of a legal system are regarded as having similar effects. From a non-instrumental or deontological perspective, such as that adopted by Amartya Sen in his book, *Development as Freedom*, an enhanced commitment to the rule of law may be justified as an end in itself. The rule of law provides greater protection of the freedoms of concern to Sen, and its existence does not need to be justified by reference to instrumental objectives but presumably can be empirically evaluated by how well these freedoms are in fact protected.[14]

III. THE RELATIONSHIP BETWEEN THE RULE OF LAW AND DEVELOPMENT

We have already noted recent empirical evidence that is often advanced to support the claim that the quality of a country's commitment to the rule of law significantly, even dramatically, impacts on its economic development

---

11 Ibid., at 23–5.

12 Ibid.

13 For an argument along these lines, see Tom Bingham, *The Rule of Law* (London: Allen Lane, 2010).

14 Amartya Sen, *Development as Freedom,* (New York: Anchor Books, 2000).

prospects. However, this claim is not new. An earlier version of this claim appeared in the 1960s in what became known as 'the law and development movement'. Based on an assumption that law is central to development, its proponents believed that educating the legal professionals of developing countries would advance the countries' reform efforts.[15] The movement did not prove enduring and shortly after its inauguration was declared dead by two of its founders, David Trubek and Marc Galanter, in a widely cited paper,[16] in which they extensively critiqued, in a development context, what they call 'the model of liberal legalism' that motivated the first law and development movement.

For Trubek and Galanter, the components of the liberal legalism paradigm are fivefold. First, society is made up of individuals, intermediate groups in which individuals voluntarily organize themselves, and the state. The state is the primary locus of supra-individual control in society, and thus state action involves coercion of individuals. Second, the state exercises its control over the individual through law – bodies of rules that are addressed universally to all individuals similarly situated. Third, rules are consciously designed to achieve social purposes or effectuate basic social principles. These purposes are those of the society as a whole, not of limited groups within it. Fourth, when the rules made through this process are applied, they are enforced equally for all citizens, and in a fashion that achieves the purposes for which they were consciously designed. Fifth, the legal order applies, interprets and changes universalistic rules. The courts have the principal responsibility for defining the effect of legal rules and concepts on individual and group behaviour and thus normally have the final say in defining the social meaning of laws. In this respect, the courts are the central institutions of the legal order. Finally, the behaviour of social actors tends to conform to the rules: officials are guided by the rules, not by personal, class, regional or other bases of decision making; and a large number of the rules will be internalized by most of the population.

However, according to Trubek and Galanter, this paradigm has little application or relevance to many, perhaps most, developing countries:

> The ethnocentric quality of liberal legalism's model of law in society is apparent. Empirically, the model assumes social and political pluralism, while in

---

[15] World Bank, 'Law and development movement', available at http://siteresources.worldbank.org/INTLAWJUSTINST/Resources/LawandDevelopmentMovement.pdf

[16] David Trubek and Marc Galanter, 'Scholars in self-estrangement: some reflections on the crisis in law and development studies in the United States' (1974) 4 *Wisconsin Law Review* 1062.

> most of the Third World we find social stratification and class cleavage juxtaposed with authoritarian or totalitarian political systems. The model assumes that state institutions are the primary locus of social control, while in much of the Third World the grip of tribe, clan, and local community is far stronger than that of the nation-state. The model assumes that rules both reflect the interests of the vast majority of citizens and are normally internalized by them, while in many developing countries rules are imposed on the many by the few and are frequently honoured more in the breach than in the observance. The model assumes that courts are central actors in social control, and that they are relatively autonomous from political, tribal, religious, or class interests. Yet in many nations courts are neither very independent nor very important.[17]

This line of critique of the relevance of even a relatively thin conception of the rule of law to many developing countries has in turn attracted criticism. For example, Tamanaha[18] points out:

> One of the major sources of oppression and rapaciousness in developing countries today is authoritarian governments. The central premise of the liberal rule-of-law system is the protection of individuals from the tyranny of the government. Law-and-development theorists should be striving to devise ways in which the rule-of-law model can be adapted to local circumstances and nurtured into maturity, rather than expending the bulk of their efforts in tearing this model down.
>
> Informative though it was, the legal liberal paradigm elucidated by Trubek and Galanter was seriously misleading insofar as it implied that all the elements described were prerequisite to a rule-of-law system. Even the United States, as they observed, did not satisfy the description. Operating around the world today are many variations of the rule of law, coexisting with individualist-oriented as well as with communitarian-oriented cultures. It has always consisted more of a bundle of ideals than a specific or necessary set of institutional arrangements.
>
> A minimalist account of the rule of law would require only that the government abide by the rules promulgated by the political authority and treat its citizens with basic human dignity, and that there be access to a fair and neutral (to the extent achievable) decision maker or judiciary to hear claims or resolve disputes. These basic elements are compatible with many social-cultural arrangements and, notwithstanding the potential conflicts, they have much to offer to developing countries.[19]

Tamanaha also points out that the critique of liberal legalism developed by Trubek and Galanter (and other scholars) often leads to a 'state law bad, folk law good' attitude, when in fact often 'folk law is the culprit'

---

[17] Ibid., at 1080–81.

[18] Brian Tamanalia, 'The lessons of law and development studies' (1995), 89 *Journal of International Law*, 470–86.

[19] Ibid., at 476.

in sanctifying various basic human rights abuses of, for example, women and ethnic or religious minorities.[20] This raises an important issue regarding the relative importance of formal and informal rules and norms. For reformers, this is often a chicken-egg problem: should informal rules come first and serve as the basis for formal rules and norms, or vice-versa? Trubek and Galanter seem to assume that informal rules should precede and support formal norms, and recent research seems to partially support their assumption. Katharina Pistor, Antara Haldar and Amrit Amirapu show, in a recent paper, that the status of women in society is relatively weakly associated with various rule of law indices and that in poor countries this association disappears altogether. They suggest that this occurs because the status of women in society is determined primarily by social norms about gender equality and that these norms are only weakly affected by legal institutions.[21] In contrast, in the excerpt above Tamanaha seems to suggest the opposite: formal rules can predominate over informal rules, even when they conflict with them. On the relationship between formal law and informal social norms, scholars such as Richard McAdams have argued that formal law and legal institutions have the potential to shape and modify social norms over time.[22] That is to say, social or cultural norms and practices should not necessarily be viewed as a timeless given.

IV. REASONS FOR THE CHRONICALLY POOR QUALITY OF THE RULE OF LAW AND RELATED LEGAL INSTITUTIONS IN MANY COUNTRIES

Rule of law deficiencies are persistent and serious in many developing countries despite the instrumental and intrinsic importance of the rule of law to development, and despite the fact that over the past 20 years external donors have invested billions of dollars in rule of law reform initiatives in many developing countries. The World Bank's Governance data on the status of the rule of law reported that only 3 out of 18 Latin American

---

20 Ibid., at 481, 484.

21 Katharina Pistor, Antara Haldar and Amrit Amirapu, 'Social norms, rule of law, and gender reality', in James Heckman, Robert Nelson and Lee Cabatongian (eds), *Global Perspectives on the Rule of Law* (London: Routledge, 2010).

22 See Richard McAdams, 'The origin, development and regulation of norms' (1997) 96 *Michigan Law Review* 338; McAdams, 'The legal construction of norms: a focal point theory of expressive law' (2000) 86 *Virginia Law Review* 1649.

countries had positive rule of law ratings in 2008 (Chile, Costa Rica and Uruguay). In sub-Saharan Africa only 6 out of 47 countries had positive rule of law ratings in 2008 (Botswana, Cape Verde, Mauritius, Namibia, Seychelles and South Africa). In all 12 countries of the former Soviet Union, ratings were negative in 2008. On the other hand, the countries of Central Europe present a far more positive picture. Asian countries present a mixed setting with its huge diversity of countries, varying enormously in size, colonial history, legal heritage, political ideology and religious complexion. Notable exceptions to generally low rule of law ratings are Singapore and Hong Kong. Over the course of the prior decade, few countries with weak ratings significantly improved their ratings and some deteriorated further.

While rule of law measures used by the World Bank in its Governance database[23] are susceptible to methodological criticisms,[24] it is unlikely that the general conclusion about serious and persistent impediments to establishing the rule of law is unfounded. Many developing countries also perform poorly on a conception of the rule of law as encompassing the protection of various civil and political rights (as Sen's conception of development as freedom does),[25] and with respect to corruption.[26] Ratings on the rule of law, freedom and corruption indices are often highly correlated.

This body of experience has led some scholars to question the value and sustainability of the entire rule of law reform enterprise. We noted in Part III that the earlier post-war law and development movement was declared by some of its founders to be a failure by the mid-1970s.[27] The most recent law and development movement faces the risk of meeting the same fate. Indeed, according to Thomas Carothers,

---

[23] The World Bank defines the rule of law as: 'Rule of law captures perceptions of the extent to which agents have confidence in and abide by the rules of society, and in particular the quality of contract enforcement, property rights, the police, and the courts, as well as the likelihood of crime and violence.' Daniel Kaufmann, Aart Kraay and Massimo Mastruzzi, *Worldwide Governance Indicators 2010*, available at http://info.worldbank.org/governance/wgi/index.asp.

[24] See Kevin Davis, 'What can the rule of law variables tell us about rule of law reforms?' (2004) 26 *Michigan Journal of International Law* 141.

[25] See Freedom House, 'Decline in rule of law seen in new data released by Freedom House' (26 June 2007), available at http://www.freedomhouse.org/template.cfm?page=70&release=521

[26] See Transparency International, 'Global Corruption Report 2008', available at http://www.transparency.org/news_room/in_focus/2008/gcr2008 .

[27] See Trubek and Galanter, *supra* note 16.

> One cannot get through a foreign policy debate these days without someone proposing the rule of law as a solution to the world's troubles. The concept is suddenly everywhere – a venerable part of western political philosophy enjoying a new run as a rising imperative of the era of globalization. Unquestionably, it is important to life in peaceful, free, and prosperous societies. Yet its sudden elevation as a panacea for the ills of countries in transition from dictatorships or statist economies should make both patients and prescribers wary. The rule of law promises to move countries past the first, relatively easy phase of political and economic liberalization to a deeper level of reform. But that promise is proving difficult to fulfill.[28]

In a similar vein, Yves Dezalay and Bryant Garth claim that:

> The rule of law has become a new rallying cry for global missionaries. Money doctors selling competing economic expertises continue to be very active on the global plane but the 1990s also witnessed a tremendous growth in rule doctors armed with their own competing prescriptions for legal reforms and new legal institutions at the national and transnational level . . . So far the rule of law industry cannot claim too many successes in the latest campaign.[29]

According to Brian Tamanaha,

> For all but the most sanguine observers, the triumphalist confidence of the 1990s has dissolved . . . Amidst this host of new uncertainties there appears to be wide-spread agreement, traversing all fault lines, on one point, and one point only: that the 'rule of law' is good for everyone . . . This apparent unanimity in support of the rule of law is a feat unparalleled in history. No other single political ideal has ever achieved global endorsement . . . Notwithstanding its quick and remarkable ascendance as a global ideal, however, the rule of law is an exceedingly elusive notion . . . If it is not already firmly in place, the rule of law appears mysteriously difficult to establish.[30]

More recently, Tamanaha, in a pessimistic assessment of the effects of the law and development movement over the past fifty years, argues that the fundamental problem confronting rule of law reformers is that factors that influence law extend far beyond law itself and include:

- the history, tradition and culture of a society;
- its political and economic system;

---

[28] Thomas Carothers, 'The rule of law revival' (1998) 77 *Foreign Affairs* 95.

[29] Yves Dezalay and Bryant Garth (eds), *Global Prescriptions: The Production, Exportation and Importation of a New Legal Orthodoxy* (Ann Arbor, MI: University of Michigan Press, 2002) Introduction.

[30] Tamanaha, *supra* note 9.

- the distribution of wealth and power;
- the degree of industrialization;
- the ethnic, linguistic, and religious make-up of the society;
- the level of education of the populace;
- the extent of urbanization; and
- the geo-political surroundings.

He calls this the 'connectedness of law principle' and argues that discrete rule of law reform initiatives typically ignore or discount interconnections with their surrounding formal and informal institutions, and also the broader social context.[31]

Even adopting a relatively minimalist or procedural conception of the rule of law and adopting an eclectic conception of the ends served by the rule of law, recent studies provide extensive evidence of how little we know as to how to go about promoting the rule of law in developing countries.[32] After reviewing the evidence, Carothers concludes:

> The rapidly growing field of rule of law assistance is operating from a very thin base of knowledge at every level – with respect to the core rationale of the work, the question of where the essence of the rule of law actually resides in different societies, how change of rule of law occurs, and what the real effects are of changes that are produced.[33]

Michael Trebilcock and Ron Daniels, in a previous writing, hypothesized that the potential impediments that countries may encounter in implementing even a limited procedural conception of the rule of law fall into three crude (and often overlapping) categories.[34]

A. Resource Constraints

The first of these impediments may be of a technical or resource-related character where, despite political will generally on the part of their lead-

---

[31] Brian Tamanaha, 'The primacy of society and the failures of law and development: decades of stubborn refusal to learn' (26 March 2010) Washington University in St. Louis School of Law, Faculty Research Paper Series.

[32] See Thomas Carothers (ed.), *Promoting the Rule of Law Abroad: In Search of Knowledge* (Washington: Carnegie Endowment for International Peace, 2006) Chapters 1 and 2; Erik Jensen and Thomas Heller (eds), *Beyond Common Knowledge: Empirical Approaches to the Rule of Law* (Stanford: Stanford University Press, 2003), especially Thomas Heller, Chapter 11: 'An Immodest Postscript'.

[33] Carothers, *supra* note 32 at 27.

[34] Trebilcock and Daniels, *supra* note 10, Chapter 1.

ership and citizens, poor countries simply lack the financial, technical or specialized human capital resources to implement good institutions generally, including legal institutions. This lack of resources impairs a country's development prospects (whatever one's conception of development), by making it poorer (in some relevant normative sense) and, in turn, further diminishes its ability to implement good institutions, hence creating a vicious downward spiral.

With respect to impediments of this character, the general orientation of reform requires either more effective or efficient deployment of existing resources devoted to a country's legal system, a re-ordering of a country's domestic priorities and reallocation of resources from other areas of expenditure to the legal system, or the infusion of resources from external donors (in the form of financial assistance or technical advice and training, and so on). Indeed, on the narrowly instrumental economic rationale for rule of law reform, governments lacking the necessary resources should be prepared to borrow the money required to finance rule of law reforms and finance borrowing costs from future economic growth and increased tax revenues. However, other obstacles are likely to exist.

B. Social–Cultural–Historical Constraints

Another category of explanation for impediments to reform relates to a variety of factors that might loosely be placed under the rubric of social–cultural–historical factors that have yielded a set of social or cultural values, norms, attitudes or practices that are inhospitable to even a limited procedural conception of the rule of law.[35] In a recent paper in which they correlate scores on World Value Surveys with scores on rule of law, democracy and corruption indices, Licht, Goldshmidt and Schwartz argue that societies that accord higher weight to social embeddedness than individual autonomy, and social hierarchy than egalitarianism, exhibit lower commitments to the rule of law, democracy and non-corrupt governance, although there is significant unexplained variance around the mean.[36] Whether culture is conceived of as a form of consciousness or as a form of law-like social norms, the policy prescriptions entailed in overcoming this class of impediment are not nearly as obvious as in the case of technical

---

35 See Rosa Ehrenreich Brooks, 'The new imperialism: violence, norms, and the rule of law' (2003) 101 *Michigan Law Review* 2275; Amy Cohen, 'Thinking with culture in law and development' (2009) 57 *Buffalo Law Review* 511.

36 Amir N. Licht, Chanan Goldschmidt and Shalom H. Schwartz, 'Culture rules: the foundations of the rule of law and other norms of governance' (2007) 35 *Journal of Comparative Economics* 659.

or resource-related impediments nor is any impact likely to be immediate, dramatic or predictable. That is to say, changing culture, however conceived, may present at least as formidable a set of challenges as changing laws and legal institutions, if the purpose is to change human behaviour.[37]

An important historical perspective on the emergence of the rule of law is presented by North, Wallis and Weingast in a recent book[38] and in a recent paper by Weingast,[39] which has parallels with path dependence theories reviewed by us in a recent paper,[40] and overlaps with political economy constraints discussed below.

According to North et al., the most common social order throughout history is the limited access order or natural state, which solves the problem of violence through rent creation, granting powerful individuals and groups valuable rights and privileges so that they have incentives to cooperate rather than fight. The resulting rents, limits on competition, and limited access to organizations hinder the long-term economic and political development of these societies. In contrast, open access orders use competition and open access to organizations and institutions to control violence and are characterized by rent erosion and long-term growth.

The authors argue that the transition from a limited access order to an open access order is a difficult process, and only two or two-and-a-half dozen states have successfully completed it. They divide the transition into two parts: the doorstep conditions and the transition proper. There are three doorstep conditions:

- rule of law for elites;
- the perpetual state (the creation of perpetually lived organizations); and
- consolidated control over violence and the military.

The transition proper occurs when sufficient numbers of people become citizens in the sense that the state treats a large category of people imper-

---

37 See Cohen, *supra* note 35.

38 Douglass North, John Wallis and Barry Weingast, *Violence and Social Order: A Conceptual Framework for Understanding Recorded Human History* (Cambridge University Press, 2010).

39 Barry Weingast, "Why Developing countries prove so resistant to the rule of law'," in James Heckman, Robert Nelson and Lee Cabatingan (eds), *Global Perspectives on the Rule of Law* (Routledge, 2010).

40 Mariana M. Prado and Michael Trebilcock, 'Path dependence, development, and the dynamics of institutional reform' (2009) 59 *University of Toronto Law Journal* 341.

sonally and identically. At the same time, processes must begin that afford citizens access to organizations in both politics and economics, granting them the ability to compete as they wish in either system.

Weingast, in a subsequent paper, emphasizes two core aspects of the rule of law:

1. The impersonal aspects of law:
   - the certainty or predictability of the law, including the absence of arbitrary actions by the state against individuals;
   - transparency; and
   - the requirement that the state treats individuals as citizens with equality before the law.
2. A dynamic aspect of the rule of law which requires that the state be able to honour these aspects of the rule of law tomorrow even if it experiences turnover in officials.

By this definition, natural states have substantial difficulties in creating the rule of law. First, the rule of law contrasts with the typical natural state dominated by personal relationships. Second, natural states have difficulty in creating the predictability necessary for the rule of law. Third, natural states often seem to act arbitrarily. Finally, and perhaps most importantly, natural states have great difficulty in providing credible enduring commitments.

According to Weingast, rule of law reforms virtually always fail for two reasons: violence and the absence of perpetuity. Transplanting open access order institutions – such as markets, elections and legal systems – cannot create an open access order. The problem is that these reforms seek to dismantle the natural state systems of privilege and limited access; they therefore threaten violence and disorder. Rather than making everyone better off, as the reformers intend, these reforms threaten to make everyone worse off. Also central to creating the rule of law is creating a perpetual state whose institutions, rules and policies do not depend on the identity of current officials or dominant coalitions. The problem with natural states in the developing world is that almost none have perpetual states. Thus, in order to gain the rule of law, natural states must enter the transition from limited access order to an open access order. This means that fragile natural states must first become basic states; basic natural states become mature states; and mature natural states begin the transition with the doorstep conditions. Only at this stage of development are states capable of beginning to create the institutional and organizational basis for the rule of law.

Even though North, Wallis and Weingast present an important historical approach to the relationship between culture and institutions, their argument exhibits a deterministic quality and has a strong modernization theory flavour to it, somewhat akin to Rostow's 'stages of growth' theory.[41] There are good reasons to call attention to the path dependence element of institutional development (which may have little to do with deep-seated cultural values), as is discussed further below. However, this does not mean that societies are stuck in a phased trajectory and will not be able to evolve unless they follow all the steps in this trajectory in a prescribed sequence. Instead, path dependence should not dissuade citizens and decision-makers in developing countries from pursuing institutional reforms, acknowledging that change will be difficult and protracted, and outcomes unpredictable. One of the core elements of path dependence is that there is no linearity: societies are complex and change will be rather unpredictable.[42] Thus, we do not subscribe to the sequence the authors offer (basic natural states, mature natural states, open access societies). There are likely to be multiple equilibria, and progress will not be as linear and predictable as North, Wallis and Weingast suggest.

C. Political Economy Constraints

A third class of potential impediments to the effective implementation of even a limited conception of the rule of law might be loosely characterized as political economy-based impediments, where lack of effective political demand for reforms, on the one hand, and vested supply-side interests, on the other, render these reforms politically difficult to realize even if (by assumption) they would render most citizens better off in terms of their own values.

On the demand side, a procedurally-oriented conception of the rule of law has many of the attributes of a public good – 'everybody's business is nobody's business' – creating a major collective action problem. In other words, diffuse citizen commitment to the rule of law is unlikely to translate into effective political mobilization for reforms. Also, one should not naively assume that all external constituencies are likely to benefit from rule of law reform. Indeed, those who derive benefits from corruption, cronyism, favouritism and so on in existing institutional arrangements and legal processes are likely to resist such reforms.[43]

---

41 For a summary of the five stages of growth theory, see Chapter 1, Section III.A; W.W. Rostow, *The Stages of Economic Growth: A Non-Communist Manifesto* (Cambridge: Cambridge University Press, 1960), Chapter 2.

42 See Prado and Trebilcock, *supra* note 40.

43 See Daniel Kaufmann, 'Rethinking governance', The World Bank, discussion draft, March 2003; Joel Hellman and Daniel Kaufmann, 'The inequality of

In a recent book[44] Curtis Milhaupt and Katharina Pistor emphasize the importance of the demand side. They argue that the economic literature implicitly considers only the supply of law in a given society, largely neglecting the role of demand. In contrast, the authors suggest that the relationship between law and markets functions according to a continuous feedback loop, so the causal connection runs both ways and there is endogeneity in the relationship between law and markets. Also, law can play an important coordination function in markets and it can enhance the credibility of state-supplied governance structures. They conclude that the demand for law as a governance device is likely to be affected by the extent to which potentially effective constituencies are allowed to participate in lawmaking and law enforcement and to promote legal adaptations to changing economic and social conditions.

On the supply side, vested or incumbent interests in institutions or processes that do not comport even with a minimalist, procedurally oriented conception of the rule of law – for example, a corrupt or incompetent judiciary, public prosecution, police, correctional system, tax administration or other specialized law enforcement, administrative or regulatory agencies, members of the private bar and legal education institutions – are likely to resist reforms that threaten their interests.

The critical relationship between the rule of law and issues of political economy is insightfully articulated by Maravall and Przeworski:[45]

> To develop a positive conception of the rule of law one must start with political forces, their goals, their organization and their context. It is not stability that distinguishes the rule of law but the distribution of power. When power is monopolized, the law is at most an instrument of the rule of someone. Only if conflicting political actors seek to resolve their conflicts by recourse to law does law rule. Rule of law emerges when self-interested rulers willingly restrain themselves and make their behaviour predictable in order to obtain sustained, voluntary cooperation of well-organized groups commanding valuable resources. In exchange for such cooperation, rulers will protect the interests of these groups by legal means . . .

---

influence', The World Bank Institute: preliminary draft, December 2002; Karla Hoff and Joseph Stiglitz, 'After the Big Bang? Obstacles to the emergence of the rule of law in post-Communist societies' (2004) 94 *American Economic Review* 753–63.

44 Curtis J. Milhaupt and Katharina Pistor, *Law and Capitalism: What Corporate Crises Reveal About Legal Systems and Economic Development Around the World* (University of Chicago Press, 2008).

45 José María Maravall and Adam Przeworski (eds), *Democracy and the Rule of Law* (Cambridge and New York: Cambridge University Press, 2003), Introduction at 2–4.

> The difference between rule by law and rule of law lies in the distribution of power, the dispersion of material resources, the multiplication of organized interests; in societies that approximate the rule of law, no group becomes so strong as to dominate the others, and law, rather than reflect the interests of a single group, is used by the many. The rule of law is conceivable only if institutions tame or transform brute power. As organized interests multiply, a society will come closer to the rule of law, power will not be monopolized, and the law will not be used by the few against the many.

Holmes similarly argues:

> Why do people with power accept limits to their power? An even more pointed formulation is: why do people with guns obey people without guns? An economic twist is: why would the rich ever voluntarily part with a portion of their wealth? In legal theory, the parallel question runs: why do politicians sometimes hand power to judges? Why do politicians allow judges, who control neither purse nor sword, to overturn and obstruct their decisions and sometimes even to send office-holders to jail? . . . Societies may approximate the rule of law if they consist of a large number of power-wielding groups, comprising a majority of the population, and if none of them become so strong as to be able thoroughly to dominate the others. We may be able to loosen the grip of a few organized interests on power by forcing them to share political leverage with a variety of other groups. This is polyarchy; it is also rough justice, the only kind human beings will ever experience. Formulated differently, the balancing of many partialities is the closest we can come to impartiality. This may not sound particularly ideal, but it is nevertheless historically quite rare and very difficult to achieve.[46]

D. Legal Origins Constraints

Another line of explanation for the puzzle of differential legal performance is associated with the rapidly proliferating body of literature, principally in the financial development field, that focuses on whether legal origins have influenced the financial development of countries, which in turn is often asserted to be a major determinant of their rates of economic growth. Beginning with a widely cited paper by LaPorta, Lopez-de-Silanes, Shleifer and Vishny, in 1997,[47] followed by later papers by the same authors (frequently referred to as LLSV),[48] the authors assert a causal

---

[46] Stephen Holmes, 'Lineages of the rule of law', in Maravall and Przeworski, *supra* note 45.

[47] Rafael LaPorta, Florencio Lopez-de-Silanes, Andrei Shleifer and Robert W. Vishny, 'Legal determinants of external finance' (1997) 52 *The Journal of Finance* 1131–50.

[48] Rafael LaPorta, Florencio Lopez-de-Silanes and Andrei Shleifer, 'The economic consequences of legal origins' (2007) National Bureau of Economic Research Working Paper 13608.

linkage between legal origins and financial development and, indirectly, economic growth. This claim is largely based on cross-country studies which purport to show that common law jurisdictions have, in general, developed more sophisticated financial institutions and financial markets than civil law jurisdictions. Amongst civil law jurisdictions, the French civil law system has lagged behind other civil law systems such as the Germanic and Scandinavian systems. They conclude that countries with more sophisticated financial markets generally recognize more extensive rights of shareholders and creditors, and that common law jurisdictions are superior in these respects to civil law jurisdictions – in particular, the French civil law system.

LLSV rely on two inter-related mechanisms through which legal origin influences finance. The political mechanism holds that (a) legal traditions differ in terms of the priority they attach to private property, vis-à-vis the rights of the state (or, as they put it in their most recent paper, 'common law stands for the strategy of social control that seeks to support private market outcomes, whereas civil law seeks to replace such outcomes with state-desired allocations'); and (b) the protection of private contracting rights forms the basis of financial development. The adaptability mechanism stresses that (a) legal traditions differ in their formalism and ability to evolve with changing conditions; and (b) legal traditions that adapt efficiently to minimize the gap between the contracting needs of the economy and the legal system's capabilities will more effectively foster financial development than more rigid systems.

This literature[49] has been persuasively critiqued in a recent book by Kenneth Dam,[50] in which he points out that the regulation of shareholders' and creditors' rights in most jurisdictions (civil and common law) is a matter mostly of relatively recent statutes and not of the common law or private civil law codes, so that drawing sharp differences between civil and common law systems on this account is unwarranted.[51] Dam also points out that France generally enjoyed more rapid per capita economic growth than Britain from 1820 to 1998; that recent governance studies by the World Bank find legal origins to have a small to non-existent impact

---

49 The surrounding empirical evidence that proponents and critics rely on is masterfully surveyed in a recent paper by Thorsten Beck and Ross Levine, 'Legal institutions and financial development,' in C. Menard and M. Shirley (eds), (2005) *Handbook of New Institutional Economics* 251–78.

50 Kenneth Dam, *The Law-Growth Nexus: The Rule of Law in Economic Development* (Washington, DC: Brookings Institution Press, 2006) Chapter 2.

51 See also Mark Roe, 'Legal origins, politics and modern stock markets' (2006) 120 *Harvard Law Review* 460.

on the quality of the rule of law or economic growth records, especially among poorer countries;[52] and that the much broader governance measures employed by the World Bank provide a much more helpful framework of analysis for an institutional reform agenda.

In a similar vein, Gillian Hadfield, in a recent paper[53] argues that the binary classification of legal systems as either common law or civil law obscures many institutional differences that do not closely track this binary categorization. Roe and Siegel argue that political economy factors best explain why some countries have weak protection of the rights of creditors and outside shareholders: incumbent firms fear that strong financial sectors will facilitate new entrants and hence intensified competition.[54]

We should also add that, drawing on recent comparative legal research with which Michael Trebilcock has been associated,[55] the performance of legal systems in former British colonies that inherited the common law from their imperial overseers varies markedly on various measures of legal activity, including contemporary measures of the rule of law. Thus, variations in performance within legal families are often much greater than variations between legal families. This suggests that many variables other than legal origins alone explain subsequent legal performance – in particular, we argue, the degree to which the British colonial authorities afforded representation to the indigenous population in legislative bodies, and the extent to which indigenous and British common law courts and animating values were integrated, fostering the development of a localized common law jurisprudence.

V. A BRIEF REVIEW OF RULE OF LAW REFORM EXPERIENCE

We now turn to a brief review (substantially elaborated on elsewhere)[56] of the efficacy of recent reforms to legal institutions in Latin America, Africa,

---

52 See Kaufman, *supra* note 1.

53 Gillian Hadfield, 'The levers of legal design: institutional determinants of the quality of law' (2006) 36 *Journal of Comparative Economics* 43; see also symposium, 'Economics and comparative law' (2009) 59 *U. of Toronto L.J.* 179–236.

54 Mark Roe and Jordan Siegel, 'Finance and politics: a review essay based on Kenneth Dam's analysis of legal traditions in *The Law-Growth Nexus*' (2009) 47 *Journal of Economic Literature* 781.

55 Ron Daniels, Michael Trebilcock and Lindsey Carson, 'The legacy of empire: the common law inheritance and commitments to legality in former British colonies' (2011) 59 *American Journal of Comparative Law* 111.

56 See Trebilcock and Daniels, *supra* note 10.

Central and Eastern Europe, and Asia, relating these reform efforts to notions of path dependence which we have reviewed elsewhere.[57] Here we focus mostly on non-instrumental rationales for the rule of law, deferring until Chapter 3 an assessment of the empirical evidence on the efficacy of instrumental (especially economic) conceptions of the rule of law.

Although path dependence in its purest form is constraining and deterministic, this does not mean that it yields the conclusion that we are prisoners of our past. Instead, we have argued that it provides insights for those promoting institutional reforms. Indeed, the path dependence literature provides a wealth of information regarding institutional change that reformers would be wise to take seriously. First, the concepts of self-reinforcing mechanisms and switching costs, for instance, can be important because they show that reforms in key institutional nodes of any system are likely to fail if they do not address both the nature and scale of switching costs faced by internal and external actors engaged in or with these institutions. Second, to the extent that particular institutions have become embedded, over time, in a broader matrix of mutually reinforcing institutional interdependencies, nodal reform that ignores these interdependencies is likely to be further compromised. Third, the concept of critical junctures shows that comprehensive or ambitious reforms in minimally functional institutions (or networks of institutions) during 'normal times' can be disruptive and are likely to be strongly resisted by affected stakeholders. Yet defining or identifying 'critical junctures' *ex ante* where more ambitious reforms may be feasible is itself a highly speculative exercise. As path dependence theory emphasizes, much institutional change will be incremental and will occur on many small margins. Indeed, attempting too much may be a recipe for achieving too little.

A prominent focus of rule of law reforms has been judicial reform such as reducing court backlogs which have been large and growing in many developing countries. Reform efforts to this end have involved improving court record-keeping through enhanced information technology and more proactive case management techniques. Complementary reform initiatives have often involved externally supported judicial training programs.[58] In some cases, these initiatives seem to have had a positive impact on court backlogs, although various scholars have noted that enhancing judicial capacity by increasing the volume of cases processed says little or nothing about the quality of judicial decision-making.[59] Judicial corruption and

---

57 See Prado and Trebilcock, *supra* note 40.

58 Trebilcock and Daniels, *supra* note 10.

59 See Jensen and Heller, *supra* note 32.

incompetence is endemic in many developing countries, particularly at lower levels of the court system and outside major urban centres. Reform efforts have barely penetrated these courts and are thus largely ineffective, since most citizens only have contact (if any at all) with courts at the lowest level of the system.[60]

One challenge confronting reforms is that they ignore self-reinforcing mechanisms at the individual level: belief systems or patterns of behaviour on the part of internal and external actors may have adjusted to the former institutional arrangement and might not readily adapt to the new regime. These forms of adaptive behaviour are likely to increase the switching costs of moving to a new system, generating resistance to reforms akin to the 'installed base problem' (for example, resistance to moving from an imperial to a metric system of weights and measures).[61]

For judicial reforms, individual belief systems or patterns of behaviour are reinforced by legal education. Historically such education in many developing countries has focused heavily on rote learning and regurgitation in exams rather than critical or interdisciplinary analysis of legal problems.[62] In Latin America, many public law schools also suffer from over-population with many part-time students and instructors.[63] While private law schools have recently proliferated in many developing countries, they are of highly variable quality, ranging from internationally recognized law schools to part-time degree or diploma mills. Legal education institutions in Central and Eastern Europe have historically been tightly controlled by the state, which has led to a standardized, inflexible and increasingly inappropriate legal curriculum.[64] In some countries in this

---

60 Ibid.

61 The term 'installed base' refers to early adopters of a technology, who will bear a disproportionate share of transient incompatibility costs and may therefore resist the adoption of a newer technology. The larger the installed base, the more inertia it will generate. Joseph Farrell and Garth Saloner, 'Installed base and compatibility: innovation, product preannouncements, and predation' (1986) 76 *Am.Econ.Rev.* 940.

62 Trebilcock and Daniels, *supra* note 10, Chapter 9; Joseph Tome, 'Heading south but looking north; globalization and law reform in Latin America' (2000) *Wisconsin Law Review* 691; Cheng Han Tan et al., 'Legal education in Asia' (2006) 1:1 *Asian Journal of Comparative Law* at 17.

63 Stephen Meili, 'Legal education in Argentina and Chile', in Louise G. Trubek and Jeremy Cooper, *Educating for Justice Around the World: Legal Education, Legal Practice and the Community* (Aldershot: Ashgate, 1999), 138–57 at 142.

64 See George E. Glos, 'Soviet law and Soviet legal education in an historical context: an interpretation' (1989) 15 *Review of Socialist Law* 227 at 257; Susan Finder, 'Legal education in the Soviet Union' (1989) 15 *Review of Socialist Law* 197 at 207.

region, with the support of international NGOs and other institutions, efforts have been made to reform the curriculum in ways that are relevant to the new economic, social and political environments in which these countries find themselves, and to reduce or eliminate the ideological connection between law and the state that prevailed in the communist era.[65]

Legal education in Africa is extremely varied with respect to institutional support, funding and curriculum development. South Africa, a relatively rich nation on the continent, has considerable legal education infrastructure, but continues to suffer from under-funding and low quality of historically black institutions. Many other African countries have much weaker legal education infrastructures that suffer from a serious lack of resources, including such basic resources as teaching and library materials. As in Latin America, many African law schools continue to emphasize rote, black-letter learning, although significant recent efforts have been made to incorporate both clinical legal education and human rights dimensions into some law school curricula.[66] In many Asian countries there are a large number of legal education institutions of widely variable quality, with a recent dramatic proliferation of these institutions in China.[67]

Resistance to legal reforms in many developing countries seems attributable in part to the vested interests of professors, judges and existing practitioners who seek to insulate themselves from changes in curriculum or reforms of substantive or procedural features of the existing legal system,

---

65 European Commission: Education and Training, 'ERASMUS and the University', available at http://ec.europa.eu/education/index_en.htm (accessed 28 June 2009); Associate Dean Louis F. Del. Duca, 'Cooperation in internationalizing legal education in Europe – emerging new players' (2001) 20:1 *Penn State International Law Review* 9.

66 Manu Ndulo, 'Legal education in Africa in the era of globalization and structural adjustment' (2002) 20:3 *Pennsylvania State International Law Review* 489; Philip F. Iya, 'From lecture room to practice: addressing the challenges of reconstructing and regulating legal education and legal practice in the new South Africa (2002–3) *Third World Legal Studies* 144 at 151.

67 Tan et al., *supra* note 62; Mei-Ying Hung, 'China's WTO commitment on independent review: an opportunity for political reform' (Carnegie Endowment for International Peace, Working Paper No. 5, 2002), citing Zhongguo Tongxun She, 'Beijing to introduce re-education through labour law this year', 19 February 2001; Vincent Cheng Yang, 'Judicial and legal training in China: current status of professional development and topics of human rights' (China-OHCHR National Workshop for Lawyers and Judges, 2002), citing 'Chinese legal aid system basically formed, 600,000 people aided in five years', *China News Net,* 29 September 2002, available at http://www.icclr.law.ubc.ca/Publications/Reports/Beijing_August_2002.pdf.

in part because these changes entail a depreciation of their existing human capital and require investments in new human capital. Lawyers who were trained and practise, adjudicate or teach in a socially dysfunctional legal system and have made substantial investments in human capital in learning how to function in such a system are often not a progressive force for legal reform.

A more general problem with judicial reforms, however, is that they do not account for relevant macro processes in a legal system that connect what happens inside the courtroom with a series of events that precede or succeed the courtroom proceedings (enforcement of judgments, for example). In particular, recent rule of law reforms have paid little attention to reforming the most relevant law enforcement agency, the police force, despite the fact that historically in many countries the police have been viewed as a form of paramilitary organization, primarily dedicated to regime maintenance in societies dominated by military or authoritarian governments.[68] This has made policing of secondary importance in many developing and transitional economies and has led incumbent political regimes to support, or at least acquiesce in, extensive human rights abuses by police forces, including torture, coerced confessions, indefinite detention without trial and rampant corruption.[69]

In an attempt to deal with these forms of abuse, modest efforts have been made in some developing and transitional economies to implement civilian police oversight mechanisms and reform of criminal procedure laws.[70] These laws, at least in theory, enable courts to act as a check on these forms of abuse through, for example, rules that deem evidence to be inadmissible where obtained illegally. However, in practice, courts in many developing and transition economies have not been assertive monitors of abuses of public office, in part because of their historical subservience to the executive branch of government in terms of appointments, promotions

---

68 Article 1of United Nations Code of Conduct for Law Enforcement Officials, adopted by the General Assembly in 1979, G.A. Res. 34/169, UN Doc. A/34/46; Rachel Nield, 'Confronting a culture of impunity: the promise and pitfalls of civilian review of police in Latin America', in Andrew Goldsmith and Colleen Lewis (eds), *Civilian Oversight of Policing: Governance, Democracy and Human Rights* (Portland, OR: Hart Publishing, 2000).

69 Mercedes S. Hinton, 'A distant reality: democratic policing in Argentina and Brazil' (2005) 5(1) *Criminal Justice* 75 at 95; Paul Chevigny, 'Defining the role of the police in Latin America', in Juan E. Mendez, Guillermo O'Donnell and Paulo Sergio Pinheiro (eds), *The (Un)Rule of Law and the Underprivileged in Latin America* (Notre Dame, IN: University of Notre Dame Press, 1999).

70 Colleen Lewis, 'The politics of civilian oversight: serious commitment or lip service?' in Goldsmith and Lewis, *supra* note 68.

and resources.[71] Attempts to strengthen judicial independence through the creation of semi-autonomous Judicial Councils to vet appointments and promotions and to maintain a disciplinary regime for judicial misconduct have often been met with fierce resistance from the executive and legislative branches of government, as well as the judiciary itself.[72]

The problem of ignoring other elements of the legal system, like the police, in rule of law reforms is replicated in penal reforms.[73] These reforms seek to improve correctional institutions in many developing countries and transition economies, but ignore their relationship with the criminal justice system. Reform efforts in this context have focused on developing correctional institutions as professional public institutions, often through training programs for correctional personnel provided by international agencies and NGOs, and the provision of paralegal advisory services to inmates to advise them of their rights relating to abuses suffered within correctional institutions, and their related legal rights under the country's criminal justice system.[74] Some countries, especially in Latin America, have appointed official ombudsmen to investigate prisoners' complaints and report thereon to government, while in other countries (such as a number of countries in sub-Saharan Africa), pursuant to regional treaty commitments, official rapporteurs make periodic visits to and report publicly on conditions in correctional institutions.[75]

The role of prisons in many countries historically was not tied principally to crime, punishment or rehabilitation, but to suppressing political opposition and/or extracting labour from vast populations of captive workers (especially in the former Soviet Union). Severe prison overcrowding has been a chronic problem, leading to a very high incidence

---

71 Nield, *supra* note 68.

72 See Linn Hammergren, 'Do Judicial Councils further judicial reform? Lessons from Latin America', Carnegie Endowment for International Peace, Working Paper 28, 2002.

73 *Standard Minimum Rules for the Treatment of Prisoners,* adopted by the First United Nations Congress on the Prevention of Crime and the Treatment of Offenders, held in Geneva in 1955, and approved by the Economic and Social Council by its resolution 663 C(XXIV) of 31 July 1957 and 2076 (LXII) of 13 May 1977, Article 10.

74 'Penal and prison reform in Africa', Vol. 13–14 (*PRI Newsletter,* April 2001) at 5.

75 The United Nations Latin American Institute for the Prevention of Crime and Treatment of Offenders, ILANUD Activities makes the reports available on their website, at http://www.ilanud.or.cr/centro-de-documentacion/biblioteca digital/181-sistemas-penitenciarios.html.

of infectious diseases such as HIV/AIDS and TB.[76] However, reforms focused on correctional institutions often ignore the fact that a significant source of overcrowding in correctional institutions in many developing countries is the high percentage of inmates held on remand awaiting trial for often lengthy periods because of inefficiencies in the broader criminal justice system. Where reforms to the criminal justice system have been undertaken, providing judges with greater discretion to impose non-custodial forms of sentence, the judiciary has often shown a reluctance to invoke these powers, particularly in contexts of widespread public concern over high and rising violent crime rates.[77] Thus, penal reform efforts need to deal with their relationship to the broader criminal justice system.

Correction, dealing as it does with a small and marginalized sub-set of the population, is (perhaps more than any other institution) inextricable from the broader successes and failures of rule of law reform. It depends, at least, on the efficiency of court processes, the effectiveness of law enforcement, the broader complex of social factors determining crime rates more generally, a vigorous legal bar willing to defend prisoners' rights, and a culture of human rights robust enough to conceptualize prisoners within its ambit.

Other institutional interconnections that are relevant to rule of law reforms involve the bureaucracy. In many developed and developing countries important aspects of the administration of justice are vested in specialized law enforcement or administrative agencies that deal with matters as diverse as tax administration, public utilities regulation, environmental regulation, competition law enforcement, election management bodies, and so on. One of the advantages of these agencies is that they are more easily detachable from the existing bureaucracy, entailing less complex or sweeping reforms that may be less likely to suffer from path dependence problems.

Tax administration is an example of a specialized law enforcement or regulatory function which all developing countries must perform, and

---

[76] See UNAIDS, *Prisons and AIDS,* UNAIDS Best Practices Collection (1997), available at http://data.unaids.org/publications/IRC-pub05/prisons-pov_en.pdf; Centre for the Study of Violence and Reconciliation, 'Annual Report 2001/2002 Criminal Justice Programme' (2002), available at http://www.csvr.org.za/docs/2001.pdf; United Nations Press Release, 'UN expert warns of overcrowded prisons as breeding grounds for AIDS', 23 July 2010, available at http://www.unmultimedia.org/radio/english/2010/07/un-expert-warns-of-overcrowded-prisons-as-breeding-grounds-for-aids/.

[77] Mark Ungar, 'Prisons and politics in contemporary Latin America' (2003) 25:4 *Human Rights Quarterly* 909 at 912.

hence provides an important example of the challenges that developing countries face with the performance of such agencies.[78] In the case of tax administration, effective performance of this function is of critical importance to all developing countries because a constrained ability to collect revenues that are legally due also constrains governments in terms of expenditure on pressing development priorities. In many developing countries the gap between taxes nominally due and taxes actually collected is extremely large – often in the range of 40 per cent – which suggests the potential margins for improved performance in tax administration.[79]

To improve the tax system, a number of developing countries have set up large taxpayer units (LTUs), with a view to developing specialized and integrated expertise in tax assessment, given that large taxpayer units are where much of the effective taxable capacity in many developing countries resides. In addition, a number of developing countries have also set up semi-autonomous revenue agencies (SARAs), designed to ensure the fiscal autonomy of the organization and much greater freedom in personnel policies and IT development.[80] Many of these reforms appear to have been successful in broadening the taxpayer base and increasing the percentage of taxes nominally due that are actually collected. However, the experience with SARAs over time has been mixed: typically, these agencies appear initially to have a significant impact on the percentage of taxes actually collected, but subsequently their performance tends to deteriorate, in some cases because of rampant corruption within the agency,[81] and in some cases because of increasing political interference from the Ministry of Finance and other executive arms of the government in personnel and assessment processes.[82] This suggests that the ability of

---

[78] Malcolm Gillis, 'Tax reform: lessons from postwar experience in developing nations', in Malcolm Gillis (ed.), *Tax Reform in Developing Countries* (London: Duke University Press, 1989) at 493; for examples from India, Indonesia, Mexico, Singapore, Spain and the Philippines, see Arindam Das-Gupta and Dilip Mukherjee, *Incentives and Institutional Reforms in Tax Enforcement: An Analysis of Developing Country Experience* (Delhi: Oxford University Press, 1998).

[79] For examples from India, Indonesia, Mexico, Singapore, Spain and the Philippines, see Das-Gupta and Mukherjee, ibid.

[80] See Trebilcock and Daniels, *supra* note 10, Chapter 6.

[81] Susan Rose-Ackerman, *Corruption and Government: Causes, Consequences, and Reform* (Cambridge: Cambridge University Press, 1999) at 86 (showing that in tax reform incentive schemes can be used only if levels of performance can be measured by external monitors).

[82] Robert Taliercio, Jr., *Unsustainably Autonomous? Challenges to the Revenue Authority Model in Latin America Tax Agencies in Developing Countries* (Washington, DC: World Bank, 2001).

these agencies to maintain themselves over time as islands of virtue in an otherwise corrupt or incompetent general public administration may be quite limited without complementary reforms, over time, of the surrounding institutional matrix.

Another similarly motivated example of reforms is the implementation of independent regulatory agencies (IRAs) for infrastructure sectors such as telecommunications, electricity and water. During the 1990s US-style IRAs were adopted in many Latin American countries.[83] They were created to insulate regulatory decisions from electoral politics. To secure this insulation, IRAs were accorded a series of institutional guarantees of independence. For instance, in presidential systems these guarantees would include fixed terms of office for commissioners, congressional approval of presidential nominations, and alternative sources of funds to ensure their financial autonomy.[84] In the context of privatization of state-owned utility companies, this insulation was intended to provide a credible commitment by the government to existing rules and norms, supposedly protecting investors from arbitrary and unjustifiable subsequent modifications to the regulatory framework.

However, the implementation of IRAs has met with a series of obstacles.[85] In some cases, their creation was resisted by bureaucrats, who were also opposed to privatization and a competitive environment in infrastructure services. This resistance may exemplify high switching costs and the installed base problem. In other cases, the transfer of civil servants from the pre-existing bureaucracy to the IRAs brought deeply embedded practices that are difficult to change, impairing some of the institutional innovations adopted by IRAs, such as those designed to insulate these agencies

---

83 Jacint Jordana and David Levi-Faur, 'Hacia un Estado Regulador Latinoamericano? La Difusión de Agencias Reguladoras Autónomas por Paises e Sectores' (2005). See also Giandomenico Majone, 'The rise of the regulatory state in Europe' (1994) 17 *West European Politics*, 77–101 (discussing the European experience).

84 Warrick Smith, 'Utility regulators – the independence debate', in *Public Policy for the Private Sector*, note 127 (October 1997). Available at http://www-wds.worldbank.org/external/default/main?pagePK=64193027&piPK=64187937&theSitePK=523679&menuPK=64187510&searchMenuPK=64187283&theSitePK=523679&entityID=000009265_3980219162756&searchMenuPK=64187283&theSitePK=523679, but see Levi-Faur, 'The Politics of Liberalisation: Privatization and regulation-for-competition in Europe's and Latin America's Telecoms and Electricity industries', *European Journal of Political Research,* 42(5), 2003, 705–740.

85 Mariana M. Prado, 'The challenges and risks of creating independent regulatory agencies: a cautionary tale from Brazil', (2008) *Vanderbilt Journal of Transnational Law* (March 2008), pp. 453–503.

from political and electoral interests. This illustrates the difficulty of mitigating self-reinforcing mechanisms, especially when they are embedded in the institutional culture. Finally, some of the institutional guarantees of independence in these agencies were not effective because they were operating in a different institutional matrix from the country of origin of the transplant. Thus, the creation of IRAs largely ignored the importance of institutional interconnections.

A related class of administrative agency is that of competition agencies.[86] Around 60 countries – mainly in transition or developing economies – have competition agencies that are 15 years or younger in age.[87] According to the World Bank, a 2000 survey found that, on average, competition authorities in industrial countries are 40 per cent more effective than competition authorities in developing countries.[88] The following challenges have been identified in recent surveys or evaluations of the experience of such agencies by the Competition Policy Implementation Working Group of the International Competition Network (ICN)[89] and the International Development Research Centre (Ottawa).[90]

First, many countries have borrowed heavily from developed countries in designing their respective laws, and the legislative framework does not address effectively the realities of the jurisdiction that these agencies are called upon to regulate. Some statutes fail to address important anti-competitive forms of conduct because of carve-outs or exceptions for industrial policy, political economy or other reasons. Others are expansive

---

[86] For a recent survey, see Michael Trebilcock and Edward Iacobucci, 'Designing competition law institutions: values, structure, and mandate' (2010) 41 *Loyola University Chicago Law Journal* 455.

[87] A recent survey and analysis of the competition laws of 102 countries finds mild preliminary support for the claim that competition law has a positive, albeit quite limited, effect on the intensity of competition within a nation. Much of the impact appears to be as a result of the strength of enforcement in particular areas rather than the scope of the substantive law, largely through reducing collusive practices. The study finds that merger or abuse of dominance law does not seem to enhance competition intensity: Keith N. Hylton and Fei Deng, 'Antitrust around the world: an empirical analysis of the scope of competition laws and their effects' (2007) 74 *Antitrust L.J.* 271.

[88] World Bank, *World Development Report 2002: Building Institutions for Markets* (Oxford University Press, 2002) at 141.

[89] International Competition Network, Implementation Working Group, 'Lessons to be learnt from the experiences of young competition agencies' (May 2006).

[90] Taimoon Stewart, Julian Clarke and Susan Joekes, 'Competition law in action: experiences from developing countries', International Development Research Centre, Ottawa, May 2007.

in their scope, but fail to establish any set of priorities for the agency consistent with its resources and capabilities. Others do not provide for compulsory *ex ante* notification of mergers, while others set notification thresholds so low that agencies are overwhelmed with merger notifications that they are not able effectively to review. In other cases, agencies are not invested with adequate investigative powers to unearth and eliminate anti-competitive conduct or are unable effectively to enforce compulsory disclosure laws, and lack powers to grant immunities to facilitate cartel investigations. In yet others, fines and other penalties are too low to induce effective deterrence, or cannot be effectively enforced.

Second, young agencies commonly report a lack of cooperation and coordination of policy and effort with particular government ministries and other regulatory bodies in their attempt to enforce and promote competition policy – in part as a result of the recent introduction of competition laws without provisions that address prior conflicting legislation or sectoral regulatory regimes. In some cases, these problems have been partly mitigated by memoranda of understanding with other agencies as to respective roles and responsibilities.

Third, many agencies in developing countries face major obstacles in dealing with cross-border anti-competitive conduct, especially international cartels, and often lack formal and informal cooperative mechanisms with other countries' authorities with more effective jurisdiction over potential wrongdoers.

Fourth, many agencies responding to the ICN survey indicated challenges relating to the interface between the competition authority and the judiciary and reported that cases have often taken years to process, partly as a result of a lack of specialized competence on the part of public prosecutors, attorneys and the local judiciary. An earlier ICN survey of competition agencies in developing and transition economies reported:

> The all but unanimous view expressed is that the judiciary is a major stumbling block in the path of effective competition enforcement – the judges do not understand competition law and are content to avoid the necessity to learn through diverting competition issues into a maze of esoteric administrative and procedural side-streets out of which the substantive matters at issue rarely emerge.[91]

Fifth, many new agencies suffer from extreme financial and human resource constraints that pose major challenges in setting priorities, as well as politi-

---

[91] ICN Working Group, 'Capacity building and technical assistance: building credible competition authorities in developing and transition economies', 23–25 June 2003, at 35.

cal cronyism in compromising the quality of key appointments. Developing and retaining specialized human capital within agencies and complementary educational and professional institutions is a pressing challenge.[92]

Finally, the studies note the lack of a competition culture in many of the jurisdictions in which these new agencies operate. This is reflected in a lack of awareness by the business community, government agencies, non-government agencies, the media, the judiciary and the general public of the rules of competition law, and their overall responsibility to ensure that such rules are observed in the interest of competition and overall economic development. Many of these new agencies are operating in economies in transition (from command to market economies), dealing with major state-owned enterprises or only recently privatized SOEs often operating in highly concentrated sectors. Many others are located in developing countries with long histories of state-led development policies – including import substitution policies that severely restrict import competition and foreign investment. These agencies have to deal with extensive state-owned enterprises and highly concentrated economic sectors, which are often subject to extensive price, entry and exit regulation. In this context, both within and outside government there are substantial vested interests in policies that are antithetical to effective competition.[93] An earlier ICN Report concluded:

> In the end, we have been persuaded that the over-arching challenge confronting competition authorities in developing and transition countries relates to their stature and standing within the ranks of key stakeholders or interest groups, as well as the public at large. In other words, all struggle to make themselves heard and it is this that constitutes the gravest challenge confronting competition authorities in these countries.[94]

VI. IDENTIFYING FEASIBLE REFORM STRATEGIES

Approaches to rule of law reforms that do not take into account adaptive behaviour with respect to the particular institutional context in question,

---

[92] See Daniel Sokol, 'The development of human capital in Latin American competition policy', in Eleanor Fox and Daniel Sokol (eds), *Competition Law and Policy in Latin America* (Oxford: Hart Publishing, 2009).

[93] See Ignacio de Leon, 'A market process analysis of Latin American competition policy', UNCTAD Regional Meeting on Competition Law Policy, Costa Rica, 03 August – 1 September 2000.

[94] ICN Working Group, *supra* note 91 at 74.

as well as mutually reinforcing effects among interdependent institutions, are unlikely to be successful. If one takes path dependence seriously, future reform strategies will be significantly constrained and shaped by the legacies of history. The lessons of path dependence lead to a conundrum. Path dependence shows that isolated institutional reforms focused on micro-processes are likely to ignore both self-reinforcing mechanisms and institutional interdependencies, and are therefore often doomed to failure. However, system-wide ambitious reforms during 'normal times' are disruptive and likely to fail because of the serious switching costs that they are likely to entail (and the resistance that these will engender). Thus, despite institutional interdependencies, all-encompassing reforms are simply not feasible. This is true during normal times and there seems to be evidence that, even in post-conflict societies (which may present more opportunities or at least greater urgency for change), all-encompassing reforms often achieve very limited success.[95]

Are reformers then left only with windows of opportunity (critical junctures) in which major reforms can be implemented successfully? Is there any way that reformers can account for the lessons of path dependence theory without being in a potentially eternal waiting period for the right moment? As Rodrik puts it, 'the challenge for the empirical literature on institutions is to explore these [path dependent] patterns without falling into the trap of reductionism or of historical and geographical determinism'.[96]

There are two potential (and complementary) strategies for dealing with this conundrum. First, reformers may be able to identify some institutions that can be more easily detached from a broader mutually reinforcing institutional matrix or be created *de novo* (such as semi-autonomous revenue agencies, new constitutional or human rights courts or commissions, semi-independent regulatory agencies, one-stop government agencies (like the Brazilian Poupatempo)[97] for issuing, for example,

---

95 Marina Ottaway, 'The post-war "Democratic Reconstruction Model": why it can't work'. Paper presented at United States Institute for Peace, 2002.

96 Dani Rodrik, 'Feasible globalizations', KSG Working Paper Series RWP02-029 (Cambridge, MA: Harvard University, 2002), available at http://web.hks.harvard.edu/publications/workingpapers/citation.aspx?PubId=935 at 6–8. See also Dani Rodrik, *One Economics, Many Recipes Globalization, Institutions, and Economic Growth* (Princeton, NJ: Princeton University Press, 2007), Chapters 5 and 6; see also Francis Fukuyama, 'Development and the limits of institutional design', Global Development Network (St. Petersburg, Russia: 20 January 2006); Francis Fukuyama, *Statebuilding: Governance and World Order in the 21st Century* (Ithaca: Cornell University Press, 2004).

97 See Mariana M. Prado and Ana Carolina Chasin, 'How innovative was the

passports, driving licences, ID cards and health cards, and alternative forms of dispute resolution).[98] This strategy may enable more ambitious stand-alone reforms that nevertheless have important showcase effects that demonstrate lower switching costs or greater benefits than sceptics had assumed, although even here the experience with semi-autonomous revenue agencies and independent regulatory agencies suggests that these institutions are likely to be fragile without complementary reforms, over time, to the surrounding institutional matrix.

The second strategy is to reform existing institutions that are interconnected and mutually reinforcing in a time sensitive manner by prioritizing a sequence of reforms, beginning with certain core reforms but recognizing that further complementary reforms will be necessary in the future to reinforce the initial reforms. This implies that reforms should be incremental, which is quite different from many current reform practices that are either stand-alone without being incremental or are so encompassing as to be infeasible.

One of the lessons of path dependence is that we are not writing on a blank slate. It is true that in abnormal times – 'critical junctures' (for example, the aftermath of economic collapse, civil war or military invasion) – the credibility and legitimacy of incumbent elites may be weakened by such crises, creating new political openings for marginalized constituencies.[99] At the same time, it is unlikely that all pre-existing economic, social and cultural factors that create costs for switching to new institutional regimes can be ignored entirely[100] (as contemporary challenges to institutional reform in, for example, Iraq and Afghanistan exemplify). Reformers should recognize not only the importance of switching costs, but also be sensitive to the different kinds of switching costs associated with reform.[101]

Poupatempo experience in Brazil? Institutional bypass as a new form of institutional change', *Brazilian Political Science Review* [forthcoming 2011].

[98] See Thomas Heller, 'An immodest postscript', in Jensen and Heller, *supra* note 32; Mariana M. Prado, 'Institutional bypass: an alternative to development reform', (April 19, 2011). Available at SSRN: http://ssrn.com/abstract=1815442.

[99] See Michael Trebilcock, 'Journeys across the divides', in Francesco Parisi and Charles Rowley (eds), *The Origins of Law and Economics: Essays by the Founding Fathers* (Cheltenham, UK: Edward Elgar, 2005).

[100] This can be true even in post-conflict societies; see Susan Rose-Ackerman, 'Corruption and post-conflict peace-building' (2008) *Ohio Northern University Law Review* 405.

[101] This section draws on the analysis developed in Ronald J. Daniels and Michael J. Trebilcock, 'The political economy of rule of law reform in developing countries' (2004) 26 *Mich. J. Int'l L.* 99.

First, in terms of political economy considerations, switching costs may be high for those who benefit from the institutional status quo.[102] These costs may be mitigated by reforms that create or strengthen a countervailing political constituency that benefits from the reforms.[103] Alternatively, vested interests may need to be bought off or grandfathered in some way to mute opposition to the reforms. Second, switching costs may also reflect individual learning costs in adapting to a new regime (the 'installed base' problem). These can be mitigated by state-sponsored public education programs and gradual processes of transition that avoid the need for abrupt adaptation to a new regime. Third, switching costs may reflect the scarcity of financial and human resources required to implement new institutional regimes, which can be mitigated by external financial and technical assistance. Finally, switching costs may reflect deeply embedded cultural benefits or practices that are resistant to change.[104] Here, reforms that adapt traditional institutions (such as traditional forms of alternative dispute settlement or communal property rights) may mitigate problems of cultural dissonance. Moreover, institutional reforms implemented over time may in turn lead to modifications in cultural belief systems.

In this respect, various forms of alternative dispute resolution (ADR) make up a class of reforms that appears to have shown significant promise, largely through demonstration effects. ADR sometimes builds on traditional or community-based forms of dispute settlement, such as adaptations of the Lok Adalat system in India, the Shalish system in Bangladesh, the Gacaca Tribunals in Rwanda in the aftermath of years of civil war and genocide, the Casas de Justicia in Latin America and Alternative Law Groups in the Philippines. These have sought to marry indigenous methods of dispute settlement with broader rule of law norms,

---

[102] Resistance to reform can also be higher if there is uncertainty regarding the identity of potential beneficiaries. The uncertainty is higher in large-scale reforms: Dani Rodrik and Raquel Fernandez, 'Resistance to reform: status quo bias in the presence of individual-specific uncertainty' (1991) 81 *American Economic Review* 1148.

[103] How much instability these reforms should generate – i.e., how much room for constant contestation would be good for future reforms – is a topic that deserves further research. For an insightful analysis, see Susan Rose-Ackerman, 'Was Mancur a Maoist? An essay on kleptocracy and political stability' (2003) 15 *Economics and Politics* 163.

[104] See, for instance, how informal institutions for contract enforcement in the footwear industry resisted the changes brought by an open trade regime when NAFTA was implemented in Mexico: Christopher Woodruff, 'Contract enforcement and trade liberalization in Mexico's footwear industry' (1998) 26 *World Development* 979.

such as equality before the law, so as to minimize cultural switching costs. In these cases, reformers have struggled to navigate the difficult compromise between two, sometimes conflicting, models of dispute resolution and the respective roles of the formal court system and informal modes of dispute settlement. Despite these difficulties, these ADR reforms have a major benefit: they acknowledge and rely on context-specific forms of institutional vindication or instantiation of rule of law values, thus reducing cultural switching costs and nurturing an increasingly robust domestic constituency for rule of law reforms more generally over time. In this sense, these reforms enable a broadly representative range of social, economic and political interests to see their interests and values as aligned with the promotion and preservation of the rule of law.

VII. THE ROLE OF EXTERNAL ACTORS IN PROMOTING RULE OF LAW REFORM IN DEVELOPING COUNTRIES

We argue that a tailored approach, overtly attentive to the domestic political context of the countries in question, will enhance the likelihood of success of external efforts at promoting rule of law reform in developing countries. If, as many commentators have persuasively argued, the rule of law is ultimately a political phenomenon, we think that such political attention only makes sense. In this regard, Michael Trebilcock and Ronald Daniels have sketched a set of hypothetical political formations with varying degrees of support for rule of law reform that are useful in considering how reforms can be sensitive to different political contexts.[105] These paradigmatic formations, each of which can be related to real-life examples, will necessarily pose different kinds of challenges for rule of law reformers, and create different openings and opportunities for an international role. Thus, the relative salience of each of the three obstacles to reform discussed above will vary as between these different formations (and almost infinite variations on them) – and with them, the role of the international community.

The first stylized formation is characterized by an environment of broad political support for the rule of law. The state that we envision has progressive-minded political leadership at the highest levels, strong support from within the ruling party and broad popular support for legal reforms. The archetypal administration is that of Nelson Mandela in

---

105 Trebilcock and Daniels, *supra* note 10.

South Africa, particularly in the early days after his election in 1994. Not only did Mandela himself have a strong mandate, but public support for legal reform was widespread as well. Another, perhaps more contentious, example is Lee Kuan Yew, Prime Minister of Singapore from 1959 to 1990 and senior government minister thereafter, who was strongly committed to a highly competent, meritocratic, non-corrupt public administration throughout his lengthy term as Prime Minister, although the independence of the judiciary in contexts involving government officials has been more problematic. Yet further examples include several countries in Central Europe following the collapse of the Soviet Union.

The second stylized formation is more ambiguous in its support for rule of law reform. This administration is marked by a strong desire for rule of law reform at the highest political levels, but more systematic opposition from a variety of complex economic and social relationships operating below the political surface. This kind of opposition might be rooted, for instance, in an entrenched ideological orientation inconsistent with the rule of law, or in powerful public or private interests with a stake in a general state of lawlessness. These administrations will often be identifiable by the rise of a charismatic or prominent leader in a time of general political or economic turmoil. Somewhat ironic examples include Mikhail Gorbachev, Boris Yeltsin and Vladimir Putin. At least in their early days, these leaders brought tremendous promise of reform, despite, among other problems, the meteoric rise of an oligarchic class of extraordinarily powerful organized criminals, rampant corruption and the pervasive influence of Communist ideology including, not least, a not insignificant degree of popular support for it.

The third stylized formation is marked by a highly corrupt political leadership with strong incentives for maintaining the status quo and no predisposition to reform. In such states there may be varying degrees of organized popular opposition in the form of NGO or other civil society activity, and there may be some degree of opposition from, or some tendency towards, or pockets of reform within, the leadership of some governing factions or government agencies. However, where the political leadership establishes any sort of lasting foothold, it will almost invariably have complex webs of support in military, administrative or judicial branches of government, and often among some segments of the public. There are myriad examples of authoritarian and kleptocratic administrations to pick from, including the long-standing regime of Robert Mugabe as Prime Minister and then President of Zimbabwe, President Mobutu in Zaire, the Duvaliers in Haiti or the stranglehold of the late Saparmurat Niyazov, self-anointed 'leader of the Turkmens', as President of Turkmenistan. While these states will very often be undemocratic or authoritarian, we emphasize that it is not an absence of democracy per se, but rather hostility to the rule of law that will place an administration in this category. Governments with nominal election procedures in an otherwise repressive context may be hostile to rule of law reform – indeed, Mugabe is an example *par excellence*. More legitimate, popular elections may also produce governments hostile to many of the characteristics of the rule of law, as with the popular election of Yasser Arafat's Palestinian Authority in 1996.

There are several ways in which this trichotomy should be viewed as merely suggestive rather than exhaustive or definitive. First, the lines between these three categories are not strictly demarcated boundaries. States may slide in and out of each category, as governments change policy and character over time. Moreover, ruling parties in any given state may have differing interests across different institutions, and therefore support reform efforts in some institutions, and in some respects, but not in others. Second, there may be substantially different political formations within each of these categories, with significant implications for rule of law reform prescriptions. Our categories do not follow the markings of democracy but rather those of the rule of law. Consequently, within each category there are likely to be widely differing political contexts, to which reformers domestic and external will have to be attentive in selecting appropriate strategies for reform. For instance, in states with authoritarian governments – even those generally in favour of reform – it may be more difficult to pursue legal remedies against the state or its representatives in court proceedings (Singapore may be an example).

As one moves along the spectrum from Type I states to Type III states, top-down, state-centric reform strategies become less feasible, and bottom-up, community-based reform strategies become a more promising option.

Type I states

In these states, where broad political and popular support for rule of law reform exists, the role of the international community should be focused most heavily on alleviating resource constraints. While socio-cultural factors and various forms of vested interests may still act as important barriers to reform, in these states it will be domestic governments, rather than the international community, who will be best placed to address these concerns.

The preferred method of intervention in the most favourable cases (admittedly rare) should be unconditional aid, leaving to the domestic government concerned the choice of reform priorities and strategies and sources of technical advice unless, for credible commitment and signalling purposes, the recipient government requests conditionality. The 'mallet'-like political pressure of accession conditions on membership of regional or multilateral economic or political associations will play little fruitful role, because the state is already generally politically aligned with the viewpoint of reformers. Similarly, because trade policy (preferences or sanctions) does not direct new resources to rule of law initiatives, it will be irrelevant in these circumstances. Because of their punitive nature, economic sanctions would be entirely misplaced.

While there is a case for conditional aid in more equivocal cases, it is important to emphasize again that government policy may be fluid, and that strongly pro-reform administrations can shift policies quickly, particularly where they come to power in a period of transition or during a key 'constitutional moment'. Donors must therefore be vigilant in monitoring the trajectory of Type I governments, and enforcing conditions where appropriate – an historical weakness of development agencies. Funding of non-state drivers of rule of law reform such as local NGOs can also play a role in these states, as they can in almost any situation. However, in these cases, NGOs that cooperate with, rather than oppose, government policies are likely to be more effective.

Type II states

In states with generally reform-minded political leadership but with a less secure political base and widespread opposition from vested interests within state agencies – including legal institutions and perhaps private sector parties who benefit from dysfunctional public institutions – a more diverse set of strategies will be necessary. In these cases, resources may still be scarce, but international agencies or external donors cannot responsibly commit to unconditional aid. Even where high-level political leadership supports reform, increased aid flows to antagonistic public or legal institutions can be misdirected and wasted, or used for regressive purposes. With respect to conditional aid, governments truly committed to reform may agree to conditional aid that binds them to a policy and protects them from internal special interests. A case can be made for conditionality through accession or trade preferences on similar grounds. Also, there may be a good case for non-state-led reforms through local NGOs or alternative law groups operating more independently from the state in institutional contexts where independence of legal institutions is likely to be problematic.

Type III states

Governments unequivocally opposed to rule of law reform will rarely be sensitive to state-level pressure mechanisms, such as trade or other economic sanctions and forms of conditionality attached to aid, debt relief, trade preferences, or accession to regional or multilateral economic or political associations. As Preeg argues in respect of US sanctions (for example, denial of most favoured nation (MFN) trading status) against China, 'the basic reason why these unilateral economic sanctions are ineffective is that the foreign policy objective is to change the oppressive behaviour of an authoritarian or totalitarian government, which constitutes a direct threat to its control if not survival'.[106] While China is not our test case – US sanctions in this case were intended to stimulate democracy more than the rule of law – the point remains the same.

In these cases, the role of non-state actors should become a central aspect of rule of law reform efforts, with a particular focus on those local and international NGOs developing reforms independent of state agencies and the provision of financial and technical assistance to them. In China and Laos, for example, NGOs have played an important role as *de facto* monitoring mechanisms for correctional institutions where the state has denied access to formal state-level monitoring channels. Properly designed and implemented non-state dispute resolution mechanisms, often based on traditional forms of community-based dispute settlement, can also be a vital element of access to justice in circumstances where courts suffer from chronic backlog, corruption or bias, and hence a lack of legitimacy.[107]

VIII. CONCLUSION

It will be obvious that over time states may evolve either negatively or positively from one stylized type to another in the foregoing typology, requiring the international community continuously to reassess its strategies for promoting rule of law reform and to readjust its menu of strategies accordingly. However, even acknowledging this, and acknowledging further that all desirable rule of law reforms cannot be realistically embarked upon simultaneously – if only because of resource constraints and pressing demands on those resources – even in the most favourable (Type I) political environments issues of prioritization and sequencing

---

[106] Ernest H. Preeg, *Feeling Good or Doing Good with Sanctions: Unilateral Economic Sanctions and the US National Interest* (Washington, DC: Center for Strategic and International Studies, 1999).

[107] UNDP, *Making the Law Work for Everyone: Report of the Commission on Legal Empowerment of the Poor,* volume 1 (New York, NY: United Nations, 2008) at 63.

will invariably arise. While these must largely be resolved by domestic constituencies committed to rule of law reform, as must the particular forms of institutional vindication or instantiation of rule of law values, nurturing an increasingly robust domestic constituency for the rule of law over time that reflects a demand-side perspective requires that a broadly representative range of social, economic and political interests come to see their interests and values as aligned with the promotion and preservation of the rule of law. In this respect, we question (along with others) the aptness of the relatively high priority often accorded to formal judicial reform by the international community in the rule of law initiatives that it has promoted in developing countries in recent years,[108] and the relative lack of attention to institutional reforms that are more likely to affect the day-to-day interactions of the citizenry with the legal system. These include police, prosecutors, specialized law enforcement and administrative agencies, including agencies of government that issue, for example, passports, driving licences, ID cards, health cards, building permits and business licences,[109] and access to justice initiatives – such as informal community-based dispute resolution mechanisms (often reflecting adaptations to and elaborations of traditional dispute settlement mechanisms) – where more visible and immediate material benefits from successful institutional reform are likely to be experienced by a wide cross-section of the citizenry. Civil justice surveys of representative samples of the population that have been undertaken in recent years in a number of developed countries[110] provide helpful examples of instruments for identifying the relative frequency and shortcomings of citizen interactions with state agencies.

While we acknowledge that the success of institutional reforms in one context ultimately often depends, to an important extent, on complementary institutional reforms in other contexts,[111] this does not realistically

---

[108] See Carothers, *supra* note 28; Stephen Golub, 'A house without foundation', in Carothers, *supra* note 32; Bryant Garth, 'Building strong and independent judiciaries for the new law and development: beyond the paradox of consensus programs and perpetually disappointing results' (2003) 52 *DePaul Law Review* 383.

[109] Famously described by Charles Reich as 'The new property' (1964) 73 *Yale L.J.* 733, lack of effective access to which in many developing countries is equally famously described by Hernando de Soto, *supra* note 4, and is increasingly well documented in various reports in the World Bank's 'Doing Business' Surveys.

[110] See, e.g., Jamie Baxter, Michael Trebilcock and Albert Yoon, 'The Ontario Civil Needs Project: a comparative analysis of the 2009 survey data', in Michael Trebilcock, Tony Duggan and Lorne Sossis (eds), *Middle-Income Access to Justice* (University of Toronto Press, forthcoming).

[111] See Rachel Kleinfeld, 'Competing definitions of the rule of law' (Carnegie Paper No. 55, Carnegie Endowment, Washington, DC, 2005).

mean that everything can be pursued at once. Judicial reforms (and, we should probably acknowledge, reforms to legal education) are likely to have longer-term and less visible social pay-offs to the citizenry at large and hence are less likely to engage their interest and support than other reforms noted above, given the many more pressing and immediate survival challenges citizens in developing countries often face. Thus, both domestic and international proponents of rule of law reform in developing countries face a hitherto under-acknowledged challenge of rendering rule of law reform politically salient to most citizens of these countries. Strategic choices on sequencing are important in addressing this challenge.

3. The property rights/contract rights development nexus

It has become conventional wisdom amongst most economists that, whatever else the state does, it should provide effective institutions and processes to protect private property rights and enforce contracts, which are regarded as prerequisites to efficient and dynamic market economies. In the words of two prominent law and economics scholars in a forthcoming book, *Solomon's Knot*, 'inadequate institutions to enforce property and contract law are the most fundamental defect in the legal framework of poor countries'.[1] On this view of the rule of law, law plays a critical instrumental role in promoting economic development and should be accorded the highest developmental priority. In the first part of this chapter, we address the property rights protection pillar of this conventional wisdom, then in the second part turn to the contract rights pillar.

I. PROPERTY RIGHTS[2]

A. Introduction

The significance of property rights for economic growth has been the subject of much writing by development theorists and policymakers alike. The so-called 'Washington Consensus' identified property rights protection as one of the major areas of reform for the developing world.[3]

---

1 Robert Cooter and Hans-Bernd Schaefer, *Solomon's Knot* (Princeton University Press, forthcoming) (manuscript at 12); see also Kenneth W. Dam, *The Law-Growth Nexus: The Rule of Law and Economic Development* (Brookings Institution Press, 2006) at 91 ('Proponents of the rule of law in the context of economic development often express the core of their position . . . by emphasizing the need to "enforce contracts and protect property rights."')

2 This discussion of property rights and development is largely derived from Michael Trebilcock and Paul-Erik Veel, 'Property rights and development: the contingent case for formalization' (2008) 30 *University of Pennsylvania Journal of International Law* 397.

3 See John Williamson, 'What Washington means by policy reform' in John

The World Bank also advocates this approach, and has supported and financed programs for the formalization of property rights and the creation of titling systems to secure such rights.[4] While some of the research emanating from the World Bank in recent years has advocated a more nuanced approach,[5] other documents have seemed to follow its traditional attitude that the formalization of property rights is virtually always desirable.[6]

Perhaps most reflective of the importance of property rights in contemporary thinking on economic development has been the success and influence of Hernando de Soto's *The Mystery of Capital: Why Capitalism Triumphs in the West and Fails Everywhere Else*, in which he argues that strong protection for private property rights is the key factor in explaining the economic success of the developed world.[7] Indeed, on de Soto's account, the potential benefits of formalization of property rights are significant. De Soto claims that 'the total value of the real estate held but not legally owned by the poor of the Third World and former communist nations is at least $9.3 trillion', which he characterizes as 'dead capital'.[8]

This broad assertion is unsatisfactory, however, as it leaves a great deal of indeterminacy in terms of the actual policies implied in achieving the objective of strengthening the protection of property rights. The theoretical and empirical literature which has emerged in support of this claim

---

Williamson (ed.), *Latin American Adjustment: How Much Has Happened?* (Peterson Institute for International Economics, 1990) at 7, 17 (noting property rights as an area of insecurity that needs to be corrected in Latin America).

4 World Bank, 'World Development Report 2005: A Better Investment Climate for Everyone' (2004) at 2, available at http://siteresources.worldbank.org/INTWDR2005/Resources/complete_report.pdf; see also Ahmed Galal and Omar Razzaz, 'Reforming land and real estate markets' (World Bank Policy Research, Working Paper No. 2616, 1999) at 20–21, available at http://papers.ssrn.com/sol3/papers.cfm?abstract_id=636201 (assessing the World Bank's experiences with formalizing property rights in developing nations).

5 See Klaus Deininger, *Land Policies for Growth and Poverty Reduction* (Washington, DC: World Bank and Oxford: Oxford University Press, 2003) at 5–6 (finding 'a considerable evolution and increased sophistication' in the recent recommendations for property reform).

6 See, e.g., World Bank, *supra* note 4 at 80–84 (portraying examples of the virtually unequivocal support for the formalization of property rights).

7 Hernando de Soto, *The Mystery of Capital: Why Capitalism Triumphs in the West and Fails Everywhere Else* (Basic Books, 2000) at 218; see also Madeleine Albright, 'It's time for empowerment, the world in 2007' (2006) *The Economist* at 65 (noting that property right reform is essential to economic success for the Third World).

8 De Soto, ibid., at 35.

has been used by some to advocate titling and registration programs as a general solution to the problem of property rights insecurity. We argue, however, that this blanket approach towards the establishment of stronger property rights is unwarranted and counter-productive and instead that a more nuanced approach is required to craft successful development policies regarding property rights.[9]

B. The Benefits and Necessity of a Formal Property Rights Regime

1. The benefits of secure property arrangements

It is important at the outset to highlight briefly some of the reasons why property has occupied such a prominent place in the development literature in recent years. Although there have been many sweeping claims made about the benefits of private property, the literature has also disaggregated the benefits by analysing a number of distinct economic benefits that private property can bring.

Exclusive use leads to resources being used efficiently There are two mechanisms through which various bundles of private property rights can lead to resources being used in the most efficient way possible. The first mechanism assumes that because private property leads individuals to internalize fully the costs and benefits of their use of an asset, private property rights will lead people to use resources in the most socially efficient way.[10] When the protection of property rights over a given resource is weak, collective

---

[9] See David Kennedy, 'Some caution about property rights as a recipe for economic development' (2011) 1 *Accounting, Economics and Law*, Article 3, at 42–8.

[10] See Harold Demsetz, 'Toward a theory of property rights' (1967) 57 *American Economic Review* 347 at 348–9 (discussing how private property rights force owners to internalize the costs of their actions as compared to communal property rights); see also Armen A. Alchian and Harold Demsetz, 'The property right paradigm' (1973) 33 *Journal of Economic History* 16 at 24 ('[P]rivate rights can be socially useful precisely because they encourage persons to take account of social costs.'); R.H. Coase, 'The Federal Communications Commission' (1959) 2 *J.L. & Econ.* 1 (discussing the creation of the FCC and the social costs of public airwaves); Garrett Hardin, 'The tragedy of the commons' (1968) 162 *Sci.* 1243 at 1245 (discussing how communal property allows people to push social costs such as pollution onto society as a whole). Proponents of new institutional economics have also examined this claim. One proponent, Douglass North, argues that private property rights raise the private rate of return of an activity closer to the social rate of return, thereby spurring economic growth: Douglass North, *Structure and Change in Economic History* (New York and London: W.W. Norton, 1981) at 6 ('The existence of a positive return to savings is also dependent on the structure of property rights.')

action problems involving significant inefficiencies in the use and exploitation of that resource can arise. First, where numerous individuals are using the same resource, that resource may be overexploited, as individuals will not consider the detrimental effects on others from their own decisions related to resource use.[11] Second, where no property rights are assigned to a resource, individuals may have an incentive to appropriate that resource as quickly as possible lest others appropriate it first; this can lead to inefficient and wasteful resource mining.[12] Third, a lack of secure property rights over a certain type of asset may lead parties to make socially suboptimal asset allocations, investing in assets which have lower returns but which are easier to protect.[13] Thus, these claims suggest that the stronger private property is, in the sense of private ownership and allowing individuals to capture the returns from their efforts, the greater the efficiency in the exploitation and use of a resource will be.

It is important to note, however, that under certain economic conditions, both open-access systems, where no one is excluded, and communal property arrangements, where non-members are excluded, can be economically efficient arrangements.[14] For example, a system of open access

---

[11] Erik Furubotn and Rudolf Richter, *Institutions and Economic Theory: The Contributions of the New Institutional Economics* (Ann Arbor: University of Michigan Press, 2nd edn, 2005) at 111–16.

[12] See Thràinn Eggertsson, 'Open access versus common property,' in Terry L. Anderson and Fred S. McChesney (eds), *Property Rights: Cooperation, Conflict, and Law* (Princeton, NJ: Princeton University Press, 2003) at 77 ('In effect, the now-or-never motive drives actors to deplete nonrenewable resources without due attention to optimal time preferences and patterns of demand.'). For a formal demonstration of this point, see Louis Hotte, 'Conflicts over property rights and natural-resource exploitation at the frontier' (2001) 66 *Journal of Development Economics* 1, who models resource use in the case of insecure ownership and shows that where landowners believe that they may lose their access to a resource in the near future, they may exploit the resource in a socially wasteful manner.

On a related point, where individuals face tenure insecurity, they may not make socially optimal investments for the long-term protection or sustainability of a particular resource or the environment generally because they are uncertain *ex ante* about their likelihood of appropriating the benefits of such investments. For example, Gebremedhin and Swinton show that the probability of farmers making long-term investments in soil conservation measures in Ethiopia was related to their perceived degree of tenure security in their land: Berhanu Gebremedhin and Scott M. Swinton, 'Investment in soil conservation in Northern Ethiopia: the role of land tenure security and public programs' (2003) 29 *Agricultural Economics* 69.

[13] See Stijn Claessens and Luc Laeven, 'Financial development, property rights and growth' (2003) 58 *J. Fin.* 2401 at 2402 ('[O]ur idea of property rights is the degree of protection of the return on assets against powerful competitors.')

[14] See Dam, *supra* note 1 at 151 ('It would be a mistake, however, to conclude

to land could be a rational response to economic forces if land were not a scarce good, as in such circumstances there is no benefit in creating formal individual property rights, while there would be a cost.[15] Similarly, if land is only somewhat scarce and a community is relatively small, communal property arrangements may combine the benefits of socially efficient alternatives through collective action with lower enforcement and transaction costs than individual property rights.[16]

The second mechanism through which strong property rights promote efficiency is that when the land over which one has strong private property rights is also alienable, the land can be transferred from less efficient users to individuals who will put it to more efficient uses.[17] Because the land is more economically valuable to the more efficient user, mutually beneficial trades should be possible wherein land is transferred from less efficient users to more efficient users (implicating the contract rights pillar of the two pillars discussed in this chapter).

Security of tenure and easy transferability of property increase access to credit The linkage between property and access to credit is another economic aspect of property that has been extensively explored. Indeed, one of de Soto's main arguments in *The Mystery of Capital* is that secure property rights allow individuals to use their possessions as sources of capital.[18] As Feder and Onchan note, creditors will be much more likely to provide credit where that credit can be secured with collateral. Property, however, whether real or personal, can only be effective collateral if creditors believe

---

that all communal ownership is so inefficient that it is an obstacle to economic development.'). See also Robert Ellickson, 'Property in land' (1993) 102 *Yale L.J.* 1315 at 1332 (noting the advantages of communal ownership); see generally Deininger, *supra* note 5 at 29 (discussing generally some of the factors which can lead group rights to be more efficient than individual rights).

[15] See Omotunde E.G. Johnson, 'Economic analysis, the legal framework, and land tenure systems' (1972) 15 *J.L.Econ.* 259 at 259 (arguing that in certain circumstances communal property systems allow for more cost savings than personal property).

[16] See Gerson Feder and David Feeny, 'Land tenure and property rights: theory and implications for development policy' (1991) 5 World Bank Economic Review 135 at 143 (discussing how voluntary collective action in a communal property arrangement enabled an efficient solution to a problem).

[17] See Klaus Deininger and Gershon Feder, 'Land institutions and land markets' (1999) World Bank Policy Research, Working Paper No. 2014, at 1 ('[T]here is some evidence that a higher degree of transfer rights provides additional incentives for investments and for more efficient use . . .').

[18] De Soto, *supra* note 7 at 6 (noting that property rights allow Western nations to 'inject life into assets and make them generate capital').

that they will be able to gain possession of this collateral in the event of the debtor's default.[19] Thus, the debtor must have secure ownership of the property and have the ability to easily transfer it to the creditor.

A lack of access to credit can significantly impair economic development. Without access to credit, the requisite capital may not be available to finance investments. According to de Soto, in the United States 'up to 70 percent of the credit new businesses receive comes from using formal titles as collateral for mortgages'.[20] Even where creditors do not require property as collateral, the interest rate on that credit may be higher, reflecting the higher risk that creditors face when making unsecured loans. Projects which would have been financed at the lower interest rate available for secured loans may become unprofitable or may be deemed too risky at the higher rate for unsecured credit.

It should be noted, however, that while formal title can increase the supply of credit, it may not immediately lead to greater borrowing if demand for credit is limited. Even complete security and alienability of land may not improve access to credit if landholders are risk-averse and perceive a risk of losing their land if it is mortgaged.[21] This problem is especially acute when landowners have no access to insurance or alternative sources of wealth.[22]

Security of tenure increases incentives for investment The increase in investment is perhaps the most discussed beneficial effect of strong

---

19 Gerson Feder and Tongroj Onchan, 'Land ownership security and farm investment in Thailand' (1987) 69 *American Journal of Agricultural Economics* 311; see also Heywood Fleisig, 'Secured transactions: the power of collateral' (1996) 33 *Fin. & Dev.* 44 at 45 (discussing how barriers to the enforceability of security interest, such as those in developing countries, make lenders less likely to extend credit).

20 De Soto, *supra* note 7 at 84.

21 Jean-Philippe Platteau, 'Does Africa need land reform?' in Camilla Toulmin and Julian Quan (eds), *Evolving Land Rights, Policy and Tenure in Africa* (London: DFID/IIED/NRI, 2000) at 51. The ability to use land as collateral may actually be detrimental to smaller farmers. Eric van Tassel's model shows that where farmers have limited income, they may not be willing to risk losing their land in order to acquire loans. Creditors, however, may be unwilling to provide unsecured loans to such farmers, as they may perceive the farmer's preference for an unsecured loan over a secured loan as indicating that the farmer poses a high risk of default: Eric van Tassel, 'Credit access and transferable land rights' (2004) 56 *Oxford Econ. Papers* 151 at 153–5.

22 See Stephen R. Boucher et al., 'The impact of "market-friendly" reforms on credit and land markets in Honduras and Nicaragua' (2004) 33 *World Development* 107 at 111 (indicating that 'land-poor households' may be unwilling to take out loans without insurance because of the risk of collateral loss).

property rights.[23] There are three distinct ways in which stronger property rights can increase investment. First, where tenure is more secure, individuals will be more likely to invest significant resources to improve their property and make it more productive. Second, where property is alienable, individuals have greater incentives to improve property because they will be able to realize a gain from that improvement upon selling it. Finally, where property is secure and alienable, the supply of credit is increased, thereby giving individuals access to the capital necessary to improve their land.[24]

Security of tenure decreases inefficient competition for resources Where property is relatively secure, two types of socially wasteful activity can be eliminated. First, where property rights are insecure, individuals may attempt to invade land or steal assets belonging to other people. Second, and in response to this threat, individuals will have to expend resources to protect their own property from such actions; perhaps the most destructive version of this type of private protection is the property protection provided by organized crime.[25] Even where outright conflict does not occur, insecurity may induce individuals to expend resources on legal action in trying to assert ownership claims to contested property.[26] This reasoning implies that more secure and well-defined property rights may lead individuals to move away from unproductive conflict over property towards productive activities.[27]

---

[23] One of the most often cited papers in the contemporary literature on the theoretical and formal underpinnings of this effect is Besley's work, in which he formally models the relationship between security of tenure and investment: Timothy Besley, 'Property rights and investment incentives: theory and evidence from Ghana' (1995) 103 *Journal of Political Economy* 903.

[24] Platteau, *supra* note 21.

[25] See Curtis Milhaupt and Mark West, 'The dark side of private ordering: an institutional and empirical analysis of organized crime' (2000) 67 *University of Chicago Law Review* 41 at 43 ('Organized crime . . . is the dark side of private ordering – an entrepreneurial response to the inefficiencies in the property rights and enforcement framework supplied by the state.')

[26] See Tim Hanstad, 'Designing land registration systems for developing countries' (1998) 13 *American University International Law Review* 647 at 654–5 (suggesting that uncertainty over land interest, like ill-defined boundaries, often leads to litigation, especially in the absence of effective land registration systems).

[27] See Erica Field, 'Entitled to work: urban property rights and labor supply in Peru' (2007) 122 *Quarterly Journal of Economics* 1561 (suggesting that formal property rights will increase household labour supply since individuals will have to spend less time informally enforcing their property claims); see also de Soto, *supra* note 7; Hernando de Soto, *The Other Path: The Invisible Revolution in the Third*

2. The necessity for a formal property rights regime

Many development scholars and policymakers contend that the benefits of private property described above are best achieved by a formal state-run property system. Indeed, the intellectual tradition of viewing the state as being necessary for the enforcement of claims to private property has a long genesis.[28] Thomas Hobbes viewed the existence of a powerful state as necessary to overcome the anarchy that would prevail in a state of nature.[29] John Locke similarly viewed the primary purpose of the state as being one of protecting individuals' property – that is, their life, liberty and estate.[30] In *The Wealth of Nations*, Adam Smith viewed administering justice as an important role for government, which in part, for Smith, meant the protection of private property rights.[31] Although David Hume viewed property rights as conventions that all would respect for the benefit of society as a whole, he also recognized that the short-sightedness of individuals might inhibit their ability to respect such conventions. He thus argued that the principal purpose of government was to overcome this short-sightedness by enforcing conventions such as property and contract.[32]

A number of modern law and economics scholars have also emphasized the importance of strong property rights in economic development. Richard Posner emphasizes the importance of developing strong property rights regimes for fostering economic growth,[33] and Douglass

---

World (June Abbott, trans., Harper & Row, 1989) [hereinafter 'de Soto, *The Other Path*'] at 160.

28 For a brief intellectual history of property rights and economics, see Edwin West, 'Property rights in the history of economic thought: from John Locke to J.S. Mill', in Terry Anderson and Fred McChesney (eds), *Property Rights: Cooperation, Conflict, and Law* (Princeton, NJ: Princeton University Press, 2003) at 20.

29 See Thomas Hobbes, *Leviathan* (1651) (Richard Tuck (ed.), Penguin Books, 1985) at 189–91 (describing a system of laws necessary to bring man out of a state of nature).

30 See John Locke, *Second Treatise of Government* (1690) (Thomas Peardon (ed.), Bobbs-Merrill Co. 1952) (stating the necessity of the state for protecting private property) at §86–88.

31 See Adam Smith, *The Wealth of Nations* (1776) (Edwin Cannan (ed.), Bantam Dell, 2003) at 901–2 (describing the importance of such government functions as taxing private property).

32 David Hume, 'A treatise of human nature' in Henry Aiken (ed.), *Hume's Moral and Political Philosophy* (Hafner Publishing Co., 1964) at 69–80, 97–101.

33 See Richard Posner, 'Creating a legal framework for economic development' (2003) 13 *World Bank Research Observer* 1 ('A modernizing nation's economic prosperity requires at least a modest legal infrastructure centered on the protection of property and contract rights.').

North suggests that strong property rights are one of the most important institutions for growth.[34] Similarly, Knack and Keefer claim that '[f]ew would dispute that the security of property and contractual rights and the efficiency with which governments manage the provision of public goods and the creation of government policies are significant determinants of the speed with which countries grow'.[35] McCloskey, in discussing England's economic development, states: 'If the word "precondition" as it is used in the literature of economic growth includes anything it must include the formation of the legal institutions of private property.'[36]

Perhaps the best-known contemporary advocate of strong formal property rights in spurring development has been de Soto.[37] Speaking of titling, he says that '[i]t is the unavailability of these essential representations that explains why people who have adapted every other Western invention, from the paper clip to the nuclear reactor, have not been able to produce sufficient capital to make their domestic capitalism work'.[38] Similarly, he writes that '[t]he formal property system is capital's hydroelectric plant'.[39]

Although these views reflect the prevalence of the belief that formal property rights are necessary for economic development, it is important to specify why formal property rights, rather than more informal property arrangements (as discussed at 3. below), are viewed as a *sine qua non* of development. Formal property regimes are considered by these authors to be essential to economic growth because, when fully functional and accessible, they provide clearer and more secure allocations of property rights than could any informal measures to protect private property.[40] Where there is a credible third party enforcer of property rights – in particular, the state – 'uncertainty is reduced or completely eliminated'.[41] Indeed, it seems intuitive that a state-backed title registry would have the capacity to provide the most secure property rights, given the extensive adjudicative and coercive capacities that one associates with a fully functioning state. Moreover, a formal property system can also reduce transaction costs in

---

[34] North, *supra* note 10.

[35] Stephen Knack and Philip Keefer, 'Institutions and economic performance: cross-country tests using alternative institutional measures' (1995) 7 *Econ. & Pol.* 207.

[36] Donald McCloskey, 'The enclosure of open fields: preface to a study of its impact on the efficiency of English agriculture in the eighteenth century' (1972) 32 *J. Econ. Hist.* 15 at 16.

[37] De Soto, *supra* note 7.

[38] Ibid., at 7.

[39] Ibid., at 47.

[40] Johnson, *supra* note 15; Dam, *supra* note 1.

[41] North, *supra* note 10 at 36.

market interactions by providing increased information to third parties about the rights that an individual has over land. Thus, many scholars contend that a formal property regime is necessary to provide the benefits of private property.

3. Informal mechanisms for securing the benefits of private property

However, a formal property rights regime may not be the only method of securing the benefits discussed above. Indeed, informal mechanisms may provide many of the same benefits as a private property rights regime. Within the literature examining informal mechanisms as a substitute for formal mechanisms, there are two strands that explore how this can occur. Although they are in many ways linked, they differ in some respects.[42] First, the *game theoretic literature* explores how cooperation can emerge as a result of repeated interactions among individuals. Second, the *law and social norms literature* examines the development of informal norms as a mechanism of social order and control. Both of these perspectives have strong implications for the possibility of efficient, informal property regimes, as they suggest that either spontaneous cooperation or informal norms can often substitute for a formal property regime maintained by the state.

Game theoretic analysis One theoretical perspective which examines the conditions under which cooperation will occur is the game theoretic perspective. The prisoner's dilemma is a quintessential model of a situation in which parties must choose whether to cooperate or not cooperate with each other based on the anticipated outcomes of each decision. While standard game theoretic models suggest that cooperative outcomes will not be achieved in a one-off prisoner's dilemma, Axelrod shows that mutually beneficial cooperative outcomes can arise in a repeated prisoner's dilemma.[43] The general requirement for cooperation is that such games

---

[42] One important difference between the game theoretic analysis of cooperation and the law and social norms literature is that while the former supposes no order and shows how people might rationally cooperate, the law and social norms literature examines some of the negative (e.g., gossip, violence) and positive (e.g., rewards) sanctions that groups may use to enforce compliance with a norm or convention. For a survey of this point as well as a substantial list of articles which examine a variety of negative sanctions, see Richard H. McAdams and Eric B. Rasmusen, 'Norms in law and economics' (7 July 2004) (unpublished manuscript).

[43] Robert Axelrod, *The Evolution of Cooperation* (Basic Books, 1984); see also Robert Axelrod, 'The emergence of cooperation among egoists' (1981) 75 *Am. Pol. Sci. Rev*. 306 at 307 (showing that '[w]ith an indefinite number of interactions, cooperation can emerge').

continue infinitely; however, David Kreps et al. show how informational asymmetries (for example, believing for some reason that the other players have a particularly cooperative disposition) can also generate cooperation in a finitely repeated prisoner's dilemma.[44] Moreover, while the models above have assumed repeated interactions between the same players, Glenn Ellison shows how even this assumption can be relaxed, as cooperation can also emerge among a small group whose members are anonymously matched in each round of the game.[45] Thus, various conditions under which cooperation have emerged are in many ways relatively robust. Experimental evidence has confirmed many of these results, showing, for example, that cooperation can occur even in a finitely repeated prisoner's dilemma as individuals try to build a reputation for themselves.[46]

These principles are readily applicable to a regime of respect for property. The issue of respecting land tenure can be thought of as a prisoner's dilemma: all parties gain when tenure is respected (because of the lower costs associated with defending one's land, and so on), but each party has an incentive not to respect other parties' tenure. The exploitation of communal resources has also been viewed in this way.[47] While the pessimistic predictions of the prisoner's dilemma have been used in the past to argue for a strong state to enforce order (dating back to Hobbes' *Leviathan*), if cooperation can emerge as discussed above, this problem can be overcome without the state's intervention.[48] Rational self-interest rather than the

---

[44] David M. Kreps, Paul Milgrom, John Roberts and Robert Wilson, 'Rational cooperation in the finitely repeated prisoners' dilemma,' (1982) 27 *Journal of Economic Theory* 245 at 245, available at http://www.edegan.com/pdfs/Kreps%20Milgrom%20Roberts%20Wilson%20(1982)%20-%20Rational%20Cooperation%20in%20the%20Finitely%20Repeated%20Prisoners%20Dilemma.pdf. While the repeated prisoner's dilemma has largely been viewed as involving a number (potentially infinite) of discrete stages, some modelling has shown cooperative results to be even more robust when the model is made continuous – something which is much closer to the reality of tenure questions addressed below. See also David M. Kreps and Robert Wilson, 'Reputation and imperfect information' (1982) 27 *Journal of Economic Theory* 253 at 275 (arguing that uncertainty about the motivations of one or more of the players in a finite game can affect cooperation).

[45] Glenn Ellison, 'Cooperation in the prisoner's dilemma with anonymous random matching' (1994) 61 *Review of Economic Studies* 567 at 568.

[46] James Andreoni and John Miller, 'Rational cooperation in the finitely repeated prisoner's dilemma: experimental evidence' (1993) 103 *Economic Journal* 570 at 571.

[47] Ellickson, *supra* note 14; Hardin, *supra* note 10.

[48] See Elinor Ostrom, *Governing the Commons: The Evolution of Institutions for Collective Action* (Cambridge, UK: Cambridge University Press, 1990).

coercive power of the state may lead parties to respect socially efficient property arrangements.

The evolutionary game theory approach also has implications for property rights considerations. Axelrod uses this approach and shows that a strategy of 'tit-for-tat' (cooperation in the first round followed by playing whatever strategy the other player played in the previous round) is a collectively stable strategy.[49] Axelrod also shows how a relatively small cluster of individuals playing 'tit-for-tat' can invade a population that is primarily comprised of defectors. In the context of property rights, this suggests a plausible mechanism for how cooperation and mutual respect can emerge and how it might be collectively stable. Cooperative play (that is, respect for land tenure) might emerge, since even small groups that decide to respect land tenure might be more successful than those groups that do not respect tenure, and thereby come to dominate larger populations.

The law and social norms literature In addition to the game theoretic framework discussed above, the law and social norms literature provides an alternative explanation of how efficient property arrangements could emerge outside of a formal, legal framework. An important perspective in this line of literature is Ellickson's examination of how various informal rules can emerge which, in certain circumstances, make the formal legal system irrelevant.[50] Ellickson predicts that when social relations are close-knit, informal norms will encourage people in non-zero-sum situations to make choices that will conjoin to produce the maximum aggregate objective pay-off to the group by minimizing deadweight losses and transaction costs.[51] This has led Ellickson to suggest that lawmakers should defer to these informal norms, as the norms are more likely to be welfare maximizing than centrally crafted rules.[52] Epstein reaches a similar conclusion, noting that 'custom should be followed in those cases in which there are repeat and reciprocal interactions between the same parties, for then their

---

[49] For a discussion of evolutionary stability in the biological context, see John Maynard Smith, 'The theory of games and the evolution of animal conflicts' (1974) 47 *Journal of Theoretical Biology* 209.

[50] Robert C. Ellickson, *Order Without Law: How Neighbors Settle Disputes* (Cambridge, MA: Harvard University Press, 1991).

[51] Ibid., at Chapter 10. See also Robert C. Ellickson, 'A hypothesis of wealth-maximizing norms: evidence from the whaling industry' (1989) 5 *J. L. Econ. & Org.* 83 at 84 (arguing that 'when people are situated in a close-knit group, they will tend to develop for the ordinary run of problems norms that are wealth maximizing').

[52] Ellickson, *supra* note 50 at Chapter 10.

incentives to reach the correct rule are exceedingly powerful'.[53] These arguments imply that customary arrangements can be sufficient to generate order between parties.

Although Ellickson's theory rather optimistically predicts that such norms will emerge, it does not provide a strong explanation of the processes that determine when and why these norms emerge and why individuals adhere to them. McAdams suggests an esteem-based theory of norms, whereby a norm arises if

> (1) there is a consensus about the positive or negative esteem worthiness of engaging in [an action], (2) there is some risk that others will detect whether one engages in [that action], and (3) the existence of this consensus and risk of detection is well-known within the population.[54]

These conditions change the costs and benefits of engaging or not engaging in an activity, and a norm will arise if the esteem benefit is greater than the cost of (not) engaging in the activity. Eric Posner presents an alternative signalling-based model of norms, whereby social norms arise from the actions of individuals who are trying to signal to others that they are a cooperative type in order to gain benefits from interactions with those individuals.[55] Although the two theories have differences, they both highlight that a cooperative and welfare enhancing norm can arise through the rational actions of a large number of individuals. Furthermore, over time these norms may become internalized such that individuals might adhere to a norm even in situations where doing so might not be economically or strategically rational.[56]

In the context of property, this would suggest that cooperation might be possible, which would lead to the emergence of norms that yield many of the benefits that are claimed to flow from formal property rights. This reasoning suggests that tenure security, for example, might arise among a close-knit group if this were a welfare maximizing rule. This type of reasoning is consistent with the literature that stresses that tenure security can increase in response to increasing relative scarcity of land,

---

[53] Richard Epstein, 'International News Service v. Associated Press: custom and law as sources of property rights in news' (1992) 78 *Virginia Law Review* 85 at 126.

[54] Richard H. McAdams, 'The origin, development, and regulation of norms' (1997) 96 *Michigan Law Review* 338 at 358.

[55] Eric Posner, 'Symbols, signals, and social norms in politics and the law' (1998) 27 *Journal of Legal Studies* 765; Eric Posner, *Law and Social Norms* (Cambridge, MA: Harvard University Press, 2000) at 18– 27.

[56] Posner, *Law and Social Norms*, ibid., at 43–4.

since the welfare gains from secure tenure increase as the scarcity of land increases.[57] Similarly, Sjaastad and Bromley have noted the presence in many African societies of a norm that dictates that when an individual loses ownership of a piece of land, the individual taking ownership must compensate the individual losing ownership for the value of improvements made to the land.[58] This norm may provide the necessary incentives to make improvements to land without some of the costs associated with greater tenure security.

It is important to note that all of the informalist theories presented above relate to property relations among individuals; none of them relate specifically to tenure security in the sense of freedom from a reasonable apprehension of expropriation of land by the state. In terms of this aspect of property ownership, it seems unlikely that an informalist would contest the fact that tenure security vis-à-vis the state is important, but the perception of tenure security against the state might be accomplished in a variety of ways. All that is required for this type of tenure security is that the individual should not fear expropriation without compensation. To this end, predictability may be more important than formal rights.

4. The empirical evidence

In an extensive recent review of the empirical evidence relating to the case for formalization of private property rights, Michael Trebilcock and Paul-Erik Veel[59] find that the evidence tends to suggest that formal regimes may lead to more efficient use of property, but that in many contexts informal regimes are often a reasonably close substitute and that mechanisms for at least limited forms of alienability often evolve without formal property rights. As to whether formalization of property rights increases access to credit, the evidence is mixed. Where informal credit markets are strong, there appears to be little benefit from formalization in many contexts. Similarly, where credit markets are weak for other reasons, formalization is likely to have limited impact on access to credit. While formal property rights seem to lead to increased investment in productive asset enhancement, this depends to an important extent on the security afforded by

---

[57] Gershon Feder and Raymond Noronha, 'Land rights systems and agricultural developments in sub-Saharan Africa' (1987) 2 *World Bank Research Observer* 143 at 143–4 (arguing that scarcity of land encourages the development of mechanisms to secure such land); see also Demsetz, *supra* note 10.

[58] Espen Sjaastad and Daniel Bromley, 'Indigenous land rights in sub-Saharan Africa: appropriation, security and investment demand' (1997) 25 *World Development* 549 at 553.

[59] Trebilcock and Veel, *supra* note 2.

informal norms.[60] Similarly, formal property rights seem to reduce inefficient forms of resource competition, but here the evidence is relatively fragmentary.

While there may be some benefits in the formalizing of property rights regimes, such regimes also entail various costs:

1. The costs are significant in setting up a land registration or recordation system, including initial surveys and the cost of updating the registry or recordation system through time to reflect changes in the composition of land-owning groups or intervening transactions.
2. Formalization and individualization of land tenure may seriously undermine the possibility of communal tenure providing an insurance role for members of the land-owning group, and through time may result in the emergence of a landless class with few, if any, other economic opportunities, sources of insurance or social safety nets.
3. Formal rules may undermine effective informal institutions by creating dysfunctional conflicts between the two classes of regime in ignoring the significance of cultural switching costs.[61] This problem is likely to be particularly acute if formal mechanisms are predicated on spatial notions of ownership, while informal regimes recognize a much more functional conception of property rights, including a wide variety of usufructuary rights, such as the right to gather firewood, collect water, gather fruit, or hunt, fish or traverse land owned by other groups or individuals.
4. Formalization programs, depending on how they are designed and

[60] For a recent review, see James Fenske, 'Land tenure and investment incentives: evidence from West Africa', Department of Economics, Yale University, Working Paper, 2009.

[61] See Daniel Fitzpatrick, 'Evolution and chaos in property rights systems: the Third World tragedy of contested access' (2006) 15 *Yale Law Journal* 996, who argues that the greater the divergence between state law and local norms, the more likely it is that attempts to enforce exclusionary claims will lead to open access rather than an authoritative property rights regime. He argues that legal and normative pluralism is a particularly common phenomenon in the Third World and is often accompanied by institutional pluralism – a fragmentation of the state into competing agencies and levels of government, and that in circumstances of legal, normative and institutional pluralism efficient property rights regimes will not necessarily emerge. He argues that the problem of establishing and enforcing property rights is closely connected to the problem of social order. Unless social order is established, most commonly through legitimate and capable government, the process of allocating and enforcing property rights will tend to cause conflict because claimants will resort to competing legal, normative and coalitional enforcement mechanisms.

implemented, can expose latent divisions between or among claimant groups that had previously lain dormant, but are likely to be provoked or exacerbated by the relative finality of formalizing property rights, and hence lead to increased social conflict.

5. Flaws in the titling process are likely to be exploited by politically or economically powerful groups at the expense of women and other marginalized groups who face various barriers to accessing a formal property rights system.
6. Even assuming that a formal property rights system is well designed, deeply entrenched informal norms may impede the successful implementation of a formal property rights regime where they are sharply antithetical to the latter and may result in the latter being largely ignored or becoming quickly outdated.
7. As in the case of rule of law reforms, there are important institutional interconnections: a land titling system is predicated on effective complementary institutions, including the judiciary, the legal profession and the police. Formalizing property rights without complementary reforms to these other institutions may therefore achieve very little.

This is not to say that informal regimes are always efficient. For example, they may only be efficient for members of close-knit groups and may entail negative externalities for non-members. Informal regimes themselves may also reflect path dependence and time lags in responding to changes in the economic or technological environment, so that there may well be efficiency gains to be realized, at least potentially, from a more formal property rights regime.

This discussion of the costs and benefits of a formal property rights regime suggests that the picture is much more complex than many commentators and policymakers have assumed. The creation of a formal property rights regime is not without cost, and it will not necessarily be the case that the benefits of such a regime will clearly outweigh the costs. Given, however, that formal property regimes are ubiquitous in the developed world, there are reasons to believe that, at a certain stage in a country's economic development, a formal property rights regime is necessary to secure further economic development. China has experienced rapid, market-driven economic growth over the past three decades without a well-defined or enforced formal property regime,[62] but

[62] See Frank Upham, 'From Demsetz to Deng: speculations on the implications of Chinese growth for law and development theory', *NYU Journal of International Law and Politics* (forthcoming).

has recently been devoting increasing attention to formalizing property rights.[63]

At relatively low levels of development, an informal regime may be adequate to realize many of the benefits of private property. Where economic life is largely organized around small units such as the village, the mobility of the population is low and resources such as land are not overly scarce, informal mechanisms are likely to be sufficient to provide the benefits of private property. Put differently, if individuals expect to be living in the same location, the expectation of repeated interactions will create the conditions necessary for cooperation. At this point, informal mechanisms are likely to suffice to bring the benefits of private property, so a formal property regime would entail significant social and economic costs without significant benefits.

As countries undergo economic changes, however, the relative benefits of a formal private property regime are likely to increase. There are three broad reasons for this consequence. First, as development increases, communities are likely to become less close-knit, leading informal norms to be less effective in maintaining order. As Feder and Feeny note, '[w]ith more advanced stages of development and increased mobility of individuals and entrepreneurs, transactions among individuals who are not members of the same community are more frequent'.[64] Where the proportion of one-off encounters increases relative to continuing encounters, traditional methods of social cohesion are likely to be strained. Moreover, as Eric Posner notes, while informal norms can often result in a strong degree of security for items which can be easily possessed, such norms will be inadequate to protect goods which individuals cannot directly possess, such as land or capital dispersed throughout a number of locations.[65]

Second, at higher levels of economic development, the value of land, goods, and investments may increase substantially, leading to more substantial benefits from more secure property rights. While informal mechanisms may be sufficient to provide an individual with the incentives to make minor investments, more capital-intensive, asset-specific investments are likely to require greater certainty and security. Moreover, as the capital-intensiveness of activities increases, formal credit is likely to play a greater role in economic development, thereby increasing the benefits of clear and secure title.

---

[63] Trebilcock and Veel, *supra* note 2 at 397; Klaus Deininger and Songqing Jin, 'Securing property rights in transition: lessons from implementation of China's rural land contracting law' (2009) 70 *Journal of Economic Behavior & Organization* at 22–38.

[64] Feder and Feeny, *supra* note 16 at 140.

[65] Posner, *Law and Social Norms*, *supra* note 55 at 179.

Third, at higher levels of economic development, the relative costs of creating a formal property regime may be lower. As a country's tax base increases, it will be relatively easier for the state to make the expenditures required for creating a formal property regime. Where insurance markets are likely to be more developed, the loss of the insurance function of customary land tenure is likely to be less severe. Similarly, where the state takes an increasingly large role in providing social benefits to its population, the equity concerns of potential landlessness are likely to be mitigated. Finally, the very forces that undermine informal tenure can also mitigate the effects of increased landlessness and social unrest. As mobility and migration opportunities increase, individuals will be more able to seek alternative economic opportunities elsewhere, thus lowering the cost to individuals of changes to property arrangements.

The above considerations suggest that the focus of certain previous titling programs may have been misguided both in terms of the targets of these titling programs as well as in the content of the formalization program. First, while many titling programs have focused on providing formal title to agricultural landowners, the above discussion suggests that, with the exception of newly settled frontier land, established social norms in rural areas may be sufficient to provide an adequate degree of informal property rights protection. Urban titling programs, especially those aimed at newly developing squatter settlements, may yield a greater social return. The greatest return from titling programs may come, however, from providing formal ownership to firms' land and assets, as informal norms may be lacking in such circumstances or inadequate to provide the certainty required for large investments or transactions entailing significant sunk costs and long pay-off periods.

Second, to the extent that there are substantial benefits to providing stronger land rights to agricultural landowners in a given case, those benefits may be largely realized through the recognition and formalization of customary land tenure.[66] This model of formalization in the agricultural sector may bring about the benefits of security of tenure at a lower social cost than would the *de novo* creation of an individual-centred system of land rights. Both of these conclusions, however, should be taken only as general propositions, as the above discussion highlights the extent to

---

[66] For an insightful exploration of many of these issues of institutional design, see Daniel Fitzpatrick, 'Best practice options for the legal recognition of customary tenure' (2005) 36 *Development and Change* 449; see generally, Deininger, *supra* note 5 at 62–5. For proposals along these lines, see UNDP, *Making the Law Work for Everyone: Report of the Commission on Legal Empowerment of the Poor,* vol. 1 (New York: United Nations, 2008) at 65.

which the analysis of the relative costs and benefits of formalization is a highly context-dependent exercise.

Finally, it should be noted that, while the above discussion has largely focused on titling, in some cases the primary source of insecure property rights is not the threat of expropriation by other households or landowners, but rather expropriation by the state.[67] Where this is the main source of insecurity, formal title per se may not be necessary to increase individuals' perceptions of tenure security. Moreover, under such circumstances, formal title may not actually improve perceptions of tenure security if individuals believe that they will not be able to enforce their property rights against a predatory state.[68] Rather, what is required in such cases to create the perception of strong property rights is a credible commitment by the state not to expropriate land or other assets.[69] This can be a significantly less costly and more effective mechanism for gaining the benefits of private property rights than formal titling programmes.

5. Gender and property rights

Giving women access to property and guaranteeing their property rights is regarded as a strategy to increase efficiency, improve the well-being of women and other family members, promote gender equality and empower women.[70] While some of these objectives favour society as a whole (efficiency and well-being), others (equality and empowerment) are specifically targeted at women, who represent the largest percentage of the world's poor. This concern with gender equality and women's empowerment was officially included in the development agenda reflected in the Millennium Development Goals. Access to land plays an important role in promoting these goals because it can provide women with income and a source of subsistence if they are able to commercialize their produce. In this context, women could potentially benefit from private property and secure title in

---

[67] See Timothy Frye, 'Credible commitment and property rights: evidence from Russia' (2004) 98 *Am. Pol. Sci. Rev.* 453 at 456 (noting that one of the largest threats to property rights in Russia was a fear that the state would expropriate private property); see also Omar M. Razzaz, 'Property rights and investment in informal settlements: the case of Jordan' (1993) 69 *Land Econ.* 341 at 352.

[68] Frye, ibid., at 457–8 (explaining a survey of Russian businessmen finding that many believe that they will not be able to enforce their property rights against the state).

[69] Furubotn and Richter, *supra* note 11 at 97–100 (discussing the implications of state ownership of land and incentives for farmers to work).

[70] Carmen Diana Deere and Magdalena León, *Empowering Women: Land and Property Rights in Latin America* (Pittsburgh: University of Pittsburgh Press, 2001), Chapter 4.

the same way as men, for the reasons set out in the previous sections of this chapter – namely, more efficient use of land, increased access to credit, incentives for investment and decreased incentives for inefficient competition over scarce resources. Thus, some of the reforms discussed earlier have the potential to help women more specifically, and to benefit society as a whole by benefiting women.

However, the proposed reforms that guarantee the benefits of private property still generate tensions and ambiguities from a gender perspective. Shahra Razavi provides a map of these tensions and ambiguities, highlighting three main areas of concern:

1. Formalization of title and liberalization policies do not consider the difficulty faced by women in accessing land through markets.
2. Context-specific reforms can be troublesome if they endorse customary systems and land management structures that are not compatible with, or conducive to, gender equality.
3. Once granted access to land, women still need equal access to non-land resources (such as credit) to benefit equally from land tenure.[71]

We discuss each of these in turn.

Formalization of title to secure land tenure is normally promoted through ostensibly gender neutral reforms. Although formalization does have the potential to increase the economic security of women by contributing to wealth creation and accumulation, such reforms alone, however, may not be conducive to increased living standards of women in developing countries. This is because inheritance, not markets, is the predominant method by which women acquire property, and markets also embody gender structures and hierarchies that are found in society.[72] As Razavi puts it, 'although the empirical base is far from comprehensive, judicious reading of the existing evidence points to the severe limitations of land markets as a channel for women's inclusion'.[73] In some cases, formalization reforms are coupled with broader legal changes. In Latin America, for instance, one of the main achievements of the women's rights movement has been the elimination of civil code provisions designating the husband as legal head of the household.[74] However, these broader reforms do not

---

[71] Shahra Razavi, 'Liberalization and the debates on women's access to land' (2007) 28 *Third World Quarterly* at 1479–500; see also World Development Report 2012, Gender Equality and Development, Chapter 5 (World Bank: 2012).

[72] Ibid., at 1487.

[73] Ibid., at 1486.

[74] Ibid., at 1481.

overcome the fact that opportunities for women to acquire land through markets are far more limited than they are for men. 'The fact that women enter the market system with no property, little cash income, minimal political power, and a family to maintain, works to their disadvantage.'[75] This suggests that gender neutral reforms based on markets might not be sufficient to promote inclusion and improve the condition of women.

In addition to limited access to the market, legal reforms to promote gender equality might not be effective for other reasons. For instance, reforms promoted in Latin America have established co-ownership of land for men and women. This provides a guarantee for women that they will also have the title to the land if they become divorced or widowed. Women's movements have pressed for the adoption of such provisions in Africa, mostly to no avail.[76] In contrast, Brazil and Colombia were pioneers in implementing co-ownership provisions for land reform titling in 1988. These countries have implemented largely successful land reforms because they relied on innovative, community-driven approaches in which communities are given grants and access to credit and 'the beneficiaries identify the land, negotiate the price, and purchase it, rather than relying on the government to hand them land acquired through expropriation'.[77] However, by the mid-1990s there was a significant discrepancy between these two countries: while in Colombia 45 per cent of the beneficiaries of land reform were women, in Brazil they were only 12.6 per cent.[78] According to Carmen Diana Deere, this discrepancy was caused by three factors: (i) co-ownership was mandatory in Colombia and optional in Brazil; (ii) the bureaucracy in charge of implementing land reform in Brazil adopted very discriminatory practices against women; (iii) it was not until recently that the land reform movements started to promote an agenda to foster gender equality.[79]

As a result of popular pressure from social movements, in 2001 the Brazilian government adopted a series of regulations aimed at promoting the inclusion of women in the land reform, but while these changes make co-ownership clauses more effective in protecting married women,

---

[75] Ibid., at 1486.

[76] Ambraeja Manji, *The Politics of Land Reform in Africa* (London: Zed Books, 2006) at 105–9 (analysing the case of Uganda).

[77] Nancy Birdsall and Augusto de la Torre, *Washington Contentious: Economic Policies for Social Equality in Latin America,* Commission on Economic Reform in Unequal Latin American Societies (2001) at 57.

[78] Carmen Diana Deere, 'Women's land rights and rural movements in the Brazilian agrarian reform' (2003) 3:1&2 *Journal of Agrarian Change* at 257–88.

[79] Ibid.

there is still a lack of efforts to promote inclusion of female-headed households.[80] Other Latin American countries have promoted affirmative action in this context to overcome the barriers imposed by past discrimination.[81] In sum, the details of institutional design matter because they will affect the incentives created by the formal law (a mandatory or optional provision can make a significant difference).[82] Moreover, governmental authorities might adopt discriminatory practices in implementing or enforcing laws[83] and unless there are institutional guarantees of public participation in the reform process and its implementation phase, there might not be effective pressure from non-governmental groups for legal changes that better reflect social values.[84]

These obstacles show that policies to promote gender equality in access to land cannot be considered isolated projects. As in the case of formalization projects and institutional reforms, policies to promote gender equality need to be part of a general framework to promote gender equality in society. In the case of formalization, we suggested above that a general framework for formalization should include a set of reforms aimed at the promotion of the rule of law. In contrast, in the context of gender equality, recent research casts doubt on the effectiveness of such reforms. Katharina Pistor, Antara Haldar and Amrit Amirapu[85] show that positive rule of law indices do not correlate with the status of women in society. The correlation *does* exist in high-income countries, but disappears in poor countries. The explanation offered by these three authors is that the status of women in society is determined primarily by social norms, which are only weakly affected by legal institutions. This resonates with many of the gender-related concerns in the context of land reforms.

The second issue raised by Razavi is the extent to which women can fully benefit from context-specific reforms that endorse customary rights and

---

80 Ibid.

81 Deere and León, *supra* note 70 at Chapter 6.

82 *Ibid.*

83 Razavi, *supra* note 71 at 1486.

84 Curtis J. Milhaupt and Katharina Pistor, *Law and Capitalism: What Corporate Crises Reveal About Legal Systems and Economic Development Around the World* (Chicago: University of Chicago Press, 2008).

85 Katharina Pistor, Antara Haldar and Amrit Amirapu, 'Social norms, rule of law, and gender reality: an essay on the limits of the dominant rule of law paradigm', in James J. Heckmann, Robert L. Nelson and Lee Cabatingan (eds), *Global Perspectives on the Rule of Law* (New York and London: Routledge, 2009). For a more optimistic view of the virtues of constitutionalizing fundamental universal rights (capabilities) of women, see Martha Nussbaum, *Women and Human Development: The Capabilities Approach* (Cambridge University Press, 2000).

local land management systems. From a gender perspective, these rights and local systems can be 'too closely intertwined with social institutions and existing power structures'. Customary law and social practices often are not gender neutral, and patriarchal tendencies can be exacerbated when formalization of title and privatization of communal land increase competition for scarce resources. Evidence from Uganda, Tanzania and South Africa illustrate the difficulties faced by women in dealing with local authorities and overcoming inequitable social practices. In this context, formalization of property and land markets can sometimes be positive, as they provide a way for women to circumvent traditional authorities.[86] Similarly, dispute resolution systems outside customary practices may also provide a beneficial option for these women. In such circumstances, a combination of formal systems and customary practices allow women to 'forum shop', combining different claims and using dispute mechanisms that will be most favourable to them on a case-by-case basis. Obstacles to the effective use of these options, however, are lack of information and low levels of education. In this regard, again, gender equality reforms need to be combined with initiatives that are conducive to granting women equal access to other resources beyond land.

The previous two concerns cast doubts on the potential for land markets, both formal and informal, to serve as effective mechanisms for the inclusion of women. Once access to land is guaranteed, yet another concern is identified by Razavi: the ability of women to create and accumulate wealth through land depends on their access to a series of non-land resources. If women hold title individually, one important obstacle for them to benefit from private property comes from the fact that women might not have equal access to fertilizers, equipment and labour. This is often connected to lack of access to credit, which is reflective of greater social practices of discrimination against women. Microcredit initiatives in Bangladesh (and other countries), such as the Grameen Bank, were created to overcome this obstacle, but this option is not available in all countries.[87] In 2001, the Brazilian land reform program established an affirmative action program in which 30 per cent of all governmental credit given to land reform beneficiaries would go to women and 30 per cent

---

86 Razavi, *supra* note 71 at 1489.

87 The World Bank, 'Using microcredit to advance women' (1998) *PREMnotes* 8; Norman MacIsaac, 'The role of microcredit in poverty reduction and promoting gender equity' (June 1997) South Asia Partnership Canada, Strategic Policy and Planning Division, Asia Branch Canada International Development Agency, available at http://www.microfinancegateway.org/gm/document-1.9.28404/3247_3247.pdf

of the positions in training programs for land reform beneficiaries are reserved for women.[88] A further related problem is that in many countries land is a complementary source of income, being combined with employment outside the household. In these cases, barriers for women to obtain jobs can hinder their ability to benefit from land tenure. This can be overcome with anti-discrimination laws in other sectors of the economy.

C. Conclusion

Because of the complex interactions between a property rights regime and the social, economic, political and legal framework within which such a regime operates, it is not fruitful simply to argue for or against the formalization of a property rights regime or for 'strong and clear' property rights. Rather, the relationship between property rights and development is much more complex, and a more nuanced approach to these issues is required. As David Kennedy writes,

> 'clear and strong' property rights is a misleading recipe. Property rights have no ideal form which will be rendered clear and strong. Their allocation everywhere is a matter of economic, social and political choice for which no formula can substitute.[89]

The context dependence of successful property regimes leads to three important considerations. First, property formalization programs cannot be considered as isolated economic development projects as one might consider certain physical infrastructure projects. Rather, such programs must be considered as part of a general framework for economic development, typically including a wider set of reforms aimed at the promotion of the rule of law.[90] Contrary to the optimistic rhetoric of de Soto's work, property formalization programs are not, standing alone, the key to unlocking the potential of the developing world.[91]

Second, in determining what role outsiders can play in helping to promote a state's formal property regime, it is essential to ask a broader question about the similarities among optimal property regimes. If the optimality of a property rights regime is context-independent, then a titling program developed by theorists in Washington or from elsewhere in the developed world may indeed be applicable and beneficial to extremely

---

88 Deere, *supra* note 78 at 257–88.
89 Kennedy, *supra* note 9 at 53, 54.
90 Dam, *supra* note 1.
91 De Soto, *supra* note 7.

diverse countries. However, while the functions performed by property rights may be similar in many countries, the characteristics of a property regime are in fact highly dependent on local context and thus it is unrealistic to expect that one model of a successful regime would be applicable across various states. In fact, one would expect that the characteristics of such regimes, as well as strategies for their implementation, will differ substantially across states. This suggests that, in practice, local or regional models of property regimes may be more successful than Western models.[92]

Finally, significant changes to property regimes should be approached with caution and drastic, uniform top-down property changes should be avoided.[93] Contrary to conventional economic thinking, the formalization of property rights is not necessarily desirable at all stages of development or for all property owners. Formalization programs can have far-reaching social and economic consequences and, under certain conditions, formalization programs can have negligible or deleterious impacts. The context specificity of property rights regimes is not, however, a reason for inaction or a reason to counsel against the formalization of property rights in all cases. As noted above, under some circumstances, formal property rights have increased efficiency and led to economic growth, and it would thus be poor policy never to support the formalization of property rights.

Because of these considerations, unless there is clear and compelling evidence pointing to the need for a systematic state-led formalization program, the optimal response may be a voluntary and sporadic system of title registration. Although a sporadic program of title registration is not without its own costs,[94] such a program brings substantial benefits relative to a systematic formalization program. As Michael Trebilcock has argued elsewhere, in the face of limited resources and state capacity, a sporadic system of land registration has the benefit of providing the additional security and clarity of formal property rights to those desiring it most.[95] By simply providing an additional vehicle for owning property, a sporadic

---

92 See Sharun Mukand and Dani Rodrik, 'In search of the Holy Grail: policy convergence, experimentation, and economic performance' (2005) 95 *Am. Econ. Rev.* 374 (which argues for implementation of appropriate policies and institutional arrangements at the local level).

93 For a classic paper exploring the importance of avoiding drastic imposed changes see Charles Lindblom, 'The science of "Muddling Through" (1959) 19 *Pub. Admin. Rev.* 79. See also James C. Scott, *Seeing Like a State: How Certain Schemes to Improve the Human Condition Have Failed* (New Haven: Yale University Press, 1998).

94 See Michael Trebilcock, 'Communal property rights: the Papua New Guinea experience' (1984) 34 *University of Toronto Law Journal* 377.

95 Ibid., at 412–13.

registration programme does not require disturbing the arrangements of those groups that are content with the status quo. Where customary arrangements limit individuals' economic opportunities, the option of formalization is present. Moreover, a voluntary system overcomes the collective action problem of providing the machinery for the enforcement of property rights by having the state provide it and allowing people to opt into it.

Perhaps the strongest benefit, however, of a sporadic and voluntary formalization system is that it avoids the myriad unforeseeable and potentially negative consequences that can result from the top-down imposition of a uniform system of property arrangements. As we have stressed, a property rights regime is not an isolated institution, but rather an institution which has strong interrelationships within a variety of other institutions. In such circumstances, and where policymakers have imperfect or limited information, it may be impossible to predict all the potential consequences flowing from drastic institutional changes, and unpredictable negative consequences may emerge from imposed changes.[96] A gradual and reversible process of voluntary change at the individual level can mitigate such potentially harmful consequences.

Even in situations where a systematic program is clearly superior to a voluntary program, drastic and irreversible changes should be avoided. Rather, changes should be incremental in nature. For example, where communal property is prevalent, rather than registering individual titles to specified plots of land to the exclusion of all others, a rudimentary titling program could be undertaken utilizing simple compass and chain surveys rather than full-scale cadastral surveys where only the base group title would be registered without prejudice to the various functional or usufructuary rights that others might possess under customary law. Land-owning groups might also be given a more formal legal structure and clearer decision or governance rules (akin to private corporations with restrictions on share transferability), while maintaining some limits on outright alienability of group land.[97] Such programs lessen the potential for serious social conflict or disruption from abrupt legal change and

---

[96] For interesting examples relating to this point, see Scott, *supra* note 93. See also Rachel Kranton and Anand Swamy, 'The hazards of piecemeal reform: British civil courts and the credit market in colonial India' (1999) 58 *J. Dev. Econ.* 1 (discussing how reform led to increased competition among lenders, and the resulting effects on the farmers of India).

[97] See generally Fitzpatrick, *supra* note 66; Trebilcock, *supra* note 94; Kathrine Dixon, 'Property: mobilizing land in Papua New Guinea the Melanesian way' (2007) 31 *Harvard Environmental Review* 219.

facilitate an evolutionary process for the emergence of strong private property rights.

While the foregoing discussion has focused on property rights in land, it is worth noting that somewhat parallel issues arise with respect to movable (or personal) property. In many developing countries, the ability to offer movable property (plant and machinery, inventory, accounts receivable, livestock) as security for credit is severely constrained by the absence of an efficient centralized, comprehensive registry system for all security interests in movable property (both specific and generic, present and future), the lack of efficient, low-cost enforcement regimes with respect to security interests, and the absence of efficient credit information systems (for example, private or public credit bureaux). According to the World Bank's annual 'Doing Business' Reports, these constraints in turn often severely constrain the cost and availability of credit to small and medium-sized business.[98]

II. CONTRACT RIGHTS[99]

A. Introduction

Nobel Laureate Douglass North advances the strong claim that 'the inability of societies to develop effective, low-cost enforcement of contracts is the most important source of both historical stagnation and contemporary underdevelopment in the Third World'.[100]

Oliver Williamson proposes that economic activity is best understood and explained by 'an examination of the *comparative costs of planning, adapting, and monitoring task completion under alternative governance structures*'.[101] He argues that neither spot market transactions nor transactions within vertically integrated firms require formal enforcement mechanisms, because both entail minimal transaction costs.[102] Conversely, the vulner-

---

98 World Bank, *Annual Doing Business Reports*, 'Getting credit'; Frederique Dahar and John Simpson (eds), *Secured Transactions Reform and Access to Credit* (Cheltenham, UK: Edward Elgar Publishing 2008).

99 This section is largely derived from Michael Trebilcock and Jing Leng, 'The role of formal contract law and enforcement in economic development' (2006) 92 *University of Virginia Law Review* 1517.

100 Douglass C. North, *Institutions, Institutional Change and Economic Performance* (Cambridge, UK: Cambridge University Press, 1990) at 54.

101 Oliver E. Williamson, *The Economic Institutions of Capitalism* (New York: Free Press, 1985) at 2.

102 Oliver E. Williamson, *The Mechanisms of Governance* (New York: Oxford University Press, 1996) at 332.

ability experienced by at least one party to long-term, non-simultaneous transactions creates a significant need for a credible third party enforcement mechanism.[103] Credible third party enforcement addresses the reluctance of private sector agents to participate in non-simultaneous economic transactions, which often entail significant sunk costs, because of a lack of assured protection of the parties' economic interests. Williamson contemplates a continuum of microeconomic activity: at either end of this continuum are types of activity that do not require a formal mechanism for contract enforcement, while in the middle lie economic activities that require some degree of external enforcement.[104]

From the perspective articulated by Williamson and North, and given the existence of transaction costs, individuals require assurances that those transaction costs will not negate the benefits they seek to derive from the transaction itself. Recalling that institutions include both the formal and informal constraints that shape human interaction,[105] and that enforcement is an important factor in determining transaction costs,[106] North first identifies self-enforcement as the primary feature of contracts used in tribes, primitive societies and close-knit small communities – settings in which personal knowledge of transacting parties about one another is extensive, and repeat dealings are pervasive.[107] North then points out the limits of self-enforcing contracts in a world of increasingly impersonal exchange. In such a world, simultaneous exchange and repeat dealings are no longer the prevailing norm; thus, self-enforcing contracts become insufficient because there no longer exists a dense social network of interactions to enable transacting to take place at low cost.[108] Instead, individual specialization and exchange expansion in both time and space require additional contract enforcement mechanisms to assure compliance.

North thus concludes that the lack of low-cost, effective contract enforcement mechanisms (in particular, effective state enforcement through coercion) is the most important contributor to economic inefficiency and low growth rates in the developing world.[109] He then cautions, however, that no one has yet successfully proposed how to develop the state into a coercive force able to protect property rights and enforce contracts effectively without also risking abuse of its coercive power to the

---

103 Ibid.; see also Dam, *supra* note 1 at 124–8.
104 Williamson, *supra* note 102.
105 North, *supra* note 100 at 4.
106 Ibid., at 54 note 1.
107 Ibid., at 55.
108 Ibid.
109 Ibid., at 54.

detriment of society.[110] As we have noted, the last two decades have seen extensive efforts by international agencies and external donors to promote rule of law reform in many developing countries and transition economies; these efforts are, in part, predicated on the instrumental, economic rationales espoused by North. Is this prioritization warranted, at least on instrumental grounds?

While the contract-formalist approach to development taken by North regards formal contract enforcement as fundamentally important for a nation's economic development, an alternative school of thought has emerged that downplays the need for a formal third party mechanism for contract enforcement. Relying on empirical evidence that emphasizes the fundamental role played by social norms and relational networks in rendering private transactions self-enforcing, scholars have argued that many economic activities that foster economic development do not need a means of formal third-party enforcement.[111] According to Avner Greif, for example, 'many exchange relations in historical and contem-

---

110 Ibid., at 59–60.

111 See, e.g., Lisa Bernstein, 'Opting out of the legal system: extralegal contractual relations in the diamond industry' (1992) 21 *Journal of Legal Studies* 115; see also Marcel Fafchamps, *Market Institutions in Sub-Saharan Africa: Theory and Evidence* (Cambridge, MA: MIT Press, 2004) (reviewing empirical evidence suggesting that contract agreements in sub-Saharan Africa are highly dependent on social networks and personal trust); Lisa Bernstein, 'Merchant law in a merchant court: rethinking the Code's search for immanent business norms' (1996) 144 *University of Pennsylvania Law Review* 1765 (studying the self-enforcing private ordering in the American grain industry); Lisa Bernstein, 'Private commercial law in the cotton industry: creating cooperation through rules, norms, and institutions' (2001) 99 *Michigan Law Review* 1724; Avner Greif, 'Contracting, enforcement, and efficiency: economics beyond the law,' in Michael Bruno and Boris Pleskovic (eds), *Annual World Bank Conference on Development Economics 1996* (1997) at 239 (challenging the neoclassical theory that only legal contract enforcement facilitates exchange); Janet T. Landa, 'A theory of the ethnically homogeneous middleman group: an institutional alternative to contract law' (1981) 10 *Journal of Legal Studies* 349 (discussing the business practices of ethnically Chinese middlemen in Malaysia and Singapore): Janet Landa finds that the tightly knit, ethnically based business community among ethnically Chinese middlemen in Malaysia and Singapore facilitated a mutual trust that obviated any need to take measures to lessen uncertainty in transactions, while exchanges between the Chinese and the indigenous non-Chinese employed primarily cash (rather than credit) in order to reduce contract uncertainty (at 350); see also Janet T. Landa, *Trust, Ethnicity, and Identity: Beyond the New Institutional Economics of Ethnic Trading Networks, Contract Law and Gift-Exchange* (Ann Arbor, MI: University of Michigan Press, 1995) 164 at 205 (proposing a theory of informal contract enforcement institutions in achieving 'ordered anarchy').

porary markets and developing economies are not governed – directly or indirectly – by the legal system'.[112] Greif argues that, in fact, much of the world's economic development has occurred in the absence of a legal system to govern private economic transactions.[113]

B. Empirical Evidence

A provisional reading of the evidence (extensively reviewed elsewhere by Michael Trebilcock and Jing Leng)[114] is that the proponents of contract formalism and the proponents of contract informalism can both point to supporting bodies of theory and empirical evidence, but both risk overstating, or at least over-simplifying, their cases.

To take first the case made by the contract formalists, it is clear that in both developed and developing countries, many contracts are self-enforcing. Often because of ethnic, religious or cultural ties, informal transacting norms arise and are enforced through informal, extra-legal sanctions. Even in the absence of such contracting networks, long-term, incomplete contingent claims contracts are commonplace between arm's length business parties in both developed and developing economies. Where these contracts include substantial investments in relationship-specific assets, there are strong incentives to maintain the relationship. Of course, even long-term relational contracts eventually come to an end and, depending on the nature of the dependencies or interdependencies that they create, these contracts are vulnerable to problems of hold up and opportunism ('end-game' problems). These problems can sometimes only be solved by complete vertical integration, although this may not otherwise be efficient.[115]

---

[112] Greif, ibid., at 241.

[113] Ibid., at 241–2.

[114] Trebilcock and Leng, *supra* note 99 at 1517.

[115] See, e.g., Robert Cooter and Thomas Ulen, *Law and Economics* (Scott Foresman & Co., 4th edn, 2004) at 225–35; Lawrence M. Friedman, *Contract Law in America* (University of Wisconsin Press, 1965) at 89; Paul Milgrom and John Roberts, *Economics, Organization and Management* (Prentice Hall, 1992) at 131–40; Charles Goetz and Robert E. Scott, 'Principles of relational contracts' (1981) 67 *Virginia Law Review* 1089 at 1090–91; Benjamin Klein and Keith B. Leffler, 'The role of market forces in assuring contractual performance' (1981) 89 *J. Pol. Econ.* 615; Stewart Macaulay, 'Non-contractual relations in business: a preliminary study' (1963) 28 *Am. Soc. Rev.* 55 at 58–9; Ian R. Macneil, 'Contracts: adjustment of long term economic relations under classical, neoclassical, and relational contract law' (1978) 72 *Northwestern University Law Review* at 889–90; Ian R. Macneil, 'The many futures of contracts' (1974) 47 *S. Cal. L. Rev.* 691 at 758–9; Anthony

As noted above, Williamson argues that both spot market and hierarchical (corporate integration) transactions require little support from the formal legal system; in contrast, middle range transactions (long-term contracting) are particularly vulnerable in the absence of credible third party enforcement mechanisms.[116] Williamson's claim implies a continuum of forms of economic coordination or cooperation, with complete vertical integration at one end, spot markets at the other, and a large vacuum in the middle.

Even with respect to Williamson's two polar cases, however, it is not true that vertical integration can completely avoid the problems of a weak formal legal system. As a number of commentators have argued, and corroborated empirically, countries with poorer investor protection, measured by both the character of legal rules and the quality of legal enforcement, have smaller and narrower capital markets; this is particularly evident when minority shareholders are subject to serious agency costs (opportunism) by managers or controlling shareholders.[117] Moreover, employment contracts and collective agreements often require a formal enforcement mechanism. In any event, as Williamson himself acknowledges, vertical integration may be less efficient than other forms of economic coordination that an effective formal contract regime may facilitate.[118] At the other pole, even spot transactions (for example, commodity contracts) may raise quality or product defect problems that require resort to the formal legal system, at least in the absence of industry or trade associations with their own codes of conduct, norms and alternative dispute settlement mechanisms.[119]

Between these two poles, Williamson exaggerates the importance of formal contract enforcement by giving insufficient weight to the role of relational contracting[120] and contract enforcement by private sector third

---

Kronman, 'Contract law and the state of nature' (1985) *Journal of Law, Economics and Organizations* 5.

116 Williamson, *The Mechanisms of Governance*, *supra* note 102 at 332.

117 See, e.g., Thorsten Beck and Ross Levine, 'Legal institutions and financial development', in Claude Menard and Mary M. Shirley (eds), *Handbook of New Institutional Economics* 251 (Springer, 2005) at 253–4; Bernard S. Black, Reinier Kraakman and Anna Tarrassova, 'Russian privatization and corporate governance: what went wrong?' (2000) 52 *Stanford Law Review* 1731; Rafael La Porta, Florencio Lopez-de-Silanes, Andrei Shleifer and Robert W. Vishny, 'Legal determinants of external finance' (1997) 52 *Journal of Finance* 1131 at 1136–9.

118 Williamson, *supra* note 102 at 235, 332.

119 See Bernstein, 'Opting out of the legal system: extralegal contractual relations in the diamond industry', *supra* note 111 at 130–35.

120 See George Baker, Robert Gibbons and Kevin Murphy, 'Relational contracts and the theory of the firm' (2002) 117 *Quarterly Journal of Economics* 39.

parties – such as credit bureaux, bourses, exchanges, arbitrators and industry associations – in both personal and impersonal relationships.

The contract informalists, in turn, risk overstating their case to the extent that they imply that most contracts are self-enforcing, rendering formal third party enforcement unnecessary or unimportant for economic development. As noted above, long-term relational contracts may lead to end-game problems that require resort to the courts for resolution. Moreover, in many contracts for large investments in non-salvageable assets (sunk costs) – such as infrastructure or complex technology – parties will seek a fully specified, contingent claims contract.

Often the investors will not share a common ethnic, cultural or religious network with counterparties to these transactions; nor will investors wish to leave subsequent negotiation of contract details or enforcement to the vagaries of arbitrary domestic political, regulatory or legal processes. For example, circumstances that arguably have facilitated Japan's economic success in the post-war years and, more recently, China's, do not readily generalize to most other developing countries.[121] Japan is a remarkably culturally homogeneous society where reliance on informal social norms and sanctions may be particularly effective.[122] In addition, Japan has been strikingly non-dependent on large-scale foreign direct investment for its economic success. While China has recently relied on large infusions of foreign direct investment, much of this investment has come from ethnic Chinese business networks (*guanxi*) outside of China or has relied on rather unique kinds of corporatist ties to local governments.[123] China's success in attracting foreign investment cannot easily be replicated in other developing economies that do not have a huge diaspora, members of which are not only capital-rich but also willing to invest in their home countries.

---

[121] Frank K. Upham, 'Speculations on legal informality: on Winn's relational practices and the marginalization of law' (1994) 28 *Law & Society Review* 233 at 237; Frank Upham, 'Mythmaking in the rule of law orthodoxy', Democracy and Rule of Law Project at the Carnegie Endowment for International Peace, Rule of Law Series, Working Paper No. 30, 2002, at 21–31.

[122] See Robert Klitgaard, *Adjusting to Reality: Beyond 'State versus Market' in Economic Development* (ICS Press, 1991) at 169–74; Pranab Bardhan, 'Method in the madness? A political-economy analysis of the ethnic conflicts in less developed countries' (1997) 25 *World Development* 1381; William Easterly and Ross Levine, 'Africa's growth tragedy: policies and ethnic divisions' (1997) 112 *Quarterly Journal of Economics* 1203 at 1206–7.

[123] Huang Shaoqin, 'A study of contract enforcement mechanisms in China during transition (zhongguo zhuangui shiqi hetong zhixing jizhi yanjiu)' (2006) 3 *J. Legal & Econ. Studies* (Hong Fan Ping Lun) 184 at 192.

For developing countries, long-term economic growth is significantly dependent on expanding international trade and on attracting large-scale foreign direct investment from parties who do not share common ethnic, cultural or social characteristics. Here, the absence of effective formal contract enforcement mechanisms is likely to entail a number of adverse implications for investment and international trade.[124]

While, as Dixit notes, '[r]elation-based governance works well in small groups that are connected by extended family relationships, neighborhood structures, and ethno-linguistic ties, because such links facilitate repeated interactions and good communication',[125] relational contracting has the potential to create significant adverse, external effects. McMillan and Woodruff acknowledge the economic weaknesses of exclusionary business networks, observing, for example, that private ordering 'sometimes harms efficiency by excluding new entrants from trading or by achieving price collusion'.[126] Gray notes a similar effect with ethnicity-based business networks, which can render it nearly impossible for an outsider to enter the circle on a business level.[127] This 'shortage of new firms and new people' and 'inability to enter into long-term contracts can inhibit the adoption and development of complex technologies'.[128] Thus, Greif recognizes that 'reputation-based institutions that support personal exchange [may] have a low fixed cost but a high marginal cost of exchanging with unfamiliar individuals'.[129]

In a tightly knit community, Bardhan notes another obvious trade-off of private ordering: 'transaction costs are low, but . . . production costs are high, because specialization and division of labour are severely limited by the extent of a market defined by the personalized exchange process of the small community.'[130] As a result, Dixit suggests, in a relation-based contract enforcement system, 'diversified conglomerates whose component

---

124 See Daniel Berkowitz, Katharina Pistor and Johannes Moenius, 'Legal institutions and international trade flows' (2004) 26 *Michigan Journal of International Law* 163 at 166–8.; Shaoqin, ibid.

125 Avinash Dixit, *Lawlessness and Economics: Alternative Modes of Governance* (Princeton, NJ: Princeton University Press, 2004) at 79.

126 John McMillan and Christopher Woodruff, 'Private order under dysfunctional public order' (2000) 98 *Michigan Law Review* 2421 at 2423.

127 Cheryl W. Gray, 'Reforming legal systems in developing and transition countries' (September 1997) *Fin. & Dev.* at 14.

128 Ibid.

129 Avner Greif, *Institutions and the Path to the Modern Economy* (Cambridge, UK: Cambridge University Press, 2006) at 58–90.

130 Pranab Bardhan, 'Institutions matter, but which ones?' (2005) 13 *Economics of Transition* 499 at 511–12.

parts have nothing in common except common ownership by a closely knit extended family or similar network' may eventually emerge.[131] Aside from trade and production, relational contracting may also create high costs for corporate finance because, under such a system, capital markets tend to be compartmentalized among linked firms through potentially inefficient related borrowing and lending.[132]

Fafchamps notes, in an African context, that 'whenever business communities are built along ethnic, religious, or gender lines, network effects result in apparent discrimination'.[133] Not surprisingly, he finds that an ethnic bias in assigning trade credit has been 'detrimental to entrepreneurs of African descent and favorable to entrepreneurs originating outside of Africa'.[134] Thus, while ethnicity-based business networks may provide the predictability that helps facilitate certain economic transactions, such transactions may come at the cost of both discrimination against individuals outside that network and inefficiency from potentially mutually beneficial exchanges forgone. Indeed, in Greif's example of the medieval Maghribi trading networks, the coalition of traders that facilitated contract enforcement 'was not dynamically efficient' because '[t]he same factors that ensured its self-enforceability prevented it from expanding in response to welfare-enhancing opportunities'.[135]

McMillan and Woodruff usefully distinguish between formal contract law in dysfunctional and functional legal systems.[136] They note that in a functional legal system, relational contracting tends to complement the formal state-enforced contract framework, while in a dysfunctional legal system, relational contracting may be an imperfect substitute for a system of formal contract enforcement.[137]

C. Conclusion

The mix of mechanisms that are likely to ensure both a fair and efficient domain of contracting in developing countries is a function of highly context-specific factors that defy easy generalizations. This caution has also been strongly voiced in recent development literature that stresses the need to adopt highly context-specific analysis in studying

---

131 Dixit, *supra* note 125 at 79.
132 Ibid., at 80.
133 Fafchamps, *supra* note 111 at 347.
134 Ibid., at 368.
135 Greif, *supra* note 129 at 88.
136 McMillan and Woodruff, *supra* note 126 at 2425.
137 Ibid.

institutions.[138] Two considerations may be of particular relevance to this exercise.

First, as noted above, growth modes and income levels matter to the extent that catch-up economies starting from low-level economic equilibria have different demands for institutions from those of middle-income economies. As Rodrik argues, while '[t]he onset of economic growth does not require deep and extensive institutional reform[,] . . . [s]ustaining high growth in the face of adverse circumstances requires ever stronger institutions' and 'the institutional requirements of . . . growth in a middle-income country can be significantly more demanding'.[139] Similarly, Daniel Klerman finds that, historically, 'economic growth often starts without strong courts, and efforts to improve the quality of the judiciary are often the consequence, not the cause, of economic development'; but, if economic growth starts without good judicial institutions, it may create a demand for quality courts at higher levels of development.[140] Moreover, new evidence from patterns of international trade also generates support for this discriminating treatment of institutional dependency. The findings of Berkowitz, Moenius and Pistor suggest that the nature of traded goods (of varying levels of complexity) can influence the relative importance of formal, as compared to informal, contracting.[141] This conclusion corroborates the view that the requirements of formal institutional quality become

---

[138] See, e.g., William Easterly, *The White Man's Burden: Why the West's Efforts to Aid the Rest Have Done So Much Ill and So Little Good*, 77, 100–101, 345–7 (Penguin Press, 2006); Greif, *supra* note 129 at 350– 52; Rohini Pande and Christopher Udry, 'Institutions and development: a view from below', Yale University Economic Growth Center, Discussion Paper No. 928, 2005, at 2–3, available at http://www.econ.yale.edu/growth_pdf/cdp928.pdf; Francis Fukuyama, 'Development and the limits of institutional design', presentation at the Seventh Annual Global Development Conference of the Global Development Network 2 (20 January 2006), available at http://www.gdnet.org/pdf2/gdnlibrary/annualconferences/seventhannualconference/Fukuyamaplenary1.pdf.

[139] Dani Rodrik (ed.), *In Search of Prosperity: Analytic Narratives on Economic Growth*, Introduction, (Princeton, NJ: Princeton University Press, 2003); see also Kenneth W. Dam, 'China as a test case: is the rule of law essential for economic growth?' (University of Chicago John M. Olin Law & Econ., Working Paper No. 275, 2nd series, 2006), available at http://www.law.uchicago.edu/Lawecon/WkngPprs_251-300/275-kd-china.pdf , at 41(stating that Rodrik's argument is supported by the example of China).

[140] Daniel Klerman, 'Legal infrastructure, judicial independence, and economic development', Univ. S. Cal. Ctr. in Law Econ. & Org., Research Paper No. C06-1, 2006, at 1, 4; see also Edward L. Glaeser, Rafael La Porta, Florencio Lopez-de-Silanes and Andrei Shleifer, 'Do institutions cause growth?' (2004) 9 *Journal of Economic Growth* 271 at 298.

[141] See Berkowitz et al., *supra* note 124.

more demanding as economies move up the development curve. This view is also corroborated by recent evidence from China that the quality of contract adjudication and enforcement has dramatically improved in rapidly growing urban centres but continues to languish in more economically backward rural areas.[142]

Second, prevailing societal structures for organizing the behaviour of individuals in the early stages of market development – such as the different modes of social interaction in communalist and individualist societies – also matter. Communalist societies tend to rely more on relation-based contract enforcement institutions that emphasize informal intra-group sanctions. Individualist societies, by contrast, tend to support more transactions across different groups with formal contract enforcement institutions.[143]

With regard to policy considerations, building contract enforcement institutions that support markets takes time.[144] In this process of institutional evolution, alternative informal solutions, although transitional at particular stages of development, can serve value-adding and welfare-improving functions before formal institutional reform has taken hold and become effective. This is especially true for countries at early stages of industrialization, as East Asian economies have demonstrated. As Dixit has observed, 'it is not always necessary to create replicas of Western-style state legal institutions from scratch; it may be possible to work with such alternative institutions as are available, and build on them'.[145] Thus, there is a legitimate justification for incorporating efficient indigenous institutions of contract enforcement into contemporary legal regimes, rendering formal and informal enforcement institutions complementary rather than substitutional, and making the law more legitimate in the perceptions of the general population, thereby facilitating its implementation on the ground.[146]

---

142 See Xin He, 'Formal contract enforcement and economic development in urban and rural China', Working Paper, School of Law, City University of Hong Kong, 2008.

143 See Avner Greif, 'Commitment, coercion, and markets: the nature and dynamics of institutions supporting exchange', in Menard and Shirley, *supra* note 117 at 727, 762.

144 John McMillan and Christopher Woodruff, 'Dispute prevention without courts in Vietnam' (1999) 15 *J. L. Econ. & Org.* 637 at 637–8.

145 Dixit, *supra* note 125 at 4.

146 In this context it is worth noting that, regarding legal transplant as an alternative path toward legal reform in developing countries, some authors propose that 'adaptation' of the transplanted law to local conditions is important for achieving legality in the recipient countries – an assessment consistent with our argument

Another transitional strategy that has already become widespread practice in international business transactions is, in effect, to outsource contract interpretation and enforcement. Many major international transactions are now negotiated in English, contracts are written in English, and choice of law and/or choice of forum clauses in such contracts stipulate that they are to be governed by the law of New York or England and that disputes will be resolved by international commercial arbitration (with arbitral awards enforceable in domestic courts where countries are signatories to the New York Convention on the Recognition and Enforcement of Foreign Arbitral Awards).[147] This strategy, reflected in the rise of global law firms, largely bypasses domestic legal institutions (except for residual risks associated with the enforcement of foreign arbitral awards) and has raised several caveats on that account: it largely removes foreign investors as a political constituency for domestic legal reform while leaving many domestic parties captive to the frailties of domestic legal institutions, including abuses of human rights beyond the domain of commercial transactions, and risks rendering a transitional strategy the permanent status quo (a low-level equilibrium trap).

---

here. See, e.g., Daniel Berkowitz, Katharina Pistor and Jean Francois Richard, 'Economic development, legality, and the transplant effect' (2003) 47 *European Economic Review* 165 at 192; Gillian K. Hadfield, 'The many legal institutions that support contractual commitments', in Menard and Shirley *supra* note 117 at 175, 181–200.

[147] See Jens Dammann and Henry Hansmann, 'Globalizing commercial litigation' (2008) 94:1 *Cornell Law Review* at 1; Kevin Davis and Michael Trebilcock, 'The demand for bijurally trained Canadian lawyers', in Albert Breton and Michael Trebilcock (eds), *Bijuralism: An Economic Approach* (Aldershot: Ashgate, 2006).

4. Political regimes, ethnic conflict and development

I. INTRODUCTION

This chapter focuses on the role that political institutions can play in promoting development. Does democracy promote economic development (growth), or vice-versa? This has been a contested terrain over the last several decades, and the evidence in favour of democracy is inconclusive at best. Evidence suggests that democracies tend to do better than autocracies on other social indicators such as infant mortality rates and access to basic education, although the correlation is not tight. The chapter also analyses the role that political institutions can play in reducing ethnic conflict. This is a pervasive problem in developing countries that takes a serious toll on social and economic development. These conflicts have complex causes, but there are reasons to believe that political institutions can play a role in mitigating ethnic tension and violence.

After reviewing the arguments and evidence that support the idea that political institutions can play a role in promoting development and reducing ethnic conflict, we analyse institutional reforms – and political reforms in particular – to show that they pose formidable challenges. Reform efforts need to acknowledge that there is no one-size-fits-all solution to the problem of governance in general and design of political institutions in particular. As with the rule of law and other institutional reforms, path dependence and institutional interconnections may significantly constrain a society's feasible reform options with respect to its political reforms. Thus, institutional change is more likely to succeed if adapted to a country's particular context and history.

II. POLITICAL REGIMES AND DEVELOPMENT

Most of the rich countries in the world are democracies and most of the poorest countries are not, or have not been for most of their histories.[1] Recently, however, this reality seems to be changing. The last quarter-century has seen a wave of democratization,[2] the most recent examples being the revolutions in Tunisia and Egypt in 2011. In 2010, some 116 countries claimed to be democracies, compared to only 39 in 1974.[3] Many of these countries have also adopted new constitutions, entrenched bills of rights and made provisions for constitutional judicial review (the so-called 'new constitutionalism').[4] Carothers identifies seven trends in the last quarter-century that were responsible for this wave of democratization.[5] They are:

> (1) the fall of right wing authoritarian regimes in Southern Europe;
> (2) the replacement of military dictatorships by elected civilian governments across Latin America from the late 1970s through the late 1980s;
> (3) the decline of authoritarian rule in parts of East and South East Asia starting in the mid-1980s;
> (4) the collapse of communist regimes in Eastern Europe at the end of the 1980s;
> (5) the break-up of the Soviet union in 1991;
> (6) the decline of one-party regimes in many parts of sub-Saharan Africa in the first half of the 1990s; and
> (7) a weak liberalizing trend in some Middle Eastern countries in the 1990s (stronger currently).[6]

Does this wave of democratization provide a basis for optimism that these countries are now on a much stronger development trajectory?

---

[1] Adam Przeworski, 'Democracy and economic development', in Edward D. Mansfield and Richard Sisson (eds), *The Evolution of Political Knowledge: Democracy, Autonomy, and Conflict in Comparative and International Politics* (Columbus: Ohio State University Press, 2004). For the African experience, see Martin Meredith, *The Fate of Africa – A History of Fifty Years of Independence* (New York: Public Affairs, 2005); for the Latin American experience, see Michael Reid, *Forgotten Continent* (New Haven: Yale University Press, 2007); and for the Asian experience, see Minxin Pei, 'The puzzle of East Asian exceptionalism' (1994) 5:4 *Journal of Democracy* 90.

[2] Larry Diamond, *The Spirit of Democracy: The Struggle to Build Free Societies Throughout the World* (New York: Henry Holt, 2008).

[3] Freedom House, *Freedom in the World 2010: Global Erosion of Freedom* (Washington, DC: Freedom House, 2010).

[4] Kevin Davis and Michael Trebilcock, 'The relationship between law and development: optimists versus skeptics' (2008) 56 *Am. J. Comp. L.* 895.

[5] Thomas Carothers, 'The end of the transition paradigm' (2002) 13:1 *Journal of Democracy* 5.

[6] See also Samuel P. Huntington, *The Third Wave: Democratization in the Late Twentieth Century* (Norman: University of Oklahoma Press, 1991). According to Carothers, the 'third wave' of democratization is over: see Thomas Carothers, 'A quarter-century of promoting democracy' (2007) 18:4 *Journal of Democracy* 112.

The relationship between political regimes and development is highly contested terrain, both theoretically and empirically. The fact that most rich countries are democracies while most poor countries are not, or have not been for most of their histories, establishes a correlation but not necessarily causation between democracy and development.

A. Some Elements of Consensus: Markets and Democracy

There appears to be some consensus on the following four propositions.[7] First, almost all modern democracies have been market economies. (Chile under Allende was an exception; India, until the early 1990s, may have been another partial exception.) Second, there are numerous cases of non-democratic market economies. Third, it seems to follow that a market economy is (almost) a necessary condition for a political democracy, but that democracy is not a necessary condition for a market economy. Fourth, when market economies are successful over a substantial period of time, pressure for democratization tends to ensue.

There also appears to be a reasonable degree of consensus in the academic literature concerning the reasons why a market economy or economic liberalization is likely to promote the emergence or survival of a democratic regime. For a market economy to function efficiently, there must be:

- reasonably broad latitude for free economic association;
- reasonable access to private and public economic information upon which investment and contracting decisions are made; and
- a level of transparency, stability and predictability in the enactment and enforcement of laws in order to reduce risk, transaction costs and information costs.[8]

---

[7] For discussion of these four propositions, see Peter L. Berger, 'The uncertain triumph of democratic capitalism', in Larry Diamond and Mark F. Plattner (eds), *Capitalism, Socialism and Democracy Revisited* (Baltimore: Johns Hopkins University Press, 1993); Jagdish Bhagwati, 'Democracy and development', in Diamond and Plattner, ibid.; Robert A. Dahl, 'Why free markets are not enough', in Diamond and Plattner, ibid.; Jose M. Maravall, 'The myth of authoritarian advantage' (1994) 5:4 *Journal of Democracy* 17; and Andrei Shleifer, 'The age of Milton Friedman' (2009) 47 *Journal of Economic Literature* 123.

[8] See Bhagwati, *supra* note 7; Dahl, *supra* note 7 at 76; Adam Przeworski and Fernando Limongi, 'Political regimes and economic growth' (1993) 7 *Journal of Economic Perspectives* 51; and J.D. Sullivan, 'Democratization and business interests' (1994) 5:4 *Journal of Democracy* 146.

Historically, the rise of a commercial bourgeoisie or merchant class tends to be associated with the pursuit of limits on the exercise of government power and subsequent political reform. A middle class dependent on commercial and professional activity is likely to resist domination by landed elites or other non-accountable political rulers who are likely to interfere with or expropriate its investments.[9] Moreover, as incomes and levels of education rise with the emergence and growth of a market economy, citizens are likely to attach an increasing intrinsic value to democratic institutions (that is, democracy is a normal economic good). According to Francis Fukuyama, these psychological imperatives reflect a desire for universal and equal recognition.[10] Finally, the emergence of mass global communication systems and much greater international mobility of goods, capital, services and people have led to the dissemination of external ideas and values into countries and cultures that were once closed.[11]

These factors may explain why economic liberalization tends to lead to political liberalization, but what effect does the adoption of democratic institutions have on subsequent economic development? Here, as we discuss below, both the academic theorizing and the empirical evidence are much more ambiguous.

B. Defining Democracy

In order to examine the relationship between democracy and economic development, it is necessary to begin by clarifying what is meant by 'democracy'. Democracy is often understood as a political regime that protects the freedom of individuals and expresses the will of the majority through free and fair elections, protection of minority rights and respect for basic human rights.[12] However, notwithstanding this general concep-

---

[9] Bhagwati, *supra* note 7; Francis Fukuyama, 'Capitalism and democracy: the missing link', in Diamond and Plattner, *supra* note 7 at 94; Kyung-won Kim, 'Marx, Schumpeter and the East Asian experience', in Diamond and Plattner, *supra* note 7 at 11; and Daron Acemoğlu and James A. Robinson, *Economic Origins of Dictatorship and Democracy* (New York, NY: Cambridge University Press, 2006) at 22–30.

[10] Fukuyama, ibid. See also John F. Helliwell, 'Empirical linkages between democracy and economic growth' (1994) 24 *British Journal of Political Science* 225 and 'Why voting is good for you' *The Economist* 332:7878 (27 August 1994) 15.

[11] Bhagwati, *supra* note 7, and Kyung-won Kim, *supra* note 9 at 11.

[12] Economist Intelligence Unit, 'The Economist Intelligence Unit's Index of Democracy 2008' *The Economist* (29 October 2008), available at http://

tion of democracy, there is no consensus on precisely how to define or measure democracy. Scholars approach democracy in at least three different ways: by giving it a thick or thin meaning; by adopting a prescriptive or descriptive approach; and by conceptualizing it as a dichotomy or a spectrum.

There are 'thin' or 'thick' definitions of democracy.[13] Thin definitions focus on the basic features that characterize democracy, while thick definitions graft a wide range of substantive and procedural elements onto the concept. An example of a thin concept is Joseph Schumpeter's definition of democracy, which is a system 'for arriving at political decisions in which individuals acquire the power to decide by means of a competitive struggle for the people's vote'.[14] On the other hand, Larry Diamond's definition of democracy is a thick concept; Diamond suggests that a system is only a democracy if it exhibits the following attributes:

- Substantial individual freedom of belief, opinion, discussion, speech, publication, broadcast, assembly, demonstration, petition, and even the Internet;
- Freedom of ethnic, religious, racial, and other minority groups (as well as historically excluded majorities) to practice their religion and culture and to participate equally in political and social life;
- The right of all adult citizens to vote and to run for office (if they meet certain minimum age and competency requirements);
- Genuine openness and competition in the electoral arena, enabling any group that adheres to constitutional principles to form a party and contest for office;
- Legal equality of all citizens under a rule of law, in which the laws are 'clear, publicly known, universal, stable, and non-retroactive';
- An independent judiciary to apply the law neutrally and consistently and to protect individual and group rights;
- Due process of law and freedom of individuals from torture, terror, and unjustified detention, exile, or interference in their personal lives – by the state or non-state actors;
- Institutional checks on the power of elected officials, by an independent legislature, court system, and other autonomous agencies;
- Real pluralism in sources of information and forms of organizations independent of the state, and thus, a vibrant 'civil society'; and

---

graphics.eiu.com/PDF/Democracy%20Index%202008.pdf; and Michael Coppedge, 'Defining and measuring democracy', IPSA/APSA Committee on Concepts and Methods Electronic Working Paper Series (April 2005), available at http://www.nd.edu/~mcoppedg/crd/ch2.pdf.

[13] Coppedge, ibid., and Diamond, *supra* note 2 at 21.

[14] Joseph Schumpeter, *Capitalism, Socialism, and Democracy* (New York: Harper, 1947, 2nd edn) at 269.

- Control over the military and state security apparatus by civilians who are ultimately accountable to the people through elections.[15]

Second, according to Robert A. Dahl, a leading scholar in this field, democracy is both a prescriptive and descriptive tool.[16] Democracy can be a prescriptive concept that sets out what countries should aspire to become. Democracy can also be a descriptive concept that measures the degree to which a country has democratized. In this regard, the status of a country's democracy is now viewed as falling along a continuum. This reflects the third approach to understanding democracy – that is, conceptualizing democracy as either a dichotomy or a spectrum.

While earlier scholars categorized countries as either democratic or non-democratic, scholars have more recently abandoned this dichotomy and replaced it with the idea that there are varying degrees of democracy.[17] For example, Collier has studied the effect of partial democracy on countries' economic policy reforms. He shows that elections are not a sufficient proxy for democracy since using elections as a proxy results in classifying countries as full democracies even though they have only nominally fulfilled election requirements.[18] Reflecting this shift in perspective, both Freedom House and *The Economist* magazine assess the degree to which countries are democratic.[19] In short, people can generally conceptualize what democracy is supposed to represent, but rarely agree on how best to define it in detail.[20]

---

15 Diamond, *supra* note 2 at 22.

16 Robert A. Dahl, *On Democracy* (New Haven: Yale University Press, 2000) at 26.

17 David L. Epstein, Robert Bates, Jack Goldstone, Ida Kristensen and Sharyn O'Halloran, 'Democratic transitions' (2006) 50:3 *American Journal of Political Science* 551–69 at 552; Edward Mansfield and Jack Snyder, 'Democratization and war' (1995) 74 *Foreign Affairs* 79; John Bacher, 'Oil and dictatorship: most oil-rich countries are dictatorships that do little for their societies or for nature' (1998) 14:3 *Peace Magazine* 8; Jack Goldstone, Ted Robert Gurr, Barbara Huff, Marc Levy, Monty Marshall, Robert Bates, David Epstein, Colin Kahl, Pamela Surko, John Ulfelder Jnr and Alan Unger, *State Failure Task Force: Phase III Findings* (McLean, VA: SAIC, 2000); and Fareed Zakaria, *The Future of Freedom* (New York: W.W. Norton, 2003).

18 Paul Collier, *Wars, Guns, and Votes: Democracy in Dangerous Places* (New York: HarperCollins, 2009) at 45.

19 See Michael Trebilcock and Poorvi Chitalkar, 'From nominal to substantive democracy: the role and design of election management bodies' (2009) 2 *L. and Dev. Rev.* 179.

20 W.B. Gallie has characterized democracy as an example of an 'essentially

C. The Case for Democracy

Adopting what Frischtak[21] refers to as the modernization theory of the 1950s and 1960s where 'all good things go together,' proponents of democracy make four contentions. First, democracy provides greater protection of property rights than non-democratic or authoritarian regimes.[22] Second, democracy exhibits an enhanced capacity for mediating intergroup and distributional conflicts. Third, democracy generates better information and more reliable feedback on the effects of present or proposed policies[23] when dissent or criticism is an avenue of recourse available to ordinary citizens and is not dependent on extraordinary, self-sacrificial heroes.[24] Finally, democratic regimes are more likely than totalitarian or authoritarian regimes to act in the general interest, or at least to reduce predatory tendencies that will often be exhibited by autocratic rulers.[25]

Some theorists focus on the connection between democracy and orthodox measures of development, such as economic growth, levels of education and infant mortality rates.[26] However, others claim that there is a positive relationship between democracy and broader definitions of human development that include improved quality of life and enhanced social welfare and individual freedoms. For example, Sen has famously argued that it is not a coincidence that there has never been a famine in a

---

contested concept'. See Walter B. Gallie, 'Essentially contested concepts' (1956) 56 *Proceedings of the Aristotelian Society* 167.

21 Leila L. Frischtak, 'Governance Capacity and Economic Reform in Developing Countries', World Bank Technical Paper No. 254 (Washington, DC: The World Bank, 1994).

22 *The Economist, supra* note 10; David Gillies, 'Democracy and economic development' (2005) 6:2 *IRPP Policy Matters* 21.

23 Maravall, *supra* note 7; Amartya Sen, 'Freedoms and needs: an argument for the primacy of political rights' (1994) 10 *The New Republic* 31; Doh Chull Shin, 'On the third wave of democratization' (1994) 47 *World Politics* 135; John Gerring, Philip Bond, William T. Barndt and Carola Moreno, 'Democracy and economic growth: a historical perspective' (2005) 57 *World Politics* 330.

24 Bhagwati, *supra* note 7.

25 Mancur Olson, 'Dictatorship, democracy and development' (1993) 87 *American Political Science Review* 567 and Sen, *supra* note 23.

26 See, e.g., Surjit Bhalla, 'Freedom and economic growth: a virtuous cycle?', in Axel Hadenius (ed.), *Democracy's Victory and Crisis* (Cambridge: Cambridge University Press, 1997); Gillies, *supra* note 22 at 22–24. On the relationship between democracy and human capital, see Matthew A. Baum and David A. Lake, 'The political economy of growth: democracy and human capital' (2003) *American Journal of Political Science* 47. On the relationship between democracy and infant mortality, see Peter Boone, 'Politics and the effectiveness of foreign aid' (1996) 40 *European Economic Review* 289.

functioning multiparty political system.[27] He argues that in a democratic country, like India, political activism and the condemnation of governments, in cases of open starvation, have been effective in preventing famine.[28] Similarly, beginning with Immanuel Kant, a number of political scientists and philosophers have claimed that democracies are highly unlikely to go to war with one another.[29]

Many of these thinkers claim that democracies generate relatively strong incentives for political leaders to promote broader goals of development.[30] For example, in *Power and Prosperity*,[31] Olson identifies three basic political regimes: roving bandits, stationary bandits and democracies, assuming that in all cases political leaders are motivated by self-interest. Roving bandits (recent examples of which include rebel groups plundering natural resources in Sierra Leone, the Sudan, Angola and the Congo) have extremely high time discount rates because of their insecurity of tenure. As a result, they prey on the local population to the maximum amount possible by confiscating all of their wealth.[32] Stationary bandits, by contrast, fully control a particular territory and, depending on their security of tenure and associated time discount rates, may have an incentive to adopt less confiscatory short-term measures. The strategy of confiscating less than maximal amounts of wealth creates incentives for the citizenry to be productive in future time periods and thus may increase the total returns to a despot with a relatively low time discount rate.[33] Democratic leaders, however, have stronger incentives to promote broad conceptions of the social interest and concomitant laws and legal institutions than either roving or stationary bandits. According to Olson,

---

27 Amartya Sen, *Resources, Values and Development* (Cambridge, MA: Harvard University Press, 1984); Amartya Sen and Jean Dreze, *Hunger and Public Action* (New York: Oxford University Press, 1989) and Amartya Sen, *Development as Freedom* (New York: Random House, 1999).

28 Sen, *Development as Freedom*, ibid. at 155–7.

29 See Immanuel Kant, 'Perpetual peace' in Peter Gay (ed.), *The Enlightenment: A Comprehensive Anthology* (New York: Routledge, 1974) and Michael Doyle, 'Kant, liberal legacies and foreign affairs, Part I' (1983) 12 *Philosophy and Public Affairs* 323.

30 For overviews of the empirical debate, see Przeworski and Limongi, *supra* note 8; Adam Przeworski, Michael Alvarez, José Antonio Cheibub and Fernando Limongi, *Democracy and Development: Political Institutions and Well-Being in the World 1950–1990* (New York, NY: Cambridge University Press, 2000); and Bhagwati, supra note 7.

31 Mancur Olson, *Power and Prosperity: Outgrowing Communist and Capitalist Dictatorships* (New York: Basic Books, 2000).

32 Ibid., at 6–7.

33 Ibid., at 7–12.

these stronger incentives flow from the fact that, unlike autocratic rulers, democratically elected rulers can often realistically anticipate returning to power at a future date, even after being defeated in an election. This prospect may induce them to place a relatively high value on enhancing the future welfare of their citizens.[34]

Several other arguments in favour of democracy do not centre on claims about incentive effects. For instance, Rodrik has argued that participatory political institutions are the most reliable 'meta-institutions' from a developmental perspective because they are best suited to elicit and aggregate the local knowledge required to develop other norms and institutions. Following thinkers such as John Stuart Mill, Rodrik has also argued that the deliberative processes typically associated with democracy tend to make people more public-spirited and willing to compromise. He argues that democracies exhibit superior qualities to autocracies in managing social conflict and in fashioning social compromises to deal with adjustment to macroeconomic shocks.[35]

For his part, Sen argues that democracy has a value in and of itself. As noted in Chapter 1, Sen's conception of development as freedom is not primarily instrumental. While democracy can be a means to better development outcomes, it also has intrinsic value.[36] Sen also argues in his recent book, *The Idea of Justice*,[37] that the relationship between public reason and justice demands some form of participatory governance, or 'government by discussion,' since government decisions must be publicly justified. He rejects the idea that democracy has a uniquely Western heritage and points to many historical examples of 'government by discussion' in widely different societies.[38]

---

34 Cf. Avinash Dixit, Gene M. Grossman and Faruk Gul, 'The dynamics of political compromise' (2000) 108 *Journal of Political Economy* 531 (the prospect of an indefinite sequence of reasonably frequent changes in power may also give democratically elected leaders an incentive to cooperate with political opponents in the hope of receiving reciprocal treatment when they are out of power). Other scholars have observed, and Olson acknowledges, that democracies are vulnerable to interest group pressures, voter ignorance and misinformation, and majoritarian forms of oppression of minorities, and that some democratic regimes are likely to be weak, unstable or corrupt. See Olson, supra note 25. See also Carothers, supra note 5.

35 Dani Rodrik, *One Economics, Many Recipes: Globalization, Institutions and Economic Growth* (Princeton, NJ: Princeton University Press, 2008), particularly Chapter 5. Gerring et al. also discuss a similar idea of 'institutionalization of power': see Gerring et al., *supra* note 23 at 333–4.

36 Sen, *Development as Freedom*, *supra* note 27 at 148.

37 Amartya Sen, *The Idea of Justice* (Cambridge, MA: Harvard University Press, 2009), particularly Chapters 15 and 16.

38 Consistent with his argument that democracy is not a uniquely Western con-

D. The Case against Democracy

Democracy is not always viewed as being conducive to promoting development. Several arguments are commonly made against democracy and in favour of more authoritarian regimes, at least in the early stages of a country's development. These arguments find their contemporary origins in writings by prominent US political scientists.[39] There are at least four major arguments against democracy.[40]

First, democracy is likely to unleash pressures for immediate consumption, which occurs at the cost of savings and investment, and hence of economic growth.[41] Second, authoritarian regimes often insulate the state from particularistic, special-interest group pressures, and are able to take a more comprehensive, single-minded and decisive approach to pro-development policies that may entail short-run pain in order to secure long-term gain.[42] Third, democracy may threaten the security of private property rights in cases where median voters (given a typically skewed income distribution) and special interests strongly favour redistributive policies.[43] Finally, democracies may exacerbate ethnic and other intergroup conflicts if parties organize themselves along ethnic, religious or regional lines and electoral competition yields dominant parties or political bodies that practise 'winner-takes-all' politics (as we discuss more fully in the third part of this chapter).[44]

On this view, citizens of countries in the early stages of economic

---

ception, Sen argues that these examples of 'government by discussion' are democratic notwithstanding the fact that they may not have taken the organizational form of modern Western competitive multiparty political regimes.

[39] Seymour Martin Lipset, 'Some social requisites of democracy: economic development and political legitimacy' (1959) 53 *American Political Science Review* 69; Samuel Huntington, *Political Order in Changing Societies* (New Haven: Yale University Press, 1968).

[40] These arguments are well reviewed in Chapter 1 of Morton Halperin, Joseph Siegle and Michael Weinstein, *The Democracy Advantage: How Democracies Promote Prosperity and Peace* (New York: Routledge, 2010, rev. edn).

[41] Bhagwati, *supra* note 7 and Przeworski et al., *supra* note 30 at 143.

[42] Ronald Gilson and Curtis Milhaupt, 'Economically benevolent dictators: lessons for developing countries' (2011) 59 *American Journal of Comparative Law* 227–88.

[43] Adam Przeworski, 'The neo-liberal fallacy', in Diamond and Plattner, *supra* note 7, 39; Dan Usher, *The Economic Prerequisite to Democracy* (New York: Columbia University Press, 1986).

[44] See section III *infra*.

development face 'a cruel choice' between democracy and development.[45] Proponents of the view 'economic development first; democracy later' often point to the post-war economic successes of East Asian autocracies, including most recently China, as evidence that democracy need not precede development.

E. The Empirical Evidence

The empirical evidence concerning the relationship between democracy and development is as contentious as the theorizing. Przeworski and Limongi summarize 18 studies containing 21 observations about the relationship between democracy and growth.[46] Eight observations favoured democracy, eight favoured authoritarianism, and five found no difference. Helliwell, in a multiple regression analysis of data pertaining to a sample of about one hundred countries from 1960 to 1985, concludes that the effects of introducing democracy on *subsequent* economic growth appear to be minimal.[47] A subsequent statistical study of 137 countries between 1950 and 1990 published by Przeworski et al. in 2000 finds that the net effect of democracy or autocracy on economic growth is zero.[48] However, a more recent study by Halperin, Siegle and Weinstein of a large sample of countries for the period between 1960 and 2001 finds that democracies (at least full liberal democracies) generally outperform autocracies in terms of economic growth by a significant margin, as well as exhibit less economic volatility and far fewer 'economic disasters'.[49] Their study also finds that democracies perform better on other social indicators such as literacy rates, life expectancy rates and infant mortality rates.[50]

Lindert suggests that the debate over the relationship between democracy and growth remains unresolved because of weaknesses in the studies of this relationship. He argues that many of the studies of the relationship between democracy and economic development (or growth)

---

45 Bhagwati, *supra* note 7; Maravell, *supra* note 7; and Stephan Haggard and Robert R. Kaufmann, *The Political Economy of Democratic Transitions* (Princeton, NJ: Princeton University Press, 1995) at 184–6.

46 Przeworski and Limongi, *supra* note 8.

47 Helliwell, *supra* note 10.

48 Przeworski et al., *supra* note 30 at 142–79; Krieckhaus argues that whether democracy may lead to economic growth depends on the country's regional context: see Jonathan Krieckhaus, 'Democracy and economic growth: how regional context influences regime effects' (2006) 36 *British Journal of Political Science* 217.

49 Halperin et al., *supra* note 40, Chapter 2.

50 Ibid., Chapter 2.

rely on a simplistic dichotomy between democratic and non-democratic regimes, and fail to discriminate between democracies that are genuine, full-franchise democracies and those that are not (what he calls 'elite-rule'). Lindert contends that cross-country studies also often ignore the fact that many democracies became effective full-franchise democracies only relatively recently.[51] He argues that the evidence tentatively suggests that genuine full-franchise democracies typically are more strongly committed to providing effective levels of support for basic universal education; he further argues that in the contemporary global economy where human capital is often the most important factor of production, genuine full-franchise democracies are likely to be a significant determinant of a country's future growth trajectory as a result of increased investment in public primary education.[52]

Proponents of democracy also argue that the economic success of East Asian autocracies has little to do with the basic political regime but rather is related to factors such as (1) the adoption of outward-oriented growth policies,[53] and (2) the insulation of the bureaucracy from day-to-day political pressures.[54] They also note that a number of economies in Asia such as Burma, Cambodia and Laos have performed poorly under authoritarian regimes.[55] Furthermore, the tendency in the region is toward the evolution of authoritarian-pluralist regimes with increasingly democratic features (for example, Japan, Taiwan, South Korea and Singapore).[56]

Although economic liberalization has often preceded political liberalization, the upheavals in Eastern and Central Europe over the past two decades followed the opposite sequence. In these cases, authoritarian regimes were replaced by democratic regimes, some of which then embarked on a process of economic liberalization. These attempts at more or less simultaneous political and economic liberalization are largely without precedent. They have sparked intense debates over whether a comprehensive package of economic reform should be implemented in the

---

[51] Peter Lindert, 'Voice and growth: was Churchill right?' (2003) 63 *Journal of Economic History* 315.

[52] Ibid. See Boone, *supra* note 26.

[53] See Bhagwati, *supra* note 7 and Robert Wade, *Governing the Market: Economic Theory and the Role of Government in East Asian Industrialization* (Princeton, NJ: Princeton University Press, 1992).

[54] Pei, *supra* note 1; Robert Wade, ibid.; World Bank, *The East Asian Miracle: Economic Growth and Public Policy* (New York: Oxford University Press for the World Bank, 1993).

[55] Pei, ibid.

[56] Kim, *supra* note 11.

short period of extraordinary politics that follows a change of regime,[57] or whether the absence of open and sustained public debate over the economic reform package undermines the political legitimacy of the economic reforms.[58]

It is similarly argued that comprehensive constitutional reform, including the adoption of a full panoply of liberal political rights, should be undertaken during this 'window of opportunity' – a 'big bang' approach to both economic and political reform.[59] It may, however, be premature to reach a judgment on whether this simultaneous process of political and economic reform will prove successful.[60] To date, the evidence is mixed. Countries such as the Czech Republic, Poland and Hungary – which enjoyed a substantial measure of political and economic liberalization earlier in their histories – and some of the Baltic states appear to have managed both processes reasonably well. By contrast, in other Central and Eastern European countries, the prospects for both economic and political reform seem to be much less encouraging.[61]

Based on this mixed body of evidence, some commentators conclude that democracy may not be conducive to the emergence of capitalism and its early growth, but that it is the regime most likely to develop and be sustainable once societies reach a certain level of economic development.[62] Other commentators contest the proposition that authoritarian governments have been better than democratic governments, at least in recent years, at pursuing major economic reforms.[63] As *The Economist*

---

57 Anders Aslund, 'The case for radical reform' (1994) 5:4 *Journal of Democracy* 63; Leszek Balcerowicz, 'Understanding post-Communist transitions' (1994) 5:4 *Journal of Democracy* 75.

58 Adam Przeworski, *Democracy and the Market: Political and Economic Reforms in Eastern Europe and Latin America* (New York: Cambridge University Press, 1991).

59 Bruce Ackerman, *The Future of Liberal Revolution* (New Haven: Yale University Press, 1992).

60 As Barbara Geddes remarks, 'political scientists spend much of their time explaining events that have not finished happening': Barbara Geddes, 'Challenging the conventional wisdom' (1994) 5:4 *Journal of Democracy* 104 at 117.

61 Joel S. Migdal, *Strong Societies and Weak States: State-Society Relations and State Capabilities in the Third World* (Princeton, NJ: Princeton University Press, 1988); Joan M. Nelson, *Economic Crisis and Policy Choice: The Politics of Adjustment in the Third World* (Princeton, NJ: Princeton University Press, 1990); and Przeworski, *supra* note 58.

62 Berger, *supra* note 7. For a review of the literature, see Halperin et al., *supra* note 40 at Chapter 1.

63 Geddes, *supra* note 60; Sen, *supra* note 23; and Halperin et al., *supra* note 40 at Chapter 3.

points out, if authoritarian governments eventually make countries rich, especially in the early stages of economic development, Africa would be or should soon become an economic colossus.[64] Instead, some of the more pessimistic prognoses for the future of Africa depict a mafia-like world of social and political disintegration characterized by war, tribute, predation and criminalization of economic activity, as local warlords struggle to extort Africa's most useful resources for sale to the highest international bidders while creating tens of thousands of refugees in the process.[65]

Other commentators argue that authoritarian regimes may be better suited to managing the economic reforms that must occur as a country moves from communism to capitalism. Leszek Balcerowicz argues, for example, that three main categories of initiatives will often have to be contemplated when implementing economic reform in post-Communist countries: first, macroeconomic stabilization; second, microeconomic liberalization; and third, fundamental institutional restructuring.[66] Macroeconomic stabilization entails radical changes in monetary and fiscal policy that are designed to counteract hyperinflationary trends and related distortions affecting consumption, savings and investment behaviour. Microeconomic liberalization is designed to remove various state-imposed restrictions on economic activity that create policy-induced price distortions by driving a wedge between prices and real resource costs, thereby undermining the price system as a signalling and incentive mechanism. These types of policy are captured by the axiom 'getting prices right'. Fundamental institutional restructuring is aimed at privatizing state enterprises, reforming the tax system and creating new financial and regulatory institutions.[67] In the face of a major economic crisis, democracies may have no choice but to address the first two classes of issues, even though this may cause serious pain for the population at large. However, democracies may encounter much more difficulty in embarking upon fundamental institutional reform, where loss of jobs, income, status and other perquisites and rents may be much more narrowly concentrated.[68] Hence, on this view, authoritarian governments may have an advantage over democratic regimes in forcing fundamental institutional restructuring.

---

[64] *The Economist, supra* note 10.

[65] Thomas Callaghy, 'Africa: back to the future?' (1994) 5:4 *Journal of Democracy* 133.

[66] Balcerowicz, *supra* note 57.

[67] Ibid.

[68] Joan M. Nelson, 'Linkages between politics and economics' (1994) 5:4 *Journal of Democracy* 49.

Focusing on the poorest billion people in the world living in 60 of the poorest countries in the world, Collier finds that democracy is actually damaging to the reform process if it means little more than elections.[69] At very low levels of per capita income, moving from despotism to a nominally democratic regime may actually increase political violence and do nothing to enhance accountability or legitimacy. In the absence of effective checks and balances, despots will engage in various forms of intimidation, repression and bribery of voters, fraud and other electoral irregularities, and then claim the facade of democracy to further entrench themselves in power.

F. Challenges to Reforming Political Institutions

Despite the euphoria in many development circles over the recent wave of democratization, Carothers offers a sobering assessment.[70] According to Carothers, of the nearly one hundred countries considered as being in transition to democracy, only a relatively small number – probably fewer than twenty – are clearly on their way to becoming successful, well-functioning democracies. According to Diamond, the 1999 Pakistani coup initiated the reversal of the wave of democratization from its peak, and there has been democratic recession ever since.[71] Diamond argues that this reversal was symptomatic of 'deep-seated problems of governance with which many other new and fragile democracies were also struggling'.[72] The troubled attempts to install democratic political regimes in Iraq and Afghanistan are some of the more prominent contemporary examples of the challenging task of democratic reform.[73] In a 2010 report, Freedom House found that liberty, human rights and the number of free democracies in the world had been declining for four consecutive years.[74]

Carothers argues that five questionable assumptions define the conventional transition paradigm. First, any country moving away from dictatorial rule can be considered to be a country in transition toward democracy. Second, democratization tends to unfold in a set pattern of stages: the opening, the breakthrough and the consolidation. Third, elections are

---

69 Collier, *supra* note 18 at 45.

70 Carothers, *supra* note 5 at 5. See also Thomas Carothers, *Aiding Democracy Abroad* (Carnegie Endowment for International Peace, 1999).

71 Diamond, *supra* note 2 at Chapter 4.

72 Ibid., at 60.

73 See Trebilcock and Chitalkar, *supra* note 19.

74 Freedom House, *supra* note 3.

of determinative importance. Fourth, the underlying conditions in transitional countries – their economic level, political history, institutional legacies, ethnic makeup, socio-cultural traditions or other 'structural' features – will not be major factors in either the onset or the outcome of the transition process. Fifth, democratic transitions making up the recent wave of democratization are being built on coherent, functioning states.

Carothers considers all of these assumptions to be problematic. In contrast, he argues that many countries in transition from authoritarianism to democracy reflect two persistent syndromes: 'feckless pluralism' and 'dominant power politics'. 'Feckless pluralism' refers to situations in which small, deeply entrenched political elites periodically alternate power and enrich themselves at the expense of the general population. 'Dominant power politics' refers to situations where one party, despite periodic elections, dominates government over long periods of time and often governs with little heed for the general interests of the population.

Some scholars caution that the deliberation, cooperation and compromise ideally associated with democracy cannot readily be imposed through top-down measures. Instead, reform must occur from the bottom up, through thick prior networks of associational activity – civil society or 'social capital' – that have already cultivated these norms, which can then be scaled up to regional or national democratic governments.[75] However, other scholars point out that many forms of social capital are parochial, exclusionary, discriminatory, or repressive, such as the social capital that resides within the Ku Klux Klan and the Mafia. These scholars argue that desirable forms of social capital cultivate a wider radius of trust and that these forms of social capital evolve organically and are not readily constructible by deliberate public policies.[76]

In designing reforms of political institutions, it is important to be sensitive to the specific characteristics of each country. Generalizations about the relationship between democracy and development or binary distinctions between democracy and autocracy[77] offer very little useful guid-

---

[75] See, e.g., Robert Putnam, *Making Democracy Work: Civic Traditions in Modern Italy* (Princeton, NJ: Princeton University Press, 1994); Peter B. Evans, 'Government action, social capital and development: reviewing the evidence on synergy' (1996) 24 *World Development* 1119; and Peter B. Evans, *Embedded Autonomy* (Princeton, NJ: Princeton University Press, 1996).

[76] Francis Fukuyama, 'Social capital, civil society, and development' (2001) 22 *Third World Quarterly* 7.

[77] Authoritarianism comes in almost as many shades as democracy, ranging from pro-development soft authoritarianism to grossly tyrannical or repressive kleptocracies.

ance or policy-relevant information on the design of particular political regimes.

Even democratic political regimes in the developed world vary vastly in their formal institutional features: some are presidential, others parliamentary; some are unicameral, some bicameral; some are unitary states, others federal states; some have tight political party structures, while others have much looser structures; some employ majority or first-past-the-post voting, while others have adopted some form of proportional representation; some tightly regulate election campaign expenditures, others subsidize these expenditures from public resources, while still others do little of either; some have adopted an entrenched bill of rights and constitutional judicial review as constraints on legislative and executive action while others have not, and so on.[78] The political arrangements that are feasible in a country will, to an important extent, be a function of each country's history, culture and institutional legacies.[79] As with the rule of law and other institutional reforms, path dependence may significantly constrain the reform options that are feasible for a country's political regime, at least in terms of the organizational form if not the underlying rationale.

III. POLITICAL REGIMES AND ETHNIC CONFLICT[80]

Ethnic conflict occurs when there is intense rivalry, disputes or clashes of interests between groups that are organized along racial, religious, linguistic or communal lines.[81] It includes (but is not limited to) political

---

[78] Francis Fukuyama, 'Development and the limits of institutional design', Global Development Network, St Petersburg, Russia, 20 January 2006.

[79] Oona Hathaway, 'The case for promoting democracy through export control' (2010) 33 *Harvard Journal of Law and Public Policy* 17.

[80] Our analysis is largely based on the literature review developed by Theresa Miedema, 'Understanding ethno-nations and ethnic conflict', unpublished manuscript (on file with the authors), and the first chapter of her doctoral dissertation, *Social Capital and Violent Conflict in Ethnically-Polarized Developing Countries,* unpublished manuscript (on file with the authors). We are also deeply grateful to her for providing comments on an earlier draft of this session. All remaining errors are our sole responsibility.

[81] For an overview of the concept of 'ethnicity', see Donald L. Horowitz, *Ethnic Groups in Conflict* (Berkeley and Los Angeles, California: University of California Press, 2000, 2nd edn). See also Pranab Bardhan, *Scarcity, Conflicts, and Cooperation: Essays in the Political and Institutional Economics of Development* (Cambridge, MA: MIT Press, 2005) at 169.

competition between ethnically-based political actors, various forms of discrimination, and violence between ethnic groups. These conflicts represent the majority of ongoing armed conflicts around the world; in 2009, the Center for Systemic Peace reported that of 30 ongoing conflicts, 19 were ethnic in nature.[82] These 19 ethnic conflicts were largely concentrated in developing countries, and 16 took place in low- and low-middle income countries.[83] Ethnic conflict not only subverts peace and stability, resulting in enormous human suffering and losses, but also destroys vital infrastructure and imposes significant economic costs. As a consequence, ethnic conflict threatens human security and well-being, undermines economic growth, and detrimentally affects many other development indicators.[84] As Collier puts it, ethnic conflict is 'development in reverse'.[85] Thus, the question of whether and how these conflicts can be avoided or mitigated is extremely important from a development perspective.

Determining whether and how ethnic conflict can be resolved or managed, and assessing the potential role of institutions in responding to such conflict requires an understanding of the root causes of ethnic conflict. This is no easy task, however. Beyond a general agreement that ethnic conflict has devastating consequences, virtually every aspect of ethnic conflict is contested in the academic literature. Scholars from fields as diverse as anthropology, history, economics, law, political science, psychology and sociology have weighed in on matters ranging from the nature of eth-

---

[82] Center for Systemic Peace, 'Major episodes of political violence 1946–2008', May 2009, available at http://www.systemicpeace.org/warlist.htm.

[83] Ibid.

[84] See, e.g., Frances Stewart, Cindy Huang and Michael Wang, 'Internal wars in developing countries: an empirical overview of economic and social consequences', in Frances Stewart and Valpy Fitzgerald (eds) *War and Underdevelopment*, Vol. 1 (Oxford, UK: Oxford University Press, 2001) at 67; Duncan Pederson, 'Political violence, ethnic conflict, and contemporary wars: broad implications for health and social well-being' (2002) 55 *Social Science and Medicine* 175; Sanjeev Gupta et al, 'Fiscal consequences of armed conflict and terrorism in low- and middle-income countries' (2004) 20 *European Journal of Political Economy* 403 at 410; Dani Rodrik, 'Where did all the growth go: external shocks, social conflicts, and growth collapses' (1999) *Journal of Economic Growth* 385; Paul Collier, 'On the economic consequences of civil war' (1999) 51 *Oxford Economic Papers* 168 at 175; Paul Collier et al., *Breaking the Conflict Trap: Civil War and Development* (Washington, DC: The World Bank and Oxford University Press, 2003) at 17; and T. Addison, A.R. Chowdhury and S.M. Murshed, 'By how much does conflict reduce financial development?' WIDER Discussion Paper No. 2002/38 (Helsinki: World Institute for Development Economics Research, United Nations University, 2002).

[85] Paul Collier, *The Bottom Billion: Why the Poorest Countries are Failing and What Can Be Done About It* (Oxford: Oxford University Press, 2007) at 27.

nicity and ethnic affiliation, to ethnic mobilization, to the sources of ethnic conflict, to the role of institutions and other social structures in triggering or mitigating ethnic conflict. There is little consensus in the literature on definitions, methodologies, causalities or conclusions. Drawing on the work of Horowitz,[86] Bardhan observes that

> existing theories of ethnic conflict are often characterized by two sharply distinguished views of ethnicity – the 'hard view', which sees ethnicity as a *primordial* condition that evokes intense passions and takes ethnic groups as exogenously defined, and the 'soft' view, which takes a more strategic *constructivist* approach where ethnicity is subject to interests and calculations and group boundaries are somewhat malleable.[87]

It is beyond the scope of this chapter to review the extensive literature on ethnic conflict in any detail. Instead, the following discussion will focus on the intersection of ethnic conflict and institutions. Based on the constructivist view that ethnicity is subject to *interests and calculations*, but also acknowledging the emotive power of ethnic affiliation, we will discuss how political systems interact with ethnicity in potentially dangerous ways; we will also analyse some institutional strategies to reduce the risk of ethnic fractionalization erupting into violent ethnic conflict. We will begin by discussing some of the distal causes of ethnic conflict – namely the factors that motivate ethnic affiliation and mobilization and the circumstances under which ethnic affiliation becomes a source of tension. We will then consider some of the immediate causes of violent ethnic conflict. While the specific causes of ethnic conflict vary from case to case,[88] there are patterns and trends that can provide some insight into common causes. In this regard, we will examine the factors that trigger and sustain conflict as ethnic rivalries spill over into violence. Finally, we will consider possible solutions.

A. Ethnic Affiliations

For those who take the strategic constructivist approach to ethnicity with its emphasis on interests and calculations, the salience of ethnic affiliation is a function of its instrumentality. Ethnicity emerges in response to societal needs and/or the interests of certain groups, often as a mechanism

---

86 See Horowitz, *supra* note 81.

87 Bardhan, *supra* note 81 at 169–70.

88 Stefan Wolff, *Ethnic Conflict: a Global Perspective* (New York: Oxford University Press, 2006).

to solve collective action problems.[89] Collier, for example, suggests that in rural societies where people live at subsistence levels, strong ethnic affiliations act as a form of insurance; in the case of a catastrophe or personal difficulties, the ethnic group provides for the needs of its members.[90] Collier argues that '[o]ver time, loyalty to the group becomes reinforced by all the normal power of morality: it is morally good to meet your obligations'.[91] Ethnic affiliations thus generate a strong and lasting expectation of loyalty, which in turn reduces the problem of free-riding; one cannot enjoy the benefits of being a member of an ethnic group during difficult times but then abandon the group as one's personal fortunes improve.[92]

Ethnic affiliation also facilitates economic activity among its members. Shared membership in an ethnic group can act as a proxy for reliability and can serve as the basis for the development of trust between people.[93] Moreover, the authority structures and norms within an ethnic group, including social sanctions for cheating and defaulting on contractual commitments, deter opportunistic behaviour and thus facilitate more complex commercial transactions and contractual arrangements.[94] Ethnic ties also

---

89 Collier, *supra* note 18 at 52–3.

90 Ibid., at 53.

91 Ibid., at 53.

92 For examples of how members of an ethnic group work together to provide social insurance-type benefits to members in need, see Thomas Heberer, 'Ethnic entrepreneurs as agents of social change – the impact of ethnic entrepreneurship on social change and ethnicity, a case study among the Yi in Liangshan Autonomous Prefecture in China', in Armin Bohnet and Matthias Hoher (eds), *The Role of Minorities in the Development Process* (Frankfurt am Main: Peter Lang, 2004) at 63; Jean-Paul Azam, 'The redistributive state and conflicts in Africa' (2001) 38 *Journal of Peace Research* 429; Sylvie Lambert, 'La migration comme instrument de diversification des risques dans la famille ivoirienne' ['Migration as a risk diversification device in the Ivorian family'] (1994) 94 *Revue d'économie du développement* 3; Paul Collier and Deepak Lal, *Labour and Poverty in Kenya, 1900–1980* (Oxford: Oxford University Press, 1986); and Ryszard Kapuscinski, *The Shadow of the Sun,* Klara Glowczewska (trans.) (Toronto: Vintage Canada, 2002) at 36.

93 See Janet Tai Landa, *Trust, Ethnicity, and Identity: Beyond the New Institutional Economics of Ethnic Trading Networks, Contract Law, and Gift-Exchange* (Ann Arbor: University of Michigan Press, 1994) at 108–13; D. Gambatta, *Trust: Making and Breaking Cooperative Relations* (New York: Basil Blackwell, 1988); Francis Fukuyama, *Trust: The Social Virtues and the Creation of Prosperity* (New York: The Free Press Paperbacks, 1995); and B. Cornell and I. Welch, 'Culture, information and screening discrimination' (1996) 104 *Journal of Political Economy* 542.

94 For examples of such norms, see Easterly's discussion of the practices of the Hausa in Ibadan, Nigeria and the overseas Chinese in Southeast Asia: William

facilitate the circulation of information about prices, market conditions and reliability of buyers and sellers.[95]

Borjas refers to the bonds between members of the same ethnic group, and the embedded norms, traditions, knowledge, and support that are inherent within those bonds, as being a form of capital.[96] However, while ethnic affiliation is a useful mechanism for organizing collective action, many of the goods and utilities provided by the ethnic group can in principle be delivered by a functioning state.[97] The problem is that many developing countries do not have well-functioning states, which heightens the importance of ethnic groups in developing countries. Azam observes that the capital existing in the bonds of ethnic affiliation ('ethnic capital') 'ensures to most African people the provision of many services that a modern state has taken over in rich countries, including security, social insurance, education, norms of behaviour, contract enforcement, justice and so on'.[98] There are therefore strong incentives to organize most facets of life along ethnic lines in countries with weak state structures. For example, a dysfunctional judiciary that offers little certainty about the ability to enforce contracts may create incentives to engage only in commercial transactions that can be monitored within an ethnic group.

Even where governmental institutions are functional, institutional structures may create incentives for political affiliation along ethnic lines. That ethnicity is used as a tool for political mobilization is not surprising given the doctrine of ethno-nationalism, which holds that the bounds of the political unit should be coextensive with that of the ethnic group.[99]

Easterly, *The White Man's Burden: Why the West's Efforts to Aid the Rest Have Done So Much Ill and So Little Good* (New York, NY: Penguin, 2006) at 82–3.

[95] Marcel Fafchamps and Bart Minten, 'Returns to social network capital among traders' (2002) 54 *Oxford Economic Papers* 173. See also Marcel Fafchamps, 'The role of business networks in market development in sub-Saharan Africa', in Masahiko Aoki and Yujiro Hayami (eds), *Communities and Markets in Economic Development* (Oxford: Oxford University Press, 2001), available at Oxford Scholarship Online: http://dx.doi.org/10.1093/0199241015.001.0001.

[96] Borjas referred to this capital as 'ethnic capital'. See George J. Borjas, 'Ethnic capital and intergenerational mobility' (1992) *107 Quarterly Journal of Economics* 123.

[97] Collier, *supra* note 18 at 56.

[98] Jean-Paul Azam, 'The redistributive state and conflicts in Africa' (2001) 38 *Journal of Peace Research* 429 at 430.

[99] Ernest Gellner provides one of the most coherent definitions of nationalism: Ethno-nationalism is 'a theory of political legitimacy, which requires that ethnic boundaries should not cut across political ones, and, in particular, that ethnic boundaries within a given state . . . should not separate the power-holders from the rest': see Ernest Gellner, *Nations and Nationalism* (Ithaca, NY:

The doctrine of ethno-nationalism infused ethnicity with the legitimate exercise of political power, thereby setting the foundation for political mobilization along ethnic lines and grounding ethnic groups' claims to the rights of autonomy and sovereignty. Proponents of modernization theory argue that ethno-nationalism developed as a result of key socio-political and economic changes that occurred as feudal and agrarian societies grew into liberal, industrialized and urban states.[100] These changes increased the importance of ethnic identity to individuals while, at the same time, creating many new opportunities for social, economic and political power. Ethnicity thus emerged as an effective vehicle for pursuing these opportunities.

Scholars who espouse resource competition theory[101] make similar arguments to those of the modernization theorists, although the former focus primarily on the competition for resources rather than the forces that fused ethnicity with the pursuit of social, political and economic power. Resource competition theory scholars argue that the need to compete for jobs, power, privilege and political influence provides individuals with strong incentives to organize along group lines in order to minimize transaction costs and to increase the benefits accruing to them. Barth pioneered the application of resource competition theory to ethnic groups. He argued that ethnicity should be viewed as 'a system of boundaries between groups whose power and relevance are determined primarily

---

Cornell University Press, 1983) at 1. For other constructivist accounts of the emergence of ethno-nationalism see Eric Hobsbawn, *Nations and Nationalism since 1780: Programme, Myth, Reality* (Cambridge, UK: Cambridge University Press, 1990, 2nd edn) and Benedict Anderson, *Imagined Communities: Reflections on the Origin and Spread of Nationalism* (London, UK: Verso, 1991, revised edn) at 5.

[100] For examples of scholars who espouse modernization theory, see Karl W. Deutsch, 'Social mobilization and political development' (1961) 55 *American Political Science Review* 493 at 493; Karl W. Deutsch, *Nationalism and Social Communication: An Inquiry into the Foundations of Nationality* (Cambridge, MA: MIT Press, 1967, 2nd edn) at 188; Gellner, ibid.; Eric Hobsbawn, ibid.; and Benedict Anderson, ibid. Each scholar has a unique view on how the forces of modernization contributed to social mobilization on the basis of ethnicity and on how modernization triggers ethnic conflict.

[101] For the pioneering work on resource competition theory and ethnic conflict, see Fredrik Barth, *Ethnic Groups and Boundaries* (Boston: Little, Brown, 1969). For more examples of the application of resource competition theory, see Joanne Nagel, 'Resource competition theories' (1995) 38:3 *American Behavioral Scientist* 442 and John Mukum Mbaku, 'Ethnicity, constitutionalism, and governance in Africa', in John Mukum Mbaku, Pita Ogaba Agbese and Mwangi S. Kimenyi (eds), *Ethnicity and Governance in the Third World* (Aldershot: Ashgate, 2001).

by the nature and scope of contact and competition for scarce resources among ethnic cleavages'.[102]

Scholars point to two types of socio-economic factors that make ethnicity the preferred vehicle for pursuing social, political, and economic opportunities – namely, historical and emergent factors. Historical factors include the cultural division of labour[103] and a split labour market,[104] while emergent factors include labour migration and immigration.[105] The coincidence of ethnic divisions with economic divisions brings ethnicity to the fore as an efficient means of collective organization in the pursuit of jobs and other opportunities. Political opportunities also serve as a basis for ethnic mobilization. The factors that act as an incentive to mobilize along the lines of ethnic affiliation include:

> (1) common language and culture, and the existence of ethnic organizational structures that can allow contenders for political office to minimize transaction costs; (2) possession of large deposits of exploitable environmental resources (e.g., petroleum, natural gas, diamonds and other minerals, etc.) by an ethno-regional group; and (3) historical domination of some groups by others.[106]

As this discussion illustrates, a variety of scholars have pointed to a connection between ethnic affiliation and the competition for scarce resources. Assuming these scholars are at least partially right, then under certain circumstances *interests and calculations* can influence and determine ethnic affiliations, as well as increase the importance of these affiliations. As we will discuss below, the use of ethnicity to pursue scarce resources is a source of tension in many states; moreover, certain institutional structures are better than others at managing ethnic tension and rivalry in this context.

---

102 Mbaku, ibid. at 60, referring to the work of Barth in *Ethnic Groups and Boundaries,* ibid. See also Nagel, ibid. at 442–3.

103 For a detailed discussion of how the cultural division of labour impacts ethnic mobilization and ethnic conflict, see M. Hechter, 'Group formation and the cultural division of labour' (1978) 84 *American Journal of Sociology* 293 and M. Hechter and M. Levi, 'The comparative analysis of ethnoregional movements' (1979) 2 *Ethnic and Racial Studies* 260. See also Mbaku, *supra* note 101 at 63–4.

104 See, e.g., E. Bonacich, 'A theory of ethnic antagonism: the split labor market' (1972) 37 *American Sociological Review* 547 and E. Bonacich, 'The past, present, and future of split labor market theory' (1979) 1 *Research in Race and Ethnic Relations* 17. See also Mbaku, *supra* note 101 at 64-65.

105 Mbaku, *supra* note 101 at 63–5.

106 Ibid. at 65.

B. Ethnic Tension and Rivalry

The literature on ethnic conflict points to three broad inter-related factors that influence the intensity of ethnic rivalry and tension in the polity: (1) contact and the fact of ethnic difference; (2) the degree of diversity; and (3) the institutional structures in which competition for scarce resources occurs.[107] Drawing on the work of Deutsch, Forbes analyses how ethnic difference contributes to conflict when ethnic groups come into contact with each other.[108] When groups that were formerly isolated from each other come into contact as a result of processes such as modernization, urbanization, centralized education and economic specialization, they must find a means of effectively communicating and coordinating their actions. In the context of development, particularly in the post-colonial period, major decisions also have to be made about how ethnic groups will order their coexistence within the polity. Coexistence and coordinated action ultimately require some degree of homogenization of the ethnic

---

[107] These factors represent the views of scholars who take a highly constructivist view of ethnicity that emphasizes interests and calculations. Other scholars who cannot properly be described as primordialists emphasize softer variables, including socio-psychological processes. Examples include categorization theory and social identity theory. For a discussion of psychological factors related to ethnic conflict (including, for example, 'belongingness want' – the need to belong to a group), see C. Hayes, *The Historical Evolution of Modern Nationalism* (New York: Russell and Russell,1968); Dusan Kecmanovic, *The Mass Psychology of Ethnonationalism* (New York, NY: Plenum Press, 1996); David Krech, Richard S. Crutchfield and Egerton L. Ballachey, *Individual in Society: A Textbook of Social Psychology* (New York: McGraw-Hill, 1962); and Donald M. Taylor and Fathali M. Moghaddam, *Theories of Intergroup Relations: International Social Psychological Perspectives* (Westport, CT: Praeger, 1994, 2nd edn). For a discussion of categorization theory, see Joshua Searle-White, *The Psychology of Nationalism* (New York, NY: Palgrave, 2001). For a discussion of social identity theory, see Henri Tajfel and John C. Turner, 'An integrative theory of intergroup conflict', in W.G. Austin and S. Worchel (eds), *The Social Psychology of Intergroup Relations* (Monterey, CA: Brooks/Cole, 1979); Henri Tajfel and John C. Turner, 'The social identity theory of intergroup behavior', in S. Worchel and G. Austin (eds), *Psychology of Intergroup Relations* (Chicago: Nelson-Hall, 1986); John C. Turner, 'Some current issues in research on social identity and self-categorization theories', in Naomi Ellemers, Russell Spears and Bertjan Doosje (eds), *Social Identity* (Oxford: Blackwell, 1999); and Henri Tajfel, 'Social categorization, social identity, and social comparison', in Henri Tajfel (ed.), *Differentiation between Social Groups* (London: Academic Press, 1978) at 63.

[108] See H.D. Forbes, *Ethnic Conflict: Commerce, Culture, and the Contact Hypothesis* (New Haven: Yale University Press, 1997). See also Deutsch, 'Social mobilization', *supra* note 100, and Deutsch, 'Nationalism', *supra* note 100.

groups' different norms, institutions, social structures, language and cultural practices. The groups that are unable to impose their language, social structures and institutions on the others must bear the transaction costs associated with learning a new language and set of institutional practices. Moreover, conceding/assimilating groups are less likely to be able to dominate social, political and economic institutions and structures of the shared polity and, consequently, have restricted access to the scarce resources available through these institutions. The process of homogenization thus engenders conflict because each group has strong incentives to resist making concessions in the determination of the common language, norms and institutions.

The degree of ethnic fragmentation in a polity also influences the intensity of ethnic rivalry and tension, likely because of the incentive structures that exist at different levels of diversity. Collier's empirical research shows that ethnically diverse societies with democratic regimes actually face fewer risks of civil conflict; by contrast, societies characterized by dominance (that is, where the largest ethnic group makes up 45 to 90 per cent of the total population) face higher risks of conflict.[109] Other authors confirm the observation that ethnic diversity per se does not increase the risk of conflict.[110]

In a truly diverse society, where there is a high degree of ethnic fragmentation, no ethnic group is large enough to secure a monopoly on power. Cross-ethnic alliances are necessary in order to secure access to political power and influence. In this context, ethnic elites have strong incentives to adopt moderate, non-ethnic positions and strategies. By contrast, in polarized polities, elections tend to divide the polity along ethnic lines, having a negative impact on electoral competition.[111] Collier suggests that electoral

---

[109] Paul Collier and Anke Hoeffler, 'Greed and grievances in civil war', World Bank Policy Research Working Paper 2355, CSAE WPS/2002-01 (Washington, DC: World Bank, 2001). For a succinct formulation of Collier's arguments on economic factors, see Paul Collier, 'Economic causes of civil conflict and their implications for policy', in Chester A. Crocker, Fen Osler Hampson and Pamela All (eds), *Leashing the Dogs of War: Conflict Management in a Divided World* (Washington, DC: United States Institute of Peace, 2007).

[110] José G. Montalvo and Marta Reynal-Querol, 'Ethnic polarization, potential conflict, and civil wars' (2005) 95 *American Economic Review* 796. But see Ravi Bhavnani and Dan Miodownik, 'Ethnic polarization, ethnic salience, and civil war' (2009) 53 *Journal of Conflict Resolution* 30 (claiming that ethnic salience is a relevant factor, especially when there are low levels of polarization).

[111] Wonbin Cho, 'Ethnic fractionalization, electoral institutions, and Africans' political attitudes', Afrobarometer Working Paper No. 66 (January 2007), available at http://next.pls.msu.edu/index.php.

competition in polarized societies can take political agendas to extremes since a candidate will draw larger support the more he or she promises to favour one group over another. Elites attempt to solidify support from their respective ethnic groups by 'rallying the faithful' through the use of ethno-centric rhetoric. In this regard, elites from the same ethnic group often attempt to 'outbid' each other for the support of their group by adopting increasingly radical platforms in order to demonstrate that they are the best protector of the group's interests.[112] Once elected, the ethnic elites in power must safeguard their own group's interests by providing access to influence and the scarce resources of the state while excluding elites from other ethnic groups from the political process. Elites must avoid the perception that they have made concessions to other ethnic groups or adopted moderate or conciliatory policies. This turns competition for political power into a zero-sum competition for resources and public goods.[113] Moreover, this competition is framed in terms of ethnic identity.[114] In sum, elites in fragmented societies have incentives to be bridge-builders between ethnic groups while elites in polarized societies have incentives to adopt ethno-centric and divisive platforms that increase the risk of conflict between ethnic groups.

The negative impact that higher degrees of ethnic polarization have on the political system may be influenced by the political structures that govern ethnically diverse societies. Rational choice theorists and public choice theorists argue that inter-ethnic violence arises or intensifies in response to a particular set of incentive structures.[115] On this view, some socio-economic and political structures are more likely to give rise to tension than others because of the incentive structures they create. Institutions that establish or perpetuate the domination of one group over another, or provide a group with a monopoly over wealth and/or power within a certain polity, tend to generate more conflict than institutions that

---

112 See, e.g., Neil Devotta, 'From ethnic outbidding to ethnic conflict: the institutional bases for Sri Lanka's separatist war' (2005) 11 *Nations and Nationalism* 141.

113 Collier, *supra* note 85 at 44–6.

114 Kenya is a recent example of how this dynamic may lead to conflict. But this is not a recent problem. See Human Rights Watch, *Divide and Rule: State-sponsored Ethnic Violence in Kenya* (New York: Human Rights Watch, 1993).

115 See, e.g., Michael Hechter and Satoshi Kanazawa, 'Sociological rational choice theory' (1997) 23 *Annual Review of Sociology* 191; Michael Hechter, 'Rational choice theory and the study of ethnic and race relations', in John Rex and David Mason (eds), *Theories of Ethnic and Race Relations* (Cambridge: Cambridge University Press, 1988); and Bhanu Mehta, 'Ethnicity, nationalism and violence in South Asia' (1998) 71 *Pacific Affairs* 377.

force ethnic groups to share power.[116] For instance, incentives to organize electoral competition along ethnic lines are higher in democratic regimes that permit ethnically-based party systems and have electoral rules such as winner-takes-all.[117] The risk of heightened ethnic tension that is associated with ethnic polarization and dominance can be managed by institutional arrangements (for example, electoral rules, constitutional provisions and property rights) that provide fair, predictable and efficient rules to govern the competition for scarce political and economic resources.[118]

In addition to political institutions, some socio-economic structures contribute to inter-ethnic rivalry. Socio-economic structures that either establish the dominance of one ethnic group over another (ethno-classes) or establish a monopoly of one ethnic group over limited resources to the detriment of others (middlemen minorities) can contribute to an increase in ethnic tension.[119]

In his book *Identity and Violence*, Sen suggests that inter-ethnic tensions only exist because people often place excessive emphasis on one-dimensional notions of identity, be it ethnicity or nationality.[120] The objective reality, however, is that each person's identity is multifaceted rather than one-dimensional and, so long as the various dimensions of a person's identity are not in conflict, they can coexist with each other.[121] Moreover, each person has the capacity and the freedom to determine which group loyalties and affiliations to prioritize.[122] On this view, the reduction of a person's identity to the single dimension of ethnicity or nationality should be avoided as it has the potential to generate conflict.

Sen's assessment seems to underestimate the importance of ethnicity in developing and developed countries alike, where ethnic groups often provide important goods and services and ethnic affiliation is still very

---

116 Donald Horowitz, 'Structure and strategy in ethnic conflict: a few steps toward synthesis', in Boris Pleskovic and Joseph E. Stiglitz (eds), *Annual World Bank Conference on Development Economics 1998* (Washington, DC: World Bank, 1999) 345.

117 Bardhan, *supra* note 81 at 183–4.

118 Mbaku, *supra* note 101 at 83.

119 Bardhan, *supra* note 81 at 171–6. See also Reed Coughlan and S.W.R. de A. Samarasinghe, 'Introduction – economic dimensions of ethnic conflict: theory and evidence', in Reed Coughlan and S.W.R. de A. Samarasinghe (eds), *Economic Dimensions of Ethnic Conflict* (London: Pinter Publishers, 1991).

120 Amartya Sen, *Identity and Violence: The Illusion of Destiny* (New York: W.W. Norton, 2006).

121 Ibid at 4–5; see also Kwame Anthony Appiah, *Cosmopolitanism: Ethics in a World of Strangers* (New York: W.W. Norton, 2006).

122 Ibid.

relevant to people's daily lives.[123] Sen does not present concrete proposals on how to mitigate the effects of these affiliations.[124] Other authors appear to advocate the deliberate choice of policies that can help to downplay ethnicity by superimposing a constructed national identity or assimilating ethnic groups into a shared, civic identity.[125] Collier cites Tanzania and Indonesia as successful examples in this regard: by using, creating or imposing a national language, Tanzanian President Julius Nyerere and Indonesian President Sukarno managed to mitigate ethnic divisions. In Tanzania, language policy was coupled with the creation of symbols of national identity, political reforms and education policies to reshape cultural identity. For example, Nyerere eschewed a multiparty system by creating village committees and prohibiting campaigns based on ethnic platforms.[126] Collier argues that, as both ethnic and national identities are constructed, these policies could be successfully replicated in other countries. Other authors, however, are more cautious about the prospects of transferability.[127] Moreover, Kymlicka argues that such policies may be sources of conflict in and of themselves since the process of forming a national or civic identity requires at least one group to assimilate to

---

[123] The perception of the United States, for instance, as a 'melting pot' where there is a large degree of cultural assimilation has been rejected by sociologists. See, e.g., Gordon Milton, *Assimilation in American Life* (New York: Oxford University Press, 1964) and Nathan Glazer and Daniel Moynihan, *Beyond the Melting Pot: The Negroes, Puerto Ricans, Jews, Italians and Irish of New York City* (Cambridge, MA: MIT Press, 1970). See also Joel Perlmann, *Ethnic Differences: Schooling and Social Structure Among the Irish, Italians, Jews, and Blacks in an American City, 1880–1935* (New York: Cambridge University Press, 1988) and Stephen Steinberg, *The Ethnic Myth: Race, Ethnicity, and Class in America* (Boston, MA: Beacon Press, 1989).

[124] To be sure, Sen presents proposals for institutional reforms both at the national and international levels, so as to address exclusion from the global economy and to reduce levels of inequality between poor and rich countries. These are not, however, related to notions of identity. Instead, they deal with the concern that grievances generated by exclusion and inequality might contribute to a rise in conflict.

[125] See Forbes, *supra* note 108 and Jon Orman, *Language Policy and Nation-Building in Post-Apartheid South Africa* (Springer Netherlands, 2009), particularly the chapter entitled 'Language policy, language planning and national identity: theoretical perspectives'. For a cautionary survey of experiences in Asian countries and some policy recommendations, see Michael E. Brown and Sumit Ganguly (eds), *Fighting Words: Language Policy and Ethnic Relations in Asia* (Cambridge, MA: MIT Press, 2003).

[126] Collier, *supra* note 18 at 67.

[127] See Will Kymlicka and Alan Patten (eds), *Language Rights and Political Theory* (Oxford: Oxford University Press, 2003).

the characteristics of whatever is deemed to be the 'national' or 'civic' identity.[128]

C. Factors that Trigger and Sustain Conflict

Why does violent conflict erupt between communities that have coexisted relatively peacefully for significant periods of time despite historical animosities? While institutional arrangements may increase tension and aggravate rivalries in ethnically diverse societies, they will not necessarily trigger conflict.[129] In many cases, there are factors that suddenly emerge, creating a shock to the social structure and triggering violent conflict. Many of these factors are not the sole cause of conflict, but when combined with political, social and economic structures that have generated tensions and rivalry for years, they may be the tipping point that triggers violence. In sum, these factors help to explain what triggers and sustains violent conflicts.

In countries where ethnic divisions coincide with class divisions, adverse consequences of international economic policies can exacerbate preexisting ethnic tensions. These economic policies may reinforce the existing dominance of a certain group and may generate resentment and precipitate a violent reaction from excluded groups.[130] According to Amy Chua, neoliberal policies for development that seek to promote free

---

[128] See Will Kymlicka, 'Misunderstanding nationalism', in Ronald Beiner (ed.), *Theorizing Nationalism* (Albany: State University of New York Press, 1999).

[129] According to Collier and Hoeffler, 'greed' seems to be a better predictor of conflict than 'grievance'. That is, economic motivations and opportunities (finding deposits of natural resources, for instance) seem to be more relevant than historical structures of dominance in predicting violence. Examples of such cases are Nigeria (oil) and Sierra Leone (diamonds). See Rachel Stohl, 'UN imposes diamond ban on Sierra Leone', Center for Defense Information, *Main Issues* (13 July 2000), available at http://www.cdi.org/program/issue/document.cfm?DocumentID=651andIssueID=93andStartRow=1andListRows=10andappendURL=andOrderby=DateLastUpdatedandProgramID=23andissueID=93, and R.T. Suberu, *Federalism and Ethnic Conflict in Nigeria* (Washington, DC: United States Institute of Peace, 2001). Regarding opportunities, conflict seems more likely to happen in places where rebels can be easily financed, which are likely to be places in which the structure of the state is weak (especially its military and police forces) and/or where there are high levels of unemployment (reducing the opportunity cost for rebels). See James D. Fearon and David D. Laitin, 'Ethnicity, insurgency, and civil war' (2003) 97 *American Political Science Review* 75. See also Paul Collier and Nicholas Sambanis (eds), *Understanding Civil War: Africa – Evidence and Analysis, Vol. 1* (Washington, DC: World Bank, 2005) at 248.

[130] Bardhan, *supra* note 81.

markets and democracy may increase these tensions significantly in cases where there is an economically dominant ethnic minority. She analyses a number of such cases to show how pre-existing tensions, combined with liberal democratic reform that empowers an impoverished majority, often became explosive.[131]

Chua's arguments are challenged by Milica Bookman (among others), who argues that the institutional protection of civil and political rights serves as an 'ethnostabilizer'.[132] According to Bookman, despite economic and social hierarchies, in liberal democracies groups are equally protected by the rule of law. Civil and political liberties, including the right to be free from discrimination, provide protection to groups when competition escalates and the pressure for discriminatory policies rises. Bookman, however, does no less explicitly address the cases highlighted by Chua – namely, countries that simultaneously implement liberal democratic and market reforms. The ability of institutions to protect ethnic groups may be weaker in new democracies. Moreover, in contrast to Chua's work, Bookman provides very little empirical evidence to support her arguments. In fact, James Fearon and David Laitin show that political democracies and states that observe civil liberties are not less civil war-prone than dictatorships.[133]

Scholars who draw on rational choice theory argue that violence may be used strategically as a modality of political action. Breakdowns in existing institutional arrangements create uncertainty and undermine the security of ethnic groups; in these circumstances, ethnic groups may resort to violence as a pre-emptive measure to safeguard their vital interests.[134] Here, 'violence can be analyzed in terms of cost–benefit analysis, theories of bargaining, game theory and rational choice'.[135] Institutions that place some ethnic groups at a competitive disadvantage in the pursuit of political and economic resources are also likely to trigger violence.[136] Proponents

---

131 Amy Chua, 'Markets, democracy, and ethnicity: toward a new paradigm for law and development' (1998) 108 *Yale Law Journal* 1; Amy Chua, 'The paradox of free market democracy: rethinking development policy' (2000) 41 *Harvard International Law Journal* 287; Amy Chua, *World on Fire: How Exporting Free Market Democracy Breeds Ethnic Hatred and Global Instability* (Toronto: Doubleday, 2003).

132 Milica Z. Bookman, *Ethnic Groups in Motion: Economic Competition and Migration in Multi-Ethnic States* (Portland, OR: Frank Cass, 2002) at 91.

133 Fearon and Laitin, *supra* note 129.

134 See Mbaku's review of rational choice theory in Mbaku, *supra* note 101 at 69–70.

135 Mehta, *supra* note 115 at 377.

136 Mbaku, *supra* note 101 at 75.

of public choice theory (a sub-set of rational choice theory) argue that institutional structures that do not create fair, stable and efficient rules to govern competition by ethnic groups for political and economic power generate incentives to resort to violence.[137]

Economic decline can also intensify inter-ethnic competition. During periods of economic decline and stagnation, groups tend to be more aggressive as they compete for a shrinking pool of resources.[138] Moreover, as with international economic policies, the consequences of economic decline can be unevenly distributed, impacting on some groups more than others. Uneven distributive effects may occur if certain sectors of the economy are more affected than others, or if a specific geographic area where one group is concentrated is especially affected by the downturn. In either case, groups that have borne the brunt of economic decline will press for policies to mitigate these effects and to redistribute resources. The risks of conflict can become especially high if the ethnic group benefiting from existing arrangements strongly resists redistributive policies. Institutional arrangements thus play an important role in mediating the competing interests of ethnic groups during periods of economic upheaval.

D. Possible Institutional Solutions

Thus far, we have examined the factors that motivate people to affiliate along ethnic lines, the circumstances that can increase tension and rivalry among existing ethnic groups, and the proximate causes that can actually trigger conflict in peaceful societies. In the discussion of all these issues, we suggested that institutions may play an important role in managing the dynamics of inter-ethnic relations. We turn now to a fuller discussion of how institutional arrangements may reduce the risk of conflict. This discussion is divided into two sections. First, we consider what types of institution may facilitate the transition from a period of violence to peace and stability within the polity; these institutions help societies to address the legacy of violence and past atrocities. Second, we examine the types of institution that can help a country to manage the coexistence of ethnic groups going forward, with a particular focus on the design of political institutions.

---

137 Ibid., at 77–79.

138 Bookman, *supra* note 132 at 31.

1. Institutions to deal with the past

As countries emerge from periods of violence, they must address the legacy of past atrocities, human rights violations, and violence that ethnic groups have committed against each other. The scholarship broadly refers to the process of moving from the former regime (typically associated with the commission of atrocities and systematic violence) to the new, typically democratic governance structure in terms of transitional justice.[139] The imperatives of 'transitional justice' are varied and include holding leaders of the former regime accountable for their actions; providing justice to the victims, including the possibility of reparations; creating a historical record of past events; promoting reconciliation; and dismantling the previous despotic regime and setting the foundation for democracy.[140] The three most common types of transitional justice institutional structures are (1) truth commissions, (2) trials (domestic and international), and (3) lustration or vetting. Each of these structures is discussed below.

Truth commissions (TCs) have become a common institutional response to past periods of violence and atrocity.[141] The use of TCs originated

---

[139] For discussion of what 'transitional justice' means and what it requires, see, e.g., Ruti G. Teitel, *Transitional Justice* (New York: Oxford University Press, 2000); Martha Minow, *Between Vengeance and Forgiveness: Facing History after Genocide and Mass Violence* (Boston: Beacon Press, 1998); Neil Kritz (ed.), *Transitional Justice: How Emerging Democracies Reckon with Former Regimes,* Vols I–III (Washington, DC: United States Institute of Peace, 1995); and Mark Osiel, *Mass Atrocity, Collective Memory, and the Law* (New Brunswick: Transaction Publishers, 1997). See also Rama Mani, *Beyond Retribution: Seeking Justice in the Shadows of War* (Cambridge, UK: Polity, 2002) and the collection of essays in Naomi Roht-Arriaza and Javier Mariezcurrena (eds), *Transitional Justice in the Twenty-First Century: Beyond Truth versus Justice* (Cambridge, UK: Cambridge University Press, 2006).

[140] There is no clear consensus about whether all of these imperatives should be included under the umbrella of 'transitional justice' or which imperatives should be given priority. See Bronwyn Anne Leebaw, 'The irreconcilable goals of transitional justice' (2008) 30 *Human Rights Quarterly* 95. Other scholars argue that the focus on transitional justice detracts from the underlying causes of conflict, such as deeply rooted inequalities. See, e.g., Zinaida Miller, 'Effects of invisibility: in search of the "economic" in transitional justice' (2008) 2 *International Journal of Transitional Justice* 266.

[141] For an excellent discussion of the history of truth commissions and their role in transitional periods, see Priscilla B. Hayner, *Unspeakable Truths: Confronting State Terror and Atrocity* (London: Routledge, 2000); Priscilla B. Hayner, *Unspeakable Truths: Facing the Challenge of Truth Commissions* (London: Routledge, 2002); Jon Elster, *Transitional Justice in Historical Perspective* (Cambridge, UK: Cambridge University Press, 2004); and Jon Elster (ed.), *Retribution and Reparation in the Transition to Democracy* (New York: Columbia

in Latin America and Africa, but they have now come to be implemented around the world, including in countries as diverse as Argentina, Chile, Germany, East Timor, Canada, South Africa, Ethiopia, Morocco, Solomon Islands, South Korea, Serbia and Montenegro,[142] and Nepal. TCs are bodies that have been established to investigate a past history of human rights violations in a particular country.[143] In general, the government (usually the executive branch) officially sanctions the work of the TC, which is an important factor in establishing the legitimacy of the TC.[144] Although each TC is unique in its structure, mandate and form, Hayner identities four primary elements common to all TCs:

> First, a truth commission is focused on the past. Second, it does not focus on just one event, but on the record of abuses over a period of time (often highlighting a few cases to demonstrate and describe patterns or large numbers of abuses). Third, a commission is a temporary body, generally concluding with the submission of a report. And finally, a truth commission is somehow officially sanctioned by the government (or by the opposition, where relevant) to investigate the past.[145]

Broadly speaking, the objectives of TCs are 'to confront, record, and acknowledge the truth about a past period of widespread rights abuses, with the hope of contributing to reconciliation, healing, and reform'.[146] Hayner notes that most TCs are created at a point of political transition within a country and often serve to underline a break with the past regime's patterns of human rights violations and to obtain or sustain

---

University Press, 2006). See also Chandra Lekha Sriram, *Confronting Past Human Rights Violations: Justice vs Peace in Times of Transition* (London: Frank Cass, 2004).

[142] Note that this truth commission never issued a report.

[143] Priscilla B. Hayner, 'Fifteen truth commissions – 1974–1994: a comparative study' (1994) 16 *Human Rights Quarterly* 597 at 600. Note that the human rights violations investigated by the TC often include violations committed by the military, but may also include violations committed by armed opposition groups (at 600).

[144] Ibid. Note that in some cases TCs have been initiated by the international community, acting through the United Nations, and by non-governmental institutions (e.g., opposition parties). See Hayner, ibid. at 604 and Michael P. Scharf, 'The case for a permanent international truth commission' (1997) 7 *Duke J. Comp. and Int'l L.* 375 at 377–8.

[145] Priscilla B. Hayner, 'Commissioning the truth: further research questions' (1996) 17 *Third World Quarterly* 19 at 20.

[146] Priscilla B. Hayner, 'International guidelines for the creation and operation of truth commissions: a preliminary proposal' (1996) 59 *Law and Contemporary Problems* 173 at 175. See also Scharf, *supra* note 144 at 379–80.

political legitimacy for a new regime. In some cases, TCs are also expected to lay the foundation for other processes in the transitional justice period, such as criminal prosecution, institutional reform and the payment of reparations to victims.[147] These goals are controversial, however, both in terms of their appropriateness for TCs and the ability of TCs to achieve such goals.[148] In particular, there is debate about whether and to what extent TCs can play a role in holding specific members of the past regime accountable for their acts, for example, by 'naming names'.[149]

Despite the proliferation of TCs, there is a paucity of scholarship that critically evaluates their successes and failures. Brahm puts the matter succinctly: 'the truth commission literature suffers from definitional ambiguity, the imprecise measurement of what are often abstract concepts, and a reliance on anecdotal evidence and perceptions to judge the impact of truth commissions'.[150] More pragmatically, Hayner notes that although TCs do provide a historical record of past atrocities, there is disagreement about whether TCs promote reconciliation or deepen resentment.[151]

Criminal prosecutions have risen to prominence since the Nuremberg and Tokyo trials at the end of World War II.[152] In general, the focus

---

147 Christopher K. Connolly, 'Living on the past: the role of truth commissions in post-conflict societies and the case study of Northern Ireland' (2006) 36 *Cornell International Law Journal* 401 at 404. See also Hayner, *supra* note 146 at 175.

148 See, e.g., Henry J. Steiner (ed.), *Truth Commissions: A Comparative Assessment* (WPF Report No. 16) (Cambridge: World Peace Foundation, 1997). See also David Mendelhoff, 'Truth-seeking, truth-telling and post-conflict peace-building: curb the enthusiasm?' (2004) 6 *International Studies Review* 355 and Stephan Landsman, 'Alternative responses to serious human rights abuses: of prosecutions and truth commissions' (1996) 59:4 *Law and Contemporary Problems* 81.

149 See Hayner 'Commissioning the truth', *supra* note 145 at 24, 26, and Hayner, *supra* note 143 at 647–50. See also Jo M. Pasqualucci, 'The whole truth and nothing but the truth: truth commissions, impunity, and the inter-American human rights system' (1994) 12 *Boston University International Law Journal* 321 at 335.

150 Eric Brahm, 'Uncovering the truth: examining truth commission success and impact' (2007) 8 *International Studies Perspectives* 16 at 17, citing Mendelhoff, *supra* note 148. See also Hayner, *Confronting State Terror, supra* note 141 at 252.

151 Hayner, 'Commissioning the truth', *supra* note 145 at 22–3. See also Hayner, *supra* note 150, and Jonathan Allen, 'Balancing justice and social unity: political theory and the idea of a truth and reconciliation commission' (2001) 49 *University of Toronto Law Journal* 315. For a case study on whether a TC has contributed to reconciliation, see Gibson's study of the South African Truth and Reconciliation Commission: James L. Gibson, *Overcoming Apartheid: Can Truth Reconcile a Divided Nation?* (New York: Russell Sage Foundation, 2004).

152 Prior to World War II, the concept of an international war crimes tribunal was virtually non-existent, as was the concept that one could be prosecuted for

of criminal prosecutions is on gross violations of human rights (such as torture, extralegal killing and forced disappearances) and war crimes (such as genocide). Prosecutions may occur in international forums, through domestic courts or both.[153] At the international level, prosecutions generally occur in the International Criminal Court (ICC) or in international war crimes tribunals such as those established to hear cases from the former Yugoslavia and Rwanda. Domestically, prosecutions are based on alleged violations of a country's laws (usually criminal laws), which can be problematic if a country has not yet enacted legislation prohibiting war crimes and gross violations of human rights. Rwanda, for example, had not at the time of the 1994 genocide enacted domestic legislation codifying criminal acts related to genocide and crimes against humanity.[154] In some cases, special hybrid war crimes courts are created; these hybrid courts are a blend of international and domestic institutions and are generally staffed by both domestic and international personnel. The Serbian War Crimes Court (WCC) in the District Court of Belgrade is an example of a hybrid war crimes court.[155]

Some countries have prosecuted alleged perpetrators of atrocities through a mix of conventional courts and traditional forms of administering justice. The most notable case is that of Rwanda, where, in addition to an international war crimes tribunal, the government instituted a community-based form of justice proceedings based on *gacaca*, a traditional

---

'crimes against humanity'. The Nuremberg and Tokyo trials played a key role in establishing the norms surrounding the prosecution of such crimes. The fairness of these trials was compromised by the retroactive application of the law to the accused. See Minow, *supra* note 139 at 30–5.

153 For a comparative analysis of the relative strengths of international and domestic prosecutions, see Donald L. Hafner and Elizabeth B.L. King, 'Beyond traditional notions of transitional justice: how trials, truth commissions, and other tools for accountability can and should work together' (2007) 30 *Boston College International and Comparative Law Review* 91.

154 Rwanda was a signatory to the Geneva Convention at the time of the genocide, however.

155 The WCC was established in 2003 as a domestic court and has exclusive jurisdiction to hear cases involving war crimes, genocide and crimes against humanity: see Law Amending the Law on Organization and Jurisdiction of Government Authorities in Prosecuting Perpetrators of War Crimes, Official Gazette of the Republic of Serbia, No. 135/2004, 21 December 2004, article 3 (amending art. 2 of Law on Organization and Jurisdiction of Government Authorities in Prosecuting Perpetrators of War Crimes, Official Gazette of the Republic of Serbia, No. 67/2003, 1 July 2003). Prior to the enactment of the Serbian War Crimes Law, prosecutions for war crimes occurred in Serbia's criminal courts.

approach to meting out justice and settling disputes.[156] While some laud the adoption of this traditional institution as a means of dealing with low-ranking *genocidaires*, others question how appropriate *gacaca* was for the task of holding these *genocidaires* to account while still others have raised concerns about deficits in due process.[157]

The availability of international forums for prosecuting gross violations of human rights and war crimes is generally regarded as a positive step in the efforts to promote accountability and to deter future atrocities.[158] These forums are also more likely to have the resources necessary to carry out prosecutions, including experienced, unbiased staff who have no political connections to the conflict in question.[159] International tribunals and the ICC thus play a particularly important role in cases where the domestic legal infrastructure is in disarray and when the legal community has been decimated.[160] Nevertheless, reliance on the ICC and international tribunals raises concerns about holding accountability proceedings in venues far removed from the country in which the alleged

---

[156] For a description of the *gacaca* process, see Phil Clark, 'Hybridity, holism, and "traditional" justice: the case of the Gacaca Courts in post-genocide Rwanda' (2007) 39 *George Washington International Law Review* 765, Mark A. Drumbl, 'Sclerosis: retributive justice and the Rwandan genocide' (2000) 2 *Punishment and Society* 288 at 292; and Alice Karekezi, Alphonse Nshimiyimana and Beth Mutamba, 'Localizing justice: gacaca courts in post-genocide Rwanda', in Eric Stover and Harvey M. Weinstein (eds), *My Neighbor, My Enemy: Justice and Community in the Aftermath of Mass Atrocity* (Cambridge: Cambridge University Press, 2004).

[157] African Rights, *Gacaca Justice: A Shared Responsibility* (London: African Rights, 2003) and Penal Reform International, 'Monitoring and Research Report on the Gacaca: information-gathering during the national phase' (London: Penal Reform International, 2006).

[158] See Neil J. Kritz, 'Coming to terms with atrocities: a review of accountability mechanisms for mass violations of human rights' (1996) 59 *Law and Contemporary Problems* 127 at 129.

[159] Ibid. It is not always the case that an international tribunal will have access to better resources and experienced legal staff: see Alison des Forges and Timothy Longman, 'Legal responses to genocide in Rwanda' in Stover and Weinstein, *supra* note 156 at 53.

[160] Kritz, *supra* note 158. The Rwandan judicial system, for example, was overwhelmed in the aftermath of the genocide. The physical infrastructure of the judicial system was in disarray: see des Forges and Longman, ibid. Moreover, the Rwandan legal community was decimated by the genocide: see Barbara Oomen, 'Justice mechanisms and the question of legitimacy: the example of Rwanda's multi-layered justice mechanisms', in Kai Ambos, Judith Large and Marieke Wierda (eds), *Building a Future on Peace and Justice: Studies on Transitional Justice, Peace, and Development* (Berlin: Springer-Verlag, 2009) at 192.

crimes occurred; there is a value in ensuring that the local population is in close proximity to these proceedings. Moreover, where prosecutions occur at both an international and a domestic level, questions have been raised about the appropriate relationship between the different proceedings and the fairness of prosecuting some perpetrators internationally and others domestically.[161]

Many scholars view prosecutions as an essential part of the transitional justice period. Orentlicher, for example, argues that the rule of law *requires* the prosecution of especially atrocious crimes.[162] She further argues that there is a duty under international human rights law to investigate and (subject to legitimate constraints) to prosecute those responsible for torture, extralegal killings and forced disappearances.[163] Even scholars who take a more limited view of the role of prosecutions suggest that prosecutions can advance an extensive array of important objectives:

> Seeking justice through the institutions of the law is the best means of determining responsibility for acts of genocide, war crimes, and other politically motivated violations of human rights. Criminal prosecutions of crimes of this magnitude not only punish the individual who committed them, demonstrating that impunity does not exist, but also help to restore dignity to their victims. They can provide a cathartic experience not only for individual victims, but also for society as a whole. By holding individuals responsible for their misdeeds, criminal trials may also deter the commission of abuses in the future. Moreover, if conducted in strict accordance with legal due process, criminal prosecutions of war crimes can help to strengthen the rule of law and establish the truth about the past through accepted legal means.[164]

The ability of prosecutions to achieve these goals remains contested.[165]

---

[161] See Melynda J. Price, 'Balancing lives: individual accountability and the death penalty as punishment for genocide (Lessons from Rwanda)' (2007) 21 *Emory International Law Review* 563.

[162] See Diane F. Orentlicher, 'Settling accounts: the duty to prosecute human violations of a prior regime' (1991) 100 *Yale Law Journal* 2537. See also Diane F. Orentlicher, '"Settling accounts" revisited: reconciling global norms with local agency' (2007) 1 *International Journal of Transitional Justice* 10. See also Minow, *supra* note 139 at 25–6.

[163] Orentlicher, 'Settling accounts', ibid.; see also Orentlicher, 'Reconciling', ibid.

[164] Timothy Phillips and Mary Albon, 'When prosecution is not possible: alternative means of seeking accountability for war crimes', in Belinda Cooper (ed.), *War Crimes: The Legacy of Nuremberg* (New York: TV Books, 1999) at 244. Remarkably, this assessment of what prosecutions may be able to achieve is put forward by *critics* of criminal prosecutions as a transitional justice measure.

[165] For an evaluation of the relative strengths and weaknesses of trials, see

Indeed, there is concern that in some cases prosecutions may represent a 'victor's justice'.[166] Moreover, as with the case of TCs, there appears to be a lack of scholarly rigour in the critical study of prosecutions.[167] More empirical analysis is necessary to determine what impact prosecutions actually have on peace-building and efforts to promote the rule of law and to better understand the factors that contribute to the ultimate success or failure of prosecutions.[168]

Lustration refers to the process of banning former state officials from holding public office as a result of the role they played in the former regime. In essence it is a form of vetting that is designed to exclude those who collaborated with the former regime from acquiring key posts in the new governance structure. Lustration has been used most prominently in Eastern and Central Europe, where it played a central role in the transitional processes of former communist countries.[169]

Landsman, *supra* note 148; Mark J. Osiel, 'Why prosecute? Critics of punishment for mass atrocity' (2000) 22 *Human Rights Quarterly* 118; and Laurel E. Fletcher and Harvey M. Weinstein, 'Violence and social repair: rethinking the contribution of justice to reconciliation' (2002) 24 *Human Rights Quarterly* 573. See also Carlos S. Nino, 'The duty to punish past abuses of human rights put into context: the case of Argentina' (1991) 100 *Yale Law Journal* 2619.

166 See Matt Rettig, 'Gacaca: truth, justice, and reconciliation in post-genocide Rwanda?' (2008) 51 *African Studies Review* 25 at 40, 45; Amnesty International, 'Rwanda: gacaca: a question of justice', AFR 47/007/2002 (London: Amnesty International, 2002), available at http://www.amnesty.org/en/library/asset/AFR47/007/2002/en/c0b61832-d769-11dd-b024-21932cd2170d/afr470072002en.html; Mark A. Drumbl, 'Law and atrocity: settling accounts in Rwanda' (2005) 31 *Ohio Northern University Law Review* 41 at 63–5; Oomen, *supra* note 160 at 194; and Allison Corey and Sandra Joireman, 'Retributive justice: the gacaca courts in Rwanda' (2004) 103 *African Affairs* 73 at 86.

167 See Laurel E. Fletcher and Harvey M. Weinstein with Jamie Rowen, 'Context, timing, and the dynamics of transitional justice: a historical perspective' (2009) 31 *Human Rights Quarterly* 163.

168 Up to this point, while there have been case studies of prosecutions, these case studies have largely focused on the choices made by particular regimes, the trade-offs that were made, and the implementation (or non-implementation) of these choices. There has been no detailed study of the actual effects of prosecutions on long-term stability and growth. See Chandra Lekha Sriram, 'Truth commissions and the quest for justice: stability and accountability after internal strife' (2000) 7:4 *International Peacekeeping* 91 at 93.

169 For case studies and discussions of lustration processes in former communist countries, see: Maria Łoś, 'Lustration and truth claims: unfinished revolutions in Central Europe' (1995) 20 *Law and Social Inquiry* 117; Jiri Priban, 'Oppressors and their victims: the Czech lustration system and the rule of law', in Alexander Mayer-Rieckh and Pablo De Greiff (eds), *Justice as Prevention: Vetting Public Employees in Transitional Societies* (New York: Social Science Research Council,

There is a broad range of approaches to lustration. David sets out a classification system that identifies two principal categories of lustration systems: exclusive systems and inclusive systems.[170] In *exclusive* lustration systems, once a person's association with the past regime is established, that individual is automatically barred from holding lustrated positions in the new political order, although the former official may hold posts that are not subject to lustration laws.[171] Exclusive systems ensure that certain key posts in the new state institutions are 'disconnected from past practices through personnel changes'.[172] Czechoslovakia, Bulgaria and Albania have adopted exclusive lustration systems.[173]

Critics of exclusive lustration systems argue that the automatic barring of officials is too arbitrary and may violate the right to be treated fairly, and that the systems therefore raise rule of law concerns. Critics also suggest that exclusive systems may violate international human rights law by, for example, breaching the right to be free from discrimination and freedom of expression.[174] Moreover, exclusive lustration systems appear to punish everyone who had affiliations with the former regime on a collective basis. Not surprisingly, the political opposition in every country that adopted exclusive lustration laws requested a constitutional review of the lustration legislation.[175] The Czech lustration law was narrowed, though upheld in its substance, following constitutional review; the Bulgarian court endorsed one lustration law, while the Albanian court struck down that country's lustration legislation.[176]

In an *inclusive* system, officials from the former regime may retain public office on the condition that they reveal their past involvement with that regime. Officials have the option of resigning if they do not wish

2007); Elizabeth Barrett, Péter Hack and Ágnes Munkácsi, 'Lustration as political competition: vetting in Hungary', in Mayer-Rieckh and De Greiff, ibid.; and Roman David, 'Lustration law in action: the motives and evaluation of lustration policy in the Czech Republic and Poland (1989–2001)' (2003) 28 *Law and Social Inquiry* 387.

170 Roman David, 'From Prague to Bagdad: lustration systems and their political effects' (2006) 41 *Government and Opposition* 347.

171 Ibid., at 353–4. David, *supra* note 169.

172 David, *supra* note 170 at 354.

173 Ibid., at 355.

174 Ibid., at 356.

175 Ibid., at 356. Following a constitutional review, the Czech law was narrowed, although upheld in its substance. The Bulgarian court endorsed a lustration law. In Albania, the court struck down the country's lustration legislation.

176 Ibid., citations omitted.

to disclose the details of their involvement with the former regime.[177] Inclusive systems aim to end the secret practices of the past regime, and operate on the assumption that the public can exercise control over an official once information about that official's past is revealed.[178] Hungary, Poland, Romania and Serbia adopted inclusive systems.[179]

David also identifies a third, hybrid category of lustration system: the mixed system. In mixed systems, 'vetting commissions' typically make lustration decisions on a case-by-case basis. An official's collaboration with the former regime is not determinative. Instead, a number of factors are considered, including the individual's past record, the requirements of a particular post, and, from a pragmatic perspective, the nature of the labour market.[180] Germany adopted a mixed lustration system as a term of the Unification Treaty.[181]

De Greiff suggests that lustration serves to end a culture of impunity and that it acts as a punitive, deterrent and preventative measure.[182] He further argues that vetting can, in some cases, facilitate application of other transitional justice mechanisms, such as TCs and trials and that it can also facilitate broader institutional reform.[183] By contrast, other scholars have argued that lustration may not be an effective tool for transitional justice given its potential for exacerbating factionalism.[184] However, there has not yet been any rigorous analysis of the impact that lustration has had on the ability of countries to manage the transition to a democratic regime.

2. Institutions to manage the coexistence of ethnic groups in the polity

Having considered how institutions may contribute to helping a country address its past, we now turn to consider how institutional arrangements may serve to reduce the risk of violent conflict in the polity in the future. This discussion focuses largely on the design of political institution.

---

177 Ibid., at 353 and 357.

178 Ibid., at 357.

179 Ibid., at 357–8.

180 Ibid., at 362. See also Serge Rumin, 'Gathering and managing information in vetting processes', in Mayer-Rieckh and De Greiff, *supra* note 169, 402 at 405–6.

181 David, 'Lustration systems', *supra* note 170.

182 Pablo de Greiff, 'Vetting and transitional justice', in Mayer-Rieckh and De Greiff, *supra* note 169, 522.

183 Ibid. But see Arthur L. Stinchcombe, 'Lustration as a problem of the social basis on constitutionalism' (1995) 20 *Law and Social Inquiry* 245 on the issue of lustration and institutional reform.

184 See Roman Boed, 'An evaluation of the legality and efficacy of lustration as a tool of transitional justice' (1998–1999) 37 *Columbia Journal of Transnational Law* 357.

The rules that govern the political system are important institutional factors that influence a country's political dynamics through the incentives they generate. These rules include, for example, the design of democratic regimes and power-sharing mechanisms, such as federalism and concurrent majorities.[185] Depending on their design, democratic governance structures may be more suitable political regimes for ethnically diverse societies than authoritarian regimes.[186] Although diversity makes democratic politics more challenging, according to some authors ethnic diversity 'is likely to make dictatorship lethal'.[187] However, not all democratic regimes will be effective in mitigating conflict: institutional design of democratic regimes is crucial to their success in managing inter-ethnic tension and preventing violent conflict. Electoral systems, for instance, may help mitigate tensions or may polarize societies even further, depending on their design.[188] The Westminster 'first-past-the-post' (or 'winner takes all') system tends to heighten tension while proportional representation is generally regarded as having a moderating effect on ethnic tension.[189]

---

185 For discussions of these and other political institutions and their role in managing ethnic conflict, see Eric Nordlinger, *Conflict Regulation in Divided Societies,* Occasional Paper No. 29 (Cambridge, MA: Harvard University Center for International Affairs, 1972); John McGarry and Brendan O'Leary (eds), *The Politics of Ethnic Conflict Regulation: Case Studies of Protracted Ethnic Conflicts* (New York: Routledge, 1993); John McGarry and Brendan O'Leary, 'The political regulation of national and ethnic conflict' (1994) 47 *Parliamentary Affairs* 94; Ian Lustick, 'Stability in deeply divided societies: consociationalism versus control' (1979) 31 World Politics 325; Arend Lijphart, *Electoral Systems and Party Systems* (New York: Oxford University Press, 1994); Timothy D. Sisk, *Power Sharing and International Mediation in Ethnic Conflicts* (Washington, DC: United States Institute of Peace, 1996); Frank S. Cohen, 'Proportional versus majoritarian ethnic conflict management in democracies' (1997) 30:5 *Comparative Political Studies* 607; Horowitz, *supra* note 81; Daniel L. Byman, *Keeping the Peace: Lasting Solutions to Ethnic Conflicts* (Baltimore: John Hopkins University Press, 2002); Wolff, *supra* note 88; and Ulrich Schneckener and Stefan Wolff (eds), *Managing and Settling Ethnic Conflicts: Perspectives on Successes and Failure in Europe, Africa and Asia* (New York, NY: Palgrave Macmillan, 2004).

186 Paul Collier, 'The political economy of ethnicity', paper prepared for the Annual World Bank Conference on Development Economics, Washington, DC, 20–21 April 1998. See also R. J. Rummel, 'Democracy, power, genocide and mass murder' 39 *Journal of Conflict Resolution* 3.

187 Collier, *supra* note 18 at 63–6.

188 McGarry and O'Leary, 'The political regulation of national and ethnic conflict', *supra* note 185 at 106.

189 Bardhan, *supra* note 81 at 183. See also Horowitz, *supra* note 81 at 628–51 and Benjamin Reilly, 'Electoral systems for divided societies' (2002) 13:2 *Journal of Democracy* 156.

Regarding the design of democratic systems, some authors support the idea that constraints on political elites, such as those imposed by systems of checks and balances, are one of the most important features of a democratic system in avoiding rent-seeking behaviour, especially when large amounts of natural resources are found.[190] The challenge, then, is to create effective mechanisms for the separation of powers. One of the major obstacles to this endeavour is institutional interconnections: creating an effective system of checks and balances and separation of powers will largely depend on:

(i) electoral rules that guarantee proportional representation or otherwise ensure a fair distribution of seats in the legislature among the different ethnic groups;
(ii) a party system that is representative of the diverse composition of the nation, such as one that features a power-sharing executive; and
(iii) the rules of standing for judicial review, which should grant ethnic minorities access to the constitutional or highest appellate court to challenge unconstitutional measures.

In other words, institutional interdependencies will determine whether separation of powers mechanisms will in fact reduce the risk of conflict and mitigate any possible negative effects of ethnic diversity.[191] Each of these features also has independent value as a means of creating incentives for cooperation and for increasing the security of ethnic groups in the polity.

An interesting development in the study of the design of democratic systems to manage conflicts is consociational democracy.[192] The concept of consociational democracy was pioneered by Lijphart, who argued that while it may be difficult to achieve and maintain a stable democratic government in a plural society, it is not impossible if the appropriate institutional conditions exist. Lijphart proposed that elite cooperation

---

190 Daron Acemoğlu, Simon Johnson and James Robinson, 'An African success story: Botswana', in Dani Rodrik (ed.), *In Search of Prosperity: Analytic Narratives on Economic Growth* (Princeton, NJ: Princeton University Press, 2003). See also Collier, *supra* note 85 at 186 (discussing the importance of a robust system of accountability).

191 For an analysis of the empirical evidence on exporting US-style separation of power systems to fragile democracies, see Hathaway, *supra* note 79.

192 Arend Lijphart, 'Consociational democracy,' (1969) 21 *World Politics* 207 at 216 and Arend Lijphart, *Democracy in Plural Societies* (New Haven: Yale University Press, 1977).

could counteract the centrifugal tendencies inherent in a plural society.[193] He identifies four essential features of a consociational democracy, each of which plays a role in promoting cooperative attitudes and behaviour among the elite:

(i) a grand coalition government which incorporates all of the political parties representing the main segments within the society;
(ii) a policy of proportionality with respect to political representation, employment, and expenditures in the public sector;
(iii) norms of self-governance and community autonomy over matters which are of the greatest concern to groups; and
(iv) constitutional vetoes for minorities.[194]

Lijphart originally presented consociational democracy as an empirical model, drawing on the experiences of a few deeply divided European democracies.[195] However, his arguments have acquired a more normative tone over time,[196] and consociational engineering (which incorporates the features described above in the design of political institutions) is regarded by many today as a way to achieve stable democracy in highly factionalized societies.[197]

Federalism is a prominent example of a power-sharing mechanism that has been adopted in a wide range of fragmented societies. The strength of federalism as a means of mitigating conflict, however, is highly contested in the academic literature. Federalism seems to have potential as an institutional arrangement for governance structures in countries that feature geographically concentrated ethnic communities within a country. A number of authors have claimed that decentralization and federalism is a potential antidote to identity-based tensions in these cases,[198] because

---

193 Lijphart, *Democracy in Plural Societies,* ibid.

194 Ibid.

195 Arend Lijphart, 'Typologies of democratic systems' (1968) 1 *Comparative Political Studies* 3.

196 By the time *Democracy in Divided Societies* was published in 1977, Lijphart was describing consociational democracy as both a normative and an empirical model. See *Democracy in Plural Societies, supra* note 192 at 1–2.

197 Ralph Premdas, 'Ethno-racial divisions and governance: the problem of institutional reform and adaptation', Research Project on Racism and Public Policy, United Nations Research Institute for Social Development (2001).

198 Donald L. Horowitz, *A Democratic South Africa? Constitutional Engineering in a Divided Society* (Berkeley, CA: University of California Press, 1991); John McGarry, 'Federal political systems and the accommodation of national minorities', in Ann L. Griffiths (ed.), *Handbook of Federal Countries, 2002* (Montreal:

they devolve power to sub-national governments, granting higher levels of political, economic and social autonomy to ethnic groups concentrated in certain geographic areas. But this claim has been disputed, given that decentralization and federalism also have the potential to reinforce ethnic identities and to increase ethnic tensions.[199] Devolving power to certain regions may ultimately lead to demands for more power, culminating in claims for secession.[200] Proponents of federalism respond to this argument by pointing out that ethnic communities are already escalating their claims for autonomy. Federalism responds to these claims by devolving a degree of power to these communities, thereby moderating demands for full secession.

Federalism can also apply to non-geographically specific matters: decision-making power over certain issues (for example, culture and social services) can be devolved to ethnic groups regardless of where the members of the group live. This unique federalist system was implemented in Belgium in the 1970s.[201] The Belgian federal system features two different forms of constituent unit – the Communities and Regions – in addition to the federal (central) government. There are three Communities: Flemish, French and German; membership of the Communities is tied to language and is determined on an individual basis. There are also three Regions: Flanders, Wallonia and Brussels. Membership of one's Region is territory-based and is determined by residence. Communities have jurisdiction over matters such as language, culture, education and various social services. Regions have jurisdiction over matters such as regional

---

McGill-Queen's University Press, 2002); A. Lijphart, R. Rogowski and R.K. Weaver, 'Separation of power and cleavage management', in R. Ken Weaver and Bert A. Rockman (eds), *Do Institutions Matter? Government Capabilities in the United States and Abroad* (Washington, DC: Brookings Institution Press, 1993) 302–44; N. Bermeo, 'The import of institutions' (2002) 13:2 *Journal of Democracy* 96; C. Hartzell and M. Hoodie, 'Institutionalizing peace: power sharing and post-civil war conflict management' (2003) 47 *American Journal of Political Science* 318; and Horowtiz, *supra* note 81.

199 E. M. Penn, 'Citizenship versus ethnicity: the role of institutions in shaping identity choice' (2008) 70 *Journal of Politics* 956 and Will Kymlicka, 'Is federalism a viable alternative to secessionism?', in Percy B. Lehning (ed.), *Theories of Secession* (New York: Routledge Press, 1998).

200 Nordlinger, *supra* note 185 at 32.

201 Formerly a unitary state, Belgium officially concluded the reforms in 1992, but the federalist system is still evolving. For an overview of the process, see John Fitzmaurice, *The Politics of Belgium: A Unique Federalism* (Boulder, CO: Westview, 1996). See also Maureen Covell, 'Federalization and federalism: Belgium and Canada', in Herman Bakvis and William Chandler (eds), *Federalism and the Role of the State,* (Toronto: University of Toronto Press, 1987).

economic development, urban planning, and public works. The federal government of Belgium has jurisdiction over financial and monetary policy, justice, social security, defence and international relations.[202]

Another power-sharing mechanism is concurrent majorities, also called 'mutual vetoes'. This mechanism grants veto powers on certain issues to minority groups that constitute a significant portion of the population. As a consequence, even if one ethnic group dominates one branch of government (or more than one), other ethnic groups have a means of exerting influence over the development and implementation of policies and of securing their interests. Practically speaking, the mutual veto creates incentives for moderation and accommodation since decisions that are not acceptable to other major ethnic groups risk being vetoed.[203] The list of protected items can range from a predefined set of basic issues (for example, basic individual rights specified in the constitution) to broader economic and political reforms. There are also different forms of veto – for example, a delaying veto, a direct veto and an indirect veto.[204] In all these cases, mutual vetoes reduce the risk of subjugation and dominance.[205]

In sum, institutions can play an important role in managing ethnic tension and rivalry. The constitution-making process by which these institutions are selected and designed in post-conflict low-trust societies is also important in ensuring inclusiveness, transparency and ultimately legitimacy for the institutional outcomes of this process. As stated at the outset of this chapter, ethnic conflicts are complex phenomena, and it is unlikely that institutional design alone can avoid the problem; often institutional reforms that were expected to reduce the risk of conflict have not proved effective. However, this should not preclude a potentially fruitful debate about which institutions in particular contexts may mitigate ethnic conflict and its potentially devastating consequences for a country's development prospects.

IV. CONCLUSION

In discussing the importance of political institutions and challenges of institutional reforms, this chapter has also underscored the important

---

202 Andre Lecours, 'Belgium', in Griffiths, *supra* note 198 at 58.

203 Nordlinger, *supra* note 185 at 24–5.

204 Ulrich Schneckener, 'Models of ethnic conflict regulation: the politics of recognition', in Schneckener and Wolff, *supra* note 185 at 28–9.

205 Bardhan, *supra* note 81 at 191. See also John C. Calhoun, *A Disquisition of Government* (New York, Liberal Arts Press, 1953) at 28.

role that lawyers, along with others, can play in the exercise of designing political institutions that can promote development and reduce the risk of ethnic conflict. Many solutions discussed here relate to details of political and legal systems that may influence whether a particular legal or political regime will promote economic and social development and/or mitigate conflict and some of the other negative consequences of ethnic diversity. There are also many interconnections between political, legal and other institutions to be considered in constructing effective systems of checks and balances. These all raise complex legal issues, inter alia, and their design requires both legal and other forms of expertise as well as an appreciation of local context.

5. Public administration, corruption and development

I. INTRODUCTION

The emergence of an institutional perspective on development over the past decade or so has entailed not only a sharper focus on the nature and quality of a country's political and legal institutions, but also on the organization of its bureaucracy or civil service. According to Salvatore Schiavo-Campo, formerly of the Public Sector Management Team at the World Bank, 'the slide of today's "failed states" can be traced back to, in part, the degradation of their public administrations'.[1]

The frailties and failures of public administration in many developing countries have long been documented or remarked upon in the development literature. According to these accounts of bad government in developing countries, to quote Judith Tendler:

> Public officials and their workers pursue their own private interests rather than those of the public good. Governments over-extend themselves in hiring and spending. Clientelism runs rampant, with workers being hired and fired on the basis of kinship and political loyalty rather than merit. Workers are poorly trained and receive little on-the-job training. Badly conceived programs and policies create myriad opportunities for bribery, influence peddling, and other forms of malfeasance. All this adds up to the disappointing inability of many governments to deliver good public services and to cope with persistent problems of corruption, poverty, and macro-economic mismanagement.[2]

This view of government is exemplified in Hernando de Soto's widely cited book, *The Other Path*,[3] in which he documents the delays, costs, bureaucratic complexities and corruption entailed in registering title to residential land or obtaining approvals to open a small business in Peru. De Soto

[1] Salvatore Schiavo-Campo, 'Reforming the civil service' (1996) 33:3 *Finance and Development* 10–13.

[2] Judith Tendler, *Good Government in the Tropics* (Baltimore: Johns Hopkins University Press, 1997) at 1.

[3] Hernando de Soto, *The Other Path* (New York: HarperCollins, 1989).

suggests that the existence of large informal economies in many developing countries is partly explained by the immense difficulties of doing business legally in these countries. These impediments to doing business in many countries have been more systematically documented in the World Bank's 'Doing Business Reports', which aim to investigate 'the scope and manner of regulations that enhance business activity and those that constrain it'.[4] The project is based on the theory that governments regulate the entry of new firms into the economy, and this can be a limiting factor on economic development.[5] The reports include detailed information about business law conditions in 175 countries, ranking countries on how easy it is to start and close a formal business, hire and fire workers, and enforce a contract. They also examine the ability of local business to access credit. In 2005, the report added the ease of registration of property and the level of investor protection, and then, in 2006, paying taxes, cross-border trading and obtaining licences.[6] The reports are highly influential, claiming to induce reforms that increase the ease of doing business in developing countries worldwide. Djankov, the former leader of the Doing Business project, claims that this research has 'led to an acceleration in reform: in 2003–2008, 193 reforms took place in 116 countries', as well as inspiring a wealth of academic literature which relies on the data compiled by the project.[7]

According to Tendler, a negative view of the performance of public administrations in many developing countries has tended to lead to advice, from donor institutions and others, directed at limiting the 'damage' that the public sector can do in developing countries. The advice falls into three categories: (1) reducing the size of government by getting rid of 'excess' workers, contracting out for services, privatizing and decentralizing; (2) terminating many of the policies and programs that provide opportunities for bureaucrats to exert undue influence on the policy process and for citizens to bribe them; and (3) subjecting public agencies and their managers and workers to market-like pressures and incentives to perform.[8]

---

[4] World Bank, *Doing Business in 2004: Understanding Regulation* (Washington, DC: World Bank, 2004) at viii.

[5] Simeon Djankov, Rafael La Porta, Florencio Lopez-de-Silanes and Andrei Shleifer, 'The regulation of entry' (2002) 117 *Quarterly Journal of Economics* 1.

[6] However, these reports have been criticized for misrepresenting and oversimplifying information by empirically quantifying legal issues that are inherently complex and difficult to measure: see Kevin Davis and Michael B. Kruse, 'Taking the measure of law: the case of the Doing Business Project' (2007) 32:4 *Law & Social Inquiry* 1095–119.

[7] Simeon Djankov, 'The regulation of entry: a survey' (2009) CEPR Discussion Paper 7080.

[8] Tendler, supra. note 2. A. Israel, *Institutional Development: Incentives to*

However, as Tendler and others have pointed out, this view of the quality of public administrations in developing countries and prescriptions and antidotes for their deficiencies ignores the fact that, even on a limited view of the appropriate functions of government, a well-functioning public administration is indispensable to the effective performance of these tasks. Moreover, the focus on the deficiencies of public administration in many developing countries ignores many examples of good performance within and among developing countries from which valuable and perhaps transferable reform lessons may be learned.

II. MEASURING BUREAUCRATIC PERFORMANCE

Beginning in the mid-1990s, systematic quantitative efforts have been undertaken to measure bureaucratic quality. For example, Knack and Keefer[9] use ratings by the International Country Risk Guide of Corruption and Government and Bureaucratic Quality in one of their indices of institutional quality, and use a rating by Business and Environmental Risk Intelligence of bureaucratic delays in the other. Mauro[10] uses ratings by Business International of 'bureaucracy and red tape' and 'corruption' in his index of bureaucratic efficiency. Others, in addition to measuring bureaucratic performance, have tried to measure the impact of bureaucratic performance on economic growth. Indeed, Knack and Keefer find positive and significant effects of both of their institutional quality indices on growth and on per capita gross domestic product (GDP). Mauro finds the same for his index of bureaucratic efficiency.[11] By focusing on outcomes, these early quantitative studies are limited by their lack of specificity regarding the particular characteristics of a public administration that predisposed it to either good or bad performance, at least in terms of impacts on economic measures of development. There are also various case studies of the high-performing East Asian economies, which

Performance (Baltimore: Johns Hopkins University Press, 1987); N. Manning, 'The legacy of the New Public Management in developing countries' (2001) 67:2 *International Review of Administrative Sciences* 297–312.

[9] S. Knack and P. Keefer, 'Institutions and economic performance: cross-countries tests using alternative institutional measures' (1995) 7 *Economics and Politics* 207.

[10] P. Mauro, 'Corruption, country risk and growth' (1995) 110 *Quarterly Journal of Economics* 681.

[11] Ibid. See also James Rauch and Peter Evans, 'Bureaucratic structure and bureaucratic performance in less developed countries' (2000) 75 *Journal of Public Economics* 49.

emphasize the positive role played by certain dimensions of East Asian bureaucracies in the region's spectacular industrialization.[12] These studies, however, tend to suffer from the limitations of most case studies – that is, their inability to be generalized.

In two more recent companion papers, Peter Evans and James Rauch examine the characteristics of core state economic agencies and the growth records of a sample of 35 developing countries for the period from 1970 to 1990, based on the assessments of country experts of key institutional characteristics.[13] They draw on the theorizing of Max Weber,[14] where Weber argued that public administrative organizations characterized by meritocratic recruitment and predictable long-term career paths will be more effective at facilitating capitalist growth. In their studies, Evans and Rauch focus on meritocratic recruitment, internal promotion and career stability, and competitive salaries, and find that the institutionalization of meritocratic recruitment (public service exams or higher educational credentials) is crucial for ensuring high levels of bureaucratic performance, while internal promotion and career stability – which may facilitate institutional coherence, long-term policy goals and counter temptations to short-term gain (including corruption) – seem to be of secondary importance. Whether or not competitive salaries have any effect on bureaucratic performance remains unclear. The authors find that these Weberian characteristics, particularly meritocratic recruitment, significantly enhance a country's prospects for economic growth, even when initial levels of GDP per capita and human capital are controlled for. There are notable regional variations in the relationship between bureaucratic performance and economic growth, with sub-Saharan Africa ranking lowest, then Latin America, and the East Asian high-performing economies ranking substantially higher (thus confirming, from a comparative perspective, the earlier findings of the East Asian case studies).

As noted in Chapter 1, the World Bank's Governance studies now regularly measure the impact of countries' governance performance (includ-

---

[12] See, e.g., Alice Amsden, *Asia's Next Giant: South Korea and Late Industrialization* (New York: Oxford University Press, 1989); Robert Wade, *Governing the Market: Economic Theory and the Role of Government in Taiwan's Industrialization* (Princeton, NJ: Princeton University Press, 1990); Jose Campos and Hilton Root, *The Key to the Asian Miracle: Making Shared Growth Credible* (Washington, DC: Brookings Institution, 1996); World Bank, *The East Asian Miracle: Economic Growth and Public Policy* (New York: Oxford University Press, 1993).

[13] See Peter Evans and James Rauch, 'Bureaucracy and growth: a cross-national analysis of the effects of "Weberian" state structures on economic growth' (1999) 64 *American Sociological Review*, 748; Rauch and Evans, *supra* note 11.

[14] Max Weber, *Economy and Society* (1904–1911).

ing 'government effectiveness', 'regulatory quality' and 'corruption') on various development outcomes, and find similar impacts to Evans and Rauch. Similarly, as noted above, the World Bank's more recent 'Doing Business' reports[15] catalogue and compare time, costs and complexities in performing many routine bureaucratic and legal activities in many countries (developed and developing). However, both groups of studies (like some earlier studies) evaluate bureaucratic outputs, rather than bureaucratic inputs or particular characteristics of a public administration.

III. ALTERNATIVE REFORM STRATEGIES

A. The New Public Management

In the late 1980s traditional Weberian bureaucratic organization theory was challenged by the New Public Management (NPM), a bureaucratic reform philosophy that derived from neoliberal ideas critical of the role of the state. NPM is a move away from traditional public sector management principles. The traditional public sector organizational theories – such as the Whitehall Model, which originated in Great Britain – emphasized hierarchy in the public service, anonymity of public servants, and input and output centred program management. NPM, on the other hand, promotes modernization through adapting private sector management techniques and market principles to the public sector.[16] This means that public servants are expected to provide customer-centric services with less emphasis on hierarchy and more emphasis on measurable outcomes, expanded use of user fees, and remuneration more closely related to outcomes, with services contracted out, wherever feasible, through competitive tendering, to private for-profit or non-profit sectors ('steering' rather than 'rowing').[17] Accordingly, NPM considers the two main duties of the civil service – policy-making and service delivery – as distinct tasks.[18]

Richard Batley's five-year review of the effects of NPM on the economies

---

15 World Bank, *Doing Business 2009* (Washington, DC: World Bank, 2008), available online at http://www.doingbusiness.org/.

16 Wolfgang Drechsler, 'The rise and demise of the New Public Management', (2005) 33 *Post-Autistic Economics Review*, available at http://www.paecon.net/PAEReview/issue33/Drechsler33.htm; Michael Trebilcock, *The Prospects for Reinventing Government* (Toronto: C.D. Howe Institute, 1994).

17 Trebilcock, ibid.

18 Manning, *supra* note 8 at 299.

of developing countries finds that the results have been ambiguous.[19] Often performance outcomes are difficult to define and measure, and contracting-out through often flawed and sometimes corrupt processes to an often thin and uncompetitive private sector is not always more efficient. Nick Manning observes that NPM was 'no more able than old public administration to provide governments with the incentives and the capacity to address poverty and provide better services'.[20] Wolfgang Drechsler further argues that there has been 'no empirical evidence that NPM reforms have led to any productivity increase or welfare maximization'.[21]

Manning highlights the importance of 'motive' and 'capability' for the successful implementation of NPM principles.[22] By motive, he means public expectations that motivate governments to take action. This assumes that the government is genuinely interested in or has sufficient incentives to care about public opinion and accountability. Democratic political regimes and 'mechanisms that incorporate civil society and local governments within the policy-making processes' create such interest in public opinion.[23] By capability, Manning means 'core public management elements', such as 'administrative systems governing policy-making and budgeting, basic service provision, and economic regulation [,which] might be inefficient, but are essentially present'.[24] Manning labels these existing mechanisms 'Old Public Disciplines'.[25]

Abu Elias Sarker also suggests that state capability is a principal precondition for NPM's successful implementation.[26] In particular, Sarker, who studied NPM implementation in Singapore and Bangladesh, adds economic capability, political commitment, effective governance, rule of law and the absence of clientelism and corruption as important preconditions to viable implementation of NPM in developing countries.[27] Since bureaucratic organizations do not exist in isolation from their surroundings, NPM does not seem to be a viable solution for states that do not have 'Old Public Disciplines'.

---

[19] Robert Batley, 'The role of government in adjusting economies' (1999), in Manning, *supra* note 8.

[20] Manning, *supra* note 8 at 303.

[21] Drechsler, *supra* note 16.

[22] Manning, *supra* note 8 at 303.

[23] Ibid., at 304.

[24] Ibid.

[25] Ibid., at 302.

[26] Abu Elias Sarker, 'New public management in developing countries: an analysis of success and failure with particular reference to Singapore and Bangladesh' (2006) 19:2 *International Journal of Public Service* 180–203.

[27] Ibid., at 189–94.

Finally, although NPM was a major reform strategy in the 1990s, both Manning and Drechsler suggest that NPM is a 'somewhat dated label'.[28] Since the late 1990s there has been scepticism about 'generalized applicability' of NPM. NPM was viewed as an imposition of 'Western organizational and institutional structures on the developing world [that has] been counterproductive', particularly to the aid-dependent countries that are 'susceptible to the pressures of the international donor agencies in formulating and reformulating [their] reform agenda'.[29]

B. The 'Old' Public Management

According to Schiavo-Campo,[30] efforts at civil service reform in developing countries have yielded a variety of practical lessons, including the following.

1. A two-tier arrangement may make it possible to recruit, at a higher salary scale, new staff who meet more demanding standards of qualification.
2. Even at low salaries, young, better trained people can be induced to take up government employment for short periods if they are given challenging responsibilities and training.
3. In practice, centralized personnel management systems are generally more cost-effective than decentralized systems.
4. Individual salary negotiations between new staff and ministries should be avoided, because they result in distortions and inequities and compromise prospects for sustainable reform.
5. The temptation to 'fence off' reform projects in order to insulate them from an inefficient system should be avoided; creating enclaves does not work, and civil service reform should be directed at the overall system.
6. For external assistance to be effective there must be genuine ownership of reform by the government as a whole if systemic reforms are attempted, or by a major government player if reforms are limited to a specific sector or function, and government must formulate – with appropriate participation by the public as well as government employees themselves – a clear, long-term vision of public sector reform in concrete detail.

---

28 Drechsler, *supra* note 16; Manning, *supra* note 8 at 297.
29 Sarker, *supra* note 26 at 195.
30 Schiavo-Campo, *supra* note 1.

Schiavo-Campo also notes that downsizing or retrenchment for fiscal reasons can often have unintended consequences if such programs encourage the best people to leave (e.g., through voluntary severance and early retirement programs) and that short-term fiscal savings from compressing wages may also lead to the departure of better or more senior employees and increased difficulty in recruiting qualified outsiders. Finally, he argues that without improvements in accountability, downsizing and more adequate compensation may result in a small and well-paid, but no less inefficient or corrupt, civil service. Hence, external accountability is essential for the civil service to become more responsive to the public (for example, through user surveys, wearing of nametags, whistle-blower laws, and public opinion polls).

C. Civil Servants as Communitarians

Tendler, in her widely cited book, *Good Government in the Tropics*,[31] explores, through detailed case studies, four programs in the state of Ceará, in Brazil's poor northeast region:

- programs in preventive health;
- public procurement from informal sector producers;
- a large emergency employment-creating public works program; and
- agricultural extension services to small farmers.

She draws several lessons from her studies of 'good government'.

First, government workers in all these cases demonstrated unusual dedication to their jobs and reported feeling more appreciated and recognized, not necessarily by superiors but by their clients and the communities in which they worked. Second, the state government contributed in an unusual and sometimes inadvertent way to the new sense of recognition by creating a strong sense of 'calling' and mission around these particular programs and their workers through public information campaigns, prizes for good performance, public screening methods for new recruits, orientation programs, and sheer boasting through the media about its successes. Third, workers carried out a larger variety of tasks than usual and often voluntarily, in part in response to their perception of what their clients needed and out of a vision of the public good. Workers were able to provide this more customized service because they had greater autonomy and discretion than usual. Fourth, the greater discretion and responsibility

[31] Tendler, *supra* note 2.

inherent in the self-enlarged jobs and their fuzzier job definitions would seem to make supervision more difficult than it already is in large public bureaucracies; however, workers wanted to perform better in order to live up to the new trust placed in them by their clients and citizens in general. The trust was a result of the more customized arrangements of their work and the public messages of respect from the state. The communities where these public servants worked watched over them more closely and the state's publicity campaigns and similar messages had armed citizens with new information about their rights to better government and how public services were supposed to work. All these features suggest that instead of approaching public servants as rational self-interested agents, as many public management proposals seem to do, reformers should think of these servants as members of a community.

From a broader institutional perspective, Tendler also draws an interesting lesson: while enthusiasm about decentralization in the development community to date portrays local government and civil society as locked in a healthy two-way dynamic of pressures for accountability that results in improved government, Tendler's case studies revealed instead a three-way dynamic that included an activist central government (in this case, the state government) as well as local governments and civil society. While Ceará was fortunate to have two reformist governors during the early years of these programs, Tendler is inclined to discount the centrality of good leadership in effective programs of this kind, in part because of the serendipity and scarcity of charismatic leadership. She notes that these programs survived the terms of initial political leaders and that, while inspired leadership is obviously an asset, it is not a necessary condition for the development and implementation of public service delivery programs staffed by dedicated and motivated public servants.

D. Institutional Bypasses

As discussed in Chapter 1, path dependence is a crucial factor that policy-makers should consider in developing institutional reform strategies. Such strategies may often depart from Schiavo-Campo's recommendations, especially his argument that one should never 'fence off' bureaucratic reform projects, but rather focus on across-the-board bureaucratic reforms, and are often more consistent with the thrust of Tendler's analysis. In recent papers, Mariana Mota Prado[32] argues that many

[32] Mariana Mota Prado and Ana Carolina Chasin, 'How innovative was the Poupatempo experience in Brazil? Institutional bypass as a new form of institutional

successful reforms have arguably one common feature: instead of trying to fix an entire set of dysfunctional institutions, as most failed reforms do, they simply bypass them. These 'institutional bypasses' can be an effective way of overcoming the three traditional obstacles to institutional reform proposed by Trebilcock and Daniels:[33] lack of financial, human or technological resources; social–cultural–historical factors; and political economy-based impediments. Moreover, it may help reformers to deal with the high levels of uncertainty related to the effects of reforms caused by institutional interconnections and path dependence-related factors.

Like coronary bypass surgery, in which transplanted blood vessels are used to create a new circulatory pathway around clogged or blocked vessels, an institutional bypass creates new pathways around ineffiient or dysfunctional institutions. Unlike other procedures that try to unblock clogged arteries or expand narrow ones, the coronary bypass simply ignores the existence of the unhealthy artery and creates a new pathway for blood flow. One example of an institutional bypass is a bureaucratic reform in Brazil called *Poupatempo* (Saving Time).[34] In 1997, the government of the state of São Paulo created a one-stop shop for bureaucratic services. In contrast to the pre-existing system, in which government services were accessed by the public at multiple service points, offices of the federal, state and, in some cases, local administration were placed in one location in order to provide easy access to a variety of services. Services were provided more quickly than within the pre-existing bureaucracy, disrupting entrenched institutional cultures.

Poupatempo became the main provider of governmental services within the state shortly after its creation. In 2007, it provided services to an average of 50 000 people a day in the state of São Paulo. In that year, 18 units together serviced 23 million people. *Poupatempo* is an example of a successful institutional bypass because it created a new pathway for the provision of the same services that were being provided by the existing bureaucracy, but in a more efficient fashion.

---

change', *Brazilian Political Science Review* (forthcoming 2011); Mariana Mota Prado, 'Institutional bypass: an alternative for development reform', available at http://papers.ssrn.com/sol3/papers.cfm?abstract_id=1815442; see also Thomas Heller, 'An immodest postscript', in Erik Jensen and Thomas Heller (eds), *Beyond Common Knowledge: Empirical Approaches to the Rule of Law* (Palo Alto, CA: Stanford University Press, 2003).

[33] Michael Trebilcock and Ronald Daniels, *Rule of Law Reform and Development: Charting the Fragile Path of Progress* (Cheltenham: Edward Elgar, 2008). For a summary, see Chapter 2, section IV, Reasons for the Chronically Poor Quality of the Rule of Law and Related Legal Institutions in Many Countries.

[34] Prado and Chasin, *supra* note 32.

E. Decentralization

Another line of thinking in much of the recent public service reform literature emphasizes the virtues of formal decentralization of government functions to sub-national levels of government (regional or local). This is based largely on the theory that decentralization moves the state closer to the people and renders it more responsive to local needs and preferences. While this, in principle, may be true, experience suggests that implementing decentralization strategies poses major design challenges.

First, a careful identification of functions that are better performed at the local rather than national level needs to be determined so as to minimize inter-jurisdictional spillovers (negative or positive externalities) which risk promoting local policies that may be at variance with or antithetical to the national interest. Such spillovers are likely to be pervasive in areas such as infrastructure, health care, education, law and order, and environmental degradation, rendering an appropriate division of power between national, regional and local governments a major challenge.

Second, once a division of functions is determined, a reallocation of financial capacity, commensurate with the reallocation of functions, is required. On the one hand, decentralizing functions without decentralizing financial capacity is likely to degrade the quality of services offered at the local level and is likely to require some form of fiscal equalization to ensure that all regions have reasonably equivalent capacity to deliver basic public services. On the other hand, decentralizing functions and decision-making authority without clearly defined and stable caps on the central government's fiscal responsibilities – through transfers or subsidies, or explicit or implicit guarantees of borrowings by sub-national levels of government – is likely to encourage fiscal irresponsibility by sub-national levels of government, as well as macroeconomic instability.

Finally, if decentralization fails to increase local citizens' influence over the public sector, the principal benefits of decentralization will be lost. One of the key determinants of local accountability is the system for electing local officials – governors, mayors and members of sub-national legislatures. Where these regimes of accountability are deficient, decentralization may simply lead to more clientelism, patronage and outright corruption (an outcome, unfortunately, too often borne out by experience).[35] As Atul

---

[35] See William Dillinger and Marianne Fay, 'From centralized to decentralized governance' (1999) 36 *Finance and Development* 19; World Bank, *World Development Report: 1999–2000: Entering the 21st Century* (New York: Oxford University Press, 1999) Chapter 5; see also 'Bringing the state closer to the people' (1997) *World Bank World Development Report*.

Kohli points out in an insightful recent paper on state capacity for development, countries like India and Brazil often possess competent national bureaucracies – or at least apex economic bureaucracies – but state or local government functions, including the provision of infrastructure and basic education and health care, are often mired in incompetence, corruption, patrimonialism or excessive influence by wealthy local elites (explaining, in part, high levels of inequality in access to these services.)[36]

F. Building on Social Capital

A variant on formal decentralization strategies is to emphasize the potential for informal collaborative arrangements between the public and private sectors – in particular the realization of synergies between contributions by government and those by community or civil society organizations (intermediaries between government and individual citizen) that are able to deploy significant forms and levels of 'social capital' amongst their members in collaborative enterprises for mutual benefit. Peter Evans argues[37] that synergies may be realized because of the differences in comparative advantage between the state and civil society organizations in the provision of different inputs to joint projects and the greater potential for embeddedness that such projects permit in terms of civil servants engaging with the concerns of local communities.

By way of examples, Evans points to successful cases of rural irrigation project developments in Taiwan, condominium sewer developments in urban areas of Brazil, and some of Tendler's case studies (for example, her study of the provision of agricultural extension services), as well as the dense public sector–private sector business networks that are often claimed to have been important ingredients in the industrialization of the high performing East Asian economies. Tendler also argues that, from this perspective, public sector unions can be seen in a more sympathetic light than they are often portrayed in the development literature, where they

---

[36] See Atul Kohli, 'State capacity for development', United Nations Development Program, Global Event Working Paper, 2010.

[37] Peter Evans, 'Government action, social capital and development: reviewing the evidence on synergy' (1996) 25 *World Development* 1119; Peter Evans, *Embedded Autonomy – States and Industrial Transformation* (Princeton, NJ: Princeton University Press, 1995); see also Michael Woolcock, 'Social capital and economic development: towards a theoretical synthesis in policy framework' (1998) 27 *Theory and Society* 151; Christiaan Grootaert and Thierry van Bastelaer (eds), *The Role of Social Capital in Development: An Empirical Assessment* (Cambridge and New York: Cambridge University Press, 2002).

are often seen as self-interested defenders of a dysfunctional status quo in public administration.

However, the East Asian example (amongst others) provides some basis for caution in assigning an indiscriminately large role to civil society in the development equation. What was once seen as an important strength of governments in the high-performing East Asian economies – that is, extensive public sector–private sector networks – quickly became derided by many commentators during and after the Asian financial crisis in the late 1990s as symptomatic of 'crony capitalism' – patronage and corruption in the allocation of credit, licences and government contracts.[38]

IV. PUBLIC ADMINISTRATION AND THE LEGAL SYSTEM

While perhaps not as obvious as the design of legal or political institutions and related constitutional frameworks, law and legal institutions do, in fact, play an important part in structuring the public administration in most countries. Public sector employment laws and collective bargaining regimes, grievance procedures, anti-discrimination laws (often enforced by courts, arbitral bodies or specialized human rights agencies), and specialized administrative agencies charged with overseeing recruitment and promotion (such as public service commissions) all play a central framework role in structuring the performance of a country's public service. Any major set of reforms to the public service must address reforms to this legal framework. In the case of specialized administrative agencies performing regulatory functions (discussed in Chapter 2), administrative law principles and judicial review have a large area of potential application in ensuring transparency, impartiality and due process in their functioning.[39]

V. CORRUPTION AND DEVELOPMENT

Corruption affects most countries around the world but the problem is especially acute, and indeed pervasive, in many developing countries. The cost of corruption is high for developing countries, because it has a

---

[38] See, e.g., David C. Kang, *Crony Capitalism: Corruption and Development in South Korea and the Philippines* (Cambridge University Press, 2002).

[39] See Susan Rose-Ackerman, *From Elections to Democracy: Building Accountable Government in Hungary and Poland* (Cambridge and New York: Cambridge University Press, 2005).

negative impact on a country's economy (impairing growth), its politics (affecting governmental regulation and policy decisions), its international relations (affecting FDI and diverting foreign aid from its intended purposes), and its society (worsening the distribution of wealth). The World Bank has identified 'corruption as among the greatest obstacles to economic and social development'.[40]

Corruption is a complex phenomenon, but academic research has shown that some of the most important underlying causes of corruption are institutional.[41] Based on this assumption, we assess the prospects for anti-corruption reforms. Given that corruption is yet another institutional factor that prevents development, it poses similar challenges to other institutional reforms analysed in this book: it requires a complex plan of action, which must be adapted to the particular circumstances of each country, and needs to take into account institutional interdependencies, self-reinforcing mechanisms that generate path dependence and political economy problems.

A. Defining Corruption

Although there are many definitions of corruption, we use the term to refer to 'the use of public office for private gain' – that is, corruption of or by public officials (political or bureaucratic).[42] This includes both 'behaviour which deviates from the normal duties of a public role',[43] and 'the violation of the formal rules governing the allocation of public resources'.[44] However, in some countries there may be a lack of formal rules governing official behaviour, or the normal duties of an official may include behaviour that would qualify as corruption in other countries, such as accepting gifts. This complicates comparison between countries.[45]

---

[40] World Bank, 'Overview of anti-corruption', available at http://go.worldbank.org/K6AEEPROC0.

[41] Susan Rose-Ackerman, *Corruption and Government: Causes, Consequences, and Reform* (Cambridge, UK: Cambridge University Press, 1999) at 226.

[42] Cheryl W. Gray and Daniel Kaufmann, 'Corruption and development' (March 1998) 35 *Finance and Development* 1; Pranab Bardhan, *Scarcity, Conflicts, and Cooperation: Essays in the Political and Institutional Economics of Development* (Cambridge, MA: MIT Press, 2005) at 138.

[43] Joseph Nye, 'Corruption and political development: a cost–benefit analysis' (1967) 61 *American Political Science Review* 2.

[44] Mushtaq H. Khan, 'Patron-client networks and the economic effects of corruption in Asia' (1998) 10:1 *European Journal of Development Research* 15–39.

[45] Michael Johnston and Arnold J. Heidenheimer, *Political Corruption* (New Brunswick, NJ: Transaction Publishers, 2001) at 26.

Generally, corruption entails an 'exchange of government property for personal gain'.[46] More often than not, economic gains are the goal of corrupt behaviour, but the term can also encompass the use of public office to obtain non-economic gains (political or personal). Although corruption comes in many forms, the common element is that an agent (usually a government official) pursues personal gain by bargaining away an item or benefit over which he or she has discretion, but which belongs to a principal (usually the public).[47] It is this principal–agent relationship that gives rise to opportunities and incentives for corruption.

Two of the most important types of corruption for economic gain are embezzlement and bribes. While embezzlement entails the misappropriation of public funds, bribes, in contrast, involve the appropriation of private funds by public officials. Officials might ask for bribes to perform their functions (for example, a city official asking for money to issue a permit that a citizen would otherwise be entitled to), not to perform their functions (for example, a police officer asking for money not to issue a ticket to the driver of a speeding vehicle), or not to perform acts that are not part of their functions but which they can threaten to perform through abuse of power (for example, a police officer asking for money not to torture a prisoner, or a tax official demanding a bribe to forego an audit). Decisions can be 'sold wholesale, as when government policies are distorted to benefit a specific interest group who has bribed policymakers . . . or retail, as is the case when public employees personally collect a payment for the granting of a permit or a license'.[48]

Forms of corruption that involve non-economic benefits, clientelism or patronage take place where public resources and political processes are manipulated to increase personal power.[49] This entails a political exchange between a politician or public official, the 'patron', who gives patronage in exchange for the vote or support of a 'client'. This is a form of 'institutional corruption', which generates gains in a way that benefits officials in their capacity as public officials rather than in their personal life (individual corruption).[50] For example, an elected official may offer high-ranked

---

[46] Andrei Shleifer and Robert W. Vishny, 'Corruption' (1993) 108:3 *Quarterly Journal of Economics* 1.

[47] Moses Naim, 'Corruption eruption' (Summer 1995) *Brown Journal of World Affairs*, 2: 2: 245–61.

[48] Ibid.

[49] Luis Ronniger, 'Political clientelism, democracy, and market economy' (2004) 36 *Comparative Politics* 3.

[50] Michael Johnston and Arnold J. Heidenheimer, *Political Corruption* (New Brunswick, NJ: Transaction Publishers, 2001) at 42.

and well-paid jobs in the bureaucracy in exchange for political support, rather than hiring based on merit.[51]

When patronage is applied to personal relationships, often referred to as 'nepotism', it results in personal gains for elected officials who use public office to provide benefits and grant privileges to people with whom they are personally affiliated in some way. In this case, public office is used to create benefits for people who belong to a particular social network to which a public official also belongs (extended family, political party or ascriptive group, such as clan, ethnic or religious group).

B. Measuring Corruption

The absence of an authoritative and universally applicable definition of what constitutes corruption limits the development of a measurement tool. This is further complicated by the absence of 'direct, simple and easily contrastable indicators'. Because it is a clandestine activity, corruption measurement requires 'much more elaborated constructions, subject to complex and, often, subjective inputs'.[52] Another problem is that the collection of data only started with the relatively recent attention to corruption in the development literature, resulting in an absence of data from before 1980.[53] Thus, there is limited capacity to analyse how corruption has evolved over longer periods of time.

Most assessments of corruption use one of three methods: (i) gathering the perceptions of stakeholders and individuals; (ii) national institutional profiles which function as a proxy for corruption (budget management or procurement practices), and (iii) auditing individual projects as a sample of likely national practices. None of these assessments are direct measures of corruption. The most direct corruption indicators gather survey information on the real experiences of individuals and businesses of corruption and paying bribes.[54]

---

[51] James A. Robinson and Thierry Verdier, 'The political economy of clientelism' (2003) Center for Economic Policy Research Discussion Paper No. 3205.

[52] Francisco Javier-Urra, 'Assessing corruption – an analytical review of corruption measurement and its problems: perception, error and utility' (May 2007), Edmund A. Walsh School of Public Service, Georgetown Washington. Available at http://unpan1.un.org/intradoc/groups/public/documents/APCITY/UNPAN028792.pdf.

[53] Andrew Williams and Abu Siddique, 'The use and abuse of governance indicators' (2008) *Economics of Governance* 9.

[54] See, e.g., M. Seligson, 'The impact of corruption on regime legitimacy: a comparative study of four Latin American countries' (2005) 64 *Journal of Politics* 408.

The most recent development in corruption measurement is the emergence of 'second-generation'[55] or 'aggregate indicators'[56] which combine several primary measurements. The most widely used measurements are the Corruption Perception Index, developed by Transparency International, and two indices developed by the World Bank: the Business Environment and Enterprise Survey and the World Governance Indicators (WGI).

The Corruption Perception Index incorporates a list of sources which have undertaken their own assessments of levels of corruption, such as the World Business Environment Survey or Freedom House, which are each given a weighting to yield an average corruption ranking. The major advantage of these indices is that they take an average rating, therefore avoiding biases in individual sources and measurement errors.[57] For example, the WGI expresses its rankings with larger confidence intervals for countries for which they have fewer primary sources. Sources are also weighted on the strength of their correlation to each other, although this has been criticized by Arndt and Oman for assuming that similarity in measurement results show higher levels of accuracy, rather than simply sharing the same errors.[58]

Criticisms of these measures reveal the complicated challenge of measuring corruption. These measures primarily focus on expert assessments, such as elite business panels, rather than local household or business sector perceptions. They have been criticized for excluding the experiences of the poor or the informal sector, while focusing too heavily on the perspectives of multinational organizations.[59] Further, a significant gap has been found between perceptions and actual levels of corruption.[60] Perceptions have been found to overestimate local experiences of corruption when compared to survey evidence of real experiences of

---

55 M. Johnston, 'Measuring the new corruption rankings: implications for analysis and reform', in A.J. Heidenheimer and M. Johnston (eds), *Political Corruption: Concepts and Context* (New Brunswick, NJ: Transaction Publishers, 2001).

56 D. Kaufmann, A. Kraay and P. Zoido-Lobatón, 'Aggregating governance indicators' (1999) World Bank Policy Research Working Paper No. 2195.

57 D. Kaufmann and A. Kraay, 'On measuring governance: framing issues for debate', Issues Paper for 11 January 2007, Roundtable on Measuring Governance, World Bank Institute and the Development Economics Vice-Presidency of the World Bank.

58 C. Arndt and C. Oman, *Uses and Abuses of Governance Indicators* (Paris: OECD, 2006) at 58.

59 Williams and Siddique, *supra* note 53.

60 D. Donchev and G. Ujhelyi, 'Do corruption indices measure corruption?' Working Paper, Economics Department, Harvard University, 2007.

corruption.[61] However, even if more objective data regarding government practices is used, it is still likely to obscure the real situation because of the difficulty of obtaining accurate measurements of a secret activity.

C. Consequences of Corruption

Transparency International has declared that 'in low-income countries, rampant corruption jeopardizes the global fight against poverty, threatening to derail the UN Millennium Development Goals (MDGs)'.[62] How does corruption negatively affect development prospects? To answer this question, it is important to distinguish between different kinds of corruption. First, the misappropriation of public funds for private use has a clear and direct effect on the amount of government finances available to be spent on development-related projects and services. Bribes, in contrast, raise more complicated questions.[63]

In the past, some authors have suggested that bribery can positively influence government functioning and development. Bribes have been considered to be supplementary to a bureaucrat's salary, and thus are similar to the government raising taxes and increasing the remuneration of public servants.[64] This would be especially true if bribes are being paid for these servants to perform their functions or to overcome bureaucratic hurdles (a form of piece-work or performance-based compensation).[65] Some scholars have argued that using bribery to fund the bureaucracy instead of taxes may reduce the tax burden paid by businesses that do not use the government service calling for these bribes, and these lower taxes may be beneficial for growth.[66]

---

[61] Mireille Razafindrakoto and François Roubaud, 'How far can we trust expert opinions on corruption? An experiment based on surveys in francophone Africa', in *Global Corruption Report* (Transparency International, 2005).

[62] Transparency International, 'Press kit: persistently high corruption in low income countries amounts to an ongoing humanitarian disaster', 23 September, 2008, available at http://www.transparency.org/policy_research/surveys_indices/cpi/2008.

[63] Gray and Kaufmann, *supra* note 42.

[64] Beatrice Weder, 'Institutions, corruption, and development and their ramifications for international cooperation', in Hans van Ginkel, Brendan Barrett, Julius Court and Jerry Velasquez (eds), *Human Development and the Environment: Challenges for the United Nations in the New Millennium* (New York: United Nations University Press, 2002) 149–59.

[65] Of course, it would not be equivalent if the bribe was being paid to stop acts in which officials are abusing their powers and positions, such as police officers who ask for bribes not to torture prisoners.

[66] G.S. Becker and G.J. Stigler, 'Law enforcement, malfeasance, and compensa-

It has also been claimed that bribery can help to overcome institutional shortcomings and foster efficiency. For example, Huntington has argued that bribery could enhance efficiency by 'oiling' the ineffective mechanisms of a poorly functioning government, thus improving governance through an informal mechanism.[67] Bribes have also been described as an allocative mechanism that allows for a kind of bidding contest for government services, which may result in an efficient allocation of resources.[68] As Bardhan explains:

> In the context of pervasive and cumbersome regulations in developing countries, corruption may actually improve efficiency and help growth. Economists have shown that in the second-best world with pre-existing policy-induced distortions, additional distortions in the form of black-marketeering and smuggling might actually improve welfare, even when some resources might have to be spent in policing such activities. (. . .) As non-economists usually point out, corruption is the much needed grease for the squeaking wheels of a rigid administration.[69]

These arguments in favour of bribery are not persuasive. A major difference between taxes and bribery is the cost of keeping corruption secret to avoid detection and punishment, with the result that corruption is more distortionary than taxation.[70] There is also evidence that suggests that the cost of capital for organizations tends to be higher where bribery is more prevalent.[71] Moreover, there is a high degree of uncertainty in corruption practices: a private party will never be sure if a corrupt official will keep

---

tion of enforcers' (1974) 3 *Journal of Legal Studies* 1.

67 Samuel P. Huntington, *Political Order in Changing Societies* (New Haven: Yale University Press, 1968).

68 An example of this type of argument was made by Nathaniel Leff, 'Economic development through bureaucratic corruption' in Monday U. Ekpo (ed.), *Bureaucratic Corruption in Sub-Saharan Africa* (Washington DC: University Press of America, 1979) at 329: 'Corruption may introduce an element of competition into what is otherwise a comfortably monopolistic industry . . . [and] payment of the highest bribes [becomes] one of the principal criteria for allocation . . . Hence, a tendency toward efficiency is introduced into the system.' Similarly economist Francis Lui has asserted that 'bribing strategies . . . minimize the average value of the time costs of the queue . . . [and the official] . . . could choose to speed up the service when bribery is allowed': Francis Liu, 'An equilibrium queuing model of bribery' (1985) 93 *Journal of Political Economy* 760.

69 Bardhan, *supra* note 42 at 139–40.

70 Ibid., at 146.

71 Daniel Kaufman and Shang-Jin Wei, 'Does "Grease money" speed up the wheels of commerce?' (December 1999) World Bank Policy Research Working Paper No. 2254.

his promises. The negative impact of bribes on economic development was first demonstrated empirically by Mauro in his 1995 paper 'Corruption, country risk and growth'.[72] In a business environment with substantial unpredictable costs, businesses will be reluctant to invest. The more variable the rates of corruption, the more negative the effect on foreign investment.[73] Instead, public investment is often increased, as larger budgets and bureaucratic structures of government provide more ample opportunities for corruption and misappropriation.[74] The argument that claims that corruption is efficiency enhancing assumes that red tape is an exogenous factor, and ignores the fact that bribes might become an incentive for the creation of pervasive and cumbersome regulation, thus exacerbating rather than solving the problem of inefficient governance.[75] Corruption may create incentives to preserve the existence of a burdensome regulatory framework, given that interest groups that benefit from the status quo will resist any type of reform aimed at reducing red tape.

Empirical evidence shows that in countries where bribery is common the amount of time private enterprise representatives spend with public officials is higher than in less corrupt countries, reflecting an inefficient use of resources that are wasted on courting political connections.[76] Moreover, those best able to utilize bribery are often not the socially optimal service recipients:

> [t]he grease argument is particularly troublesome in this context [where laws and regulations serve productive social objectives, such as building codes, environmental controls, and prudential banking sector regulations] since bribes can override such regulations and cause serious social harm, such as illegal logging of tropical rain forests or failure to observe building codes designed to ensure public safety.[77]

Corruption negatively affects the ability of the government to regulate market activity effectively by distorting the decision-making process of

---

[72] Mauro, *supra* note 10.

[73] S.-J. Wei, 'Why is corruption so much more taxing than tax? Arbitrariness kills' (1997) National Bureau of Economic Research Working Paper 6255 (Cambridge, MA).

[74] V. Tanzi and H. Davoodi, 'Corruption, public investment, and growth'(1997) International Monetary Fund Working Paper, 97/139.

[75] Vito Tanzi, 'Corruption around the world: causes, consequences, scope and cure' (1998) 45 *IMF Staff Papers* 4; Gray and Kaufmann, *supra* note 42 at 8; Bardhan, *supra* note 42 at 141.

[76] Raymond Fisman and Roberta Gatti, 'Bargaining for bribes: the role of institutions' (2006) Discussion Paper No. 5712, CEPR.

[77] Gray and Kaufmann, *supra* note 42 at 8–9.

government officials. Anti-corruption detection and punishment efforts are also costly for the state. Finally, the distributive effect of corruption is negative: while a tax system can have progressive features, bribes are likely to exclude the poor from the bribery system altogether, increasing inequality and perpetuating vested interests. Corruption increases levels of inequality by limiting access to beneficial government activities to an already privileged group.[78] In sum, corruption is a major obstacle to development. However, it is not fully clear whether causality between corruption and development runs in only one direction. Corruption can reduce the GDP per capita, but at the same time poorer countries have fewer resources to fight corruption, and the lack of resources creates more incentives to be corrupt,[79] which suggests that growth may reduce corruption.

D. Causes of Corruption

Corruption has not always been a prominent issue on the development agenda. Until recently, there was resistance to discussing the prevalence of corruption in developing countries because this could suggest that it was part of the culture of these countries – a claim that could be perceived as racist, discriminatory or morally patronizing.[80] Some studies have linked levels of corruption to such factors as more hierarchical social structures or social embeddedness, which can be detrimental to individual civic engagement – a factor which should help to reduce corruption.[81] Although culture may not be able to explain fully the presence of corruption in developing countries, it is clear that reforms targeting corruption must take cultural factors into account.[82]

The importance of culture has been documented in a recent study by

---

78 For a pioneering study, see Mauro, *supra* note 10. For an extensive review of the literature, see Johann Graf Lambsdorff, 'Consequences and causes of corruption – what do we know from a cross-section of countries?', in Susan Rose-Ackerman (ed.), *International Handbook on the Economics of Corruption* (Northampton, MA: Edward Elgar Publishing, 2006).

79 Ibid.

80 Robert Klitgaard, *Controlling Corruption*, (Berkeley: University of California Press, 1988) at 208–9.

81 Rafael La Porta, Florencio Lopez-De-Silanes, Andrei Shleifer and Robert W. Vishny, 'The quality of government' (1999) 15:1 *Journal of Law, Economics and Organization* 222–79; Lambsdorff, *supra* note 78; Amir Licht, Chanan Goldschmidt and Shalom Schwartz, 'Culture rules: the foundations of the rule of law and other norms of governance' (2007) 35 *Journal of Comparative Economics* 659.

82 B. Husted, 'Wealth, culture, and corruption' (1999) 30:2 *Journal of International Business Studies* 339–60.

Raymond Fisman and Edward Miguel.[83] They measured how likely it was for diplomats from different countries working for the United Nations in New York to comply with parking rules. These diplomats have immunity and therefore cannot be fined when they park illegally (they can be issued tickets, but they do not have an obligation to pay them). Their study shows that diplomats from corrupt countries are more likely to park illegally and, whenever fined, these same diplomats are less likely to pay these fines than diplomats from less corrupt countries. The lesson, as Fisman and Miguel put it, is 'that reformers of government institutions – whether local officials or World Bank hotshots – must be aware that values and social norms can undermine their attempts at change. In other words, altering the law is unlikely to be sufficient in the presence of a pervasive culture of corruption'.[84]

Corruption is more commonly explained as rampant in developing countries 'not because their people are different from people elsewhere, but because conditions are ripe for it'.[85] Institutional arrangements create opportunities and incentives for corruption, making the problem more pervasive in these nations. As Gray and Kaufmann explain:

> The motivation to earn income is extremely strong, exacerbated by poverty and by low and declining civil service salaries. (. . .) Not only motivation is strong, but also opportunities to engage in corruption are numerous. Monopoly rents can be very large in highly regulated economies, (. . .) The discretion of many public officials is also broad in developing and transition countries, and this systemic weakness is exacerbated by poorly defined, ever-changing, and poorly disseminated rules and regulations.[86]

Institutional arrangements that are often perceived to be conducive to corruption are size of the government and the degree of state intervention in the economy.[87] There are, of course, exceptions: large governments in Scandinavian countries are associated with some of the lowest levels of corruption in the world. But there seems to be a clear pattern otherwise. It is possible that this is simply because the larger the role of the govern-

---

[83] Raymond Fisman and Edward Miguel, 'Corruption, norms and legal enforcement: evidence from diplomatic parking tickets' (2007) 115 *Journal of Political Economy*.

[84] Raymond Fisman and Edward Miguel, *Economic Gangsters: Corruption, Violence, and the Poverty of Nations* (Princeton, NJ: Princeton University Press, 2008) at 102.

[85] Gray and Kaufmann, *supra* note 42.

[86] Ibid., at 9.

[87] Lambsdorff, *supra* note 78.

ment, the more opportunities will be available for abuse of that power.[88] Corruption is also encouraged where economic activity is highly regulated by the government (less true of governments in Scandinavian countries who place greater emphasis on social programs), as substantial rents will accrue to organizations that are able to attract the favour of government decision makers.[89] This is exacerbated in closed economies where international competition for markets is limited.[90] Natural resource rents may also encourage corruption,[91] as may the presence of highly corrupt neighbouring countries.[92]

Poor government quality can be either a cause or a consequence of corruption. Sometimes they reinforce each other and the causal arrow runs in both directions. There are, however, certain institutional arrangements that are more often correlated with higher levels of corruption, as Lambsdorff shows in a detailed review of the literature.[93] Centralized states seem to be more corrupt than federal states with a high level of fiscal decentralization. This seems especially true if decentralization reforms take place in countries that have civic cooperation, trust among people, and well-developed sub-national units. The relationship between democracy and corruption is non-linear: democratic practices inhibit corruption after a country has a robust, fully functional democratic regime; however, corruption in medium-democratic regimes is higher than in totally authoritarian countries. Within democracies, smaller voting districts, proportional representation and presidential systems are correlated with higher levels of corruption. After reviewing the studies that support these findings, Lambsdorff summarizes the lessons for reformers, as follows:

> In sum, democracy reduces corruption, but not the lukewarm type, not the type with little electoral participation and not immediately after its implementation. Before transforming authoritarian systems into halfhearted democracies it is worthwhile considering whether such systems have established their peculiar methods of honoring integrity and how these might be endangered during

---

88 Ibid., at 14.

89 D.R. Henderson, 'Power corrupts – editorial comment', *Wall Street Journal*, 19 April 1999.

90 J. Sachs and A. Warner, 'Economic reform and the process of global integration' (1995) 25:1 *Brookings Papers on Economic Activity* 1–118.

91 A. Ades and R. Di Tella, 'Rents, competition, and corruption'(1999) 89 *American Economic Review* 982–94.

92 W. Sandholtz and M. Gray, 'International integration and national corruption' (2003) 57:4 *International Organization* 761–800.

93 Lambsdorff, *supra* note 78.

> transition. Thinking about an ideal type of democracy, there is evidence that presidential systems fare worse with respect to corruption as compared to parliamentarism. But it remains to be seen whether presidentialism might be a second best option where political parties are of poor quality. Finally, but less strong in magnitude, electoral systems of proportional representation are associated with higher corruption than plurality rule with single-member districts. Westminster democracy would be the model best capable of reducing corruption.[94]

It is not very often, however, that reformers find themselves in a position to change a country's political regime. The windows of opportunity for state-building exercises are rare and more often than not reformers will be able to do little to change the political institutions along the lines suggested by Lambsdorff. With this in mind, we turn to potential reform options that take into account the fact that the reformers are not writing on a blank slate.

E. Potential Cures

Institutional reforms can reduce the opportunities and incentives to use public office for private gains and therefore have significant potential to reduce overall levels of corruption. In this regard, Susan Rose-Ackerman provides the following categories of reform strategies that are available for tackling corruption:

(a) the redesign of government programs to limit the underlying incentives for corruption by limiting the pay-offs available from corruption;
(b) increasing accountability and transparency of government actions to increase the likelihood of preventing corruption;
(c) more radical reforms of government structure, such as constitutional re-engineering, to limit opportunities for corruption.[95]

In addition to these strategies, a common proposal is the creation of anti-corruption watchdog bodies, such as the Hong Kong Independent Committee against Corruption (ICAC), which was created in 1974 in response to perceived high levels of corruption in Hong Kong society.[96]

---

94 Ibid.

95 Rose-Ackerman, *supra* note 41.

96 Daniel Kaufman, 'Revisiting anti-corruption strategies: tilt towards incentive driven approaches?' in *Corruption and Integrity Improvement Initiatives in Developing Countries* (New York: UNDP, 1998).

This body conducts high-profile investigations and prosecutions which have led to a significant decrease in corruption levels since its creation.[97] The results have been particularly striking in the Hong Kong Police Department, where the ICAC, operating completely separately from regular law enforcement bodies, was able to launch a strong anti-corruption offensive, including the investigation, arrest and interrogation of police management and officers. The success of these efforts was largely as a result of maintaining routine investigations, regardless of the presence of specific reports of corruption.[98]

As well as focusing on enforcement and prevention, the ICAC also included mass public education campaigns, which informed citizens about the role of the ICAC, and the illegality of corruption and what this comprised. Reporting of corruption was also encouraged, and this served to increase social disapproval of corrupt activities. This fundamental change in the attitudes of the Hong Kong community was coupled with the institutional changes necessary to increase public perceptions of corruption control, especially within the police.[99] The results of these efforts was the eradication of syndicated police corruption by the end of the 1970s, and a clear reduction in corruption in government by the late 1980s.[100] This created 'a new equilibrium of clean government', and the public expectation that this should remain the norm.[101]

It is important to acknowledge, however, that the creation of an anti-corruption body alone is unlikely to be an effective measure to tackle corruption. As in other cases of reform, there are important institutional interconnections that require more than stand-alone reforms. For instance, there is little that a watchdog can do without strong anti-bribery legislation and an effective independent court system to enforce the applicable sanctions. There is also a more indirect connection between reform success and incentives and opportunities for corruption. Some reforms may increase the risk of punishment, but they are less likely to be effective if strong incentives and opportunities for corruption remain. Indeed, a great deal of the Hong Kong experience is also based on a variety of specific institutional reforms including, for instance, the legalization of

---

97 Bertrand de Speville, *Hong Kong: Policy Initiatives against Corruption*, (OECD Development Centre Publishing, 1997).

98 Melanie Manion, *Corruption by Design: Building Clean Government in Mainland China and Hong Kong* (Cambridge, MA: Harvard University Press, 2004) at 41.

99 Ibid., at 44.

100 Ibid., at 72.

101 Ibid.

off-track betting, which eliminated an opportunity for police officers to extract bribes from citizens.[102]

Another challenge for institutional reforms is that they need to account for self-reinforcing mechanisms in corruption practices. As Bardhan explains,[103] adopting a game theoretic approach, social norms can settle in multiple equilibria, making the problems of corruption relatively rare, widespread or systemic. The basic assumption is that expected gains from corruption depend on the number of other people who are expected to be corrupt. In this context, there are three possible equilibria: (i) nobody is corrupt, and it does not pay to be corrupt; (ii) everyone is corrupt, and it does not pay to be non-corrupt; (iii) there are both corrupt and non-corrupt officials, who are indifferent between being corrupt or non-corrupt. While the first and the second equilibria are stable, the third is not: if more and more officials decide to be corrupt, this can tip the equilibrium to one where everyone is corrupt.[104] Self-reinforcing mechanisms will be an obstacle for institutional reform in cases in which there is an equilibrium where everyone is corrupt and these social norms are very stable. In cases 'where there is systemic corruption, the institution's rules and norms of behavior have already been adapted to a corrupt modus operandi, with bureaucrats and other agents often following the predatory examples of, or even taking instructions from, their principals in the political arena'.[105]

On the other hand, small changes in an unstable equilibrium can tip the balance in the opposite direction, towards the point where nobody is corrupt. In this regard, reformers can use self-reinforcing mechanisms to move the equilibrium towards lower levels of corruption. For instance, the functions of an anti-corruption watchdog can be reinforced by the creation of various kinds of accountability mechanisms, such as 'an independent office of public auditing, an election commission to limit and enforce rules on campaign contributions in democratic elections, (. . .) an office of local ombudsman with some control over the bureaucracy, citizens' watchdog committees providing information and monitoring services and pursuing public-interest litigation'.[106]

In addition to institutional interconnections and self-reinforcing mechanisms, there is yet another similarity between reforms to tackle corruption and other pro-development institutional reforms: the problem of an

---

[102] Robert Klitgaard, *Controlling Corruption* (University of California Press, 1988) at 116.
[103] Bardhan, *supra* note 42 at 152.
[104] Ibid., at 154.
[105] Gray and Kaufmann, *supra* note 42 at 8.
[106] Bardhan, *supra* note 42 at 162.

uncongenial political economy in which interest groups that benefit from corruption are likely to resist reform.[107] Systemic corruption means that many powerful groups are likely to fall in this category, making it difficult to identify the possible beneficiaries from reform who might be mobilized to promote the necessary changes. In these cases, for example, it might be necessary to wait for a window of opportunity where a dramatic change in political regime or a major public scandal makes it politically feasible to promote reform.[108]

In the case of bribery, one possible solution is to promote reform focused on multinational companies based in developed countries, but which operate within developing countries, often engaging with corrupt governments. Bribes involve two parties: the public official demanding the bribe (the demand side) and the private party willing to pay for it (the supply side). Thus, in addition to reforms that reduce opportunities and incentives for corruption among public officials, it is also possible to reduce opportunities and incentives for corruption among multinational corporations, thus reducing the supply side. These companies can be controlled by extraterritorial legislation in their countries of origin, which would also govern their acts outside the home country's territory. This would overcome some of the institutional complexities of promoting reform in developing countries.

One of the first countries to enact legislation against these practices was the United States. The 1977 Foreign Corrupt Practices Act (FCPA) forbids American companies from bribing foreign officials, or from knowingly arranging for a bribe through an intermediary.[109] However, there are limitations on its scope: the Act does not forbid payments to speed up bureaucratic processes (facilitation or 'grease payments') and in 1988 the Act was amended to expand the list of what qualifies as facilitation. This list now includes 'all payments to foreign officials to expedite procedures, such as customs procedures or permits, that would otherwise occur without a bribe, but more slowly'.[110] The Act applies to all US nationals, or entities established under US law or operating principally in the United States. Since the enactment of the FCPA, the United States has put considerable pressure on other countries to follow its actions.

---

107 See Chapter 1, section IV, E. Why are Some Countries Afflicted with Persistently Bad Institutions?

108 William Dillinger and Marianne Fay, 'From centralized to decentralized governance' (1999) 36 *Finance & Development* 4.

109 Foreign Corrupt Practices Act, 15 U.S.C.78 m, 78dd-2, 78dd-3, 78ff.

110 Alvaro Cuervo-Cazurra, 'The effectiveness of laws against bribery abroad' (2008) 39:4 *Journal of International Business Studies* 636.

In 1997, the OECD promulgated the first multilateral convention to combat bribery of foreign officials – the OECD Anti-Bribery Convention – which was also signed by Argentina, Brazil, Bulgaria, Chile and the Slovak Republic.[111] This document is fundamentally consistent with the basic principles of the anti-bribery provisions of the FCPA.[112] The Convention also includes the provisions of the 1995 Recommendation on the Tax Deductibility of Bribes of Foreign Public Officials, which recommended that member countries make bribes paid to foreign officials no longer tax deductible as a business expense, which has since been implemented by all signatories.[113] Although the implementation of the Convention has been heralded as significant progress in advancing anti-corruption efforts, its efficacy is limited by the allocation of minimal resources in many countries to monitoring compliance and enforcement, and often limited incentives to undertake such actions against a state's own businesses competing with foreign businesses for contracts in other countries. Also, major foreign investors such as China are not signatories; this creates collective action problems. Thus it may be a weak substitute for domestic institutional reform.[114]

A major source of the supply of bribes comes from multinational companies (MNCs) in natural resource extraction sectors. The result is often that 'bribery, cheating and imbalanced negotiating all cut into what rightfully ought to go to the developing country', as the MNCs are able to gain control of the desired resource without paying the country the full value which it would have received in a fair and competitive market.[115] Greater transparency in oil, gas and mining contracts would greatly increase the opportunities for developing countries to receive full value for their natural resources. The Extractive Industries Transparency Initiative is

---

111 OECD Convention, OECD Doc. DAFFE/IME/BR(97)20, reprinted in 37 I.L.M. 1 (1998).

112 Stuart H. Deming, *Foreign Corrupt Practices Act and the New International Norms* (American Bar Association, 2010, 2nd edn).

113 OECD Convention, OECD/C(96)27/Final, (1996), reprinted in 35 I.L.M. 1311 (1996).

114 Ben W. Heineman, Jr. and Fritz Heimann, 'The long war against corruption,' (May/June 2006) *Foreign Affairs*; Kevin Davis, 'Self-interest and altruism in the deterrence of transnational bribery' (2002) 4:2 *American Law and Economics Review* 314–40; Kevin Davis, 'Does the globalization of anti-corruption law help developing countries?' in Julio Faundez and Celin Tan (eds), *International Economic Law: Globalization and Developing Countries* (Cheltenham, UK: Edward Elgar, 2010).

115 Joseph Stiglitz, *Making Globalization Work* (New York: W.W. Norton & Co., 2006) at 140–41.

a recent initiative involving a coalition of governments, companies, civil society groups, investors and international organizations that 'supports improved governance in resource-rich countries through the verification and full publication of company payments and government revenues from oil, gas and mining'.[116] Governments and companies that sign the Initiative do so voluntarily, and are then bound to publish all payments made, or payments received, which are independently verified by a multi-stakeholder group. How effective such a voluntary initiative is likely to prove remains to be tested by experience.

VI. CONCLUSION

It seems clear that there is not a single bureaucratic regime that represents an ideal for all countries, at least at an operational or organizational level, notwithstanding the importance of Weberian characteristics as general benchmarks. The same can be said for anti-corruption reforms. As Fukuyama has pointed out, even amongst developed countries with well-performing bureaucracies, operational and organizational details vary vastly and are the legacy of the particularities of history, culture, politics and economic imperatives, and are not readily transplantable to or adaptable by other countries.[117] Civil service reform initiatives need to take the legacies of the past seriously if they are to be both feasible and predictable in their effects in the context in question.[118] Hence, as with the design of legal and political institutions, a premium attaches to adaptive and incremental strategies in advancing the agenda for bureaucratic and anti-corruption reform. These initiatives cannot effectively be imposed by 'outsiders' but require domestic leadership and mobilized local political constituencies to promote and support them. Lessons from comparative experience and external financial and technical resources may usefully complement such initiatives but cannot substitute for them. As with the conclusion reached in other chapters, lawyers have an important role to play in this complex exercise of designing institutional solutions that meet the needs and address the particular challenges of each country.

---

116 Extractive Industries Transparency Initiative, 'What is the EITI?' Available at http://www.eitransparency.org/eiti.

117 Frances Fukuyama, *State-Building, Governance and World Order in the 21st Century* (Ithaca, NY: Cornell University Press, 2004).

118 Kohli, *supra* note 36.

6. State-owned enterprises, privatization and development[1]

I. INTRODUCTION

In the 1980s and 1990s a wave of privatizations swept the world. State-owned enterprises (SOEs) in many countries were sold to private investors in sectors as varied as steel, mining, banking, telecommunications, electricity and water. From 1977 to 1999 there were 2459 privatization deals in 121 countries.[2] Privatization, together with a number of other reforms that constituted the so-called 'Washington Consensus',[3] was part of an internationally accepted strategy for fostering economic growth. Before these privatizations, governments (especially those in developing countries) assumed many of the economic functions pursued by the private sector in other countries, as exemplified by the prominent role played by SOEs in delivering infrastructure services in some developed and most developing countries. Privatization reforms were driven by the assumption that these functions could be more efficiently performed by the private sector. However, in many cases, privatization fell short of delivering the expected results. These outcomes, combined with the pitfalls of other 'Washington Consensus' policies, have forced reformers and academics to revisit many of their original assumptions and adopt a more cautious perspective on privatization. In some cases, privatization may be a solution, but in others it is not. And even in those cases where it may be a solution to the inefficiencies of the public sector, it is not the only one. Many alter-

---

[1] Portions of this chapter are adapted and updated from two previous publications by one of the authors: D. Andrew, C. Smith and Michael J. Trebilcock, 'State-owned enterprises in less developed countries: privatization and alternative reform strategies' (2001) 12 *European Journal of Law and Economics* 240; and Ronald J. Daniels and Michael J. Trebilcock, 'The private provision of public infrastructure: an organizational analysis of the next frontier' (1996) 46 *University of Toronto Law Journal* 393.

[2] Bernardo Bortolotti, Marcella Fantini and Domenico Siniscalco, 'Privatization around the world: evidence from panel data' (2003) 88 *Journal of Public Economics* 305.

[3] See Chapter 1.

natives to privatization can and should be considered in implementing reforms.

The discourse about privatization may have changed, but the challenge remains the same. On one hand, state-owned companies may provide social and political benefits to a country, but this may come at significant economic and fiscal costs because of operational inefficiencies. On the other hand, private companies may be able to deliver essential and basic services, such as electricity or telecommunications, but there are significant challenges in ensuring that these companies will provide universal service, and foster other social and political goals. Reducing the inefficiencies of state-owned companies can provide infrastructure for other economic activities, thus fostering economic growth. However, this goal cannot be decoupled from alleviating poverty and providing universal access to essential services. This is especially true in developing countries. As a consequence, alternatives to privatization are still prominent on the development agenda.

This chapter analyses the arguments for and against privatization of state-owned companies, reviews the evidence from the most recent privatization experiences around the world, discusses possible reasons for the failures and assesses the possible alternatives. The conclusion is that there are at least two strong institutional components in privatization processes. The success or failure of privatization is connected both with a country's broader institutional environment (a healthy private sector, effective regulation, lack of corruption, a stable political system) and with the institutional details of the specific privatization strategy adopted by reformers. The same is true for alternatives to privatization, such as public–private partnerships for the development of new infrastructure. Thus, reforms to improve the delivery of basic services in developing countries are intrinsically connected to the reforms discussed in other chapters of this book.

II. STATE-OWNED ENTERPRISES AND DEVELOPMENT

A. Rationales for State-Owned Enterprises

State-owned enterprises emerged in the developing world for a mix of political, ideological and economic reasons. They were often formed (and subsequently expanded) to marshall support for new and fragile governments in developing countries: the larger an SOE sector, the larger a government's direct influence over its economy. Developing country governments were also influenced by the spread of socialist ideology following World War II, which dictated that the state should control the 'commanding heights' of its economy.[4] Nationalism, often in the form of sovereignty concerns following decolonization, similarly fuelled the desire for developing countries to control the strategic sectors of their economies. SOEs were also advocated as a workable method of income redistribution – for example, by reducing prices of goods primarily consumed by the poor – especially in developing countries with large informal sectors in which income redistribution could not practically be accomplished through a progressive tax system. Profitability often was not the most important goal behind their creation.

The primary economic motivation behind SOEs was increased capital investment. Several constraints hindered capital investment in developing countries in the years following World War II, the most important of which was low domestic savings rates. Developing countries also often lacked the institutions, such as effective financial intermediaries, necessary to facilitate allocative efficiency in capital markets. Moreover, developing countries suffered from market failures, such as low-level investment traps and a lack of basic infrastructure. In addition to ostensibly addressing these problems, SOEs also served other economic purposes, including combating inflation, controlling industries susceptible to natural monopolies, protecting fragile developing country economies from external shocks, and promoting regional development within a developing country. Thus, SOEs were not created exclusively to generate revenue for the nation state but were also intended to yield economic and social benefits above and beyond any financial reforms.[5] When assessing the success of SOEs,

---

4 See, e.g., Mehdi Haririan, *State-Owned Enterprises in a Mixed Economy: Micro versus Macro Economic Objectives* (London: Westview Press, 1989) at 10; Russell Muir and Joseph P. Saba, *Improving State Enterprise Performance: The Role of Internal and External Incentives* (Washington, DC: World Bank, 1995) at 11; R.C. Dutt, *State Enterprises in a Developing Country: The Indian Experience 1950–90* (New Delhi: Abhinav Publications, 1990) at 4; Dieter Bös, *Public Enterprise Economics* (Amsterdam: North-Holland, 1986) at 26; Thomas J. Trebat, *Brazil's State-Owned Enterprises: A Case Study of the State as Entrepreneur* (New York: Cambridge University Press, 1983) at 65; Malcolm Gillis, 'The role of state enterprises in economic development' (1980) 47: 2 *Social Research* 248 at 263.

5 For some less developed countries (LDCs), SOEs operated as an institutional bypass, as these countries suffered from a lack of bureaucratic capacity, more specifically an inability to tax and regulate private enterprise at arm's length, and state ownership offered an alternative means of taxation: World Bank, *World Development Report 1991: The Challenge of Development* (New York: Oxford University Press, 1991) at 130.

particularly in comparison to private enterprises, it is important to evaluate an SOE in the light of its putative social purposes.

B. The Cost of Poor SOE Performance

Between 1986 and 1991, an increasing number of SOEs in developing countries were unable to generate the resources needed to finance their operations, expansion and the servicing of their debts.[6] While it may be efficient to invest with borrowed money where an investment is expected to generate positive gains in the future, it is inefficient to finance low productivity investments with borrowed money, which has been the case with many developing country SOEs.

The persistent deficits of SOEs trigger derivative social costs. First, SOEs receive a disproportionate amount of domestic investment, significantly increasing the cost of capital of private enterprises in developing countries. More generally, inefficient levels of production in SOEs result in the withdrawal of resources from areas of the economy in which they might be more productively employed. An SOE sector typically represents about 11 per cent of GDP in developing economies, rising to an average of 14 per cent in the poorest developing countries. The SOE share of gross domestic investment (GDI) is generally much higher: in 1991 accounting for about 18 per cent of GDI in developing economies and about 27 per cent in low-income countries.[7] By way of contrast, SOE sectors typically represented about 8 per cent and 13 per cent of GDI respectively in high-income economies in 1988, and is now much lower as a result of privatizations.[8] Second, developing country governments, which are often reluctant to cut social expenditures, tend to cut expenditures with long-term benefits (such as infrastructure) in order to finance SOE deficits.[9] The direct and indirect losses attributable to poor SOE performance have been estimated at between 5 and 8 per cent of GDP in the typical developing

---

[6] In this period, the savings-investment (S-I) deficit averaged 1.7 per cent of GDP in the typical low-income economy and 0.8 per cent of GDP in developing countries generally: Mary M. Shirley et al., *Bureaucrats in Business: The Economics and Politics of Government Ownership* (Washington, DC: World Bank, 1995) at 42–3. Available at http://www-wds.worldbank.org/external/default/WDSContentServer/IW3P/IB/1995/09/01/000009265_3961219104659/Rendered/PDF/multi0page.pdf

[7] Ibid., at 34.

[8] Ibid., at 33.

[9] For example, average capital expenditures in sub-Saharan Africa fell from 8.7 to 6.1 per cent of GDP during the 1980s: World Bank, *Private Sector Development in Low-Income Countries* (Washington, DC: World Bank, 1995) at 50.

country and, where an SOE sector is relatively large, as high as 8 to 12 per cent of GDP.[10]

Small gains in SOE efficiency could have a sizable impact on developing economies. Jones has estimated the impact that a 5 per cent increase in SOE efficiency would have had upon the GDP of several developing economies over the period 1980 to 1981: Pakistan would have experienced a 1 per cent increase in GDP, while Egyptian GDP would have grown by 5 per cent, and South Korean GDP would have grown by 1.7 per cent.[11] Another study, conducted by the World Bank, produced similar results – for example, a 5 per cent increase in SOE efficiency would have improved GDP in Turkey, Tanzania, Bolivia and Mali by 2 per cent, 1.5 per cent, 1.4 per cent, and 2.2 per cent, respectively.[12] To place the benefits of SOE reform in context, by diverting SOE operating subsidies to basic education, the central governments of Mexico, Tanzania, Tunisia and India could increase central government education expenditures by 50, 74, 160 and 550 per cent, respectively. Similarly, redirecting SOE subsidies to health care would permit the central government of Senegal to more than double health care expenditure in that country, and the central governments of Turkey, Mexico (and Tunisia) and India to increase health care expenditure threefold, fourfold and fivefold, respectively.[13]

SOEs have often not delivered the social benefits they were intended to achieve.[14] For example, notwithstanding that one of the key economic rationales behind the creation of SOEs was an increase in capital investment in infrastructure so as to make private investment in developing countries more attractive, the World Bank estimates that the poor quality of utilities and infrastructure adds 10 to 25 per cent to an organization's costs in sub-Saharan Africa.[15] If SOEs do provide positive social externalities (a benefit not necessarily specific to public enterprise), they do so at a significant cost to organizational efficiency. Academics have argued that

---

10 Russell Muir and Joseph P. Saba, *supra* note 4 at vii.

11 Leroy P. Jones, 'Performance evaluation for state-owned enterprises', in Ravi Ramamurti and Raymond Vernon (eds), *Privatization and Control of State-Owned Enterprises* (Washington, DC: World Bank, 1991) at 179; Leroy P. Jones, *Efficiency of Public Manufacturing Enterprises in Pakistan* (1981), prepared for Pakistan Ministry of Production, and Pakistan Division, World Bank.

12 World Bank, *World Development Report 1983* (New York: Oxford University Press, 1983) at 75.

13 Shirley et al., *supra* note 6 at 48.

14 V.V. Ramanadham, *The Economics of Public Enterprise* (New York: Routledge, 1991).

15 World Bank, *Private Sector Development in Low-Income Countries* (Washington, DC: World Bank, 1995) at 39.

there are two key factors that could potentially explain this inefficiency: (i) the ownership effect; and (ii) the competition effect.

C. The Ownership Effect

In terms of management performance, the ideal ownership structure is the owner/operator because all efficiency gains of the enterprise accrue to the owner/operator, who then has powerful incentives to operate the organization efficiently. However, this type of ownership structure obviously places severe limits on the potential for expansion and growth. Thus, in the modern larger corporation, there is a division between principals (the owners or shareholders) of the organization and the agents (the management and employees). The governance structure of the corporation is then designed to guarantee that the principal has effective control over the agent's actions, and the interests of the agent are aligned with those of the principal.[16] Also, the potential lack of managerial incentives to improve the organization's performance is, to some extent, alleviated by the market which, in theory, rewards proven management skills and punishes inadequate performance through product markets, markets for corporate control, markets for managerial talent and bankruptcy laws.[17]

In the context of SOEs, however, often both the governance structure of SOEs and the market have a much more attenuated impact on managerial performance. This is because SOE managerial appointments are often made on the basis of politics rather than merit, and because SOEs are not subject to traditional market risks such as takeovers or bankruptcy. In the private sector, shareholders often monitor the activities of a corporation, because they expect returns from their investments in monitoring. In the case of SOEs, the owner is the state and thus, in some sense, each citizen can be considered a shareholder. However, since these ownership interests are not transferable, the returns to any one citizen as a result of monitoring will never be greater than the opportunity cost of the time invested in such activities and citizens face major collective action problems in coordinating their monitoring efforts.[18]

---

[16] Roy Hrab, *Private Delivery of Public Services: Public–Private Partnerships and Contracting Out*, Report prepared for the Ontario Panel on the Role of Government, Research Paper No. 21, 29 January 2004 (on file with the authors).

[17] See John Vickers and George Yarrow, *Privatization: An Economic Analysis,* (Cambridge, MA: MIT, 1998).

[18] See, e.g., Louis de Alessi, 'The economics of property rights: a review of the evidence' (1980) 2 *Research in Law and Economics* 1 at 27–8; Shirley et al., *supra* note 6 at 36; B. Stevens, 'Prospects for privatization in OECD countries' (August

Further, unlike private sector shareholders, citizens, even as voters, have very little control over the composition of the state's executive. Government ministers are not held liable for the corporate failings of the organizations they monitor in the same way as corporate directors. A final important factor is that, unlike private corporations, SOEs often face multiple economic and non-economic objectives.[19] This makes it difficult for SOE monitors to properly assess the performance of managers, who can blame poor enterprise financial performance on non-commercial objectives. This is not to say that such control is impossible, but well-managed SOEs tend to be the exception, rather than the rule. In sum, private enterprise often offers better management incentives, better monitoring incentives and better monitoring capabilities than government ownership.

D. The Competition Effect

Another possible explanation for the inefficiencies of SOEs is the fact that, in the absence of natural monopoly, private enterprise encourages competition whereas government ownership tends to encourage monopoly. Competition engenders allocative efficiency by removing the ability to set prices from the monopolist and placing it in the market. In theory, where producers in a competitive market are earning economic profits, other producers will enter the market and supply consumers with the same goods until the price of the product has been driven down to the marginal cost of production. In this way, consumers' demands are brought in line with the marginal costs of supply and the deadweight loss associated with monopoly production is eliminated.

In theory, competition also engenders productive efficiency by encouraging producers to minimize costs. Where cost reductions permit producers to earn economic profits, new producers will enter the market, once again driving prices down to the marginal cost of supply. In these circumstances, constant attention to productive efficiency becomes a matter of an organization's very survival. In contrast, monopolists are not faced with the threat of being priced out of the market place, and so do not have the

---

1992) *National Westminster Bank Quarterly Review* 2 at 20; Michael J. Trebilcock and J. Robert S. Prichard, 'Crown Corporation: the calculus of instrument choice', in J. Robert S. Prichard (ed.), *Crown Corporation in Canada: The Calculus of Instruments Choice* (Toronto: Butterworths, 1983) at 34.

[19] In fact, a manager will often face as many sets of multiple objectives as government officials/bodies having control over his or her SOE (e.g., senior bureaucrats, ministers of state, the head of state, etc.), Jones, 'Performance evaluation for state-owned enterprises', *supra* note 11 at 181.

same incentives to increase productive efficiency. An additional benefit of competition is that it provides clear information on relative management performance to corporate monitors. Competition also tends to increase dynamic efficiency (innovation) over time more than monopolistic market structures.

III. PRIVATIZATION

The term 'privatization' is often used ubiquitously to cover a wide range of different policy options. However, generally speaking, it refers to the transfer of productive assets from the state sector to the private sector.[20] Depending on the way it is implemented, privatization may be one, but not the only, solution to the sizable social costs inflicted by poor SOE performance.

A. Historical Context

While there were isolated cases prior to the 1980s,[21] privatization as a broad-based economic policy did not truly come of age until its implementation under the UK Thatcher administration during the 1980s when, between 1979 and 1997, the Conservative government reduced the SOEs' share of GDP from approximately 10 per cent to nearly nothing.[22] It was not until the 1990s, however, that privatization programs outside the United Kingdom truly began to accelerate. As a result, privatization represented a major policy change in the economies of the world: from 1980 through 1999, governments throughout the world generated over US$1 trillion in revenue from privatization.[23]

With respect to developing countries, divestitures in the first part of the 1980s involved relatively small SOEs, primarily in commerce, services,

---

[20] David Parker and Colin Kirkpatrick, 'Privatisation in developing countries: a review of the evidence and the policy lessons' (2005) 41 *Journal of Development Studies* 4 at 514.

[21] For example, the German Christian Democrat governments of the 1950s and 1960s: William Megginson, Robert Nash and Matthias van Randenborgh, 'The financial and operating performance of newly privatized firms: an international empirical analysis' (1994) 49 *Journal of Finance* 403 at 406; and the Pinochet government of Chile following the overthrow of President Allende.

[22] William L. Megginson and Jeffrey M. Netter, 'From state to market: a survey of empirical studies on privatization' (2001) 39:2 *Journal of Economic Literature* 321 at 324.

[23] Ibid., at 326.

light manufacturing and agribusiness.[24] Subsequently, they have also included the sale of large SOEs in major infrastructure sectors, such as utilities and transportation.[25] At the beginning of the privatization movement, there were wide regional variations in government divestiture in developing countries: Latin America accounted for 55.1 per cent of the value of all divestitures occurring in the developing world between 1988 and 1993, while in the same period divestitures in Asia and Africa, respectively, accounted for just 19.7 and 3.2 per cent of the value of total divestitures of developing countries.[26] The landscape, however, has since changed. According to the World Bank, Latin America's share of the global total value of privatization fell from nearly 60 per cent in the 1990s to 3 per cent in 2006. East Asia now leads the developing world in privatization value, raising US$74 billion in 2007 – an increase of 45 per cent from 2006 and a staggering 236 per cent from 2004–05,[27] which is primarily attributable to initial public offerings (IPOs) in China.

B. Theory versus Practice

The theory behind SOEs holds that the ownership and competition effects undermine the performance of SOEs. However, it is important to examine the empirical evidence to test whether these theoretical conjectures are borne out in practice, first by comparing the relative performance of SOEs and private organizations in the same sectors, and then comparing pre- and post-privatization performance. It is important to note that evaluating the impact of privatization on organizational performance is extremely difficult in transition or developing economies partly because of the challenges in obtaining accurate information. A greater problem, however, is that it is difficult to isolate the impact of one variable, privatization, when a society may be undergoing numerous economic, political and social changes, all of which can impact on organizational performance and lead to erroneous or misleading conclusions.

---

24 Shirley et al., *supra* note 6 at 27; Christopher Adam, William Cavendish and Percy S. Mistry, *Adjusting Privatization: Case Studies from Developing Countries* (London: James Currey, 1992) at 39–40.

25 Shirley et al., *supra* note 6 at 27.

26 *Ibid* at 28.

27 Sunita Kikeri and Verena Phipps, 'Privatization trends: a record year for initial public offerings in 2007', in World Bank Group, Financial and Private Sector Vice Presidency, October 2008, Note 321.

1. Relative sectoral performance

According to Parker and Kirkpatrick, most sectoral studies involving developing countries have focused on reform in utilities, particularly telecommunications.[28] This is due to two factors: first, telecommunications have been particularly affected by privatization[29] and, secondly, data is readily available from annual reports published by the International Telecommunications Union (ITU) in Geneva. While there are some differences between the specific conclusions of the numerous studies,[30] researchers have mostly found that privatization impacted positively on the telecommunications industry in terms of teledensity levels (service coverage),[31] decreases in service costs[32] and profitability.[33] Perhaps more

---

28 There have been studies conducted in other utilities sectors, such as energy and water and sewage. In terms of energy, Zhang, Parker and Kirkpatrick conducted two studies modelling the impact of privatizing electricity generation in developing countries, looking at 51 economies between 1985 and 2000/01. They found that, while competition increased service penetration, capacity expansion and labour productivity, the effect of privatization alone was statistically insignificant except for capacity utilization. They also found that sequencing the reforms was vital to achieving improvements. Case studies conducted by Gray in 2001 and Estache, Gomez-Lobo and Leipziger in 2000 both found that electricity privatization resulted in fewer blackouts, higher labour productivity and lower electricity costs. However, other studies such as those by Sravat in 1998 yielded more equivocal results, finding that privatization of energy can result in disputes that are very costly. Studies of the water and sewerage sector, which was privatized largely by concessions, have been generally positive with respect to the impact of privatization. Concessions have led to improved services, higher productivity, reduction in tariffs and new connections. For details see Parker and Kirkpatrick, *supra* note 20 at 519.

29 According to Li et al., in 1980, approximately 2 per cent of telecommunications firms were privatized but that number rose to 42 per cent by 1998. See Parker and Kirkpatrick, ibid.

30 For a detailed and comparative explanation of the findings and methodological differences and shortcomings of the various studies, see Parker and Kirkpatrick, ibid.

31 See D. Petrazzini and T.H. Clark, 'Costs and benefits of telecommunications liberalization in developing countries' (1996) Working Paper, Hong Kong: Hong Kong University of Science and Technology; A.J. Ros, 'Does ownership or competition matter? The effects of telecommunications reform on network expansion and efficiency' (1999) 15 *Journal of Regulatory Economics* at 65.

32 See S.J. Wallsten, 'An econometric analysis of telecom competition, privatization and regulation in Africa and Latin America' (2001) 43 *Journal of Industrial Economics* 1 at 1.

33 B. Bortolotti, J. D'Souza, M. Fantini and W.L. Megginson, 'Privatization and the sources of performance improvement in the global telecommunications industry' (2002) 26 *Telecommunications Policy* at 243.

importantly, however, some of the studies also concluded that privatization alone was insufficient to yield such benefits: to improve organizational performance privatization must be combined with other structural changes, notably effective competition or effective and independent sectoral regulation.[34] While there is a need for more detailed research on the various sectors undergoing privatization, the results from the telecommunications industry suggest that divestiture, coupled with the necessary institutional reforms, is likely to result in improvements in terms of organizational profitability and efficiency.

2. Pre- and post-privatization relative performance

A number of studies have compared the pre- and post-privatization performance of a variety of divested SOEs. The results of these studies largely support the argument that privatization generally increases social welfare when implemented in the appropriate environment, but where such an environment is absent, privatization offers greatly reduced social benefits.[35]

There seems to be a connection between the benefits of privatization and the broader institutional environment of the country conducting the reforms. An analysis of non-transition economies offers support for the conclusion that privatization is correlated with improvements in the operation and financial performance of divested organizations. In contrast, in transition economies the change in ownership was insufficient to improve a country's macroeconomic performance and that improvement only resulted when ownership changes were combined with other reforms such as incentive and contracting issues, hardened budget constraints, removal of barriers to entry, an effective legal and regulatory framework, as well as the introduction of new management.[36]

While the results of these studies suggest that privatization offers substantial social welfare improvements to middle and upper-middle income developing countries, they do not suggest that privatization is a universal

---

34 Wallsten, *supra* note 32 and Bortolotti et al., ibid., at 243. See also Parker and Kirkpatrick, *supra* note 20.

35 Megginson and Netter, *supra* note 22; Ahmed Galal, et al., *The Welfare Consequences of Selling Public Enterprises: Case Studies from Chile, Malaysia, Mexico and the U.K.* (New York: Oxford University Press, 1994) at 22–23.

36 Megginson and Netter, ibid. See also Clifford Zinnes, Yair Eilat and Jeffrey Sachs, 'The gains from privatization in transition economies: is "change of ownership" enough?' (2001) *IMF Staff Papers*, Vol. 48 – *Transition Economies: How Much Progress?* 146–70; and Clifford Zinnes, Yair Eilat and Jeffrey Sachs, 'Benchmarking competitiveness in transition economies' (2001) 9 *Economics of Transition* 315.

remedy for poor SOE performance. Indeed, evidence suggests that the benefits of privatization are much less significant in low income and lower-middle income developing countries than in wealthier developing countries.[37] Although low income developing countries would benefit greatly from the increased capital investment, among other things promised by privatization, the consequences of low income LDC market structures in terms of privatization possibilities are clear: unless privatization is coordinated with significant private sector reform (including the regulation of anti-competitive behaviour), the lack of competition in these economies may ensure privatized SOEs (and the individuals and corporations who control them) monopoly profits; society will gain little or nothing.

In sum, the evidence suggests that often the impact of privatization on the performance of SOEs is dependent upon the broader institutional environment in which the privatized organizations will operate. In this regard, institutional reforms are key. For instance, in infrastructure sectors such as telecommunications many of the benefits of privatization are largely dependent upon appropriate roles for competition and regulation. Establishing competition and securing an effective regulatory framework, in turn, depends on a non-corrupt bureaucracy and competent regulatory agencies. Building these institutions, however, is not an easy task, as we have suggested earlier in this book. Similarly, broader institutional reforms, such as judicial and bureaucratic reforms and anti-corruption policies, seem to be relevant in transition economies and low income countries contemplating privatization, reinforcing the importance of institutions in this process.

C. Prerequisites for effective privatization

While many academics and practitioners agree that privatization is a preferable strategy to maintaining SOEs, privatization is not advisable or advantageous in every situation. In addition to a country's institutional environment, certain conditions and prerequisites are necessary for privatization not only to improve economic efficiency within a given undertaking or industry, but for it to contribute positively to long-term and sustainable economic and social development. These preconditions can be divided broadly into two categories – economic and political – although it must be noted that these factors are not only country-specific, but

---

[37] Christopher Adam, William Cavendish and Percy S. Mistry, *Adjusting Privatization: Case Studies from Developing Countries* (London: James Currey, 1992) at 71.

also industry-specific. As we suggest below, both economic and political factors are institutional in nature.

1. Economic prerequisites

The four primary and interconnected economic prerequisites are: (i) a healthy private sector; (ii) effective regulatory structures; (iii) macroeconomic stability; and (iv) an absence of corruption.

First, privatizing SOEs into a non-competitive environment may result in economic losses, including deadweight losses associated with monopoly pricing and possibly the further crowding out of the indigenous private sector as private monopolists exploit their economic power. One solution to the absence of a competitive private sector, especially in the case of natural monopolies, is regulation. The absence of effective regulation has been a major cause of mediocre post-privatization performance in lower-income developing countries.[38] While designing an effective regulatory regime is an extremely complex exercise that is dependent on context, it is important that these regulatory arrangements should be finalized prior to divestiture. Changes in the regulatory structure following privatization undermine the government's credibility with potential investors, and thus impact negatively on levels of investment.

With respect to macroeconomic instability, the dangers of privatizing in a crisis are obvious. Macroeconomic instability increases economic uncertainty and therefore investment risk, and thus results in decreased interest by domestic and foreign investors in the SOEs of a developing country. Perversely, developing country governments often face increased incentives to privatize in times of economic crisis as a result of a dire need for revenue. With severely constrained bargaining power, such developing countries may be forced to accept terms that are far less attractive than they could have achieved in the absence of a crisis. Moreover, in order to maximize revenue from privatization, developing countries may be tempted to turn public monopolies into private monopolies. Decisions to privatize should be made on the basis of an analysis of the long-term social benefits of a given divestiture, not the state's need for immediate revenue.

The final economic prerequisite is the absence of corruption. Prima facie, one might think that corruption in the public sector would make privatization desirable. However, privatizing SOEs in developing coun-

---

38 Boubraki, Narjess and Jean-Claude Cosset, 'The financial and operating performance of newly privatized firms: evidence from developing countries' (1998) 53 *Journal of Finance* 1081; Colin Kirkpatrick, David Parker and Yin-Fang Zhang 'An empirical analysis of state and private-sector provision of water services in Africa' (2006) 20:1 *World Bank Economic Review* 143.

tries with highly corrupt public sectors can greatly increase the costs of such corruption. These include the more obvious costs such as kickbacks in the privatization process, but also involve problems such as officials making and implementing privatization decisions on the basis of personal or political gain rather than social benefit (which, arguably, militates in favour of a centralized, specialized agency with well-developed protocols for privatization), or the fact that widespread corruption undermines investor confidence. Moreover, corruption may not only impede original investment in SOEs, but may also impede subsequent investment in the divested enterprise, thereby destroying one of the key benefits promised by privatization: increased capital investment.

These prerequisites are institutional in nature because they depend on a complementary set of private and public sector institutions. For instance, a healthy private sector requires a functioning financial system, an appropriate regulatory framework depends on a functioning bureaucracy, and a stable macroeconomic environment depends on a functional and competent central bank (inter alia).

2. Political prerequisites

Even where a developing country has the institutions in place to make privatization welfare-increasing, privatization will only succeed if it is politically practicable. This involves two considerations: (i) whether key policy-makers in developing countries are desirous of implementing privatization; and (ii) if so, whether privatization can succeed in the face of political opposition.

Shirley, in a study examining the success of SOE reform in 12 developing countries, found that both political desirability and political feasibility were necessary elements of SOE reform.[39] According to Shirley, however, privatization will be politically desirable in only two circumstances: (i) where a developing country government has experienced a change in leadership and the new leader is not dependent on SOE interests for his or her support; and (ii) where privatization is demanded by an economic crisis.[40] Although, in Shirley's research, an economic shock alone was insufficient, Campos and Esfahani found – in studying SOE reform attempts in 15 LDCs over the period 1972 to 1991 – that 19 of the 24 reform attempts studied were preceded by a crisis (although this involves the serious dangers noted above).[41]

---

39 Shirley et al., *supra* note 6 at 175–6.

40 Ibid., at 178–9

41 Jose Edgardo Campos and Hadi Salehi Esfahani, 'The political foundations

In terms of political feasibility, this often not only includes placating opposition parties, but also garnering the support of the workforce. Ultimately, however, political feasibility is affected by the credibility of the developing country government, especially where the government seeks to win the workers' support, for example, with the carrot of shares in the divested SOE. Unless a government's reform plans are credible, workers are unlikely to give up the rents they may be receiving from their public sector jobs for shares, which have some probability of being worthless. However, where workers are permitted to purchase underpriced shares in a divested enterprise, the government instantaneously creates a constituency that will oppose a reversal of the divestiture.[42]

D. Shock Therapy versus Gradualism

In determining how to shift from an economy dominated by SOEs, there are two primary schools of thought: the shock therapists and the gradualists. Shock therapy is based on the premise that both markets and market institutions will quickly and spontaneously appear with rapid economic liberalization. According to leading proponents, such as Anders Aslund,[43] shock therapy includes a broad range of policies aimed at reducing government involvement in the economy. Such measures include price and exchange rate liberalization (including the break-up of currency zones), privatization of SOEs, macroeconomic stabilization, and the removal of export and import subsidies and wage and price controls.

Rapid reform advocates consider a gradual approach to transition to be needlessly costly, both in terms of time and lost output. In part, this set of economic prescriptions has been predicated on a set of political assumptions – a kind of political Coase theorem of privatization: (i) the initial owners of privatized assets do not matter much as the market will soon reallocate the assets to efficient owners; and (ii) appropriate laws and legal institutions will follow private property rather than the other way around. This view assumes a critical interaction between economic

---

of public enterprise reform in developing countries' (World Bank, 1994, unpublished) at 23.

42 Ibid., at 9.

43 See, for example, Anders Aslund, 'Why has Russia's economic transformation been so arduous?' World Bank Annual Bank Conference on Development Economics, Washington, DC, 28–30 April 1999. See also, Jeffrey Sachs, 'The transition at mid-decade' (1996) 86 *American Economic Review* 128; Jeffrey Sachs, 'Reforms in Eastern Europe and the former Soviet Union in light of the East Asian experience' (1995) 9 *Journal of the Japanese and International Economies* 454.

and political reforms – namely that economic reforms create pressure for political reforms and that business pressures are likely to play a critical role in political and consequential legal reforms. The underlying presumption is that such pressures did not exist before the economic reforms.[44]

By contrast, gradualists such as Joseph Stiglitz and Kenneth Arrow caution that rapid liberalization will be impractical to implement because privatization requires a broad social consensus, and generating such consensus is a long-term process.[45] Gradualists tend to favour an extended period of state intervention: price and wage controls, fixed exchange rates, gradual privatization and nurturing of market institutions are key elements of this process. Gradualists also tend to emphasize the importance of the institutional infrastructure of a market economy, including competition, entrepreneurship, regulation of financial markets, social capital and a strong legal system.[46]

Both shock therapists and gradualists claim that the performance of transition countries proves the relative success of their reform agenda. Poland, Kyrgyzstan, the Czech Republic and the Baltic states, as radical liberalizers, have grown faster than 'go-slow' countries such as Belarus and Ukraine.[47] On the other hand, China has created its own path of gradual transition from a planned to a market economy, and has enjoyed enormous economic success. Russia's economic decline in the period following the break-up of the Soviet Union is cited by both sides to prove their point: gradualists argue that the Russian experience proves that shock therapy was seriously misconceived, while advocates of shock therapy reclassify Russia as a go-slow reformer because they believe reforms were partial at best.

IV. TYPES OF PRIVATIZATION

Several conclusions can be drawn from the above discussion of SOEs and privatization. First, SOEs in the developing world are often sources

---

44 Andrei Shleifer and Robert Vishny, *The Grabbing Hand: Government Pathologies and Their Cures* (Cambridge, MA: Harvard University Press, 1998) Chapter 11.

45 See, e.g., Joseph E. Stiglitz, 'The insider' (17 April 2000) *The New Republic*; Joseph E. Stiglitz, 'Whither reform? Ten years of the transition,' World Bank Annual Bank Conference on Development Economics, Washington, DC, 28–30 April 1999; Joseph E. Stiglitz, *Globalization and Its Discontents* (W.W. Norton & Co., 2002); Kenneth Arrow, 'Economic transition: speed and scope' (2000) 156 *Journal of Institutional and Theoretical Economics* 9.

46 Stiglitz, 'Whither reform?' ibid.

47 Schleifer and Vishny, *supra* note 44 at 228.

of major inefficiency and, moreover, typically have not generated the economic or social benefits they were created to provide. Privatization offers a possible solution, if implemented in a congenial environment (including an efficient post-privatization competitive and regulatory environment).

Assuming that privatization is desirable and that various economic and political prerequisites are to a greater or lesser extent in place, there are numerous methods of privatization that are available as models for implementation. In 1996, Josef C. Brada categorized various methods[48] and, while not an exhaustive list, it provides a useful framework within which to understand the different ways in which privatization can be undertaken. Building on Brada's taxonomy, this section will survey four different types of privatization, assessing both the costs and benefits of each.

A. Post-Soviet Privatization: Restitution and Vouchers

Privatization by restitution has primarily been employed in former Soviet states in Eastern Europe as it involves returning land or other property that was expropriated by the state to the original owners or their heirs. This method of privatization can be difficult because of the need to identify original owners and often the required evidence of ownership is unavailable or has been destroyed. Moreover, there is a disconnection between theory and practice. While, in theory, returning land and property to its original owners or their heirs should afford them the right to determine its use and alienability, in practice privatization through restitution has often incorporated numerous restrictions and stipulations that preclude the exercise of full and free ownership.

Another category of privatization identified by Brada that has been used primarily in Central and Eastern Europe is mass or voucher privatization. This involves the distribution of vouchers for free, or at a nominal cost, that enable eligible citizens to bid for shares of SOEs or other assets that are being privatized. Effectively, vouchers 'create a stock of savings that matches the stock of state assets being privatized'.[49] Although the scheme has resulted in fundamental changes to the ownership of business assets, often it did not change the effective control over these assets because of the wide diffusion of share ownership, thus leaving incumbent managers

---

48 Josef C. Brada, 'Privatization is transition – or is it?' (1996) 10 *Journal of Economic Perspectives* 2 at 67.

49 Ibid.

or small concentrated groups of shareholders in control of the assets with little accountability to the new owners.[50]

B. Management Buy-Outs (MBOs)

Employee buy-outs involve the transfer of the rights of ownership of industrial or commercial facilities to those who are employed in them. However, in the case of MBOs, the existing management is the buyer.[51] MBOs have been advocated in situations involving small- and medium-sized enterprises (such as those formed by the dissolution of former combines or large enterprises) and as a way to draw upon a substantial pool of 'privatization demand' from the very people who work in the enterprise.[52]

However, given the importance of new human capital to the success of a divested SOE documented in many studies, MBOs are often a poor method of privatization (since enterprise management typically does not change as a result of a MBO). There are a number of other reasons why MBOs are often not an optimal method of divestiture:

- MBOs are often highly leveraged, leaving the new enterprise vulnerable to macroeconomic shocks;
- managers of SOEs, given their information advantages and political influence, may be able to purchase their SOEs for less than fair market value; and
- management may not be able to secure adequate financing, leaving the developing country government (acting as a de facto guarantor or lender) bearing the risk of enterprise failure.

Thus, notwithstanding that MBOs often have the support of the workforce, the MBO is not generally an efficient method of divestiture.

C. Privatization through the Sale of State Property

The sale of state property is the method by which a government 'trades its ownership claim for an explicit cash payment'.[53] As discussed by Megginson and Netter, this category can be subdivided into two different

---

50 Megginson and Netter, *supra* note 22.

51 Harald Sondhof and Markus Stahl, 'Management buy-outs as an instrument of privatization in Eastern Europe,' (1992) 27 *Intereconomics* 5 at 210.

52 Sondhof and Stahl, ibid.; Anthony Bennett, *How does Privatization Work?* (London and New York: Routledge, 1997).

53 Megginson and Netter, *supra* note 22.

approaches. The first is *direct sale* whereby a SOE, or one of its component parts, is sold to an individual, a corporation or a group of investors. The second option is *share issue privatization* (also known as an SIP), where some or all of the government's holding in an SOE is sold through a public share offering. The sale of state property serves several concrete objectives, including producing revenue for the state, restructuring organizations and attracting foreign investors.[54]

This method of privatization can be controversial, however, as foreign investment represents a paradox to developing governments: while capital-starved developing countries are in need of foreign capital, foreign investment has often been perceived as a neo-colonialist threat to newly emergent states attempting to fashion their own societies rather than be absorbed into the political economy of the developed world. Thus, domestic investment may be more attractive to many developing economies, implying that a country's savings rate (savings as a percentage of GDP) will be a significant factor in the determination of the mode of divestiture adopted. This suggests that a developing country with a higher savings rate is likely not only to rely to a greater degree on domestic investment, but also to employ the public offering more frequently as a means of placing some portion of large SOEs in domestic rather than foreign hands.

Moreover, developing countries with higher savings rates are more likely to have the financial institutions necessary to facilitate a public offering. To date, direct sales to the domestic private sector in developing countries have been concentrated in smaller-scale activities associated with the commercial, manufacturing, service and agricultural sectors. The divestiture of larger enterprises, such as utilities, has relied more on foreign direct investment and public share issues.

D. Partial Privatization

Partial privatization of an SOE may be a desirable interim option for governments for whom full privatization is not politically desirable or feasible. Partial privatization may take the form of a partial public offering that, if the stock is widely traded, will introduce stock prices (and changes thereto) as a benchmark of an SOE's performance, as well as creating a private constituency with a direct stake in SOE efficiency. Alternatively, government could sell a minority interest to a single commercial partner or joint venture partner with needed capital and expertise and a role in the

---

54 Brada, *supra* note 48.

SOE's governance, again with a direct stake in enhanced SOE performance. Under both options, full privatization may ultimately be rendered more politically feasible. Government credibility may, however, prove a serious problem with both of these options, in that the stakes of the minority investors are at risk of expropriation or devaluation by changes in policies by the controlling shareholder or government, being motivated by considerations other than efficiency. Hence, minority shareholders may be difficult to attract at all, or only at severely discounted acquisition prices, reflecting political risk.

V. ALTERNATIVES TO PRIVATIZATION

While there are many options in terms of how to privatize SOEs, there are also reform alternatives to privatization that should be identified. While developing countries work towards improving their institutions and strengthening their private sectors in preparation for divestiture, they can also improve their economies by implementing several public sector reforms. The following reforms, to a greater or lesser extent, seek to benefit from the ownership and/or competition effect.

A. Management Contracts

A management contract is an agreement between a government and a private party (often enforceable through international arbitration or governed by the law of a recognized centre of commerce) by which the private party agrees to operate the assets of an existing SOE for a fee, which will often be tied to performance. In other words, management contracts privatize SOE management without divesting the SOE's assets. Variations of the concept of management contracts for the development of new infrastructure are discussed more fully below (in section VI) in our discussion of public–private partnerships. Basic types of management contract in potentially competitive sectors are typical in only a handful of industries and in small numbers.

According to Shirley in a 1995 study, a worldwide search for management contracts revealed only 202 contracts, with 68 per cent of them concentrated in certain sectors: 46 contracts in agriculture (24 in sugar, 22 in Sri Lankan tea and rubber plantations), 44 in the hotel industry, 23 in infrastructure, 13 in food processing and beverages, and 12 in extractive sectors. Moreover, if one does not consider Sri Lanka (with 22 contracts in total), or the hotel industry contracts (which are spread all over the world), the remaining management contracts in the sample (136) were concentrated in Africa, which accounted for two-thirds (91 of the 136) of the contracts identified by Shirley.[55]

While there is evidence providing some support for the use of management contracts as a means to improve SOE efficiency,[56] they have their drawbacks. First, in order for management contracts to yield significant benefits from the incentive of private management, remuneration under the contract must be tied to organizational performance. In practice, contracts often include fixed fees, and some do not even attempt to relate fees to performance. Secondly, the limited term of a management contract may create perverse management incentives. Because of uncertainties over whether the contract will be renewed – a problem compounded by the lack of credibility of many developing country governments – management may be tempted to maximize short-term gains (by degrading assets, for example), often at the cost of long-term performance.[57] And while a well-drafted management contract may mitigate such perverse incentives by including longer contract terms, technological uncertainties and uncertainties relating to market demand and surrounding government policies may negatively affect the risks associated with a project over the long term, making longer contract terms relatively unattractive to private organizations.[58]

An important question concerns the relative efficiency of the management contract and divestiture. As stated earlier, privatization – assuming appropriate post-divestiture competition and regulatory policies – takes full advantage of both the ownership effect and the competition effect of private ownership. Management contracts, on the other hand, do not take advantage of the ownership (or often the competition) effect, and hence may be less effective than divestiture. This is because of a number of factors:

- private ownership is more likely to result in increased capital investment than management contracts,

---

55 Shirley et al., *supra* note 6 at 134–6.

56 Ibid., at 136–9. Shirley studied the experience of 20 contracts in several countries and industries, measuring their impact on SOE performance in terms of increases in post-contract profitability and productivity, and found that 13 out of the 20 SOEs, or 65%, were successes. Moreover, profitability *or* productivity improved in three other organizations.

57 See Daniels and Trebilcock, *supra* note 1 at 404.

58 See Daniels and Trebilcock, ibid., at 405; although the management contracts of the most successful organizations in the Shirley study generally have longer terms.

- divestiture is a much stronger signal to the investment community of a government's commitment to market liberalization, and
- provided that the privatized SOE does not have monopoly power, divestiture may not result in the same level of transaction costs as management contracts (for example, the costs of ongoing negotiations and monitoring).[59]

Thus, where the economic and political prerequisites for privatization are present, privatization is likely to be a better reform alternative than management contracts. However, the key benefit of management contracts is that they can be successfully implemented in circumstances where privatization is not feasible.

B. Performance Contracts

A key distinction between private and public enterprises is that private enterprises are generally motivated by one clear objective – profit maximization – whereas SOEs typically face multiple, sometimes conflicting, objectives. Poorly defined and shifting corporate objectives severely inhibit the evaluation of management performance in SOEs, while a lack of autonomy from government decision-makers and a failure to tie management compensation to organizational performance deter good management performance. These are problems that *may* be resolved by a performance contract.

The three major components of a performance contract system are:

- a performance evaluation system, in which national goals are translated into explicit SOE objectives and quantified in performance criteria;
- a performance information system which monitors actual achievements; and
- an incentive system, in which the welfare of the managers and workers of the SOE is linked to its objectives by a pecuniary or non-pecuniary reward system based on the achievement of particular target values.[60]

By the mid-1990s, performance contract systems had been implemented in 28 developing countries – mostly in Asia and Africa – but, unfortunately,

---

[59] Shirley et al., *supra* note 6 at 149.

[60] A. Hartman and S.A. Nawab, 'Evaluating public manufacturing enterprises in Pakistan' (September 1985) *Finance and Development* 27 at 28–30.

despite some successes there have also been many failures. Obstacles to successful implementation of performance contracts include ensuring that SOE managers, who enjoy a significant information advantage over their government monitors, do not use this advantage to negotiate easily attainable performance targets, and ensuring that management remuneration is effectively tied to SOE performance. In one study,[61] only five of the twelve sample companies offered pecuniary bonuses as a performance award. This study also found a tendency for the governments of developing countries to breach their performance contract commitments with impunity, thereby seriously derogating from the significance attached to them by SOE managers.

Thus, the implementation of performance contracts does not appear to be a broad solution to the problem of SOE inefficiencies. Relative to privatization, performance contracts do not increase competition and they face serious obstacles in their attempt to induce good management. However, improvements can be made to the system, such as reducing bargaining inequality by channelling performance contracts through a centralized specialized agency, or using published and frequently updated benchmarks from comparable organizations in other sectors or countries to lower transaction costs. If these changes and assurances can be made to the performance contract systems in LDCs, SOEs that cannot (or should not) be privatized for economic or political reasons may still benefit from improved enterprise management.

C. Increased Competition

While management contracts and performance contracts attempt to improve SOE performance largely through improvements in management incentives and monitoring, these types of SOE reform have little impact on the level of competition faced by an SOE. There are four means by which governments of LDCs may introduce greater levels of competition in their SOE sectors: (i) the unbundling of monopolies; (ii) the reduction of import barriers; (iii) performance-based price regulation using competitive benchmarks from other jurisdictions; and (iv) competition laws.

As in the case of the other alternative reform options, they are still a less effective option than privatization, which takes advantage of the ownership effect as well as the competition effect. However, such a strategy

---

[61] Nichola Dyer Cissé, *The Impact of Performance Contracts on Public Enterprise Performance* (Washington, DC: World Bank, 1994), Background Paper, Policy Research Department, World Bank.

may be a preferable interim measure in situations where, for political or economic reasons, privatization is not a viable option. Like privatization, however, these strategies depend on the existence of strong institutions, including effective and competent competition and regulatory authorities. The challenges in building these institutions in developing countries, however, are not negligible.

VI. PRIVATE PROVISION OF PUBLIC INFRASTRUCTURE SERVICES: PUBLIC–PRIVATE PARTNERSHIPS

Having recognized the benefits of privatization and the circumstances that best engender the divestiture of SOEs, we also must acknowledge that there are some sectors that may not be well suited to privatization, notably public infrastructure. Public infrastructure, unlike other sectors, is often likely to be a natural monopoly in which competition is often neither feasible nor desirable. Moreover, infrastructure involves the creation or provision of basic and vital services such as water, electricity, communications and roads, where failures in service delivery or project completion can have a disastrous impact on consumers and users. Infrastructure is also a central component for the entire development enterprise, and therefore a form of public good. Poor physical infrastructure can undermine and impede other efforts towards economic growth and social progress while good infrastructure raises productivity and lowers production costs.[62] According to the World Bank, a 1 per cent increase in the stock of infrastructure is associated with a 1 per cent increase in GDP across all countries.[63]

However, maintaining and enhancing the quality of physical infrastructure requires massive capital infusions, which developing countries often lack in terms of their own resources. In 1994 the World Bank reported that inadequate maintenance was an almost universal (and costly) failure of infrastructure providers in developing countries. For example, it reported that timely road maintenance expenditures of US$12 billion would have saved road reconstruction costs of US$45 billion in Africa during the preceding decade. More recently, the OECD estimated that maintaining existing infrastructure and undertaking necessary extensions of its

---

[62] World Bank Development Report, *Infrastructure for Development* (Washington, DC: World Bank, 1994).

[63] Ibid.

coverage would entail costs of about 7 per cent of the GDP of developing countries, equivalent to about US$600 billion per year, while public spending on infrastructure in developing countries is presently around 3 per cent per year.

With this in mind, we consider alternative arrangements that maximize efficiency within infrastructure sectors, avoiding the endemic inefficiencies of SOEs and the risks associated with privatization, while attracting the capital investment necessary to finance the projects.

Generally speaking, the term 'public–private partnership' (PPP) refers to an arrangement that is aimed at harnessing private sector capital and expertise in designing, financing, building, managing and maintaining infrastructure projects through various mechanisms without entirely divesting the government of its ownership. In understanding PPPs it is useful to consider a continuum of service delivery arrangements. At one end is complete government provision of services (via SOEs and/or government departments) and at the other end is complete divestiture or privatization. PPPs are located somewhere in the middle, where the government retains some ownership or assets in a sector but divests other functions to private enterprises. More technically, the OECD defines a public–private partnership as

> an agreement between the government and one or more private partners (which may include the operators and the financers) according to which the private partners deliver the service in such a manner that the service delivery objectives of the government are aligned with the profit objectives of the private partners and where the effectiveness of the alignment depends on a sufficient transfer of risk to the private partners.[64]

In the absence of a significant transfer of risk, private service delivery can be viewed as a form of traditional public procurement.[65]

A. The Innovative Aspects of PPPs

Ronald Daniels and Michael Trebilcock argue that the most distinctive feature of many of the larger public–private sector infrastructure partnerships that have emerged in recent years is the integration within a single private sector organization or consortium of all or most of the functions of financing, designing, building, operating and maintaining the facility

---

[64] OECD, 'Public–private partnership: in pursuit of risk sharing and value for money' (2008) 17.

[65] Ibid., at 18.

in question.[66] Extensive integration is the main feature that brings about efficiency gains from PPPs in contrast with traditional government procurement, where the government specifies the quality and quantity of particular goods or services required and buys inputs from private sector organizations. However, the lack of effective integration of functions has often resulted in attenuated incentives to optimize the efficiency of the overall project.

A PPP's extensive integration of functions, on the other hand, allows the partners to coordinate and allocate resources more efficiently. The vertically integrated private-sector model might undertake various functions, such as project identification, design, financing, construction, operations and maintenance. With the extensive vertical integration of these functions in the provision of infrastructure, organizations may be able to coordinate these functions at lower costs than the government, yielding superior performance to more discrete forms of contracting out. The empirical evidence suggests that vertically integrated private providers of infrastructure services can complete initial infrastructure construction far more quickly than can be done under the traditional mode of public provision with discrete contracting out of particular functions. This is largely because of reductions in transaction and coordination costs and greater freedom from stringent government budget allocation and procurement regulations.[67]

An important offsetting feature of vertical integration may be a marked reduction in competition for infrastructure contracts. Very few organizations or consortia are likely to be able to assemble all the relevant specialized inputs required to bid on large integrated infrastructure projects.[68] Empirical evidence generally suggests that increasing the number of bidders from three to four can result in savings of up to 18 per cent; from seven to eight, up to 4 per cent; and from ten to eleven, up to 2 per cent.[69] A more competitive bidding process may be facilitated by less vertical integration.

---

66 Daniels and Trebilcock, *supra* note 1.

67 Issaka Ndekugri and Adrian Turner, 'Building procurement by design and build approach' (1994) *Journal of Construction and Engineering and Management* 120 at 250.

68 David Sappington and Joseph Stiglitz, 'Privatization, information and incentives' (1987) 6 *Journal of Policy Analysis & Management* 572.

69 R. Preston McAfee and John McMillan, *Incentives in Government Contracting* (Toronto: University of Toronto Press, 1988) at 151.

B. Types of Public–Private Partnership

Public–private partnerships in the development and operation of infrastructure that are proliferating throughout the world vary in both scale and nature. The OECD has categorized the various forms such arrangements may take:[70]

1. Service contracts: the least integrated form of PPP. The public sector retains overall operational responsibility and risks, while the private sector provides a bundle of services to a public utility. The two most common forms are:
   (a) *Management support*: the private partner provides the government with human and technical resources.
   (b) *Operation and management*: the private operator is responsible for the daily maintenance of the facilities following government performance criteria. In some cases the private operator may be in charge of operating the facilities.
2. Delegated management contracts: 'the public sector retains overall ownership of the assets, but delegates the responsibility for their operation to a private operator for a definite (often long) period of time'. The two most common forms are:
   (a) *Affermage or lease agreements*: the private operator manages, maintains and renews the facilities for a period of time. It is responsible for all existing assets but is not required to finance new facilities. The government is in charge of all new investment and ensuring compliance with existing laws.
   (b) *Concessions*: the private operator is entirely responsible for managing the services and all necessary investment for the length of the concession (for example, 20 years or more). Consumers are directly charged by the private operator, while the public authorities determine service terms and all key decisions related to charges.[71]
3. Construction support: the most integrated form, where the private operator participates in 'the design and construction phases of new infrastructure and carries at least some of the risks associated therewith'.

---

[70] This categorization is provided by the OECD report. Please see the full report for greater details: OECD, 'Encouraging public–private partnerships in the utilities sector: the role of development assistance', in NEPA/OECD Investment Initiative, *Investment for African Development: Making it Happen* (2005).

[71] OECD, ibid., at 6.

(a) *Build Design Operate* (BDO): 'the private operator, for a fixed period of time, designs, constructs and operates new facilities, which remain the property of the public authorities. The private operator assumes the risks linked to design and management of the facility. It is paid a fee by the public authorities and commits to an overall cost for the facility's construction and operation'.

(b) *Build Operate Transfer* (BOT): 'the private operator designs, finances and builds infrastructure. While formal ownership of the assets is assigned to the government, the private sector operates the project long enough to service any debt incurred and to earn a suitable return'.

(c) *Build Own Operate* (BOO): 'the private investor retains ownership and control of the project. The public sector has no obligation to purchase the facility'.

Table 6.1 Characteristics of alternative forms of PPP

	Operation and maintenance	Ownership	Investment	Commercial risk	Duration (years)
Management support	Public and private	Public	Public	Public	1–2
O&M	Private	Public	Public	Public	3–5
Leasing	Private	Public	Public	Semi-private	8–15
Concession	Private	Public	Private	Private	20–30
BDO	Private	Public	Public	Private	20–30
BOT/BOO	Private	Public/private	Private	Private	20-30

Source: OECD, 'Encouraging public–private partnerships in the utilities sector: the role of development assistance', in NEPA/OECD Investment Initiative, *Investment for African Development: Making it Happen* (2005).

C. PPPs and the Developing World

Since the early 1990s, PPPs have been implemented in various sectors and with varying degrees of success in almost all developing countries.[72] They have become common as a result of the well-documented inefficiencies of SOEs in the infrastructure sector where it was estimated that public sector

[72] Ibid.

monopolies in energy, road, water and rail in developing countries generated losses of US$55 billion a year.[73] According to the OECD, between 1990 and 2003 there were over 2750 projects involving private participation in infrastructure in developing countries, with total public and private investment in these projects amounting to US $786 billion.[74]

Although PPP agreements have become increasingly common throughout the developing world, the OECD reports that private investors in infrastructure have favoured certain countries over others, generally those with 'relatively large, wealthy or fast-growing markets'.[75] The top 25 destinations for investment in PPPs in infrastructure together account for almost 90 per cent of total PPP investment in the developing world, and the 64 countries at the bottom of the list account for only 1 per cent of total investment in PPPs in developing and transition economies since 1990.[76] PPPs have been most prominent in Latin America, reflecting the greater degree of economic liberalization undertaken in most of that region.[77] The IMF further notes that PPPs have been more common in Latin American countries because of the relatively strong institutional framework that is necessary for the successful establishment and execution of a PPP.[78]

D. Challenges in Designing a Successful PPP Project

Formidable contracting problems arise both *ex ante* in negotiating and drafting the initial contract and *ex post* in ensuring compliance with its terms and in renegotiating the contract at relevant contract renewal junctures. It is important to keep in mind that these problems exist in all PPP arrangements, but that their impact and impediment is often amplified in developing countries where governments often lack the information, expertise, resources and capacity to deal with these problems, and may be in a position of inequality of bargaining power vis-à-vis the private sector partners.

The OECD identifies three principal challenges in designing successful projects: (i) competition in the awarding of contracts; (ii) falling demand and consumer dissatisfaction; and (iii) non-compliance with contractual

---

73 Philip Gray, *Private Participation in Infrastructure: A Review of the Evidence* (World Bank: 2001) at 1.

74 OECD, *supra* note 70.

75 Ibid.

76 Ibid.

77 Ibid.

78 IMF, Fiscal Affairs Department, *Public–Private Partnerships* (Washington DC: IMF, 2004).

terms. In terms of the first challenge, when the host country is a developing country and lacks the administrative capacity to properly evaluate and award contracts, a large number of project negotiations are often abandoned. According to one source, cited by OECD, only 11 per cent of potential investment negotiations were concluded.[79] Such a dismal probability of concluding projects may render bidding uncompetitive which, in turn, undermines the very purpose of creating PPPs. A World Bank study estimates that the typical number of bidders for a project in the transport sector is two or three – a level that may not be sufficient to elicit strong competition, nor likely to engender significant innovation.

The second challenge is failing demand and consumer dissatisfaction. In order to gauge consumer demand properly, market research is necessary, which many developing countries simply do not have the resources to undertake. Moreover, while stable macroeconomic conditions are crucial for the success of PPPs, many developing countries experience macroeconomic shocks, such as currency crises, which can impede the likelihood of successful project completion and operation and compromise investor confidence in the country. Moreover, given that the primary concern of PPP investors is post-investment cash flow, which is largely dependent on macroeconomic conditions, unfavourable shocks may render the project no longer profitable without a price change.[80] Large fluctuations in prices, in turn, will lead to consumer dissatisfaction, which can further impact on the ultimate success of the PPP.[81]

The third challenge arises when contractual terms are not adhered to. This may be related to public resistance, political circumstances, macroeconomic shocks, or may be as a result of one party's inability to comply with the contractual terms. Often, when the private party cannot comply with the negotiated terms it is because it has understated the expected costs in order to win the contract and subsequently claims 'special circumstances' to demand a variation of the contractual terms.[82]

In the light of these problems it comes as no surprise that the number

---

[79] OECD, *supra* note 70 at 20. See also D. Jamali, 'Success and failure mechanisms of public private partnerships in developing countries: insights from the Lebanese context' (2004) 17 *International Journal of Public Sector Management* 414.

[80] OECD, *supra* note 70 at 21.

[81] Recent prominent examples include Bolivian water projects: see Willem Assies, 'David versus Goliath in Cochabamba: water rights, neoliberalism and the revival of social protest in Bolivia' (2003) 30 *Latin American Perspectives* at 19; and Lebanese mobile phone concessions: see Jamali, *supra* note 79.

[82] OECD, *supra* note 70 at 22.

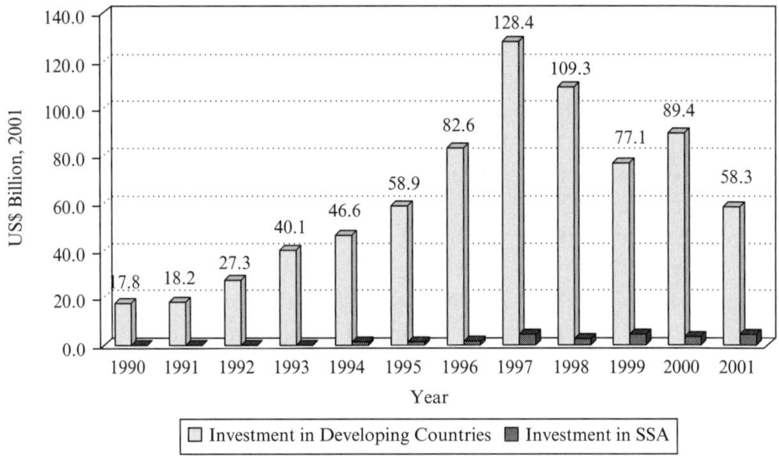

Source: World Bank PPI Projects Database.

Figure 6.1 PPI projects entered into by developing countries, 1990–2001

of PPPs that developing countries have entered into has been declining in recent years, as is shown by Figure 6.1. Indeed, in 2005, infrastructure projects involving PPPs were back to the level of a decade earlier.[83]

VII. CONCLUSION

Privatization was originally conceived as a strategy to address the inefficiencies that generally plague SOEs, attract much needed private investment to poor economies and mitigate the fiscal deficits that were crippling developing countries. It was believed that the revenues from the sale of SOEs, together with the reduced need for governmental investment in inefficient and often unprofitable companies, would promote fiscal responsibility and might allow governments to channel available resources to other sectors, such as education or healthcare. The outcomes of the privatization process in the 1990s, however, fell short of achieving these objectives.

This chapter has provided some insights into the reasons for these pitfalls. Evidence shows that richer countries benefit more from privatization than poorer countries. In some cases, privatization can only be successful

[83] Ibid., at 7.

if properly coordinated with significant private sector reform, which would entail the creation of credible competition policies and regulatory structures, macroeconomic stability and the reduction of corruption. This means that a country's broader institutional environment will be an important factor in the success of privatization processes. This broader institutional environment can also impact on the political feasibility of privatization.

However, even if the broader institutional environment is in place, and there is political willingness to move forward with privatization, the institutional details of the privatization process still present a formidable set of challenges. The chapter has illustrated this issue with an analysis of the costs and benefits of major privatization strategies, such as restitution and voucher, privatizations, management buy-outs, outright sale of state property and partial privatizations. The chapter also considers the advantages and disadvantages of alternatives to privatization, such as management contracts, performance contracts, increased competition, and public–private partnerships in the context of new infrastructure projects.

This chapter has underscored the point that there are important interconnections between privatization and other elements of the broader institutional environment. For instance, a healthy private sector with robust competition requires a well-functioning financial system, an appropriate regulatory framework depends on a competent and non-corrupt bureaucracy, and a stable macroeconomic environment depends on a functional and competent central bank (inter alia). In addition, privatization itself is a challenging exercise in detailed institutional design requiring high levels of legal, financial and management expertise, which many developing countries lack. While this expertise can often be obtained externally, external consultants often lack the detailed knowledge of a developing country – its history, culture and politics – to provide relevant advice, thus rendering external expertise an imperfect substitute for indigenous expertise in the long run (although combinations of indigenous and external expertise may be a short-term solution).

7. International trade, foreign direct investment and development

I. INTRODUCTION

In the next two chapters, we address features of the international economic order that bear importantly on the economic prospects of developing countries: – trade and foreign direct investment in this chapter, and foreign aid in Chapter 8.

To put these features in perspective, global exports from developing countries amounted to US$1 717.7 billion in 2000.[1] In 2008, investment inflows to developing countries reached US$517 billion,[2] and official development assistance (foreign aid) US$119.8 billion.[3] These figures show that international trade and foreign direct investment (FDI), are clearly the most substantial sources of external income for developing countries.

From the perspective of developed countries, they can either import goods or services from low-wage developing economies (like China or India), or they can maintain very liberal immigration policies with respect to not only skilled workers but also unskilled workers, and maintain relatively low-wage industries in developed countries. Alternatively, they can view trade and FDI as complements and invest in manufacturing facilities in low-wage developing countries and use these as an export platform either to their home country or other developed or developing economies around the world (as exemplified by the growth of global supply chains and intra-firm trade). Or, again, they can view trade and FDI as

---

1 William R. Cline, *Trade Policy and Global Poverty* (Washington DC: Peterson Institute, 2004) at 20.

2 UNCTAD, 'Assessing the impact of the current financial and economic crisis on global FDI flows', 19 January 2009, available at http://www.parl.gc.ca/Content/LOP/ResearchPublications/prb0710-e.htm.

3 Jennifer Paul and Marcus Pistor, 'Official development assistance spending', 13 May 2009, Parliamentary Information and Research Service Library of Parliament. Available at http://www.parl.gc.ca/information/library/PRBpubs/prb0710-e.pdf.

substitutes and, instead of exporting to large developing country markets, invest in manufacturing facilities in these countries to service their domestic markets.

From a developing country perspective, emigration is a poor substitute for trade in that developing countries risk losing their most highly skilled workers to developed countries through a brain drain – which is, to some extent, offset by the substantial remittance flows that expatriates often send back to their home countries (estimated to be in excess of US$300 billion per year), and sometimes also offset by trade and investment networks that develop between home countries and diasporas in developed countries (Silicon Valley in the United States, for example).[4] As to whether trade and FDI are substitutes or complements, FDI may provide the capital and technical and managerial expertise required to promote major export-oriented sectors in developing countries and hence are complements, but this will entail host countries sharing the benefits of these investments to a greater or lesser extent with the foreign direct investors involved (as will be explored later in this chapter). Where import substitution policies are adopted by developing countries, trade and FDI are likely to be substitutes.

II. TRADE AND DEVELOPMENT

A. Trade Policy and Development: An Historical Perspective

International trade has a long history, both in terms of intellectual thought[5] and in terms of actual practice. Countries, or more accurately merchants in these countries, have been trading with each other for millennia;[6] however, it was not until the Enlightenment and the writings of political economists – such as Adam Smith in *The Wealth of Nations*[7] and David Ricardo in *The Principles of Political Economy*[8] – that the basic

---

4 See Michael Trebilcock and Matthew Sudak, 'The political economy of emigration and immigration' (2006) 81:1 *NYU Law Review* 234. Ian Goldin, Geoffrey Cameron and Meera Balarajan, *Exceptional People: How Migration Shaped Our World and Will Define Our Future* (Princeton, NJ: Princeton University Press, 2011).

5 See Douglas Irwin, *Against the Tide* (Princeton, NJ: Princeton University Press, 1996).

6 See Nayan Chanda, *Bound Together: How Traders, Preachers, Adventurers and Warriors Shaped Globalization* (New Haven, CT: Yale University Press, 2007).

7 Adam Smith, *The Wealth of Nations* (1776).

8 David Ricardo, *The Principles of Political Economy* (1817).

economic theory of international trade was first formulated. Adam Smith emphasized the gains from specialization and that these gains were limited only by the extent of the market. He pointed out that very few families find it economically rational to produce all the goods and services that they require, but in fact they produce goods or services for some of their needs and otherwise purchase goods or services from others who are better qualified to provide them. Smith argued that, just as this makes sense in the case of the family, it also makes sense in the case of a nation. It is easy to appreciate the force of this argument for free trade within nation-states. For example, in a large federal state like the US, Michigan specializes in producing automobiles (*inter alia*), Florida citrus fruit and tourism, Texas oil and beef, and California wine and high technology products. If each state of the US were to have attempted to become self-sufficient in these and all its own needs, the US would today be immeasurably poorer. It equally follows, on Smith's theory, that similar specialization is likely to generate mutual gains from trade in international exchanges – the division of labour is limited only by the extent of the market. According to Ricardo's theory of comparative advantage, countries should specialize in exporting goods where their comparative advantage is greatest and import goods where their comparative disadvantage is greatest, implying that all countries will find it advantageous to trade with other countries, even though they may lack an absolute advantage in any product.

It is conventional wisdom amongst trade scholars that a liberal world trading system in which countries are free to exploit or develop distinctive forms of comparative advantage is a key to increased productivity, economic growth and development. This thinking was evident in the original Bretton Woods Agreement which gave birth to the post-war international economic architecture, including the IMF, the World Bank and the GATT. In other words, conventional economic thinking was that, with the emergence of a liberal world trading system, a rising tide would lift all boats. Unfortunately, this has not proven to be the case. As Williamson shows,[9] over the past two centuries there has been a dramatic divergence in incomes around the globe, which has been driven overwhelmingly by the rise of between-country rather than within-country inequality.[10]

A number of developing countries have successfully integrated themselves into the world trading system and have benefited enormously from

---

[9] Jeffrey Williamson, 'Winners and losers over two centuries of globalization' (2002) World Institute for Development Economics Research Annual Lecture (WIDER) at 9–10.

[10] See more generally Branko Milanovic, *Worlds Apart: Measuring International and Global Inequality* (Princeton, NJ: Princeton University Press, 2005).

Figure 7.1 Global inequality of individual incomes, 1820–1992

it (the most prominent contemporary examples being China and India). However, many other developing countries have largely been left behind by the process of globalization. In *The Bottom Billion*,[11] Paul Collier documents the stagnation or absolute decline in real incomes of a number of very poor countries around the globe: most are concentrated in sub-Saharan Africa, but a number are located in Central Asia and Latin America, which are home to the bottom billion of the world's population, living on less than one dollar a day. These countries – about 60 on Collier's count – comprise almost a third of the countries in the world (mostly small) and one-sixth of the world's population. While foreign aid sometimes mitigates their economic decline, minimal exports and foreign direct investment preclude significant growth. According to Collier, these are countries caught in various traps – the conflict trap, the natural resource trap, the landlocked with bad neighbours trap, and the bad governance trap.

The multilateral trading system has not been oblivious to the special economic challenges facing developing countries.[12] Almost from the beginnings of the GATT in 1947, developing countries were accorded a

[11] Paul Collier, *The Bottom Billion* (New York: Oxford University Press, 2007).

[12] For useful introductions to the GATT/WTO, see Bernard Hoekman and Petros Mavroidis, *The World Trade Organization: Law, Economics and Politics* (London: Routledge, 2007); Michael J. Trebilcock, *Understanding Trade Law* (Cheltenham: Edward Elgar Publishing, 2011).

form of exceptionalism in terms of the application of standard GATT disciplines (referred to as 'special and differential treatment' – SDT). In 1955, Article XVIII of the GATT was extensively revised so as to permit developing countries to

- maintain a flexible tariff structure to promote a particular industry, even where previous tariff bindings had been entered into;
- limit imports by quantitative restrictions to address balance of payments problems; and
- impose tariff and quantitative restrictions to promote the establishment of a particular industry with a view to raising the general standard of living.

These extensive dispensations from GATT disciplines (that can be compendiously characterized as infant industry or import substitution rationales for protectionism) were justified on various grounds. First, it was widely argued by many developing countries – and indeed by many mainstream development economists in developed countries and international agencies at that time – that developing countries had often inherited truncated economies from their colonial overseers, where they had been largely restricted economically to the role of hewers of wood and drawers of water, leaving them with large, traditional and inefficient agricultural sectors where the marginal product of labour was often thought to be negligible or even zero. As with most developed countries earlier in their histories a major transformation in developing country economies was called for in reallocating resources from traditional agricultural sectors to more productive industrial or manufacturing sectors. To facilitate and encourage this, it was argued that at least temporary protectionism was required for these fledgling manufacturing industries in order to enable them to achieve minimum efficient scale and become competitive in both domestic and export markets.

Second, it was widely argued that infant industry protectionism had been aggressively pursued by many developed countries early in the process of their economic development including the United States, Canada, Germany and many other currently developed countries – and that developing countries which found themselves at similar stages of development in their early post-independence histories should not be denied similar policy flexibility. Third, it was often argued that adjustment costs faced by many developing countries in moving to a fully open international trading regime were likely to prove far more severe than those facing developed countries embarking upon a similar strategy of trade liberalization, because of low levels of education, poor physical infrastructure, inadequately developed financial, credit and insurance markets, and inadequate or non-existent social safety nets. Fourth, it was also argued that, at least for smaller and poorer developing countries, their share of world trade, and in particular imports, was typically so small that protectionist policies on their part were likely to have negligible adverse impacts on world prices in the commodities affected by these policies, and thus any terms of trade externalities from the pursuit of such policies were likely to be small to non-existent.

Despite these arguments for infant industry protection or import substitution policies, it was also widely recognized in the early years of the GATT that increasing export earnings was also an important impetus to economic development, which would be facilitated by enhanced access to developed countries' markets for exports of both primary and manufactured products from developing countries. Therefore, in 1965, Part IV (Articles XXXVI to XXXVIII) was added to GATT. These provisions called on developed countries to provide favourable market access to products of export interest to developing countries on a non-reciprocal basis. Following the adoption of Part IV, in 1968 the United Nations Conference on Trade and Development (UNCTAD) established a generalized system of preferences (GSP), by which developed countries could, on a voluntary basis, provide non-reciprocal preferential tariff reductions for products of export interest to developing countries. Since such preferential tariff reductions violated the most favoured nation (MFN) provisions of the GATT, a waiver from MFN obligations was provided by the GATT in 1971, initially for ten years and, in 1979, was extended permanently by the so-called Enabling Clause which permits – and indeed encourages – the extension of 'generalized, non-reciprocal and non-discriminatory preferences' to developing countries. Pursuant to the initial GATT waiver and subsequently to the Enabling Clause, many developed countries have extended preferential treatment to many exports from developing countries.

In the course of the Uruguay Round of multilateral negotiations (from 1986 to 1993), the general orientation of negotiations was to integrate developing countries more fully into the world trading system.[13] This was pursued in a number of ways:

(a) by insisting on the developing countries binding and at least modestly reducing most of their typically very high tariff rates;
(b) by narrowing the scope of the balance of payments exception;

---

13 See Trebilcock and Howse, ibid., Chapter 15.

(c) by treating almost all of the Uruguay Round agreements[14] as a single undertaking to which all members of the GATT (now the WTO) would be required to commit themselves, albeit – in the case of developing countries – typically with longer implementation periods and promises of technical assistance in meeting their compliance obligations.

The so-called 'Grand Bargain' reflected in the Uruguay Round agreements was that developing countries would commit to additional responsibilities in the areas noted above, in return for

- continuing the liberalization of tariffs on industrial exports to developed countries;
- more stringent safeguards regimes;
- a significant start on liberalizing international trade in agricultural products, including some constraints on export subsidies, domestic measures of support, and some reduction in tariffs; and
- the gradual liberalization and elimination of the Multi-Fibre Arrangement (MFA).

Since the close of the Uruguay Round, many developing countries have become disenchanted with the so-called 'Grand Bargain'. They point out that they still face disproportionately high tariffs on their industrial exports, increasingly frequent invocation of contingent protection mechanisms (anti-dumping, safeguards and countervailing duties), still numerous barriers in exporting their agricultural products to developed countries – including high tariffs, substantial subsidies, escalating tariffs on processed agricultural products, and onerous technical standards.

In the case of the MFA, while quotas have been reduced or eliminated in stages, high tariffs still often remain; moreover, since the expiration of the MFA, major importers such as the United States and the European Union have imposed safeguards or negotiated new limits on imports of textiles and clothing from major developing country exporters, in particular China. In turn, developing countries argue that the new responsibilities that they have assumed in areas such as TRIPS have imposed unforesee-

[14] The Uruguay Round agreements included the Trade-Related Intellectual Property Rights Agreement (TRIPS), the Trade-Related Investment Measures Agreement (TRIMS), the Subsidies and Countervailing Measures Agreement (SCM), the General Agreement on Trade and Services (GATS), the Sanitary and Phyto-Sanitary Standards Agreement (SPS Agreement) and the Technical Barriers to Trade Agreement (the TBT).

ably burdensome compliance requirements on them in setting up sophisticated western-style intellectual property regimes, but have produced negligible benefits, and indeed in many cases adverse impacts on them in terms, for example, of access to essential medicines.

The Doha Multilateral Round of trade negotiations that was launched in 2001 was intended in part to provide a forum for addressing these concerns. Indeed, at its launch the Doha Round was officially characterized as the Doha Development Round. In the course of negotiations during this Round, the future status of SDT for developing countries on both the import side and the export side has emerged as a major fault-line between developing and developed countries, and along with other and often related issues (such as agricultural liberalization) has brought negotiations to the brink of collapse. In this Round – unlike earlier Rounds where developing countries were largely marginalized from being significant participants in the negotiations – developing countries (especially larger states such as China, India, Brazil and Mexico) have formed loose negotiating coalitions.

At the Cancun Ministerial of the WTO in November 2003, a group of 20 developing countries articulated extensive demands for major revisions of the multilateral trading architecture, including special and differential treatment, which many developed countries equally strenuously resisted, leading to the collapse of the Ministerial. Progress on many of these issues has since then been extremely modest.

B. Special and Differential Treatment: An Assessment[15]

The two limbs of special and differential treatment (SDT) referred to above need to be seen as inherently interrelated. The much greater policy flexibility extended to developing countries on the import side necessarily implies that, in securing better access to developed countries' markets for

---

[15] For excellent reviews of special and differential treatment see Bernard Hoekman, Constantine Michalopoulos and L. Alan Winters, 'Special and differential treatment of developing countries in the WTO: moving forward after Cancun' (2004) 27 *The World Economy* 481; M. Pangestu, 'Special and differential treatment: special for whom and how different?' (2000) 23 *The World Economy* 1285; T.N. Srinivasin, 'Developing countries in the world trading system: from GATT 1947 to the Third Ministerial Meeting of WTO' (1999) 22 *The World Economy*; M. Hart and B. Dymond, 'Special and differential treatment and the Doha "Development" Round' (2003) 37 *Journal of World Trade* 395; and J. Michael Finger and L. Alan Winters, 'What can the WTO do for developing countries?', in Anne O. Krueger (ed.), *The WTO as an International Organization* (Chicago: University of Chicago Press, 1998).

their exports, they cannot be expected to offer reciprocal trade concessions (without undermining their policy flexibility on the import side). Hence the second limb of SDT contemplates non-reciprocal and preferential treatment of exports from developing countries by developed countries. While it was assumed that this combination of policies would substantially enhance the economic prospects of developing countries, this assumption has come under increasingly searching scrutiny in academic research.

On the import side, much research beginning in the 1960s and increasing through the 1970s found that import substitution policies were not achieving their goals and were actually hindering the growth of developing countries.[16] For example, research by Balassa found that protectionist policies had hurt developing countries by encouraging industrialization at the expense of agriculture, worsened income distribution, reduced domestic savings, increased unemployment, and led to a very low rate of capital utilization. Little et al. demonstrated the high and indiscriminate levels of protectionism in many developing countries, and research by Krueger revealed the rise of rent-seeking behaviour and corruption that accompanied highly discretionary protectionist trade policies and related policies such as foreign exchange controls. More recent literature has provided further evidence of the positive relationship between trade openness and growth, stemming from gains from improved resource allocation, greater

---

[16] See, for example, Ian Little, Tibor Sctivosky and Maurice Scott, *Industry and Trade in Some Developing Countries* (Oxford: Oxford University Press, 1970); Bela Balassa, *The Structure of Protection in Developing Countries* (Baltimore: Johns Hopkins University Press, 1971); Anne O. Krueger, *Foreign Trade Regimes and Economic Development: Liberalization Attempts and Consequences* (Lexington: Ballinger, 1979); and Jagdish Bhagwati, *Foreign Trade Regimes and Economic Development: Anatomy and Consequences of Exchange Control Regimes* (Lexington: Ballinger, 1978). Writing in 2002, Jeffrey Williamson reports that the World Bank has conducted over 41 studies of developing countries and contrasted the performance of relatively open and relatively closed economies, concluding that trade openness and growth are positively correlated: see Jeffrey Williamson, 'Winners and losers over two centuries of globalization' (September 2002) NBER Working Paper No. W9161 at 9. See also Jeffrey Sachs and Andrew Warner, 'Economic reform and the process of global integration' (1995) 1 *Brookings Papers on Economic Activity* 1; David Dollar, 'Outward-oriented developing economies really do grow more rapidly: evidence from 95 LDCs, 1976–1985' (1992) 40 *Economic Development and Cultural Change* 523; Sebastian Edwards, 'Productivity and growth: what do we really know?' (1998) 108 *The Economic Journal* 383; Romain Wacziarg and Karen Horn Welch, 'Trade liberalization and growth: new evidence', Stanford Graduate School of Business Working Paper (2003). For a critique of this literature, see Francisco Rodriguez and Dani Rodrik, 'Trade policy and economic growth: a skeptic's guide to the cross-national evidence' (1999) National Bureau of Economic Research Working Paper 708.

Table 7.1 Trade-policy orientation and growth rates in the Third World, 1963–92

	Average annual rates growth of GDP per capita %		
Trade policy orientation	1963–73	1973–85	1980–92
Strongly open to trade	6.9	5.9	6.4
Moderately open	4.9	1.6	2.3
Moderately anti-trade	4.0	1.7	−0.2
Strongly anti-trade	1.6	−0.1	−0.4

Note: In all periods the three strongly open economies were Hong Kong, South Korea and Singapore. The identities of the strongly anti-trade countries changed over time. In 1963–73 they were Argentina, Bangladesh, Burundi, Chile, Dominican Republic, Ethiopia, Ghana, India, Pakistan, Peru, Sri Lanka, Sudan, Tanzania, Turkey, Uruguay and Zambia. For the two overlapping later periods, the strongly anti-trade countries were the previous 16, plus Bolivia, Madagascar and Nigeria, minus Chile, Pakistan, Sri Lanka, Turkey and Uruguay.

Source: Peter H. Lindert and Jeffrey G. Williamson, 'Does globalization make the world more unequal?' in M. Bordo, A.M. Taylor and J.G. Williamson (eds), *Globalization in Historical Perspective* (Chicago: University of Chicago Press, 2002).

potential to realize economies of scale, improved access to technology, greater domestic competition and increased domestic savings and foreign direct investment. While measuring trade openness is not unproblematic, these findings are reflected in Table 7.1.[17]

These findings are often reinforced by reference to the trade policies adopted by the so-called East Asian miracle economies – beginning with Japan in the early post-war years, followed by Hong Kong, Singapore, Taiwan, Korea, Malaysia, Thailand and more recently by Vietnam, China and India, or in Africa countries such as Botswana and Mauritius, or in Latin American countries such as Chile. In one respect or another all these countries have pursued policies of export-led growth (outward rather than inward-looking policies that were adopted in many countries that adopted import substitution policies). It must be acknowledged, however, that there is ongoing and, to some extent, unresolved controversy as to the extent to which this export-led growth has been managed by interventionist trade and related policies designed to protect infant industries in their early stages and to support selectively export-oriented industries (various

[17] Williamson, ibid.

versions of so-called 'strategic trade theory'). At the very least, it is true that most of these countries have pursued somewhat idiosyncratic paths to integration with the global economy.[18]

As to the second limb of SDT – non-reciprocal trade preferences – much recent research suggests that these preferences have not proved to be as useful to developing countries as they had hoped for the following reasons:

1. The benefits of the preferences seem to be concentrated on the more advanced developing countries, which needed them least. For example, a 1987 study found that four beneficiaries – Brazil, Hong Kong, Korea and Taiwan – derived more than 50 per cent of all GSP benefits.[19]
2. GSP market access preferences have tended to become less valuable as margins of preference have been eroded through successive negotiating rounds which have reduced MFN tariff levels.
3. Preferences are also not durable since they have often been tied to the level of a country's economic development; countries that are successful in increasing per capita incomes are often graduated out of the programs.
4. Donor countries often reserve the right to withdraw preferences if imports become too competitive with domestic products.
5. Many import-sensitive products of major export interest to developing countries have been excluded from GSP schemes.
6. Preferences have increasingly been subject to various forms of conditionality (such as human and labour rights and environmental standards) and ideological or geo-political factors (such as the perceived efforts of countries to combat terrorism).
7. Complex rules of origin have often diluted the value of GSP preferences, preventing developing countries from producing goods most efficiently.
8. Preferences cause trade diversion from developing countries that do not receive preferences to those that do. Thus, while preferences may benefit some developing countries in the short term, they are unlikely to benefit developing countries overall and they create inducements to distort comparative advantage, which puts the recipients of pref-

---

[18] See Dani Rodrik, *One Economics, Many Recipes* (Princeton, NJ: Princeton University Press, 2007).

[19] G. Karsenty and S. Laird, 'The generalized system of preferences: a quantitative assessment of the direct trade effects and of policy options' (UNCTAD Discussion Paper No. 18, Geneva, 1987).

erences at risk in the long term if and when the preferences are withdrawn.[20]

9. Finally, and most importantly, because these preferences are non-reciprocal, developing countries have forsaken significant bargaining leverage in negotiations with developed countries – without a *quid*, there is often a very meagre *quo*. This is simply to acknowledge the *réal politique* of trade negotiations – one has to give in order to get.

Despite these reservations about the past and prospective efficacy of SDT, some prominent and respected commentators continue to defend its continuing vitality and indeed argue for its strengthening and expansion. For example, Nobel Laureate Joseph Stiglitz, in two recent books,[21] argues that the empirical evidence demonstrating the economic benefits of a liberal trading regime for most developing countries is much more ambiguous than conventional thinking acknowledges. He points to the gradualist and sometimes strategic approach to trade liberalization adopted by most of the high-growth East Asian economies, the relative failure of the so-called Washington consensus to stimulate high and sustainable growth in much of Latin America, and the devastating short-term economic consequences of 'shock therapy' in Russia.

Stiglitz argues that even if, in the long run, an open trading regime is to the benefit of developing countries, the absence of most of the adjustment cushions that exist in developed countries means that many developing countries face relatively more severe adjustment costs from trade liberalization. From these premises, he argues for a radically expanded form of SDT, where countries would be divided into various per capita income tranches; countries in higher income tranches would be required to liberalize all trade with countries in lower income tranches and amongst themselves, while countries in lower income tranches would only be required to liberalize trade with countries in even lower income tranches and amongst themselves but not with respect to trade with countries in higher income

---

[20] G.M. Grossman and Alan O. Sykes, 'A preference for development: the law and economics of GSP' (2005) 4 *World Trade Review* 41.

[21] Joseph Stiglitz and Andrew Charlton, *Fair Trade for All: How Trade Can Promote Development* (Oxford: Oxford University Press, 2005); Joseph Stiglitz, *Making Globalization Work* (New York: W.W. Norton & Co., 2006), Chapter 3 'Making trade fair'; See also, Ha-Joon Chang, *Bad Samaritans: The Myth of Free Trade and the Secret History of Capitalism* (New York: Bloomsbury Press, 2008); Dani Rodrik, *The Globalization Paradox: Democracy and the Future of the World Economy* (New York: W.W. Norton & Co., 2011). For a more radical recent critique of conventional economic rationales for free trade, see Roberto Unger, *Free Trade Reimagined* (Princeton, NJ: Princeton University Press, 2007).

tranches. Proposals such as this, which have been vigorously endorsed by prominent international NGOs such as Oxfam, have significantly widened the fault-line between developing and developed countries in the multilateral trading system, and therefore it is difficult not to be pessimistic about the prospects of finding any consensus or middle ground.

With the multilateral trading system in this state of stasis, it is important to note a relevant and rapidly growing phenomenon – the proliferation of preferential trading agreements (PTAs), entered into between or among developed and developing countries, and between or among developing countries themselves. Since Cancun, for example, the United States has announced that it will aggressively pursue PTAs with friendly developing countries, and indeed has done so. As to whether this strategy provides an effective response for developing countries to the fault-lines between developing and developed countries in the multilateral system noted above, there are reasons for pessimism.

Negotiations between large developed countries and small, poor developing countries on a bilateral basis entail much greater inequalities of bargaining power than developing countries encounter in the multilateral system, at least if they strategically negotiate as blocks or informal coalitions, exploiting the consensus decision principle that governs the multilateral system. Indeed, they are likely to end up assuming so-called WTO-plus commitments in areas such as intellectual property and investment. In turn, PTAs between or among developing countries cannot, for the most part, ensure greater access to their most important potential export markets in developed countries.

Moreover, a world trading system that is dominated by (in Jagdish Bhagwati's terms)[22] a 'spaghetti bowl' of preferential trading arrangements, apart from the transaction costs entailed in negotiating and maintaining a host of these agreements and the complex rules of origin that are required as a predicate of these agreements, stands in sharp antithesis to the non-discriminatory world trading system that the architects of the Bretton Woods system (such as John Maynard Keynes) envisaged at the beginning of the post-war era as a response to the political and economic factionalism that characterized international relations in the inter-war years – with catastrophic consequences.[23]

---

22 Jagdish Bhagwati and Arvind Panagariya, 'Bilateral trade treaties are a sham', *Financial Times* (28 July 2003) 17; Bhagwati and Panagariya (eds), *The Economics of Preferential Trade Agreements* (Washington DC: AEI Press, 1996).

23 See, more generally, Jagdish Bhagwati, *Termites in the Trading System: How Preferential Agreements Undermine Free Trade* (Oxford: Oxford University Press, 2008); Sally Razeen, *New Frontiers in Free Trade: Globalization's Future and Asia's*

In our view, in the current Doha Round member countries should agree to provide immediate, unconditional and non-reciprocal duty-free access to their markets for all exports (without exceptions) from the least-developed countries that are the focus of Collier's concerns. Developing countries in higher income tranches, in contrast, should follow a different path. It is likely to be in their long-term interests to phase out reliance on SDT and bargain reciprocally for enhanced access to developed countries' markets, albeit with longer transition periods, more gradual reductions in trade barriers, more expansive safeguard protections, and cross-issue bargaining where reductions in developed country trade barriers can be exchanged for not only reductions in developing country trade barriers but also a relaxation of restrictions on foreign direct investment and services. In addition, specialized agreements like TRIPS and TRIMS should in future generally be plurilateral rather than multilateral in nature (as they were prior to the Uruguay Round), leaving more policy flexibility for developing countries on the scope and timing of commitments beyond the general GATT principles.

C. Institutional Implications of Trade Policy

A growing body of literature finds a positive two-way relationship between trade policy and domestic institutional quality: countries with better domestic institutions (especially legal institutions) tend to be more successful exporters (especially of more complex products) because of credible commitments they can offer to their customers,[24] and in turn more open

---

Rising Role (Washington DC: Cato Institute, 2008) Chapter 5; Kyle Bagwell and Robert Staiger, *The Economics of the World Trading System* (Cambridge, MA: MIT Press, 2002) Chapter 7. For a more sympathetic view of PTAs see Arie Reich, 'Bilateralism versus multilateralism in international economic law: applying the principle of subsidiarity' (2010) 60 *University of Toronto Law Journal* 263 (arguing that PTAs can better accommodate differences in regional conditions than the multilateral system).

[24] See James Anderson and Douglas Marcouiller, 'Trade insecurity and home bias: an empirical investigation' (1999) National Bureau of Economic Research Working Paper 7000; Joseph Francois, Johannes Kepler and Miriam Manchin, 'Institutions, infrastructure and trade' (2007) World Bank Policy Research Working Paper 4152; Marion Jansen and Hildegunn Kyvik Nordas, 'Institutions, infrastructure and trade flows' (April 2004) World Trade Organization Staff Working Paper ERSD-2004-02; David Dollar and Aart Kraay, 'Institutions, trade and growth' (2003) 50 *Journal of Monetary Economics* 133; Daniel Berkowitz, Johannes Moenius and Katharina Pistor, 'Legal institutions and international trade flows' (2004) 26 *Michigan Journal of International Law* 163. For a recent collection of essays on PTAs see Kyle Bagwell and Petros Mavroidis (eds), *Preferential Trade*

trade policies tend to strengthen domestic institutions because of the ability of traders to vote with their feet if the domestic institutional environment is not conducive to trade (thus enhancing inter-jurisdictional competition).[25] This evidence once again places a premium on domestic institutional quality – this time in external economic relations. The positive feedback effects of more open trade policies on domestic institutions suggest a case for a general orientation to trade openness. However, even with such an orientation, domestic institutional capacity constraints argue for less developed countries placing a priority on enhancing their bargaining power (often in coalitions with larger, more sophisticated developing countries) in the multilateral trading system rather than attempting to negotiate and administer a plethora of bilateral PTAs. Such constraints also suggest that, to the extent that developing countries feel a need to protect various economic sectors from international competition, a premium should attach to very simple, broad gauge policies – a common tariff across all such sectors, for example, rather than a highly calibrated tariff structure that lends itself to rent-seeking and corruption in its formulation and administration.

Unfortunately, many poor developing countries that have pursued import substitution (infant industry protection) policies, especially those with small domestic markets, have become captive to a form of path dependency where, once having implemented these policies, they have become saddled with a range of increasingly costly, uncompetitive and inefficient industries, along with interest groups and rent-seekers with a vested interest in their perpetuation. These interests are a severe impediment to a shift of focus to an outward-oriented, export-led growth strategy that holds out the only prospect for long-term economic growth. Even less poor developing countries with large potential domestic markets have very mixed experiences with import-substitution policies, enjoying some successes in promoting infant industries, but also being saddled with costly and increasingly uncompetitive industries in the face of vested interests that demand ongoing and often increasing support.[26]

Agreements: Law, Policy and Economics (Cambridge: Cambridge University Press, 2011).

[25] Shang-Jin Wei, 'Natural openness and good government' (2000) National Bureau of Economic Research Working Paper 7765; Dani Rodrik, Arvind Subramanian and Francesco Trebbi, 'Institutions rule: the primacy of institutions over geography and integration in economic development' (2004) 9 *Journal of Economic Growth* 14.

[26] See Peter Evans, *Embedded Autonomy: States and Industrial Transformation* (Princeton, NJ: Princeton University Press, 1995) Chapter 6 ('State firms and high technology husbandry').

Beyond issues bearing on the relationship between domestic institutional quality and trade policy, major international institutional issues arise in the formulation of international trade policy. According to Joseph Stiglitz, developed countries impose far higher – on average four times higher – tariffs against developing countries than against developed countries. Rich countries have cost poor countries three times more in trade restrictions than they give in total development aid.[27] Data like this provides fodder for dependency theories noted in Chapter 1 that attribute the plight of many or most poor countries to an unfair international economic system that is rigged in favour of developed countries.

Professor Gerald Helleiner, a distinguished development economist, in his Praul Prebisch lecture[28] argues that developing countries, accounting for over 85 per cent of the world's population, are severely under-represented in current governance arrangements for the global economy. Decision-making on key global economic issues remains highly concentrated in the major industrial powers and the major international financial institutions which they control. The selection processes for the leadership of key multilateral financial institutions demonstrate no regard for the principles of due process, with the presidencies of the IMF and the World Bank vested with the EU and the US respectively. Groups such as the G7 countries exclude entirely developing countries from their membership. Even the G20, which includes some larger developing countries, entirely excludes smaller and poorer developing countries. Whereas developed countries account for only 17 per cent of voting strength in the United Nations and 24 per cent in the WTO, they account for almost three-quarters of total World Bank membership, where they hold 40 per cent of total votes.[29]

While we do not share the view that all or most of the problems that afflict poor countries are attributable to the international economic system, it is easy to be persuaded that substantial reforms are required to this system in order to more fully integrate developing countries into the global economy, and on a fairer and more efficient basis.

In the case of the WTO, at least in principle, decision-making authority is distributed equally, with each of the 153 member countries entitled to a vote (from smallest to largest), and most major decisions taken by

---

27 Stiglitz, *supra* note 21 at 78.

28 Gerald Helleiner, 'Markets, politics, and globalization: can the global economy be civilized?' 10th Praul Prebisch Lecture, Geneva, 11 December 2000.

29 The South Centre, 'Reform of World Bank governance structures' (September 2007), available at http://www.southcentre.org/index.php?option=com_docman&task=cat_view&gid=45&Itemid=182&lang=en&limitstart=140.

consensus. However, the reality has been that negotiations in the late and critical stages of previous negotiating rounds under the GATT, and more recently the WTO, have typically been dominated by the so-called triad – the US, the EU and Japan – and the results of their three-way negotiations in the so-called 'Green Room' simply presented to other countries as largely a *fait accompli*. As with the domestic formulation and administration of trade policy, the multilateral trade regime has been afflicted with a form of path dependency reflected in the serious difficulties the regime has experienced in outgrowing its institutional origins as a small, 'rich man's club' to a genuinely multilateral organization, the vast majority of whose members are developing countries, including some of the largest, most rapidly growing economies in the world (China, India and Brazil).

However, developing countries have struggled to play an effective role in this regime. Multilateral trade negotiations have become increasingly complex and protracted, with an ever-expanding agenda of issues – the Uruguay Round took seven years to complete (1986 to 1993) and the current Doha Round, which began in 2001, has still not reached a conclusion ten years later. Negotiations place an enormous strain on the expertise, resources and institutional capacity of smaller and poorer developing countries, many of which cannot afford even to maintain delegations in Geneva. Those countries that have such delegations expect these delegations to assume responsibility for many more matters than trade policy issues vested in various other international agencies located in Geneva. Even delegations with a more limited mandate confront the fact that WTO processes involve at least 45 meetings per week in Geneva, most of which are technically complex and highly legalized, and find it next to impossible to get clear, consistent and informed directions from their home governments, which typically lack the institutional capacity to provide informed judgments or directions on the complex trade-offs that are often required. In the past, developed countries have often pursued a divide-and-conquer strategy with various groups of developing countries, further weakening their negotiating leverage. Only in recent years have developing countries been able to form more effective negotiating coalitions that hold out considerable promise for redressing bargaining inequalities between developing and developed countries.

Once negotiations have been concluded and countries have made various commitments to each other, adherence to these commitments raises the possibility of disputes. The WTO maintains a sophisticated dispute settlement system for adjudicating formal disputes between member countries, beginning with informal consultations, followed by formal proceedings before ad hoc panels, and then appeals on matters of law to a standing Appellate Body. Again, many smaller and poorer developing countries find that they lack the resources, expertise and institutional capacity to be effective litigants, either as complainants or respondents, in this sophisticated and demanding dispute settlement process. Even in the event of a small developing country prevailing in a dispute against a large developed country, the ultimate sanction for non-compliance is the imposition of authorized retaliatory trade sanctions against the non-compliant country. For large developed countries that prevail in disputes against small developing countries, this is a serious threat, but obviously the converse does not apply, implying yet a further asymmetry in the multilateral institutional arrangements governing international trade.[30]

These various asymmetries between developing and developed countries in the institutional arrangements governing international trade require urgent attention, but they should not obscure the imperative that for developing countries to participate effectively even in a fairly designed international trading system and its governance, effective domestic institutional capacity that facilitates such participation is an essential pre-condition – in other words, fair international institutions and effective domestic institutions are complements, not substitutes.

III. FOREIGN DIRECT INVESTMENT AND DEVELOPMENT

A. Policy Concerns

Foreign direct investment (FDI) should be distinguished from portfolio investment. FDI typically involves some form of effective control and active management of assets in host countries, while portfolio investment typically involves passive investments in enterprises or government bonds in host countries. Over the last several decades, there has been a dramatic increase in FDI around the world, much of it between developed countries, but increasingly developing countries have been major recipients of FDI, including countries such as China, and in some cases have themselves become exporters of FDI (again, China is a prominent example).[31]

---

30 See Chad Bown, *Self-Enforcing Trade: Developing Countries and WTO Dispute Settlement* (Washington, DC: Brookings Institution Press, 2009).

31 See generally, Americo Zampetti and Pierre Sauvé, 'International investment', in Andrew Guzman and Alan Sykes (eds), *Research Handbook in International Economic Law* (Cheltenham, UK: Edward Elgar, 2007); Ha-Joon Chang, *Bad Samaritans: The Myth of Free Trade and the Secret History of Capitalism* (New York: Bloomsbury Press, 2008); Dani Rodrik, *The Globalization Paradox:*

More than 40 per cent of world FDI inflows are directed to developing countries and FDI flows to developing countries now exceed foreign aid flows by a factor of about 5 to 1.[32]

In their early post-independence years, many former colonies viewed FDI with scepticism and, in some cases, outright hostility, viewing it as holding the potential for creating a new form of economic imperialism (reflected in dependency theories of development that were influential in many developing countries in the 1950s and 1960s). More recently, many developing countries have come to see FDI as having at least the potential for making significant contributions to their economies – as a source of investment in infrastructure, as a source of technology transfers and spillovers, as a source of investment in human capital and skills upgrading, as a source of investment in major natural resource extraction projects, and as a major source of local employment in low-wage, low-skilled manufacturing activities.[33] Foreign direct investors, in turn, sometimes see international trade in goods or services and FDI as complements and in other cases as substitutes. Where host countries have large protected domestic markets, FDI may be the most effective way of accessing these markets behind prevailing tariff walls – particularly the case with host countries with large growing populations and hence significant potential demand for the goods or services that foreign investors can produce. In this case, FDI is a substitute for trade. In other cases, foreign investors are able to expand their opportunities for international trade in goods or services by accessing lower cost inputs (for example, natural resources or low-cost labour) in host countries and thereby gain a comparative advantage in export markets. In this case, FDI and trade are complementary.

Democracy and the Future of the World Economy (New York: W.W. Norton & Co., 2011). See also Deborah Brautigam, *The Dragon's Gift: The Real Story of China in Africa* (Oxford, New York: Oxford University Press, 2011), showing that sometimes China's involvement in Africa cannot be clearly classified either as FDI or as foreign aid, but suggesting nevertheless that it has a positive impact in the region.

32 UNCTAD, 'Assessing the impact of the current financial and economic crisis on global FDI flows', 19 January 2009.

33 See, e.g., Theodore Moran, 'Enhancing the ability of developing countries to attack and harness FDI for development', in Theodore Moran (ed.), *Harnessing Foreign Direct Investment: Policies for Developing Countries* (Washington, DC: Brookings Institution Press, 2006); Theodore Moran, Edward Graham and Magnus Blomstrom (eds), *Does Foreign Direct Investment Promote Development?* (Washington, DC: Peterson Institute, 2005); OECD Report, *Foreign Direct Investment for Development: Maximizing Benefits, Minimizing Costs* (Paris: OECD, 2002).

In principle, the theory of comparative advantage should apply as much to international movements of FDI as to international trade in goods or services – capital is likely to gravitate to where its marginal productivity is greatest. If unqualified, this presumption would suggest the case for an international regime that facilitates the free movement of FDI, and constrains countries from adopting domestic policies designed either to encourage it – for example, through subsidies, tax breaks or tax incentives – or to discourage it – for example, through regulations pertaining to local sourcing, minimum export requirements, restrictions on exports, trade balancing requirements that restrict the value or volume of imports to the value or volume of exports, technology transfer requirements, and so on. In fact, many countries have adopted a wide range of domestic policies that either encourage or restrict FDI either generally or, more commonly, in particular sectors.

Restrictions on FDI by host countries may be motivated by a range of concerns.

1. There are likely to be concerns about foreign investors acquiring domestic organizations where the nature of the activities in question raise national security issues – concerns that have been exacerbated by the rapid growth of Sovereign Wealth Funds.[34] Foreign governments who control these funds may gain access to sensitive national security technology or information, through foreign acquisitions.
2. While there are few inherent legal constraints on the application of domestic jurisdiction to the activities that foreign investors engage in within a particular country, there may be significant practical constraints in the effective application of domestic laws where the bulk of the organization's assets, many of its senior personnel, and much of the information about its activities and decision-making are located abroad.
3. There may be concerns about attempts by home country governments to enforce their laws and foreign jurisdictions through foreign subsidiaries of home country parent corporations – that is, the extraterritorial application of the laws of the home country.
4. There may also be concerns that foreign subsidiaries will be managed in such a fashion as to reflect home country bias in business decisions – for example, by purchasing inputs from home country affiliates or

[34] See Jackie Van Der Meulen and Michael Trebilcock, 'Canada's policy response to foreign sovereign investment: operationalizing national security exceptions' (2009) 47 *Canadian Business Law Journal* 392.

using personnel from home country or other affiliates rather than local personnel, perhaps in some cases motivated by a desire to appear to be a 'good corporate citizen' in the home country in order to maximize political influence in that jurisdiction.
5. There may be concerns that foreign investors will seek to protect their investments in specialized technology and know-how by restricting access to them by domestic organizations or individuals in the host country, thereby reducing the benefits of technological spillovers and human capital enhancements in the host country.
6. There may be cultural and political sovereignty concerns with permitting FDI in certain sectors such as the print and electronic media.

Foreign direct investors, in turn, are likely to confront their own set of concerns in contemplating investments in a foreign country. These may include political and policy instability (including macroeconomic instability); where investments are sunk, subsequent governments may have incentives to behave opportunistically towards foreign direct investors who lack direct political voice in host countries[35] by unilateral *ex post facto* re-specification of the terms on which the initial investment was made; weak protection of private property rights and ineffective enforcement of contracts; law and order; and corruption in the administration of state functions (including legal functions).

B. Multilateral Regulation of Foreign Direct Investment[36]

Historically, the GATT was almost exclusively focused on international trade in goods, and not international trade in services or international movement of capital. However, a GATT panel decision in 1984[37] – in response to a complaint by the United States relating to various undertakings obtained from foreign investors pursuant to Canada's Foreign Investment Review Act – held that certain features of domestic foreign investment regulations may fall within the purview of the GATT where these affect international trade in goods. In this case, the US challenged undertakings that required foreign investors to commit to certain local

---

[35] A proposition that is challenged by David Schneiderman, 'Investing in democracy? Political process and international law' (2010) 60 *University of Toronto Law Journal* 909.

[36] See generally M. Sornarajah, *The International Law on Foreign Investment* (Cambridge: Cambridge University Press, 2010).

[37] *Canada: Administration of the Foreign Investment Review Act* BISD 305/140 (1984).

sourcing and minimum export requirements as a condition for approval of their investments in Canada. The Panel held that the local sourcing requirements violated the National Treatment principle in Article III of the GATT by treating local suppliers of these inputs more favourably than foreign suppliers, although it held that minimum export requirements did not violate any provision in the GATT.

At the beginning of the Uruguay Round in 1986, the US proposed that the multilateral negotiating agenda for this round should include a comprehensive agreement on foreign investment. The Agreement on Trade-Related Investment Measures (TRIMS) that emerged from the round is, in fact, much more modest than the initial US proposals, and builds on the prior GATT Panel ruling in 1984 by prohibiting domestic regulations that would violate the National Treatment principle in Article III.4 of the GATT, including local sourcing requirements, trade balancing requirements, or export restrictions. This illustrative list is non-exhaustive. The TRIMS Agreement has attracted very little subsequent formal dispute settlement activity, in large part because it does little more than reaffirm the application of Article III.4 of the GATT to certain forms of regulation or FDI that may influence imports or exports of goods by foreign direct investors.

Disaffected with this modest outcome from the Uruguay Round, the US and other developed countries sought to shift the venue for multilateral negotiations on a comprehensive investment treaty from the WTO to the OECD, where it was assumed that the predominance of developed countries would yield a readier consensus on liberalizing restrictions on FDI than the WTO, where the preponderance of developing country members with more sceptical, or at least cautious, views of the merits of FDI was likely to preclude achievement of a consensus on a more ambitious set of international disciplines. The expectation was that non-OECD members would be able to accede to any resulting treaty, and that there would be strong inducements to do so in order to compete effectively for FDI. From 1996 through to 1998 negotiations on a multilateral agreement on investment (MAI) proceeded within the OECD, but negotiations were non-transparent, even clandestine, and the leaking of a draft of the agreement to various NGOs precipitated an international firestorm of criticism of the draft agreement and the process by which it was being negotiated. The principal criticism was that it would confer extensive rights on foreign direct investors but with few, if any, concomitant obligations on their part to host countries or their citizens, for example, with respect to technology transfer, health and safety, the environment, labour standards and international human rights. In the face of these criticisms, the MAI negotiations were formally abandoned in December 1998. Proposals to include negotiations over FDI in the Doha Round of the WTO were also abandoned at the Cancun Ministerial in September 2003 in the face of opposition from developing countries.

C. Bilateral Investment Treaties

While attempts at negotiating a comprehensive multilateral treaty on FDI appear to have been abandoned, at least for the time being, a notable contrasting phenomenon has been the dramatic proliferation since 1990 in the number of bilateral investment treaties (BITs) or international investment agreements (IIAs) that have been negotiated – from just over 400 in 1990 to more than 2600 today.[38] The primary impetus behind this proliferation of BITs appears to be that in the competition for foreign direct investment, many countries, especially developing countries, feel obliged to provide investors with certain legally enforceable protections of their investment, although BITs are not limited to developed–developing country dyads (only about 40 per cent); about a quarter of all BITs are between pairs of developing countries.[39]

BITs typically include provisions on the scope and definition of foreign investment; admission of investment; national and most favoured nation treatment; fair and equitable treatment; guarantees and compensation in respect of expropriation and compensation for war and civil disturbances; guarantees of free transfer of funds and repatriation of capital and profits; subrogation on insurance claims; and dispute settlement, both state-to-state and investor-to-state (typically by international arbitration, most often the International Centre for Settlement of Investment Disputes (ICSID) affiliated with the World Bank).

The proliferation of BITs has raised a number of controversies:

1. The 'fair and equitable' standard of investment protection lacks precision and consistent interpretation or clearly articulated exceptions or qualifications for measures by host countries to address health, safety, and environmental concerns or financial crises, which has led to criticisms of BITs as unduly constraining the political sovereignty of host countries.
2. The expropriation provisions in most BITs also lack clear definition

---

[38] See Gus Van Harter, *Investment Treaty Arbitration and Public Law* (Oxford: Oxford University Press, 2007) Chapter 2; Stephan Schill, *The Multilateralization of International Investment Law* (Cambridge: Cambridge University Press, 2009).

[39] UNCTAD, 'Recent developments in international investment agreements', IIA Monitor No. 3 (2009).

and may be interpreted as extending beyond outright transfer of title to foreign investors' assets or physical dispossession of those assets to various forms of regulatory 'takings' that can be viewed as significantly impairing the value of these assets; this again is criticized for constraining or 'chilling' legitimate spheres of regulatory autonomy.

3. Given that many countries have signed multiple BITs with various other countries, each of which typically contains a most favoured nation clause, major disputes have arisen as to when foreign investors are able to invoke ('cherry pick') either substantive or procedural provisions in BITs other than the BIT to which their home country is a party which are more favourable to their claims than their own BITs.
4. The National Treatment principle, which is contained in most BITs, also gives rise to ambiguity as to when foreign investors have been treated less favourably than domestic investors in 'like circumstances'.
5. The international arbitral dispute resolution system has been criticized as lacking transparency, consistency and scope for effective third party (amicus) interventions, and in general being biased towards the interests of foreign investors.[40]
6. It is argued that BITs largely remove foreign investors as a political constituency for domestic legal reform in host countries by providing them with privileged supra-national legal protections.[41]

A new generation of BITs attempts to strike a finer balance between the interests of investors and the interests of host countries by adding interpretive provisions, general exceptions clauses, and new preambular language as to the purpose of the agreements,[42] but how arbitrators are likely to interpret such provisions and whether they are effectively justiciable in a consistent and credible manner remains to be tested by experience. As to

---

40 For a review of many of these critiques, see David Schneiderman, *Constitutionalizing Economic Globalization: Investment Rules and Democracy's Promise* (Cambridge: Cambridge University Press, 2008).

41 Tom Ginsburg, 'International substitutes for domestic institutions: bilateral investment treaties and governance' (2005) 25 *International Review of Law and Economics* 107. For a contrary view, see Susan Franck, 'Foreign direct investment treaty arbitration and the rule of law' (2007) *Pacific McGeorge Global Business and Development Law Journal* 337.

42 See Suzanne Spears, 'The quest for policy space in a new generation of international investment agreements' (2010) 13 *Journal of International Economic Law* 1037; see also Peter Muchlinski, 'Holistic approaches to development and international investment law: the role of international investment agreements', in Julio Faundez and Celine Tan (eds), *International Economic Law, Globalization and Developing Countries* (Cheltenham, UK: Edward Elgar, 2010).

whether BITs actually increase FDI flows to host countries that are signatories to them has yielded a rather mixed body of empirical evidence.[43] The most recent and comprehensive study[44] finds (contrary to some earlier studies) that BITs do promote FDI flows to developing countries (although yielding declining marginal impacts as more BITs are signed) and may even substitute for weak domestic institutions, though probably not for unilateral measures such as opening up previously restricted industries, removing foreign ownership restrictions, promotional efforts and tax and fiscal inducements.

Nevertheless, the extent to which BITs can substitute for weak domestic institutions is limited in part because arbitral awards still need to be enforced in the domestic courts of host countries, and in part because purely private disputes may still need to be resolved in these courts unless the parties have contracted out of the jurisdiction through (increasingly common) choice of law and choice of forum clauses – although even in these cases foreign judgments or arbitral awards need to be enforced in host countries' courts.[45] It needs to be acknowledged more generally that the empirical evidence on how important a host country's legal system is as a determinant of FDI is contested terrain, with scholars pointing, as counter-evidence, to the case of large recent inflows of FDI into China, despite relatively weak legal institutions, at least on conventional criteria.[46]

Chapter 11 of NAFTA, while involving three parties, exemplifies many of the issues and controversies that have arisen with respect to BITs and has been a prominent lightning rod for critics of NAFTA. When Chapter 11 was initially negotiated, it was thought likely to apply in practice mostly to Mexican laws and regulations pertaining to FDI, given a long and somewhat tangled history in Mexico of cycles of nationalization and liberalization of FDI. However, Chapter 11 has provoked a number of formal complaints (in excess of 30 to date), including a number against measures adopted in Canada and the US.

Chapter 11 of NAFTA contains a National Treatment provision in

---

[43] For a review of this evidence, see Amnon Lehavi and Amir Licht, 'BITs and pieces of property', 36 *Yale Journal of International Law* 115 at 126–8.

[44] Matthias Busse, Jens Koniger and Peter Nunnenkamp, 'FDI promotion through bilateral investment treaties: more than a bit?' (2010) 146 *Review of the World Economy* 147.

[45] See Jans Damman and Henry Hansmann, 'Globalizing commercial litigation' (2008) 94 *Cornell Law Review* 1.

[46] See Amanda Perry, 'Effective legal systems and foreign direct investment: in search of the evidence' (2000) 49 *International and Comparative Law Quarterly* 779; cf. Agnes Benassy-Quere, Maylis Coupet and Thierry Mayer, 'Institutional determinants of foreign direct investment' (2007) 30 *The World Economy* 5.

Article 1102 (subject to reservations that the three parties have entered in schedules to NAFTA) and a most favoured nation treatment provision (Article 1103). Article 1105 (Minimum Standard of Treatment) requires that each party shall accord to investments of investors of another party treatment in accordance with international law, including fair and equitable treatment and full protection and security. Article 1106 (Performance Requirements) prohibits a long list of performance requirements, including those contained in the TRIMS Agreement but extending to other performance requirements such as technology transfer requirements. Article 1110 (Expropriation and Compensation) provides that no party may directly or indirectly nationalize or expropriate an investment of an investor of another party in its territory or take a measure tantamount to nationalization or expropriation of such an investment except (a) for a public purpose; (b) on a non-discriminatory basis; (c) in accordance with due process of law and Article 1105; and (d) on payment of compensation.

Chapter 11 then sets out a procedural regime for the resolution of disputes which permits private investors to file complaints with international arbitral panels, primarily the International Centre for Settlement of Investment Disputes (ICSID). Awards issued by such arbitral panels – which provide for monetary compensation for foreign investors who have been able to satisfy an arbitral panel that the host country's measures in question violate one of the substantive provisions of Chapter 11 – are enforceable in the domestic courts of host countries.

The arbitral case law that has emerged under Chapter 11 has raised major uncertainties as to the interpretation and application of key substantive provisions in Chapter 11, especially the international minimum standard of treatment requirement in Article 1105 and the expropriation provisions in Article 1110, which different arbitral panels have interpreted both expansively and narrowly but without a system of appellate review or precedent to resolve inconsistencies. Critics of Chapter 11 argue that its provisions and the investor-driven complaints dispute settlement process have undesirably constrained the domestic political autonomy of member countries and imposed a regulatory chill on legitimate environmental and health and safety measures that host countries have sought or might seek to adopt.[47] Moreover, the expropriation provisions of Chapter 11 risk standing the National Treatment principle on its head by requiring

---

[47] See Chris Tollefson, 'NAFTA's Chapter 11: The case for reform', in John Kirton and Peter Hajnal (eds), *Sustainability, Civil Society, and International Governance* (Aldershot: Ashgate Publishing Limited, 2006) Chapter 10.

compensation of foreign investors in circumstances where similarly situated domestic investors may lack any such entitlement.[48]

Other commentators take a more benign view of the operation of Chapter 11, and regard the few decisions that have led to liability as properly sanctioning protectionist or abusive behaviour by host country governments.[49] While some of the procedural shortcomings of the dispute settlement process under Chapter 11 have recently been mitigated (i) by member countries in an Interpretive Statement, and (ii) by reforms by arbitral panels themselves in authorizing the release of the written pleadings of the parties at the time they are filed with an arbitral panel, authorizing *amicus curiae* briefs, and making the oral hearings open to the public, concerns remain about the extent of the substantive constraints on the jurisdiction of host countries to regulate FDI, particularly given the absence of any provision in Chapter 11 analogous to Article XX (the general exceptions clause) of the GATT.

D. Conclusion

The proliferation of BITs stands in stark contrast to successive failures to negotiate a multilateral agreement on investment. However, BITs entail a risk of collective action problems and a race to the bottom among host countries (especially developing countries). This argues for a further attempt at negotiating a multilateral agreement (where coalition bargaining is possible), probably under the aegis of the WTO, building on the new generation of BITs that attempt to strike a better balance between the interests of foreign investors and host countries.

---

[48] See David Schneiderman, 'NAFTA's takings rule: American constitutionalism comes to Canada' (1996) 46 *University of Toronto Law Journal* 499; Michael Trebilcock, 'Trade liberalization, regulatory diversity, and political sovereignty', in Kirton and Hajnal, ibid., at 224–5.

[49] See Julie Solway, 'NAFTA's Chapter 11: investor protection, integration, and the public interest', in Kirton and Hajnal, ibid., Chapter 9.

8. Foreign aid and development: the aid-institutions paradox

I. INTRODUCTION

Foreign aid programs in the post-war period find their genesis and inspiration in the Marshall Plan mounted by the United States to reconstruct the war-torn economies of Europe, complemented by similar forms of assistance to Japan during the period of US occupation. In both cases, this assistance contributed to a rapid and dramatic reconstruction of many of these economies, with Germany and Japan quickly emerging as major economic powers in the post-war era.

However, these two countries possessed highly educated work forces, well-developed infrastructure, high levels of technological sophistication, and well-established institutional and organizational capacity in the public and private sectors. Very few of these conditions were replicated in developing countries, many of whom were granted independence by their former colonial powers (sometimes with very little in the way of advance preparation or transition), beginning in the mid-1950s.

Moreover, the motivations of developed countries in providing foreign aid to developing countries were subject to a number of serious distortions. First, with the onset of the Cold War in the late 1940s, many developed countries were inclined to provide aid at levels and in forms that reflected judgments about the ideological affinities of recipient states with either communism or capitalism, or other geo-political considerations, irrespective of whether this aid well served basic development priorities. Second, many developed countries, in their aid policies, showed strong preferences for their former colonies, reflecting historical ties, again according secondary importance to whether the aid was being effectively utilized by the recipient countries. Third, many donor countries saw aid partly as an export promotion strategy through 'tied aid' conditions. Thus, as we explore in more detail below, evaluations of the efficacy of foreign aid to developing countries over the post-war period range from mixed to disappointing.[1]

[1] For a comprehensive and balanced description and evaluation of the history

In recent years, most developed countries have officially committed themselves to increasing levels of foreign aid to 0.7 per cent of GNP.[2] Currently, aid levels, on average, are running at about half of this number.[3] Current official development assistance and debt relief, from multilateral, regional and bilateral sources, was about US$100 billion in 2007.[4] To put this number in perspective, this is about the annual expenditure budget of the Ontario provincial government in Canada, serving the needs of about eleven million people. By way of contrast, almost three billion people in developing countries live on less than US$2 per day. About 70 per cent of aid is provided on a bilateral basis and 30 per cent on a multilateral basis.[5] About 70 per cent of all official development assistance is provided directly to recipient governments. NGOs account for about another US$24 billion in development assistance, and emergency and humanitarian aid for about another US$15 billion a year, on average.[6]

A number of major controversies surround the foreign aid–development nexus, which we briefly review below, largely drawing on a spirited (and at times vitriolic) debate between two leading contemporary development economists, Jeffrey Sachs and William Easterly. Sachs, in his book, *The End of Poverty: Economic Possibilities of Our Time*, argues for a much more expansionary foreign aid policy (in fact, a trebling of aid over the next two decades).[7] William Easterly, in his book, *The White Man's Burden: Why the West's Efforts to Aid the Rest Have Done So Much Ill and So Little Good*, argues that foreign aid in the past has done little to improve the long-term well-being of the citizens of developing nations (beyond short-term emergency or humanitarian aid, which itself has been subject to trenchant criticism for often being afflicted by a lack of coordination amongst multiple donors and corruption in its

---

and efficacy of foreign aid in the post-war period, see Roger C. Riddell, *Does Foreign Aid Really Work?* (Oxford: Oxford University Press, 2007).

2 Karina Rollins (ed.), *The Index of Global Philanthropy* (Washington DC: Center for Global Prosperity, 2007) at 7.

3 Ibid., at 10.

4 Organization for Economic Co-operation and Development (OECD), Development Co-operation Directorate, 'Debt relief is down: other ODA rises slightly' (4 April 2008).

5 Organization for Economic Co-operation and Development (OECD), Development Co-operation Directorate, 'Reference DAC statistical tables', available at http://www.oecd.org/dac/stats/reftables.

6 See Riddell, *supra* note 1 at 259, 317.

7 Jeffrey Sachs, *The End of Poverty: Economic Possibilities for Our Time* (New York: Penguin Group, 2005).

delivery)[8] and that there is no reason to suppose that a dramatic expansion of aid is likely to have a larger impact in the future.[9] Sachs regards Easterly 'notorious as the cheerleader for can't-do economics', while Easterly portrays Sachs as a hopelessly utopian global central planner. More recently, Dambisa Moyo has joined the debate taking an even more critical view of aid in the case of Africa.[10] In her book, *Dead Aid*, she suggests that foreign aid has undermined development by providing external funding for developing country political regimes, which has propped up venal, repressive or incompetent governments by rendering them unaccountable to their citizens for their tax and expenditure policies.[11] These authors represent three fundamental perspectives which frame more specific debates about foreign aid: Sachs advocates substantially increased aid; Easterly is critical of increasing aid, at least without a major re-orientation of current aid strategies, while Moyo believes aid is damaging and should be eliminated completely.

Other recent assessments by long-time aid practitioners of the efficacy of foreign aid in promoting long-term economic development support a generally pessimistic view, in large part because foreign aid (which is mostly government-to-government) has done little or nothing to transform dysfunctional institutions in developing countries and may indeed have helped to perpetuate them,[12] leading to what some commentators have called an 'aid-institutions paradox'.[13]

---

8 See Linda Polman, *War Games: The Story of Aid and War in Modern Times* (London: Viking, 2010).

9 William Easterly, *The White Man's Burden: Why the West's Efforts to Aid the Rest Have Done So Much Ill And So Little Good* (Oxford: Oxford University Press: 2006); see also Easterly, 'Introduction', in William Easterly (ed.), *Reinventing Foreign Aid* (Cambridge, MA: MIT Press, 2008).

10 For an example of this debate see Jeffrey Sachs, 'Aid ironies', *Huffington Post* (24 May 2009), available at http://www.huffingtonpost.com/jeffrey-sachs/aid-ironies_b_207181.html; Dambisa Moyo, 'Aid ironies: a response to Jeffrey Sachs', *Huffington Post* (26 May 2009), available at http://huffingtonpost.com/dambisa-moyo/aid-ironies-a-response-to_b_207772.html; William Easterly, 'Sachs ironies: why critics are better for foreign aid than apologists', *Huffington Post* (25 May 2009), available at http://www.huffingtonpost.com/william-easterly/sachs-ironies-why-critics_b_207331.html.

11 Dambisa Moyo, *Dead Aid: Why Aid is Not Working and How There is a Better Way for Africa*, (New York: Farrar, Strauss, Giroux, 2009).

12 See Ashok Chakravarti, *Aid, Institutions and Development* (Cheltenham, UK: Edward Elgar, 2005); Mary Shirley, *Institutions and Development* (Cheltenham, UK: Edward Elgar, 2008), Chapter 4; for a more optimistic recent assessment of the efficacy of foreign aid, see Charles Kenny, *Getting Better* (New York: Basic Books, 2011).

13 See Todd Moss, Gunilla Pettersson and Nicholas van de Walle, 'An aid-institutions paradox? A review essay on aid dependency and state-building in sub-Saharan Africa', in William Easterly (ed.), *Reinventing Foreign Aid*, *supra* note 9.

II. NORMATIVE RATIONALES FOR FOREIGN AID

Many people feel there is a moral duty to assist those in need, including those living in conditions of extreme deprivation in developing countries. For libertarians, as exemplified by the views of Canadian philosopher Jan Narvedson,[14] this duty is limited only to those who suffer from evils which donors have inflicted on them, no matter where, and donors owe these people compensation. In a foreign aid context, one might argue that in the case of developing countries that were formally colonies, there may be a duty of compensation on the part of the former colonial powers. In this analysis, a debt is owed to countries where development was inhibited by colonial powers which adopted policies that undermined traditional belief systems and forms of social organization – including, in some cases, the promotion of slavery, the exhaustion of natural resources or the drawing of arbitrary borders that created dysfunctional states. However, this argument does not account for aid given to contemporary developing countries that were never colonies such as China, Ethiopia, Iran and Thailand. Furthermore, many decolonized countries have become very successful middle or high income developing countries post independence (for example, Singapore, Hong Kong, Taiwan, South Korea, Malaysia, Chile, Botswana), so there is not a close correlation between earlier colonial experience and a contemporary need for foreign aid.

From a utilitarian perspective – or at least a global utilitarian perspective – it seems obvious that global well-being is likely, in principle, to be increased by the wealthy in developed (and some developing) countries, making what for them is likely to be modest sacrifices to dramatically enhance the well-being of the most destitute in poor countries. Peter Singer, in a recent book,[15] takes this view, arguing from the analogy of a stranger encountering a child drowning in a pool of water who can be easily rescued, perhaps at the minor expense of a new pair of shoes that the stranger is wearing. However, these arguments, which rest on a moral obligation to assist those living in developing countries, are critically contingent on a demonstration that such transfers of wealth will in fact make the needy in poor countries better off. Whether this is true or not is essentially an empirical question on which (as we have noted) the evidence is not generally encouraging. The utilitarian case for foreign aid

---

[14] Jan Narvedson, 'We don't owe them a thing: a tough minded but soft hearted view of aid to the faraway needy' (2003) 86 *The Monist* 419.

[15] Peter Singer, *The Life You Can Save: Acting Now to End World Poverty* (New York: Random House, 2009).

may be strengthened when aid results in a peace or security dividend for donor countries by stabilizing recipient countries whose failure may lead to military conflicts, a major exodus of refugees that require resettlement, or provide a haven for international terrorists.

A theory of global distributive justice might also seem to be implied by Rawlsian social contract theory,[16] although in later writing Rawls ascribes a very limited role to the application of principles of distributive justice among nations, in the absence of a world government to oversee the social contract[17] – a position strongly contested by other political philosophers.[18]

The normative case for expansive forms of foreign aid is perhaps strongest when based on some notion of intrinsic universal human rights and basic universal individual freedoms – a kind of Kantian categorical imperative of mutual support for basic human dignity by virtue of our common humanity – as articulated, for example, by Amartya Sen in his book, *Development as Freedom*.[19] In this case, the argument in favour of aid does not assume that its primary goal is directly to promote economic growth or to reduce global inequalities of wealth between nations. Rather, it suggests that aid may enhance the agency and dignity of individuals in developing countries, although whether it actually does so rests again on empirical judgments,[20] and where the state is the major source of deprivation of these freedoms makes institutional reform, again, a central objective of foreign aid (however intractable).

---

16 John Rawls, *A Theory of Justice* (Cambridge, MA: Harvard University Press, 1971).

17 John Rawls, *The Law of Peoples* (Cambridge, MA: Harvard University Press, 1999).

18 See, for example, Charles Beitz, *Political Theory and International Relations* (Princeton, NJ: Princeton University Press, 1999, revised edition), and Thomas Pogge, *Realizing Rawls* (Ithaca, NY: Cornell University Press, 1989).

19 Amartya Sen, *Development as Freedom* (New York: Alfred A. Knopf, 1999).

20 A recent trend in this field suggests that foreign aid should be based on trials and randomized experiments, as many policies that are well-designed in theory do not work in practice. Based on that, some argue that collecting empirical evidence through randomized control trials of certain policies should precede any foreign aid investment. See, for instance, Dean Kaplan and Jacob Appel, *More than Good Intentions: How a New Economics is Helping to Solve Global Poverty* (New York: Dutton, 2011); and Abhijit Banerjee and Esther Duflo, *Poor Economics: A Radical Rethinking of the Way to Fight Global Poverty* (Public Affairs, 2011).

III. IS THE CURRENT AMOUNT OF FOREIGN AID ENOUGH?

Sachs argues that many developing countries are caught in a 'poverty trap' which prevents self-sustaining growth.[21] The trap results from a lack of investment as a result of low or non-existent savings rates, accompanied by disinvestment caused by depreciation of existing capital and population growth. Large infusions of foreign aid can break this trap by facilitating investment in human capital, business capital, infrastructure, natural capital, public institutional capital and knowledge capital (although the existence of poverty traps has been strongly contested).[22] Sachs argues that successes with foreign aid programmes to date warrant confidence that they can be effectively scaled up to help developing countries escape the poverty trap. In this respect he identifies as successes the Green Revolution in Asia, the eradication of smallpox, the global alliance for vaccines and immunization, the control of African River Blindness, the eradication of polio, the spread of family planning, the development of export processing zones in East Asia, and the mobile phone revolution in Bangladesh and elsewhere.

Sachs argues that incremental investments of foreign aid often fail to address all the links in a causal chain that explain chronic poverty. For example, if children of primary school age lack access to schools, aid donors could build classrooms, but these would be of little or no value without teachers to staff them. In turn, teachers are of little or no value if they have not received proper training or if children lack basic textbooks. In turn, classrooms and teachers are of little value if young children are unable to attend school because of poor roads or debilitating diseases or economic imperatives within the family that they work rather than acquire an education. To mitigate these family pressures, expanded economic opportunities need to be provided to parents or other forms of financial support, and in order to motivate both parents and children to attend school and take education seriously they need to be offered economic opportunities after an education has been acquired to justify the investments in this education.[23]

Sachs notes that Americans in public opinion polls regularly report on

---

21 Sachs, *supra* note 7.

22 For sceptical views on the existence of 'poverty traps', see William Easterly, 'Reliving the 1950s: the big push, poverty traps, and takeoffs in economic development' (2006) 11 *Journal of Economic Growth* 289; Aart Kraay and Claudio Raddatz, 'Poverty traps, aid, and growth' (2007) 82 *Journal of Development Economics* 315.

23 Sachs, *supra* note 17.

average that foreign aid accounts for 20 per cent of the federal budget, roughly 24 times the actual figure.[24] Peter Singer argues that if we accept the premise that all lives have equal value, wherever they are lived, the small amount that Americans contribute to foreign aid is morally indefensible.[25] He starts with the top 0.01 per cent of US taxpayers, earning an average of US$12 775 000 per year and assumes that they could each give a third of their annual income. For the next 0.1 per cent, he assumes they could give a quarter of their income; the next 0.5 per cent could give one-fifth of their income; the next 1 per cent could give 15 per cent of their income; and the remainder of the nation's top 10 per cent could give 10 per cent of their income, producing a total of US$404 billion from just 10 per cent of American families. If such a scheme were extrapolated worldwide it would generate revenue of US$808 billion annually for development aid – vastly in excess of the figure that even Sachs thinks is required to lift most developing countries out of poverty.

Easterly, on the other hand, while not necessarily opposed to increases in levels of aid, views such increases as an exercise in futility unless there are reasons for assuming that they will be more effective than the US$2.3 trillion in aid provided to developing countries over the past five decades, including US$568 billion to Africa over the past 45 years.[26] He favours piecemeal or incremental initiatives that are subject to rigorous independent evaluations of their efficacy. Instead of funding 'grand plans' administered by poorly functioning aid agencies and corrupt recipient governments, foreign aid should focus on small-scale social or business entrepreneurs, or 'searchers' (rather than 'planners') as he calls them, who seek out innovative development solutions. He advocates more emphasis on demand-driven aid initiatives by citizens and communities in developing countries, rather than supply-driven initiatives from external donors. By funding these alternative development agents, inadequate governance can be bypassed, which will allow modest development advances through gradual and small-scale change. Only when institutional stability

---

24 Jeffrey Sachs, 'The Development Challenge', *Foreign Affairs* (March/April 2005).

25 Peter Singer, 'What Should a Billionaire Give – and What Should You?', *New York Times* (December 17, 2007), subsequently slightly modified in Singer, *The Life You Can Save: Acting Now to End World Poverty* (New York: Random House, 2009).

26 Easterly, *The White Man's Burden*, *supra* note 9; Easterly, 'Introduction', in Easterly (ed.), *Reinventing Foreign Aid*, *supra* note 9. But see Joseph Hanlon, Armando Barrientos and David Hulme, *Just Give Money to the Poor: The Development Revolution from the Global South* (Sterling, VA: Kumarian Press, 2010).

allows for expectations to develop which promote domestic savings and investment can large-scale foreign aid make fundamental changes to the economic systems of developing countries. This again depends on success and stability in institutional reform.

Once donors make aid commitments, it is crucial to development efforts that they are fulfilled.[27] As noted above, the gap between commitments and actual aid flows can be dramatic, and the aid that is delivered is often volatile and unpredictable, as donor priorities change or agency capacity to disburse funds varies. This prevents long-term policy formation and creates expectations of volatility which establish perverse incentives for recipient governments to focus spending on short-term consumption, rather than investment. This has a generally negative effect on aid effectiveness, and undermines government policy in recipient countries.

IV. WHICH COUNTRIES SHOULD RECEIVE AID?

If one takes the view that an expansion in levels of aid should be predicated on reasonable assurances of efficacy, it is then appropriate to turn to factors that have limited the efficacy of aid in the past (other than the factors noted at the outset of this chapter) as a prelude to consideration of reforms of the institutional architecture of the foreign aid system. Are some aid environments more supportive of effective foreign aid than others? In a widely cited World Bank study reviewing the post-war aid experience, published in 1998,[28] the authors conclude from the empirical experience that aid works best in good policy and institutional environments and is often wasted or dissipated in other environments. This conclusion, as a matter of intuition, seems compelling, although it has been challenged empirically,[29] but even if well founded it raises a major foreign aid dilemma: developing countries with good policy and institutional environments will often have less pressing claims for aid, as measured on many common economic and social indicators, than developing countries that lack these environments.[30] As Moises Naim puts it (perhaps rather

---

[27] Oya Celasun and Jan Walliser, 'Predictability of aid: do fickle donors undermine aid effectiveness?' (2008) *Economic Policy* 545.

[28] David Dollar and Lance Pritchett, *Assessing Aid: What Works, What Doesn't and Why* (Oxford: Oxford University Press, 1998).

[29] See William Easterly, 'Can foreign aid buy growth?' (2003) 17 *Journal of Economic Perspectives* 23; and Riddell, *supra* note 1 at 232.

[30] See Jakob Svensson, 'Absorption capacity and disbursement constraints', in Easterly (ed.), *Reinventing Foreign Aid*, *supra* note 9.

too dramatically), 'the paradox is that any country capable of meeting such stringent requirements is already a developed country'.[31] Failed or fragile states present this dilemma in its most acute form, but many developing countries exhibit a mix of good and bad policies and good and bad institutions.

According to Paul Collier, in his book, *The Bottom Billion*,[32] foreign aid should be concentrated on the 60 or so developing countries comprising the poorest billion citizens of the world and suffering from one or more of the various traps that Collier describes – the natural resource trap, the landlocked-with-bad-neighbours trap, the civil conflict trap and the bad governance trap. But, of course, these countries are precisely those where the good aid environment described by the World Bank in its review of the post-war foreign aid experience generally does not exist. For multilateral, regional and bilateral aid agencies already facing a significant level of public scepticism in donor countries as to the efficacy of aid, this may be viewed as an extremely high risk aid strategy if providing aid to countries that need it most is unlikely to have the desired effects because of institutional and policy failures.

V. HOW SHOULD AID BE COORDINATED?

Coordination problems manifest themselves in a wide range of dimensions in the foreign aid field. First, within large multilateral aid organizations – such as the World Bank and a plethora of UN agencies, and replicated to some extent in regional and bilateral aid agencies – personnel and budgets are typically organized into various subject area groupings, for example, rural development, infrastructure, governance reform, sustainable development and gender issues, which in turn are overlaid by geographic groupings by country or region. Aid dispensers experience strong incentives to disburse money quickly, as a readily observable measure of activity, while resisting both independent evaluations of outcomes and acknowledgements of failure (from which lessons for the future may be learned).[33] Within recipient governments, there is a somewhat parallel set

---

[31] Moises Naim, 'Washington Consensus or Washington Confusion', *Foreign Policy* (Spring 2000) 87 at 96.

[32] Paul Collier, *The Bottom Billion: Why the Poorest Countries are Failing and What Can Be Done About It* (New York: Oxford University Press, 2007).

[33] See Lant Pritchett, 'It pays to be ignorant: a simple political economy of rigorous program evaluation', in Easterly (ed.), *Reinventing Foreign Aid*, *supra* note 9.

of organizational issues, with various line ministries of government – for example, health, education and infrastructure – often in some tension with central ministries such as finance in competing for donors' assistance, again with similar incentives to 'move the money', while avoiding honest and rigorous evaluations of results.

On the donor side of the equation, these problems are compounded horizontally by donor proliferation, where many donor agencies (recalling that most aid is bilateral) are active in the same subject areas and countries or regions, each reflecting its own citizens' or taxpayers' preferences or priorities[34] (or else there would be only one global aid agency). Each country's aid agency has strong political incentives to 'plant the flag' on as many visible projects as possible, and in many cases in as many countries as possible, even though the result is often dozens or even hundreds of donors or their agents involved in various aid projects in a given developing country.[35] Each aid recipient country receives official development assistance from an average of 26 different official donors and upwards of 30 substantial NGOs.[36] Donor agencies are often unaware of the multiple donor agencies working on similar projects, and thus make aid allocation decisions with imperfect information about the overall funding going to a particular sector. On the recipient side, disbursing aid from multiple sources burdens recipient governments with high transaction and managerial costs in complying with each donor's reporting and accountability requirements, reducing general governmental capacity and undermining the government's ability to attend to basic functions.[37] Problems of horizontal coordination on the recipient side are compounded when subnational levels of government, community organizations, local or foreign NGOs, or 'ring-fenced' aid projects are involved in the aid delivery process (such problems are often compounded by 'poaching' by these organizations of some of the most knowledgeable employees of the host government at much higher salaries). From the recipient side, Ashraf Ghani, the first Minister of Finance in the post-Taliban government in Afghanistan, describes how the central budgetary process was undermined by the

---

34 See Ritva Reinikka, 'Donors and service delivery'; Stephen Knack and Aminur Rahman, 'Donor fragmentation'; Berton Martens, 'Why do foreign aid agencies exist?' in Easterly (ed.), *Reinventing Foreign Aid*, *supra* note 9.

35 See Polman, *supra* note 8.

36 Riddell, *supra* note 1, at 52, 54; Ashraf Ghani and Clare Lockhart, *Fixing Failed States: A Framework for Rebuilding a Fractured World* (New York: Oxford University Press, 2008), Chapter 5.

37 Nancy Birdsall, 'Seven Deadly Sins: reflections on donor failings' (2005) Center for Global Development, Working Paper No. 50.

proliferation of donors, contractors and sub-contractors, NGOs and projects. This confusion undermined government attempts to establish a coherent set of strategic priorities.[38]

Individual donor agencies also face problems of vertical coordination, when aid is delivered through a chain of contracts and sub-contracts with local or foreign contractors or NGOs. There would seem to be obvious gains in aid effectiveness to be realized by bilateral aid agencies developing substantial expertise in a few sectors in a few developing countries (and hence achieving a comparative advantage in these sectors and countries). However, there appear to be powerful institutional and political incentives driving in the opposite direction, such as desire for donor visibility within many recipient countries and the international aid community.[39]

Here again we confront the 'aid-institutions' paradox identified earlier in this discussion of foreign aid: bypassing governments in recipient countries (even those with weak governments) poses various risks. Many charities and NGOs suffer from their own problems of transparency, accountability and effectiveness.[40] Setting up a composite body of government, donor and NGO representatives ('independent service authorities') in recipient countries to address the problems of coordination (as Collier and Riddell propose)[41] raises similar issues of transparency and accountability, as well as the risk of dysfunctional internal politics within such bodies and the creation of a parallel *de facto* government that further undermines the legitimacy and effectiveness of the *de jure* government.[42] However, channelling all aid through weak governments – in its purest form, simply enhancing the central government's budgetary capacity – runs its own set of risks: the risk of gross misallocation, even misappropriation, of aid resources and, even in more favourable circumstances, being unappealing to donor countries whose domestic political constituencies may be unimpressed by the seeming irresponsibility of writing blank cheques to foreign governments in developing countries without visible projects to point to as the result of aid expenditures.

---

[38] Ghani and Lockhart, *supra* note 36.

[39] Danielle Goldfarb and Stephen Tapp, 'How Canada can improve its development aid: lessons from other agencies' (Toronto: CD Howe Institute, Commentary No. 232, April 2006); John Richards, 'Can aid work? Thinking about development strategy' (Toronto: CD Howe Institute, Commentary No. 231, April 2006).

[40] See Polman, *supra* note 8.

[41] Collier, *supra* note 32 at 118–20; Riddell, *supra* note 1 at 396.

[42] See Reinikka, *supra* note 34.

VI. SHOULD AID BE CONDITIONAL AND ON WHAT?

An attempt to address the conflicting relationship between the interests of aid donors and those of developing country governments is the use of conditionality in the terms on which aid is provided to encourage recipient governments to comply with donor interests or expectations. Some forms of aid conditionality are, on their face, quite perverse from a development perspective. In particular, tied aid – whereby donors require recipient governments to commit to purchasing inputs, goods or services from firms in donor countries – has been found to diminish the value of aid by 15 to 30 per cent relative to what the amount of aid could purchase on the open market. This also freezes out local suppliers in developing countries from the growth opportunities which arise from participating in the aid delivery process. Tied aid still accounts for a significant percentage of bilateral aid (approximately 50 per cent), although substantial progress has been made in recent years, through the OECD, in reducing this percentage.[43]

In other cases, aid conditions reflect what donor agencies believe recipient countries should accord a high priority to in development objectives, regardless of whether these priorities are shared by the population or governments of the recipient countries. Just as there are problems of non-alignment of preferences among donors, there are often problems of non-alignment of preferences between donors and recipients; these problems reflect broken information (accountability) feedback loops where citizens/taxpayers in donor countries are ill-informed as to the effects of aid in recipient countries, and citizens in recipient countries have no political voice in donor countries.[44] If governments in recipient countries are weak, incompetent, corrupt or unaccountable to their citizens, there may be reasons for circumspection about recipient governments' articulation of aid priorities. Thus, in many cases, governments in developing countries are the problem, not the solution. In such cases, aid conditions should ideally be informed by some broader canvassing of priorities amongst representative groups of citizens of the developing countries in question if the problem of broken information (accountability) feedback loops is to be mitigated. This is not easy for external donor agencies to orchestrate in the absence of established broadly based consultative mechanisms, and in the face of potential resistance from the recipient country's government itself. Thus, in many cases, aid conditions are routinely violated or imper-

---

[43] See Riddell, *supra* note 1, at 100–101.

[44] See Martins, *supra* note 44; Svensson, *supra* note 30.

fectly followed by the governments of recipient countries, and almost as routinely ignored by many donor agencies facing imperatives to continue to disburse the aid to meet expenditure commitments, regardless of the unmet conditions.[45]

This phenomenon is exacerbated by the problem of conditions imposed by different donors at cross-purposes with one another, and by the problem of effective monitoring of compliance with aid conditions because of the fungibility of money. For example, if a country commits itself to allocating aid that it receives to primary school education, it may simply reallocate resources of its own that it would otherwise have spent on primary school education to other purposes (military expenditure, for example), while claiming that the aid received has been allocated to its intended purpose. In some cases, aid conditionality, particularly when a new reform-oriented government in a recipient country has taken office, can serve the useful function of providing a credible commitment to an agreed agenda of policy and institutional reform, as well as sending credible signals to domestic and foreign economic agents (including foreign investors) that the new government is committed to a well-defined, long-term development strategy. These cases, however, seem very much the exception rather than the rule.

VII. WHAT ENDS SHOULD AID ATTEMPT TO SERVE?

One view of the purposes of foreign aid (largely espoused by Easterly) is that aid should be confined to serving basic humanitarian needs at the grassroots levels and attempt to relieve the most severe forms of destitution or deprivation. On a different view (largely espoused by Sachs), aid should serve much more ambitious purposes and espouse an activist pro-development agenda that sets poor developing countries on a self-sustaining path to greater economic prosperity in the future.

These two views have important implications for how aid should be delivered. On the first view, much humanitarian aid might be most effectively delivered through local community organizations and local and international NGOs, largely sidestepping governments, at least in failed or fragile states, although problems of coordination will remain a daunting challenge. On the second view, this much more ambitious

---

45 Jakob Svensson, 'Why conditional aid does not work and what can be done about it?' (2003) 70 *Journal of Development Economics* 381.

pro-development agenda requires a capable, activist and well-motivated state to coordinate major investments in infrastructure such as roads, ports, communications systems, education and health care systems and the administration of justice. Incongruously in our view, Singer – who supports Sachs' arguments for much larger volumes of foreign aid – seems to imagine that this objective can be achieved solely or primarily through the local, decentralized initiatives of community organizations, charities and NGOs (which resonates much more closely with Easterly's more modest views of the ends of foreign aid).

A yet further view, espoused by Hubbard and Duggan, is predicated on the premise that very few societies throughout history have become prosperous without a thriving private sector. According to them, akin to the Marshall Plan, aid should be focused single-mindedly on promoting the growth of the private sector and providing complementary inputs in the form of physical and institutional infrastructure that are preconditions to its growth, on the assumption that greater revenues from growth can then finance various social investments in, for example, health and education. However, one might question whether some of these investments are indeed pre-conditions to the emergence of a thriving private sector.[46]

VIII. FOREIGN AID AND INSTITUTIONAL REFORM

It is useful to place the institutional capacity issues noted above primarily in the context of the Sachs–Easterly debate about foreign aid. Sachs, in arguing for a 'big push' on foreign aid, largely ignores these institutional issues, rather casually pointing to the fact that there are several governments in sub-Saharan Africa that possess the institutional competence and integrity to use more aid effectively (leaving as an unanswered mystery what should happen in the many other cases). Easterly, on the other hand, in the face of these institutional dysfunctions, seems largely to throw up his hands in despair and resign himself to aid being deployed on the margins of the development enterprise in small, incremental, local initiatives (such as drilling wells for local villages, providing mosquito nets and vaccinating against various tropical diseases). Singer attempts to skirt

---

46 R. Glenn Hubbard and William Duggan, *The Aid Trap: Hard Truths About Ending Poverty* (New York: Columbia University Press, 2009); see also Kurt Hoffman, 'Placing enterprise and business thinking at the heart of the war on poverty', in Easterly (ed.), *Reinventing Foreign Aid*, *supra* note 9; see Polman, *supra* note 8.

issues of institutional capacity entirely by focusing on private, voluntary donations to NGOs and charities. For Moyo, aid has mostly pernicious effects, so the less aid the better, making irrelevant any question of how to reform aid policies.

The enormous challenge, largely unaddressed by these authors, is whether limitations on institutional capacity and legitimacy can be addressed effectively so that a much larger volume of aid can responsibly be provided to developing countries with some reasonable confidence in its likely efficacy.[47] Setting these institutional issues to one side, or treating them as of second-order importance, in debates over foreign aid is largely to condemn aid to ineffectiveness in precisely those environments where citizens are the victims of the most severe forms of deprivation. However, confronting these issues requires donors to forego the illusion that aid is a largely technocratic rather than political exercise and that tensions with traditional Westphalian notions of state sovereignty can be avoided. We can no longer persist with the fallacy that poorly performing governments in developing countries simply lack information, technical expertise and resources (which aid can provide), but are otherwise well motivated towards their citizens.[48]

Our starting point is to acknowledge that aid agencies require, as committed clients, self-identified agents of institutional reform with self-identified agendas for reform supported by significant and broadly representative constituencies within developing countries. In some (rare) cases this may be the government itself, but is more likely to be pockets of reformers within agencies of government, or constituencies outside government, who are committed to an institutional reform agenda. This agenda cannot be imposed from outside by pretending that 'Djibouti is Denmark' or by 'skipping straight to Weber',[49] but requires an authentic domestic political constituency with a reform agenda that is sensitive to the particularities of its country's context, history, politics and culture.

Given such a reform constituency, foreign aid donors can provide both financial and technical support to such constituencies to assist them in pressing their reform agenda and also exert leverage on government and its agencies by withholding or terminating government-to-government aid for failure to respond to this reform agenda against well-specified milestones. Increasing the percentage of aid channelled through multilateral

---

47 See Riddell, *supra* note 1 at 373–7.

48 See Chakravarti, *supra* note 12.

49 Lant Pritchett and Michael Woolcock, 'Solutions where the solution is the problem: arraying the disarray in development', in Easterly (ed.), *Reinventing Foreign Aid*, *supra* note 9.

institutions is likely to increase this leverage (although at the risk of larger systemic policy errors and less policy experimentation at the level of the individual donor). Reforming the governance structure of such institutions to make them more fairly representative of the developing and developed world is also likely to enhance the legitimacy of exerting such leverage. Invoking accession negotiations for membership of trade or broader economic cooperation regimes, offering valuable long-term benefits (as the EU has done with some success with new member countries from Central and Eastern Europe) to extract, monitor and enhance meaningful institutional reform commitments that enjoy support from substantial domestic constituencies is an analogous strategy that has some promise (but has been insufficiently exploited more generally).[50]

At the end of the day, if one believes that institutions matter to development, to give up on foreign aid as an important agent of institutional change is to condemn the citizens of many of the world's poorest and most misgoverned countries to a future of more or less perpetual deprivation. Rethinking the most effective bundle of 'carrots and sticks' to drive institutional change is the central unmet challenge on the foreign aid agenda. Until this 'aid-institutions' paradox is unlocked, foreign aid will largely fail to advance long-term development objectives.

---

[50] Michael Trebilcock and Ron Daniels, *Rule of Law Reform and Development: Charting the Fragile Path of Progress* (Cheltenham, UK: Edward Elgar, 2008), Chapter 10.

9. Conclusion: in search of knowledge

I. INTRODUCTION

This book has sought to provide a concise introductory survey of the current state of academic knowledge about development, with a special focus on the ways in which development relates to institutions. As we conclude this task, the reader may be tempted to ask one of the most important questions faced by those concerned with development today: where does one start, if one wants to contribute further to the global discourse about institutional solutions to development problems?

In the first chapter we surveyed a number of theories of development, showing how each of them ascribes development to a different cause (the economy, geography, culture or a country's institutional arrangements). Despite their differences, all these theories share the belief that one can find a common set of factors that will determine a country's development prospects. There are, however, scholars who refuse to engage in such an exercise, rejecting the idea that there can be a single determinant of development and being sceptical as to the possibility of developing a 'universal theory' of development. In the view of these scholars, a country's fate will be determined by a series of factors that are quite unique and particular to that country. For these authors, the search for a general theory of development is futile: we should instead be trying to discuss separately the particular circumstances of, for example, Brazil, China and the Sudan.[1]

This divergence of views regarding the existence of a 'universal theory' of development can also be found in microcosm in institutional theories of development. Some scholars believe that it is possible to conceive a general theory of institutional development or institutional change.[2] In contrast, strong scepticism is espoused by those who see the institution-building exercise as a complex and dynamic phenomenon, informed by a variety of

[1] David Booth, 'Marxism and development sociology: interpreting the impasse' (1985) 13 *World Development* 761–87; M. Edwards, 'The irrelevance of development studies' (1989) 11:1 *Third World Quarterly* 116–36.

[2] The most emblematic example would be the work of Douglass North, founder of the new institutional economics. For a more detailed discussion of this work, see Chapter 1.

societal factors – such as politics and culture – that are beyond the reformers' (or perhaps anyone's) knowledge or control.[3] While the first view subscribes to the idea that we can collectively engage in an institution-building exercise, the second view either sees this exercise as unique and particular to each country or each institution, or it rejects altogether the idea that it is possible to conceive of 'institution building': institutions grow organically and cannot be intentionally created or modified. The latter view rejects the possibility of conceiving of a theory of institutional change, while the former is based on the assumption that observable patterns or regularities should allow us to find a common path according to which all institutions are created and evolve.

This book lies somewhere in between these two extremes. If one believes that it is not possible to conceive of a theory of development, it would be impossible to talk about development in general. We reject that view. We believe instead that middle level generalizations are possible.[4] While it may not be very useful or illuminating to compare Brazil with most low-income countries in Africa, we argue that Brazil has commonalities with Mexico or other middle-income countries that allow for comparison and limited generalization.

These middle level generalizations are also possible at the institutional level. It may be difficult to support the idea that every single institution emerges and evolves according to a universal pattern. Nevertheless, there may be useful commonalities that can be found among institutions performing similar functions in different countries.[5] This is especially true when the political, social and economic circumstances under which these institutions are operating are very similar.

The possibility of middle level generalizations at the country level and at the institutional level are the two main assumptions that underlie this

---

[3] Brian Z. Tamanaha, 'The primacy of society and the failure of law and development' *Cornell International Law Journal* [forthcoming], available at http://papers.ssrn.com/sol3/papers.cfm?abstract_id=1406999; Duncan Kennedy, 'Three globalizations of law and legal thought: 1850–2000' in D. Trubek and A. Santos, *The New Law and Development* (Cambridge: Cambridge University Press, 2006).

[4] See also Michael Todaro and Stephen Smith, *Economic Development* (London: Longman Group, 2012, 11th edn) at 56–70 (calling these 'diversity within commonalities'); Frans Schuurman (ed.), *Beyond the Impasse: New Directions in Development Theory* (London: Zed Books, 1993); P. Vandergeest and F. Buttel, 'Marx, Weber and development sociology: beyond the impasse' (1998) 16:6 *World Development* 683.

[5] Mariana Prado and Michael Trebilcock, 'Path dependence, development and the dynamics of institutional reform' (2009) 59:3 *University of Toronto Law Journal* 341.

book. Each chapter suggests that lessons can be learned from institutions performing similar functions in other countries, while at the same time being mindful that comparisons among countries that have similar characteristics are likely to be more fruitful than comparing, for instance, institutions in developing countries with those of developed countries.

II. SHOULD REFORMERS FOLLOW BEST PRACTICES?

It seems intuitive that one could look at successful practices and functional institutions in other countries and try to mimic them. Successful institutions can be perceived as possible solutions to development problems, and may inspire reformers to replicate these institutions in other countries. It is this very basic intuition that informs the practice of many multilateral organizations, such as the World Bank or the OECD. These organizations often seek to identify best practices in order to translate them into recipes that are replicable in other contexts. The idea seems to work for some public policies and anti-poverty programs: microcredit has now expanded to more than a hundred countries after the initial success of the pilot project in Bangladesh.[6] Similarly, conditional cash transfers are generating positive outcomes in Latin America, after the initial success of *Progressa* in Mexico.[7]

Best practices or blueprints, however, have not been so successful with institutional reforms.[8] Scholars have claimed that the main reason for this is the complex interaction between formal and informal institutions (often referred to as 'culture' throughout this book). This interaction does not leave room for blueprints or justify assumptions that transplanted institutions are likely to work in the same fashion as they do in their country of origin. A growing number of scholars currently argue that culture is the 'black box' of theories of development, and our lack of knowledge about culture often translates into a lack of knowledge about how to change dysfunctional institutions.[9] The extreme position held by some of these

---

[6] Muhammad Yunnus, *Banker to the Poor: Micro-Lending and the Battle against World Poverty* (New York: Public Affairs, 2003).

[7] Ariel Fiszbein and Norbert Schady, 'Conditional cash transfers: reducing present and future poverty', *World Bank Research Reports*, 2009.

[8] Michael Trebilcock and Ronald Daniels, 'The political economy of rule of law reforms in developing countries' (2004) 26 *Michigan Journal of International Law* 99.

[9] Amir N. Licht, Chanan Goldschmidt and Shalom H. Schwartz, 'Culture rules: the foundations of the rule of law and other norms of governance' (2007) 35:4 *Journal of Comparative Economics* 659.

scholars suggests that, because of these cultural factors, any institution-building exercise based on best practices from elsewhere is likely to be in vain.[10]

Again, this book lies somewhere between these two extreme views. We believe that in certain cases it may be worthwhile to borrow ideas and insights from successful experiences in other countries or contexts. In this process, however, reformers should be mindful of the fact that institution-building requires a great deal of adaptation to the particular conditions of each country.[11]

III. WHAT SHOULD BE THE SCOPE OF INSTITUTIONAL REFORMS?

A number of scholars subscribe today to the idea that a country needs 'good governance' or the 'rule of law' in order to develop.[12] How to achieve these objectives, however, is a fiercely debated matter. On the one hand, some argue that institutional interconnections are likely to render ineffective partial or piecemeal reforms.[13] As institutions depend on each other to function effectively, reforms are unlikely to be effective unless they are all-encompassing and comprehensive. In sum, reformers need to 'think big'. In contrast, there are those who are sceptical about the possibility of promoting all-encompassing reforms.[14] As a result of path dependence, political economy and other obstacles to institutional reform, some scholars believe that it is not possible to promote an institutional overhaul that will amount to something that we call 'good governance'

---

[10] Lawrence E. Harrison and Samuel P. Huntington (eds), *Culture Matters: How Values Shape Human Progress* (New York: Basic Books, 2000); Lawrence E. Harrison, *The Central Liberal Truth: How Politics Can Change a Culture and Save It from Itself* (Oxford: Oxford University Press, 2006); Lawrence E. Harrison and Jerome Kagan, *Developing Cultures: Essays on Cultural Change* (London, New York: Routledge, 2006).

[11] See also Kevin E. Davis, 'Legal universalism: persistent objections' (2010) 60:2 *University of Toronto Law Journal* 537.

[12] See Chapters 1 and 2.

[13] See, e.g., Rachel E. Kranton and Anand V. Swamy, 'The hazards of piecemeal reform: British civil courts and the credit market in colonial India' (1999) 58 *Journal of Development Economics* 1; William C. Prillaman, *The Judiciary and Democratic Decay in Latin America: Declining Confidence in the Rule of Law* (Westport, CT: Praeger, 2000).

[14] Prado and Trebilcock, *supra* note 5. Mariana Prado, 'The paradox of rule of law reforms: how early reforms can create obstacles to future ones' (2010) 60:2 *University of Toronto Law Journal* 555.

or the 'rule of law'. Instead, reformers should confine their agenda to one institution at a time. For these scholars, the assumption is that 'thinking small' is the most promising strategy to making a particular institution functional.[15] This dispute is often translated into divergent policy prescriptions, where the first perspective favours an all-encompassing approach to reforms whereas the second prefers to focus on piecemeal reforms and may question an overall agenda to promote 'good governance' or the 'rule of law'.

Yet again our book lies somewhere in the middle. We acknowledge that reformers are not writing on a blank slate. Path dependence is likely to create significant obstacles to any attempt to promote 'big bang' reforms (Chapter 1). This is a reason to favour piecemeal reforms in general, but not in absolute terms. In some cases, institutional interconnections will not allow for effective piecemeal reforms. Moreover, reformers need to be mindful that sequencing matters – in other words, piecemeal reforms should be conceived of as a part of a larger plan to promote more ambitious reforms over time.

Finally, we do not reject the idea that sometimes it is possible to promote all-encompassing and drastic reforms. Windows of opportunity for reforms may appear – a revolution, for instance, or the emergence of a charismatic leader. The problem is that reformers cannot count on those contingences, as they cannot be artificially created, are often unpredictable, and may not always be immediately identifiable.[16] Thus, reformers are more likely than not to find themselves in circumstances that will require piecemeal reforms, although these will require attention to sequencing and to institutional interconnections. And even when there are windows of opportunity, we suggest that institution-building cannot be considered as a one-shot process. It is very unlikely that any institution will be functional from the beginning and will remain so for its entire existence. Instead, adjustments will be constantly needed, and it is the process of fixing one problem at a time that is likely to increase the chances – in the long term – that developing countries will be able to benefit from functional winstitutions.

---

[15] We are using here the term coined by Jessica Cohen and William Easterly (eds), *What Works in Development? – Thinking Big and Thinking Small* (Washington, DC: Brookings, 2009).

[16] See also Prado and Trebilcock, *supra* note 5.

IV. HOW CAN WE BEST EQUIP AND PREPARWE FUTURE REFORMERS?

The central assumption of this book is that institutions matter for development and we have emphasized that, in this context, lawyers have an important role to play. The intricacies of institutional design set the context that will allow reformers to address the issues of middle-level generalizations, adaptability to context, sequencing and awareness of institutional interconnections noted above. The question that follows, then, is how to best train lawyers to engage in institutional reforms for development in a way that can potentially enhance the prospects of developing countries benefiting from them.

Contrasting theory with practice is a good way to learn how to avoid sweeping generalizations, while at the same time testing the limits of theory. By consulting the most comprehensive empirical evidence available, one can assess the validity of theoretical generalizations and possibly limit their scope.[17] In this regard, lawyers should rely in part on the expertise of economists and political scientists in collecting and compiling empirical data in a systematic fashion.[18] This can avoid many of the pitfalls that unwarranted generalizations may give rise to in the development context. There may be little point, however, in training lawyers to do this type of work themselves. Instead, lawyers should rely on what they do best: comparing cases.[19] This skill set can be built into institutional analysis and institutional reforms in at least three promising ways.

First, while empirical evidence will confirm or not *whether* a certain claim is true or is able to be generalized, case studies are likely to illuminate *why* that claim is not true or cannot be generalized. This is a way in which empirical research can offer insights that may feedback into the theory and help improve and refine it. Thus, case studies are helpful in

---

[17] For a popular instantiation of this argument, see Ian Ayres, *Super Crunchers: Why Thinking-by-Numbers is the New Way to be Smart* (New York: Bantam, 2007).

[18] For a useful contribution that is likely to be helpful to lawyers, see Thomas Ulen, Robert M. Lawless and Jennifer K. Robbennolt, *Empirical Methods in Law* (New York: Aspen, 2010).

[19] For an acknowledgement of the value of case studies in development studies, see Dani Rodrik, *In Search of Prosperity: Analytical Narratives of Economic Growth* (Princeton, NJ: Princeton University Press, 2003). See also Mary M. Shirley, *Institutions and Development – Advances* (Cheltenham, UK and Northampton, MA: Edward Elgar, 2008) at 4 (indicating how cross-country institutional analysis of institutions offers little guidance to reformers).

illuminating under which circumstances middle-level generalizations are possible or not.[20]

Second, case studies may help to illuminate what kind of cultural, political and economic factors are likely to interact with formal institutions and under which circumstances. This will help lawyers work towards adapting institutional reforms to local contexts.[21] In this regard, sociological, anthropological and political studies may be an additional tool that can help lawyers understand the context and identify the relevant factors that may affect reform in different countries. While the analysis here builds on socio-anthropological and related studies, it is aimed towards possible middle-level generalizations that will allow a legal scholar not only to understand what has transpired in a particular country, but to what extent this can yield lessons that are applicable to countries that face similar conditions.

Third, case studies can also indicate the relevance of institutional interconnections and sequencing, and may call attention to the different possible configurations that an institutional reform may take, and the possible outcomes that each of these configurations is likely to generate. Indeed, by looking at what worked and what did not work in other reforms, lawyers can begin to accumulate a tool set that can potentially be helpful in future reforms.[22] The idea here is not of a blueprint of best practices. Instead, a particular case study can illuminate the effectiveness of a certain institutional feature, or a mechanism that could potentially be creatively adapted to another context, or could inspire innovations in other reforms. If this exercise is coupled with an awareness of the uncertainty and risks involved with institutional adaptation, the importation of limited and constrained insights from other reforms can be a fruitful exercise.

---

[20] In this aspect, we subscribe to the argument supported by Shirley, ibid. On the value of randomized control trials in many policy contexts, see Dean Kaplan and Jacob Appel, *More than Good Intentions: How a New Economics is Helping to Solve Global Poverty* (New York: Dutton, 2011); and Abhijit Banerjee and Esther Duflo, *Poor Economics: A Radical Rethinking of the Way to Fight Global Poverty* (Public Affairs, 2011).

[21] See also Dani Rodrik, *One Economics, Many Recipes: Globalization, Institutions and Economic Growth* (Princeton, NJ: Princeton University Press, 2007) (arguing that we may have universal tools to identify problems, such as welfare economics, but institutional reforms and economic policies to address such problems need to be adapted to particular contexts). See also Dani Rodrik, *The Globalization Paradox: Democracy and the Future of the World Economy* (New York: W.W. Norton & Co., 2011).

[22] For an interesting proposal to achieve this by creating a clearing house of academic knowledge and on-the-ground experience, see UNDP, *Making the Law Work for Everyone: Report of the Commission on Legal Empowerment of the Poor*, Vol. 1 (New York: Unites Nations, 2008) at 87.

V. AN AGENDA FOR FUTURE RESEARCH

The proposition that institutions are a major determinant of a country's development prospects is, in many respects, self-evident – the very conception of a 'failed state' exemplifies this proposition. While it has been helpfully validated by much recent empirical work, the mantra 'institutions (or governance) matters' is unhelpful in three key respects. First, it is often so coarse-grained as to lack policy-relevant implications. Second, it is not helpful in understanding the antecedent causes of, or contributors to, dysfunctional institutions, which will often be a necessary predicate to prescribing effective and feasible cures in particular contexts. Third, it is unhelpful in developing detailed reform strategies on the ground that are sensitive to prevailing path dependency, political economy, cultural and other impediments to reform in particular contexts.

This book has sought to demonstrate that broadening institutional perspectives on development to address these three key concerns is critical to progress on an institutional agenda for development.[23]

[23] See also Lindsey Carson and Ronald J. Daniels, 'The persistent dilemmas of development: the next fifty years' (2010) 60:2 *University of Toronto Law Journal* 491.

Index